PITMAN OFFICE HANDBOOK

Joan I. Campbell ◆ Pat Smith ◆ Pamela Hay-Ellis

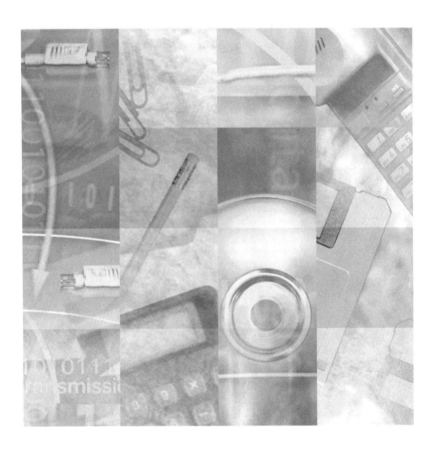

Addison
Wesley
Longman

Toronto

Canadian Cataloguing in Publication Data

Campbell, Joan (Joan I.)
  Pitman office handbook
5th ed.
Previous editions written by: Pat Smith, Pamela Hay-Ellis, Joan Campbell.
Includes index.

ISBN 0-201-74677-8

Office practice - Handbooks, manuals, etc. I Smith, Pat. II Hay-Ellis,
Pamela J. III. Title. IV. Title: Office handbook.

HF5547.S5S.2002 651   C2001-930452-8

ISBN 0-201-74677-8

Vice President, Editorial Director: Michael Young
Acquisitions Editor: Samantha Scully
Marketing Manager: Cas Shields
Associate Editor: Veronica Tomaiuolo
Production Editor: Gillian Scobie
Copy Editor: Dianne Broad
Production Coordinator: Patricia Ciardullo
Page Layout: Hermia Chung/Christine Velakis
Permissions/Photo Research: Susan Wallace-Cox
Art Director: Julia Hall
Interior Design: Lisa LaPointe
Cover/Interior Design: Monica Kompter
Cover Image: Monica Kompter

2 3 4 5   06 05 04 03 02
Printed and bound in Canada.

Your handbook is designed to make life easy for you. The first letter of the word(s) in each unit title usually gives you the location code. For example, information in Records Management has RM1, RM2, etc., as its locators.

There are three ways to find information quickly in this book. Use whichever one best suits your needs.

1. Go to the index at the back of the book. Find the subject that interests you. Beside the index entry for that subject, you will find a page number and a locator code. Go to the page, look at the left-hand side for the locator code, and you will find the information you seek. For example, E-mail etiquette/netiquette, 190 EM14 (190 is the page;EM14 is the locator code on that page).

2. Refer to the **Table of Contents** on the next page for major unit titles, and the table of contents page(s) preceding each unit for topics within it.

3. We have combined a Table of Contents and Unit Locator Guide to provide information about where each unit begins and how each is coded. Unit titles are aligned using thumb tabs, which are also printed on the outside edge of every text page. Use the tabs to find the unit you want.

TABLE OF CONTENTS

·····*PREFACE*········

Workplaces and work styles are continually changing and presenting new challenges. To help you manage your workload, we have updated and expanded the already comprehensive information in the *Pitman Office Handbook*. Full of productivity tips and the most up-to-date data, this fifth edition is an ideal "quick reference" tool for anyone working in an academic or business environment.

The *Pitman Office Handbook* has always been easy to use and the fifth edition retains its familiar format. Among the features that our faithful readers appreciate are:

◆ A second colour that highlights headings, illustrations, and examples;

◆ A table of contents that appears at the beginning of each unit;

◆ A comprehensive index for quick reference of terms and topics;

◆ Colourful tabs that guide readers to specific data;

◆ Alphabetical locator codes that help readers find each entry;

◆ Subheadings and concise point-form notes that make it easy to quickly find and retain key information;

◆ Special binding called Otabind that makes it easier to lie open pages flat; and

◆ A handy, compact size that makes it both lightweight and portable.

In the fifth edition of the *Pitman Office Handbook*, we have also rewritten several sections to ensure that the information is even clearer and easier to understand.

The modern workplace relies heavily on technology; therefore, it is continually striving to keep up with rapid technological advances. Rather than homing in on specific changes in technology, the *Pitman Office Handbook* takes a generic approach to inform you about technology's uses and its ability to improve productivity. In this edition you will find greater coverage of computer systems and company intranets. You will also learn how to use the Internet for such tasks as conducting job searches, making travel arrangements, and planning conferences and other events. Electronic mail (e-mail) can be a valuable communications tool in the workplace; therefore, this handbook discusses the pros and cons of e-mail correspondence; offers many suggestions about drafting effective e-mail messages; and provides guidelines regarding online etiquette (*Net*iquette).

Because a day at the office involves much more than "pointing" and "clicking" at your computer terminal, this edition features revised coverage of such units as Communications: Language Skills (Unit 1); Human Resources Management (Unit 8); Job Search Skills (Unit 11); and Social and Interpersonal Skills, Front Line Reception, and Public Relations Skills (Unit 18). Misused words, memo and résumé writing, conflict resolution, and presentation techniques are just a few of the topics that we have expanded. Financial Management (Unit 6) helps readers to locate information about marketplace terminology and tips about banking and investments. In Efficiency, Time Management, and Ergonomics (Unit 3), readers learn how to better manage time and stress levels. In this unit, you can also find out how to increase awareness of health and safety in the workplace. And Telephone Techniques and Services (Unit 19) features expanded coverage of cell phone etiquette.

Whether you are an office employee, business administrator, manager, entrepreneur, or student, we hope that you enjoy using the *Pitman Office Handbook, Fifth Edition*. We invite you to share your comments about the handbook with us by writing to webinfo.pubcanada@pearsoned.com

ACKNOWLEDGEMENTS

To compile the *Pitman Office Handbook, Fifth Edition*, we consulted with many people and sources. We would like to express our thanks to the following people and organizations for their help:

Bell Canada, Canada Customs, Canada Post Corporation, David Akin, *The Hamilton Spectator*, Kelly Darling, Hamilton Teachers' Credit Union, and Jenny McCartney and Marilyn McDermott of Mohawk College.

Special thanks also goes to members of the editorial and production team at Pearson Education Canada, including Samantha Scully, Acquisitions Editor; Veronica Tomaiuolo, Developmental Editor; Trish Ciardullo, Production Coordinator; Gillian Scobie, Production Editor; Dianne Broad, Copy Editor; and Julia Hall, Assistant Art Director.

We also gratefully acknowledge the assistance of the following reviewers:

Judith Barber, Saskatchewan Institute of Applied Science & Technology
Heather Armstrong Mohawk College
Veronica Weir, Mohawk College
Ruth Johnson, Fanshawe College
Wendy Burton, Algonquin College
June Harper, Holland College

Dedication

This comprehensive handbook is dedicated to students, office employees, and entrepreneurs who need up-to-date basic office or technology reference information for success in college courses or in business.

An educated person is a literate person and is usually successful through hard work and a thirst for knowledge. May this handbook be one of the tools that helps you to attain your goals. Enjoy!

J.I.C.

1

COMMUNICATIONS: LANGUAGE SKILLS

C

CONTENTS

C

The ability to communicate well is essential to success in business. A successful communication—either oral or written—is one that is understood by the receiver exactly as the sender intended it to be. If the sender puts him- or herself in the receiver's position, uses appropriate language, structures sentences with care, and adopts the right tone, the sender will produce an effective communication.

Clarity in language is becoming increasingly important. Canada is welcoming more and more immigrants and trading more globally than ever before. Considerable care must be taken, then, to ensure that communications are easy to understand by those whose first language is not English. This unit shows how to communicate successfully.

Part 1 is concerned with the technicalities or workings of the language. It provides the information needed to help you:

◆ choose and spell words with precision

◆ be knowledgeable about the rules of grammar

◆ punctuate accurately

◆ follow the conventions of style

Part 2 looks at the written and oral expression of language. Through it, you will learn to produce communications to fit most business situations.

NOTE This unit is not designed to provide you with a detailed analysis of the English language, but rather to increase your knowledge and help you solve day-to-day language problems.

 **1**

THE TECHNICALITIES OF LANGUAGE

This section will help you with choosing the right words, spelling, grammar and usage, punctuation, and style.

C1 CHOOSING THE RIGHT WORDS

Send clear messages by keeping your words simple and by using them with precision and care. Avoid clichés, slang, and jargon. Stay away from overused and dated expressions. Be very careful to steer clear of ambiguities, redundancies, and inaccuracies.

If in doubt, search it out!

Tap into the richness of the language to make your communications more expressive and effective. A dictionary, a thesaurus, and a handbook of English usage are invaluable reference books (see Unit 10 for details of these and other information resources).

C2 CLICHÉS TO AVOID

Do not use clichés or hackneyed, old-fashioned expressions in the hope they will make a good impression. Let one word do the work of three or four.

C

Avoid	Use	Example
(We) acknowledge receipt of	Thank you	Thank you for your letter...
At all times	Always	We always enjoy our business associations with you.
At an early date	Soon; immediately	We expect to have an answer soon.
At this point in time; at this time	Now; at present	Your representative is here now.
Due to the fact that	Because; since; as	Because the workers are on strike...
Enclosed please find; enclosed herewith	We enclose; enclosed is	Enclosed is a cheque for...
Encounter difficulty	Have trouble; need help	If you need help, please call us.
For the purpose of	For	The software was needed for inventory control.
In a position to	Can	We can mail the contract today.
In due course	As soon as; when	My client will pay as soon as she can.
In re	Regarding; about	Your suggestion regarding the annual bonus...
In the amount of	For	Your cheque for $100 arrived...
In the event that	In case; if	If it rains, the games...
In the near future	Soon; shortly	You can expect to hear from us soon.
In view of the fact that	Because; since	Because it was a fair solution, they all agreed.
May we anticipate an early reply?	May we expect	May we expect to hear from you soon?
Of the opinion that	Think	They think this is a good time to buy.
Until such time as	Until	Until an agreement is reached ...

C3   FREQUENTLY CONFUSED WORDS

The complexity of the English language sometimes causes confusion because some words that sound alike have different meanings. Consult the following chart if you are in doubt about the correct word to choose.

Word	Meaning	Example
accede	agree to	I will accede to the manager's request.
exceed	to go beyond	Please do not exceed the speed limit.
accept	to receive	Please accept this gift.
except	not including	Everyone except the newest member was present.
accent	a distinctive manner of pronunciation	Silvia has a delightful accent.
ascent	act of rising	Climbers take months to prepare for the ascent of Mount Everest.
assent	consent	She gave a nod of assent.
access	entry	The office did not have street access.
excess	too much; surplus	The excess paper was cut off.
ad	abbreviation for advertisement	We placed three ads in the local newspaper.
add	extend; make larger	Let's add Fran's name to the list.
adverse	hostile	Unemployment has an adverse effect on business.
averse	opposed	Politicians are averse to being blunt.
advice (n.)	recommendation	Their advice was freely given.
advise (v.)	inform; recommend	The lawyer was eager to advise the client.
affect (v.)	influence	Praise will affect an employee's productivity.
	put on, assume	She affected an air of confidence.
effect (n.)	consequence	Meeting the prime minister had a profound effect on Ginette.
effect (v.)	accomplish	We will do all we can to effect speedy delivery.
aid (n.)	help	Send aid to Somalia.
aid (v.)		Will you aid their cause?
aide	helper; assistant	He wants to be a nursing aide.
ail	to feel sick	What is it that ails her?
ale	a bitter beer	He did enjoy a cold ale on occasion.
aisle	a passageway	The supermarket aisle was too narrow.
I'll	contraction for *I will*	I'll be here.
isle	an island	Bermuda is a lovely isle to visit.
allowed	permitted	They were not allowed to go to the club.
aloud	audibly; not silently	Loretta should have kept her thoughts to herself instead of saying them aloud.

(continued...)

C

Word	Meaning	Example
altar (n.)	sacred part of a church	The bride and groom approached the altar.
alter (v.)	to change	We had to alter our plans.
alternate	one of two choices	She took the scenic route; we took the alternate one.
alternative	choice of several	He had three alternatives: turn right, turn left, or go straight ahead.
appraise	to estimate	The real estate agent was asked to appraise the property.
apprise	to inform	Please apprise me of the changes.
are (v.)	the plural and second person singular of *to be*	They are going to college.
hour (n.)	sixty minutes	The meeting lasted an hour.
our (adj.)	shows ownership	Our parents live in Toronto, but our aunt lives in Montreal.
assistance	help; aid	Give your assistance to those nurses, please.
assistants	helpers	The managers and their assistants were present.
attendance	presence	Your attendance is appreciated.
attendants (n.)	people who provide a service	The hospital attendants enjoyed helping people.
bail	a security guarantee	Bail was set at $5000.
bale	a large bundle of material	The bale of hay was too heavy.
bare	naked	The winter wind stripped the leaves from the trees, leaving them bare.
bear (n.)	large animal	They went to the zoo to see the white polar bear.
bear (v.)	support	The thin ice cannot bear your weight.
bases	plural of base	The bases were loaded.
basis	the main part	The basis of the medicine is an oil. The basis of the cake is flour.
berry	a fruit	We picked berries off the bushes.
bury	put in the earth	Erika wanted to bury the dead mouse.
berth	a place to sleep	They reserved a berth on the train.
birth	being born	She gave birth to a healthy baby boy.
beside	next to; adjacent	Please sit beside me.
besides	also; moreover	Besides a computer, he also wanted a scanner.

(continued...)

C

Word	Meaning	Example
biannual	twice a year	The biannual pay period (June and December) was approved.
biennial	occurring every two years	It was a biennial celebration (1998, 2000, 2002, etc.).
board	a piece of wood	They needed a board for the display.
	group	The board of directors met today.
bored	to be made weary by tiresome behaviour	The audience was bored and began to leave.
bloc (n.)	a group of people	The Quebec bloc attended the conference.
block (n.)	a solid piece of material	Maxine cut up the block of wood.
block (v.)	to prevent passage	The main idea was to block the entrance.
brake (n.)	a mechanical part of a vehicle	The brake on the car was found to be defective.
break (v.)	to cause to come apart	How did the child break the vase?
buy	to purchase	What did you buy today?
by	a preposition; near or beside	The theatre is by the lake.
bye	informal for goodbye	She sadly said bye to her friend.
	the odd person/team not required to play a game or match	The team had a bye in the first round and went on to win the cup.
cache	hiding place	The cache was not easy to locate.
cash	money	Mary had $20 in cash with her.
canvas	a strong cotton cloth	We will use the canvas tent when we go camping.
canvass	to solicit subscriptions or votes or to fundraise	It is hard work to canvass door-to-door for charities.
capital	invested money	The company had a huge capital investment in its steelmaking facilities.
	city	Ottawa is the capital of Canada.
	upper case when keying text	Use a capital "O" when keying the word Ottawa.
Capitol (n.)	Congress or state legislature building	The U.S. Congress meets at the Capitol in Washington, D.C.
carat	a measure used for precious stones	The ring had a half-carat diamond.
caret	a proofreader's symbol	A caret symbol (^) indicates an insertion.
carrot	a vegetable	She needed a carrot for the salad.

(continued...)

C

Word	Meaning	Example
cast	a group of entertainers	The cast for the new musical started rehearsals right after the holiday.
	a mould	The cast on her broken arm was made out of plaster.
caste	a distinct class of society	He was a member of a Hindu caste.
census	statistics of an area	The census is taken every 10 years.
senses	normal, sound condition of mind	The children quickly came to their senses after hearing the joke.
cent	a unit of currency	His change from the purchase was one cent.
scent	an odour or smell	The scent of the perfume was very pleasant.
sent	dispatched	The letter was sent out two days ago.
cereal	grain food	Cereal is good for breakfast.
serial	arranged in a series	Soap operas are serials.
choose	select	Which car did you choose?
chose	selected	I chose the newest model.
cite (v.)	to quote from an author	The student did not cite anything by Atwood in her report.
sight (n.)	vision or act of seeing	Glasses or contact lenses help many whose sight is not 20/20.
site (n.)	a position or place	The site for our new home has been chosen.
coarse	rough; common	The unfinished table has a coarse surface.
course	path; way	The safe course has no challenge.
	part of a meal served at one time	We ate the seven-course meal slowly.
	outline of a subject to be learned	The teacher prepared the Grade 11 English course of study.
complement	complete or make perfect	Use these paintings to complement your office decor.
compliment	polite expression of praise	It is kind to pay a compliment.
confidant(e)	friend; counsellor	She was a loyal confidante.
confident	sure of oneself	Tamara was confident she would succeed.
conscience	the sense that one should do right	Her conscience bothered her all day because she had lied.
conscious	aware	The accident victim was still conscious.
council (n.)	a group of people	They introduced the newly elected council.
counsel (n.)	advice	She sought counsel from her lawyer.

(continued...)

C

Word	Meaning	Example
counsel (v.)	advise	A lawyer was called to counsel the group.
consul	an official in a foreign country	One of the Canadian consuls is located in Japan.
credible	believable	Their story was barely credible.
creditable	deserving credit	That was a creditable presentation.
currant	a berry	Carole made delicious red currant jam.
		You must cut off the electrical current before repairing the toaster.
current	a flow of water or electricity	The current near the dam was dangerous.
current	of or at the present time	Are turtlenecks the current fashion?
decent	respectable	Study hard to earn a decent salary.
descent	downward movement	The descent from the mountaintop was difficult.
dissent (n. or v.)	disagree(ment)	The dissent among players caused their team to lose.
defective	faulty	The defective computer was returned to the store.
deficient	incomplete	His diet was deficient in protein.
defer	to postpone	Will we defer the meeting until next week?
defer to	respect the opinion of	Young people usually defer to older people.
differ	be unlike	Because their opinions differed, they compromised.
desert (n.)	barren land	Sand is everywhere in the desert.
desert (v.)	to abandon	The leader was deserted by his supporters.
dessert	sweet course	Dessert will be tartufo.
device (n.)	item designed to achieve a particular purpose	An X-acto knife is a very useful device for cutting paper.
devise (v.)	to invent	Let's devise a new strategy for the campaign.
discreet	tactful	Be discreet with your comments.
discrete	separate; distinct	The workshop had three discrete segments.
elicit	to draw out	The teacher tried very hard to elicit the correct answer from the student.
illicit	not legal	As a result of illicit financial dealings, the accountant was dismissed.
eligible	fit to be chosen	Your training makes you eligible for the job.
illegible	unreadable	That person's writing is illegible.

(continued...)

C

Word	Meaning	Example
emigrant	person leaving country	Sanjay is an emigrant from Kenya.
immigrant	person entering country	Joe Chan is an immigrant to Canada.
eminent	distinguished	Canada's Governor General is an eminent person.
imminent	about to happen	They were told that a merger was imminent.
emanate	come out (from)	The article emanated from last week's *Time* magazine.
ensure	to make sure or certain	We must proofread carefully to ensure there are no errors.
insure	to protect	They were advised to insure the property against fire and theft.
envelop (v.)	wrap; surround	They let the warm Caribbean envelop them.
envelope (n.)	container for letter	Use a No. 10 envelope, please.
fair	favourable or just	Our instructor is always fair when she marks tests.
	festivity: exhibition of goods or services	The Summerhill Fair takes place every June.
fare	cost of transportation	The bus fare increased in January.
	food	Cucumber sandwiches make a dainty fare.
farther	refers to actual distance	He lived three kilometres farther down the road.
further	extending beyond; in addition	Nothing could be further from the truth.
feat	an act of skill	The daring circus feat was breathtaking.
feet	plural of foot	He danced as if he had two left feet.
foreword	preface	A book often contains a foreword.
forward	in front	Veronica was asked to step forward ten paces.
formally	according to form, rule	Please dress formally for the dinner.
formerly	previously	She was formerly an administrative assistant.
forth	forward	Go forth in peace!
fourth	ordinal for four	Our company placed fourth in the competition.
golf	a game played with a small hard ball and a club	Tiger Woods won the Canadian PGA golf tournament at Glen Abbey on September 10, 2000.
gulf	large bay; ocean	She requested accommodation on the gulf side of the resort.
	large gap	There was a gulf between them.

(continued...)

Word	Meaning	Example
guessed	formed opinion without knowledge	She guessed his age to be around 50.
guest	a visitor	We had a special guest dine with us on the holiday.
hail (n.)	frozen rain	We had a severe hailstorm.
hail (v.)	to call	She will hail a cab.
hale (adj.)	healthy	For all his 80 years, he was a hale and hearty man.
hall	a passageway	The school hall was bright and cheerful.
haul	to drag or pull	They had to haul the tree from the river.
hear	perceive by ear	Praise is pleasant to hear.
here	in this place	Bring the files here, please.
hole	an open area	He dug a hole in the ground.
whole	complete	It was cheaper to purchase the whole package than one piece at a time.
incite	stir up	The speaker incited the workers to strike.
insight	understanding	The article provided a useful insight into the possibilities.
its	possessive form of *it*	The lion protects its young.
it's	contraction for *it is*	It's the end of the year on December 31.
key	instrument to lock or unlock	Hard work is one of the keys to success.
quay (pronounced "key")	dock	We'll meet your boat at Queen's Quay tomorrow.
knew	past tense of *know*	Kevin knew he had to attend the ceremony.
new	recent; not old	This was the new edition of the textbook.
last	final	The last train left at 2:30 p.m.
latest	most recent	What is the latest news on world food supplies?
later	further on in time	The later we dine, the more we will eat.
latter	second of two	Sue and Carol came to the party together; the latter drove.
lay	to set, to place	Please lay the books on the desk.
lie (n.)	a falsehood	He told a lie.
lie (v.)	to recline	He had to lie down.
lead (n.)	a soft metal	Art students sketch using lead pencils.
lead (v.)	to show the way	You lead; I'll follow.
led (v.)	guided	The guide led the group to safety.

(continued...)

Word	Meaning	Example
lean	not upright	The shed tended to lean to the right.
	thin	The lean dog was begging for food.
lien	a legal claim	There was a lien on the property because the taxes were in arrears.
leased	rented	They leased the property, but they may purchase it next year.
least	less than any other	I paid $20; Jane paid $15; but Betty paid the least, only $10.
lessen (v.)	diminish	Don't lessen pressure on that cut yet.
lesson (n.)	exercise	How was your economics lesson today?
lightening	making lighter	Lightening the load made a big difference.
lightning	a sudden flash of light	Lightning is often followed by thunder during a storm.
loan	a debt	You must pay interest on a loan.
lone	alone	There was a lone wolf out on the ridge.
loose	free	The wheel cover came loose and fell off.
lose	be deprived of	They may lose the contract if their quote is too high.
mall	a public place to shop	The new mall is opening today.
maul	to handle in a rough way	Often a male bear will maul its own cub.
medal	a decoration	Elvis Stojko won a silver medal at the Olympics.
meddle	to interfere	It was hoped that no one would meddle with the display.
might (v.)	expresses possibility	The weather forecaster said it might rain.
might (n.)	a force	The might of the tornado was frightening.
mite	a small bit; small object	It didn't make a mite of difference.
	a small child	Although she was very rushed, the shopper stopped to help the crying mite who had somehow lost his way.
	a small bug	There were mites on the plants and in the carpet.
miner	mine worker	He was a coal miner's son.
minor (n.)	person under legal age	Susie was the only minor in the group.
minor (adj.)	of lesser importance	Luckily, the error was only a minor one.

(continued...)

Word	Meaning	Example
moral	concerned with distinction between right and wrong	The moral behaviour of children is patterned after that of adults.
morale	mental condition or attitude	The morale in our office is higher with the team approach.
overdo	go too far	If you overdo the exercise, you may become ill.
overdue	late; past the due time	The March payment is long overdue.
packed	wrapped or tied	The luggage was packed for travel.
pact	an agreement	The boys made a pact to be friends forever.
pail	bucket	Donna carried the pail of water for the animals.
pale	whitish in colour	She looked so pale that they asked her to sit down.
pair (n.)	a couple or two	She purchased a pair of shoes.
pare (v.)	to cut or peel	You can pare the potatoes for the dinner.
pear (n.)	a fruit	I had a pear for dessert.
passed	past tense of *to pass*	Every student passed the exam.
past	beyond in time or place	It is now long past midnight.
patience	endurance; tolerance	A teacher needs plenty of patience.
patients	sick clients	My doctor sees 25 patients each day.
peak	top of mountain or hill	They climbed to the peak of Mount Everest.
peek	a quick look	The child took a peek into the sack.
personal	one's own	Each member is entitled to a personal opinion.
personnel	body of workers	All of our personnel are happy.
perspective	viewpoint	Your perspective will influence your decision.
prospective	anticipated	Daniel interviewed three prospective employees.
peruse	examine carefully	Please peruse the report when you have time.
pursue	follow with intent to catch	The wolf pursued the deer.
plaintiff	one who brings legal suit	Jane was the plaintiff in the lawsuit.
plaintive	mournful or sad	The music of the pipes was plaintive, reminding everyone of those lost in battle.
poor (n.)	the needy	A benefit concert was held to help thc poor.
pour (v.)	cause to flow in a steady stream	The waiter poured the coffee as he spoke.
pray (v.)	as in worship	They were asked to pray for the sick child.
prey (n.)	a hunted animal	The lion stalks its prey.

(continued...)

C

Word	Meaning	Example
precede	go before	*A* precedes *B* in the alphabet.
proceed	go on	Let us proceed with the meeting.
principal	chief; major	A principal cause of car accidents is careless driving.
principle	personal code of truth	His high principles won him the respect of his co-workers.
quay (*see key*)		
quiet	silent	Everyone was quiet for two minutes.
quite	absolutely	That is not quite
	– *or* –	correct.
	to a considerable degree	I hiked quite a distance.
quit	stop; give up	Did you quit work at 5 p.m.?
real	true	It did not look like a real diamond.
reel	a device for winding	The film was put on a reel.
receipt	proof of purchase	You will need a receipt if you wish to return the goods.
recipe	a set of directions; formula	Please follow the recipe as written.
recent	not long past	Masami was a recent graduate.
resent	feel offended	We resent his constant interruptions.
reign (v.)	to rule	The Queen of England may reign for a long time.
rain (n.)	water drops from clouds	It may rain today.
rein (n.)	bridle part	The rein broke during the race.
right (adj.)	correct	You made the right choice.
right (n.)	fair claim	You have the right to be silent.
rite	ritual; ceremony	Welcoming rites in Guinea are fascinating.
wright	creator; maker	Shakespeare was a playwright.
role	a part in a play	He was wonderful in the leading role.
roll	to move by turning over	She had to roll the bread dough quickly.
root	part of a plant	The root of the tree was rotting away.
route	a course/way in travel	That was the safest route to take.
sail	piece of canvas	The new sail flapped in the breeze.
sale	reduced price	Sophie purchased the sweater on sale.
scene	the time or place	The scene of the crime was close to the lake.
seen	past participle of see	Have you seen the latest statistics?
sew	to use needle and thread	She had to sew her torn jeans.
so	in a way; stated	Was that really so?

(continued...)

C

Word	Meaning	Example
sole (adj.)	only one	She was the sole heir to the estate.
sole (n.)	the bottom of a shoe	There was a large hole in the sole of his shoe.
	fish	She ate sole for lunch.
soul	spirit	Sabrina put all her soul into the acting role.
stair	one of a series of steps	Please take one stair at a time.
stare	look with a fixed gaze	It is not polite to stare at a person.
stalk (n.)	the stem	She cut the celery stalk into small pieces.
stalk (v.)	follow	Wild animals stalk their prey.
stock (n.)	a supply	We should add to our stock of canned goods.
stationary	unmoving	A statue is stationary.
stationery	writing materials	Most firms have printed stationery.
statue	figure covered or moulded	Michelangelo's *David* is an impressive statue.
statute	a law	A recent statute permits extended opening hours.
straight	not broken	The garment did not have a straight hem.
strait	narrow channel	The sailboat just made it through the narrow strait.
suite	an apartment	The rented suite had a wonderful view.
sweet (adj.)	a pleasant taste	The drink was very sweet.
sweet (n.)	candy	He offered her a sweet.
tail	rearmost part of an animal's body	The dog wagged its tail.
tale	a story	The tale of the two competitors was unbelievable.
tear (n.)	water from the eye	She shed a tear or two.
tear (v.)	to come apart	The mother asked her son not to tear his new shirt.
than (conj.)	used in comparisons	Steve was taller than Troy.
then (adv.)	indicates time	Marion knew then that the prophecy had come true.
their	possessive form of *they*	Their house is very large.
there	in that place	Take this computer over there, please.
they're	contraction for *they are*	They're late for the meeting.
threw	past tense of *throw*	The winning team threw five touchdown passes.
through	by means of	Their success came through hard work.

(continued...)

Word	Meaning	Example
thorough	from beginning to end complete	He came through the entire assignment unscathed. Your assistant did a thorough job for us.
verses versus	literary expressions against	The poet wrote several verses for the poem. The trial involved Smith versus (vs.) Robinson.
waist (n.) waste (adj.) waste (v.)	middle of the body useless material to make poor use of	You have a small waist. They inspected the disposal of the company's waste materials. We are advised not to waste electricity.
wait weight	to stay heaviness	It was not necessary to wait for the mail. The weight of the luggage caused the shelf to collapse.
waive wave (v.) wave (n.)	to give up to make a signal with a hand motion a swell of water	They decided to waive their rights to the property. It was sad to wave goodbye. The huge wave almost toppled the boat.
ware (n.) wear (v.) were (v.) where (adv.)	usually *wares* or part of a compound word: product put on past tense of *to be* place at which	Kitchenware is colourful these days. Wear your best suit for the interview. All of the managers were friends. Who knows where we're going?
weak week	not very strong seven days	The presentation was weak and lacked substance. They had one week to prepare the report.
weather whether	atmospheric conditions which of two alternatives	The weather forecast called for rain. Whether they come or not is unimportant.
whose who's	possessive form of *who* contraction for *who is*	Whose pen is this? The one who's first gets the prize.
your you're	possessive form of *you* contraction for *you are*	Make sure you use your dictionary. When you're in Spain, speak Spanish.

C

C4   MISUSED WORDS

Certain words and phrases are frequently misused. The following is a list of commonly misused expressions and examples of how they ought to be used.

a* and *an (articles) [see also Articles, p. 43]
Use *a* before words beginning with consonant sounds, including those spelled with an initial pronounced *h* and those spelled with vowels that are sounded as consonants.

> Greg was a historian.
> Sandra had a one-o'clock appointment.
> Gail had a university degree.

Use *an* before all vowels sounds including those spelled with *an* initial silent *h*.

> It was an organization with an excellent productivity record.
> What an honour to be invited to the opening.

accept* and *except
Accept is a verb that means "to receive."

> Please accept this gift as a token of appreciation.

Except is a verb or a preposition that means "to exclude."

> They were all going to attend except Leonard.

affect* and *effect
affect (v.) to influence

> The rainy weather did affect attendance at the concert.

effect (n.) result

> The effect of downsizing has been to create unemployment for many people.

effect (v.) to bring about or make happen

> The supplier promised to effect delivery by the date required.

among* and *between
Use *between* when referring to two items; *among* for more than two.

> The argument is between you and me.
> Please sort out the problem among the six of you.

and etc.* and *etc.
etc. means "and the rest" or "and so forth"; therefore, *and* is redundant.

> Travel agents can arrange flights, hotels, theatre tickets, etc., on request.

anyplace* and *anywhere
Use *anywhere* only. *Any* and *place* are always used separately.

> Is there a foreign exchange counter anywhere near here?

C

anyways and *anyway*

There is no such word as *anyways*.

> He had to be present anyway.

at and *to*

At indicates position.

> The branch managers were at the convention all week.

To indicates motion or direction towards something.

> The managers went to the meeting on Wednesday morning.

behind and *in back of*

Use *behind* not *in back of*.

> Place the information sheet behind the test papers.

NOTE *in front of* is correct as well.

> Place the information sheet behind, not in front of, the test papers.

beside and *besides*

Beside means "by the side of."

> She will sit beside the chairperson.

besides means "in addition to."

> Do we have any more copies besides these?

bring and *take*

Use *bring* to this place (here); and *take* to that place (there).

> Will you please bring the report when you come?
> Take these books home with you.

can and *may*

Can implies capability; *may* signifies permission sought or granted, possibility, or uncertainty.

> An athlete can usually run very fast.
> May my friend join me at the reception?
> The Games may take place in Canada.

come and *go*

Use *come* when implying "here," *go* when meaning "there."

> The president is expecting 20 guests to come for lunch.
> I am planning to go to Cape Breton Island for my holidays.

currently and *presently*

Use *currently* when meaning at the present time or now.

> We are currently using the revised schedule.

Use *presently* when meaning before long or soon.

> The taxi will arrive presently.

different from
Ordinarily, use the preposition *from* after *different* when making comparisons.

> Dale's costume was *different from* Barbara's.

When a clause follows, either *than* or *from* may be used.

> The costume was *different than* (or *from what*) she had expected.

every which way and in all directions
Every which way is slang.

> The traffic seemed to be moving *in all directions* at the same time.

from, off, of
From is generally used with persons.

> Did she borrow money from Alice?

Off is used with things. *Off* can only be used with persons when something is physically resting on them and is being lifted away.

> The plane took off as scheduled.
> He was asked to take off his hat.

Never use *of* for *from* after *off*.

> The team ran off the field. *Not* The team ran off of the field.

Never use *of* when you mean *have*.

> Troy could have been more careful with the new car.

good and well
The adjective *good* must modify a noun; *well* is used as an adverb or an adjective.

> She did a good job.
> He did well.
> I am well.

have and of
Use *have*, not *of*, after helping verbs such as *could, should, would, may,* and *might.*

> You should have (not *should of*) told me.

in, into, in to
In means position or movement within a place.

> Sharon has been in hospital for two weeks.

Into means entry or change of form.

> She was asked to take the food into the cafeteria.
> Please convert the figures into table form for the publisher.

In to (two separate words). *In* is used as an adverb; *to* is used as a preposition.

> Please take this report in to Mrs. Rodgers.

C

in regards to and *in regard to*
In regard to is correct. *In regards to* is *never* used.

Call me soon in regard to the annual meeting.

lay and *lie*
Lay means to place and requires a direct object; *lie* means to recline and can stand alone.

Yan was asked to lay the documents on the desk.
Robert had to lie down every afternoon while recuperating from his illllness.

like and *as*
Like is a preposition; it should not be used as a conjunction to join clauses.

Her skin felt like sandpaper.

If a conjunction is needed, use *as, as if,* or *as though.*

Try to proofread as carefully as Keri does.
Miss Weir smiled as though she knew what was going to happen.

none and *no one*
None is the singular pronoun standing for not one; it should always take a singular verb. *No one* is used in place of not one person; it also takes a singular verb.

None of those machines is working properly.
No one was visible in the dense fog.

on, onto, on to
On means position or movement over.

We were asked to wait on level one for the next performance.

Onto means movement towards or over.

They can get onto this train or wait for the next one.

On to (two separate words). *On* is used as an adverb; *to* is used as a preposition.

They were asked to move on to the next platform.

per, a, an
Per is a preposition usually used before Latin nouns or weights and measures.

The mortgage rates were set at 7 percent per annum. (Latin expression)
The paper comes in 500 pages per package.

NOTE   Whenever possible, use *a* or *an* instead of *per*. Never use *per* to mean "according to" or "in accordance with." See page 17.

He was earning $10 an hour for his time on the job.

C

real and *really*

Real is an adjective that describes a noun; *really* is an adverb.

> She bought a real Picasso.
> He ran really well.

seeing as how and *since*

Seeing as how is slang and should be avoided.

> Since you like chocolates, here is a large box for you.

shall and *will*

Used in formal English in the first person to indicate future action, *shall* is now so rare as to be almost obsolete. In modern usage, *will* is used in all persons to express both future and determination.

> I expect I will have a good trip. (future)
> I will complete this report if it kills me. (determination)

should of — see *have, of* (page 20)

some place and *somewhere*

Some place is incorrect.

> I left my glasses somewhere.

than and *then*

Use *than* for making comparisons; use *then* when referring to time.

> Entrepreneurs usually work longer hours than their employees do.
> First came the soup, then came the main course.

there is and *there are*

Is refers to a singular noun; *are* refers to a plural one.

> There is only one space after a comma.
> There are many voters here today.

to, too, two

To may be a preposition or part of an infinitive.

> Few people walk to work today.

Too is an adverb meaning "also" or "more than enough."

> The summary was far too long.

Two is a number used as a noun or adjective.

> She was told to give two references on her résumé.

who and *which* (relative pronouns)

Who refers to a person; *which*, to a thing.

> The person who delivered the computer was very polite.
> The telephone, which is near the door, is within easy reach.

C5   DOUBLE NEGATIVE WORDS

No, not, nobody, and other negative words.

No is known as a negative word. It is the kind of word used to refuse or deny something or to contradict someone. Other negative words are:

◆ *not, nothing, none, nowhere, and nobody*

◆ verbs combined with not: hasn't, don't, wouldn't, etc.

◆ words combined with **un-: unable, unwilling,** etc.

Avoid using double negative words by following this simple rule:

Rule: To express a negative idea, use no more than *one* negative.

Correct: He does *not* need any money.
He needs *no* money.

Incorrect: He does *not* need **no** money.

Correct: I said *nothing.*
I *didn't* say anything.

Incorrect: I *didn't* say *nothing.*

Correct: It *doesn't* mean anything.

Incorrect: It *don't* mean *nothing.*

Correct: She is *unwilling* to make any apology.
She is willing to make *no* apology.

Incorrect: She is *unwilling* to make *no* apology.

Special Negatives

Like *no, not, and nobody,* the following are negative words: *never, neither, hardly, neither . . . nor, scarcely, without,* and sometimes *but* and *only.*

Correct: There had *never* been anything like it before.

Incorrect: There had *never* been *nothing* like it before.

Correct: She has *scarcely* anything to show for her effort.

Incorrect: She has *scarcely nothing* to show for her effort.

NOTE   The combination *neither... nor* is treated as if it were a single negative.

Rule: *Never, hardly, scarcely,* and similar words follow the same rule as do other negatives. To express a negative idea, use only one negative.

C6   ONE WORD OR TWO?

If you are in doubt, refer to the list below.

Word(s)	Meaning	Example
a lot	many	There was a lot of work left to be completed.
allot	distribute	They had to allot portions of the donations to various charities.
a part	a section or piece; a member	Are you a part of this group?
apart (adv.)	separate from	They stood three feet apart from each other.
a while (n.)	a period of time	Lee Ming worked here for a while.
awhile (adv.)	for a period of time	The candidates had to wait awhile.
all ready	prepared	They are all ready to go.
already (adv.)	past the time	It is already too late for lunch.
all right	acceptable, satisfactory	Everyone agreed that the office layout was all right.
(*alright*: incorrect spelling of *all right*)		
all together	in unison	The choir should sing all together.
altogether (adv.)	entirely	Your holiday was altogether too expensive.
all ways (n.)	all methods	They tried in all ways to win the game.
always (adv.)	at all times	Our members always do a good job.
any body	a noun modified by *any*	Can you reach any body of government?
anybody	indefinite pronoun	Can anybody call that number?
any more	no more	She doesn't want any more.
anymore	now	Bill doesn't live here anymore.
any time	used with a specific time in mind	If you have any time next week, please call.
anytime (adv.)	used when no specific time is intended	You are welcome here anytime
any way	a way	Is there any way in which we can help?
anyway (adv.)	in any case	Anyway, the job had already been completed.
(*anyways* is not a word)		
burnout	stressed out	The social workers are suffering from burnout.
checkmark	a mark	Please put a checkmark beside each correct answer.
every day	each day	It is good to practise every day.
everyday (adj.)	daily	Meetings are an everyday occurrence.

(continued...)

C

Word(s)	Meaning	Example
every one	each person	Every one of them wore casual clothes on Fridays.
everyone	everybody	It's correct to show appreciation to everyone who participated.
filename	name of document	The document's filename was missing.
high school	school of higher learning	Stacey will be going to high school soon.
in to	to a place	All reports are to be handed in to me before the weekend.
into (prep.)	to the inside of	The visitor walked straight into my office.
mailbox	holder of mail	The mailbox was incorrectly labelled.
may be	could be	The children may be going this afternoon.
maybe (adv.)	perhaps	Maybe the children will go out soon.
no body	no substance; no physical structure	No body was found in that murder case.
nobody (pronoun)	no one	Nobody came to work last Saturday.
shortcut	a shorter way	They took a shortcut to school.
some time	a period of time	It will take some time to arrange the conference.
sometimes (adv.)	at times	Sometimes it's difficult to sit up straight.
touchtone	a phone	The touchtone phone comes in many colours.
turnover	a business transaction	A quick turnover of merchandise was necessary to make a profit.
workplace	a place where one works	Safety in the workplace is a major concern.
worksheet	a page on which work is created	Please hand in your worksheet with the test.
workstation	location of equipment/desk	She was asked to clean up her workstation.

C7   WORDS WITH ACCOMPANYING PREPOSITIONS

Certain English words must be accompanied by a particular preposition. In the following examples, the correct prepositions are italicized.

accompanied *by*	She was accompanied by her mother.
according *to*	According to the news, the damage was great.
account *for*	David was unable to account for the missing items.
account *to*	David will have to account to the auditors for the discrepancy in figures.
agree *on/upon*	They could not agree on a settlement.
agree *to*	Did they agree to the terms of the contract?
agree *with*	I agree with your proposal.
capable *of*	Our new recruit is capable of doing that job well.
comply *with*	If you agree, please comply with my request promptly.
concur *in* (something)	Everyone did not concur in that decision.
concur *with* (people)	The president concurred with the manager.
conform *to*	The building does not conform to specifications.
different *from* (not *to* or *than*)	Bill is quite different from Ned.
plan *to* (not *on*)	We plan to expand our office space next month.
superior *to* (not *than*)	One twin is superior in intelligence to the other.
surrounded *by*	That farmhouse is surrounded by fields.
try *to* (not *and*)	Please try to see it my way.

C8   WORDS WITH UNNECESSARY PREPOSITIONS

Omit prepositions that add nothing to the meaning of the sentence.

Examples: Where is he [at]?
Where did that book go [to]?
The car is too near [to] the garage.
Jack's house is opposite [to] hers.
Why don't we meet at about seven o'clock? (Omit either *at* or *about*.)
The box fell off [of] the truck.

C9   SPELLING

Because English is derived from so many languages and has undergone so many changes, words are sometimes spelled in unusual ways. Here are some rules to help you become a better speller, as well as a list of commonly misspelled words.

NOTE   Most software is equipped with a spell check feature. This is extremely useful, but remember that it cannot spot homonyms (words that sound alike) or words that have been correctly spelled but misused.

C

▶C10   Rules for spelling

A number of rules can help you become a good speller, but there are also many exceptions to these rules. You can improve your spelling if you try to develop a word sense, increase your vocabulary, and become a proficient dictionary user. Use memory aids such as:

◆ The **ice** in adv**ice** is a noun.

◆ The **is** in adv**ise** is a verb.

◆ A popular rhyme helps with *ei* and *ie* words:
  I before *e*
  Except after *c*,
  Or when sounded as *eh*,
  As in neighbour and weigh.

Normal use:	ach**ie**ve	bel**ie**f	bel**ie**ve	relief	yield
After c:	conc**ei**t	rec**ei**ve	c**ei**ling		
The eh *sound:*	fr**ei**ght	w**ei**ght	sl**ei**gh		

Common exceptions: counterfeit
forfeit
height
seize
neither
their
weird

Adding suffixes

Adding suffixes to words is a spelling process that seems to cause some difficulty. The standard guideline is simply to add the required suffix to a word, as in these samples:

bulk-y	depend-ent	reason-able	thought-ful
care-less	express-ed	report-ing	
citizen-ship	pack-age	retire-ment	

Several words, however, require special treatment when suffixes are added to them. The following rules will help you form endings correctly.

For one-syllable words ending in a consonant preceded by a vowel, double the final consonant:

bat	batted	drag	dragging
cut	cutting	star	starry

Exceptions: buses, boxed, fixing

For words with two or more syllables that end in a consonant and have the accent on the last syllable, double the final consonant:

control-ler   prefer-ring

C

Words ending in a silent *e* usually drop the *e* to add the suffix *y* or a suffix beginning with a vowel:

believe	believing	believable
desire	desirable	desirous
ice	icing	icy
propose	proposal	proposition

A notable exception is *mileage*.

NOTE For words ending in *ce* or *ge*, keep the *e* before the suffix *-able*:

charge   chargeable   replace   replaceable

For words ending in *y* preceded by a consonant, change the *y* to *i* before adding the suffix:

apply   applicable   carry   carrier   forty   fortieth

For words ending in *y* preceded by a vowel, simply add the suffix:

display   displayed   enjoy   enjoyable   enjoyment

For words ending in *c*, add a *k* before the suffix to retain the hard *c* sound:

picnic   picnicking   traffic   trafficked

▶C11 Word Variants

Word variants according to *Gage Canadian Dictionary* (Gage Educational Publishing Company, Toronto, ON), the *Concise Oxford Dictionary of Current English* (Clarendon Press, Oxford, England) and *Webster's New World Dictionary of American English* (Prentice Hall, New York, U.S.):

Words ending in *er* and *re* (all spellings are acceptable)

Gage	Oxford	Webster
calibre	calibre	caliber
centre*	centre	center
litre	litre	liter
lustre	lustre	luster
manoeuvre	manoeuvre	maneuver
metre	metre	meter
sabre	sabre	saber
theatre	theatre	theater

*(Note: the names of most buildings in Canada use *re* in their names, while the U.S. generally uses *er*).

Examples: Dalhousie Arts Centre
Quebec City Convention Centre
Harbourfront Centre
Saskatchewan Indian Cultural Centre
The Volunteer Centre of North Vancouver
The World Trade Center (U.S.)

(Note: Always use the proper designated name of the building.)

▶C12 Frequently misspelled words

The words listed here frequently pose spelling problems. If you have difficulties with spelling, consult a dictionary often, refer to this section, or compose your own list of troublesome words (and practise two or three of them every day). Use the spell check that comes with your software; spell check will not always identify situations in which a word is spelled correctly but is the wrong word in that context (e.g., *he* when *her* is intended). Some software with grammar-check features **will** identify correct word usage, and this is a bonus for the user.

absence	biased	controversy	exaggerate
access	bilingualism	convenience	exceed
accessibility	bookkeeper	correspondence	exercise
accidentally	brand name	courteous	exhaustible
accommodate	brochure	courtesy	extension
achievement	bulk	criticism	extraordinary
acquaintance	bulletin	cursor	facetious
acquiesce	business	database	facsimile
acquisition	calendar	debt	familiar
advantageous	campaign	deceive	fascinating
advisable	Caribbean	deductible	February
affidavit	carriage	defendant	feedback
aggressive	carriers	deficit	financier
aisle	catalogue	definitely	foreign
all right	category	dependant (n.)	foresee
amateur	Celsius	dependent (adj.)	forty
amortize	chaise longue	desirable	fourteen
analyse	champagne	development	fourth
analysis	changeable	dilemma	friend
anonymity	chauffeur	disappoint	fulfil
apparel	chronological	discreet	gauge
apparently	collateral	discrete	government
architect	colonel	dissatisfied	grammar
argument	column	dividend	grateful
arrears	commitment	domain	grievance
ascertain	committee	drawback	guarantee
assessment	commonplace	efficiency	guise
assistance	communicator	eighth	hacker
attendant	compatible	eligible	hacking
attitude	competency	ellipsis	handkerchief
attributions	copyright	embarrass	harass
bachelor	concede	enrolment	height
bankruptcy	congratulate	en route	hindrance
beginning	conscience	entrepreneur	hors d'oeuvre
believe	conscious	environment	hundredth
beneficiary	consolidation	etiquette	hypocrisy

(continued...)

C

inasmuch as	mortgage	privilege	status
incidentally	movable	procedure	subpoena
incompetent	necessary	proceed	substantial
indictment	neighbour	professor	subtle
indispensable	neither	program	subtlety
innovation	niche	promissory	subtly
installing	nickel	prompt	succeed
intercede	niece	pronounce	surgeon
interfering	ninety	pronunciation	surprise
interim	ninth	psychiatric	susceptible
irrelevant	noticeable	psychology	synonym
itinerary	nuclear	pursue	tariff
jeopardy	obsolescent	query	technique
knowledgeable	occasion(ally)	questionnaire	temperament
laboratory	occurred	queue	temperature
ledger	occurrence	receipt	thoroughly
leeway	offered	receive	toggle
liaison	omission	recipient	trademark
licence (n.)	omitted	recognize	transmit
license (v.)	ongoing	recommend	truly
lien	overhead	reference	unanimous
lieutenant	oversight	regulatory	unique
lightning	pamphlet	reinforce	usable
loose (adj.)	paperwork	relevant	vacuum
lose (v.)	parallel	resistance	vast
lying	patience	restaurant	via
maintenance	perceive	résumé	vice versa
management	permissible	rhetoric	volume
meantime	perseverance	rhythm	warehouse
mediocre	personal	satellite	Wednesday
megabyte	personnel	schedule	weekend
microcomputer	persuade	scissors	weird
microprocessor	phase	sector	whether
microtranscription	physician	seize	wholly
mileage	playback	separate	widespread
milestone	possession	sergeant	wield
millennium	practically	similar	withhold
millionaire	practice (n.)	simultaneous	woollen
miscellaneous	practise (v.)	sincerely	worldwide
mischievous	precede	skilful	wraparound
miscommunication	preferable	souvenir	writing
misspell	prejudice	speedy	
mobile	prerogative	sponsor	
modem	preside	spreadsheet	

NOTE The word *you* for *your* is one of the most common keyboarding errors.

C

C13 WORD MEANINGS

Words are formed by starting with a *root* word (**port** = carry) and then adding to it a prefix (**ex**-port = carry out of) or a suffix (port-**able** = able to be carried). Knowledge of the root meaning is the key to understanding the word; also, if you become familiar with common prefixes and suffixes, you will develop greater expertise as a language user. English root words are derived from several other languages. Some common root words are shown below.

Root	Meaning	Words derived from root
ceed	go	pro**ceed**, suc**ceed**, pre**ceed**
ject	throw	re**ject**, pro**ject**ion
mit/mis	send	dis**mis**s, re**mit**tance
mote	move	de**mot**ion, **mot**ivate
pend	hang	sus**pend**, de**pend**
port	carry	im**port**ant, trans**port**
scribe	write	sub**scribe**, tran**scribe**, de**scribe**
serve	guard/serve	re**serve**, **serv**ice
spect	look	a**spect**, re**spect**
tend	stretch	at**tend**, ex**ten**sion
vent	come	pre**vent**, ad**vent**ure
vert	turn	extro**vert**, con**vers**ion

When you first encounter a word and do not know the root meaning, try to think of a familiar word that has the same root. For example, a**pathetic**; think of sym**pathetic**—something to do with feeling; a- (ab = from) and -pathetic = away from feeling. This approach will increase not only your vocabulary but also your enjoyment of English.

Prefixes, which *change the meanings of words*, come largely from Latin, French, and Greek. Depending on usage, the original prefix sometimes changes slightly. Common examples are as follows.

Prefix	Meaning	Word example	Meaning
a/ab	from	**ab**sence	being away from
ad	to	**ad**vise	give advice to
bi	two	**bi**annual	twice a year
com/con	with	**com**mit	pledge oneself with
		concede	go along with
con	against	**con**test	witness (go) against
de	from	**de**ceive	take from
en/in	in	**en**trance	coming in
		induce	(lead in) persuade

(continued...)

Prefix	Meaning	Word example	Meaning
ex	out	**ex**ceed	go out or beyond
pre	before	**pre**judice	judgment before
pro	for	**pro**mise	(send for or on behalf of) assurance
super	over	**super**sede	(go over) take the place of
trans	across	**trans**port	carry across or over
un/in	not	**un**able	not able
		inactive	not active

Suffixes, which *do not change the meanings of words*, change the functions of words (i.e., parts of speech). For example, love (a verb or noun) can be changed to love**ly** (adjective) without losing the root meaning. Some common suffixes are the following.

Suffix	Meaning	Word example	Meaning
able/ible	able to	(in)dispens**able**	(un)able to be done without
		permiss**ible**	able to be permitted
ance/ence	act or condition/ state	acquaint**ance**	someone known
		correspond**ence**	communication
ant/ent	one who/ that which	defend**ant**	one who is defended
		depend**ent**	that which depends on
ary/ery	one who/that which/state	benefici**ary**	one who benefits
		arch**ery**	using bows and arrows
ful	full of	skil**ful**	full of skill
ion/sion/ tion	condition/ act/ result of	opin**ion**	view held as probable
		posses**sion**	ownership holding;
		reten**tion**	keeping in place
ive	quality of/ tending to	exhaust**ive**	thorough
ment	condition/ quality/state	develop**ment**	growth
ous/ious	full of/having qualities of	unanim**ous**	agreed by all
		conscient**ious**	ruled by conscience
ure	act/process/being	proced**ure**	actions in a certain order

C14 GENDER-INCLUSIVE LANGUAGE

C

Language that excludes one gender is no longer appropriate. Examples of inclusive and exclusive language follow.

Exclusive (undesirable)	Inclusive (use this)
anchorman	anchor
brotherhood	association
businessman	businessperson or executive
foreman	supervisor
manmade	manufactured; machine-made
saleswoman	salesclerk/salesperson/sales associate
chairman	chairperson

◆ Some words (such as sportsmanship and workmanship) are difficult to amend. Use completely different expressions in such cases:

   Instead of: The dress showed fine workmanship.
   Use: The dress was well made.

◆ Terms such as doctor, lawyer, professor, nurse, teacher are free of gender discrimination. Do not use such expressions as male nurse and lady doctor unless there is a reason for doing so as in:

   There will be a meeting for all male nurses at 3:30 p.m.

◆ Avoid feminine suffixes (-ess, -ette):

   She is a fine actor (not actress).
   Ask the flight attendant (not stewardess).

◆ Constructing sentences that avoid gender discrimination can sometimes result in clumsiness. Use plurals if you can or try to restructure your sentences to avoid the use of "he/she":

   Instead of: A teacher can be an excellent role model for his/her students.
   Use: Teachers can be good role models for their students.

   Instead of: The average Canadian drinks his/her coffee black.
   Use: The average Canadian drinks black coffee.

Bias and discrimination

Sensitive people will be careful to avoid, in speaking and writing, all types of biases and discrimination, including racism, ageism, and gender role stereotyping:

   Instead of: Leave it with the old man at the desk.
   Say: Leave it with the person at the desk.

C15 GRAMMAR AND USAGE

Good grammar is the result of choosing the right words and putting them in the right order to produce a clear, correctly phrased message. To help develop your understanding of grammar, this section provides information on the sentence and its parts, types of sentences, and parts of speech.

Phrases and clauses	*Sample sentence*
Introductory phrase:	In a small business,
Independent (main) clause:	(the owner or manager) (can keep
	in close touch with everything
Subordinate (auxiliary) clause:	that goes on [in the firm.])

Parts of a sentence (example indicated within marks shown)	*Parts of speech (example indicated by underscoring shown)*
Subject	Noun _____
Predicate (verb plus	Adjective ....
complement)	Preposition =====
Object	Verb _____
	Pronoun ....
	Connective =====

Components of grammar, identified in a sample sentence

C16 THE SENTENCE

A sentence is a group of words that contains a subject and a predicate (verb or verb and complement containing an object) and expresses a complete thought. Sentences can include a variety of devices to stress points, create excitement, or evoke a reaction. Well-constructed sentences are the result of correct word choice and careful word order. This unit provides all of the details you need to compose interesting, accurate, and effective sentences. It also shows you how sentences are blended and developed into paragraphs.

▶ C17 Parts of the sentence

C18 Subject—noun(s) or pronoun(s)

The subject is a noun or pronoun that governs the verb. The verb must agree with the subject in *number* (singular or plural) and *person* (first, second, or third).

C

Simple (single) subject—one noun/pronoun

The <u>manager</u> is a good administrator. (singular)
Our <u>managers</u> are good administrators. (plural)
I am working hard to qualify for a promotion. (first-person singular)
<u>We</u> were pleased to hear about your promotion. (first-person plural)
Will <u>you</u> deliver the mail, please? (second-person singular)
<u>She</u> deserves a raise. (third-person singular)
<u>They</u> work late nearly every Monday. (third-person plural)

Person	Singular	Plural
1st	I	we
2nd	you	you
3rd	he/she/it	they

Compound (combined) subject—two or more nouns/pronouns combined to make one subject

◆ requires a plural verb whether the combined subject has two singular, two plural, or one singular and one plural noun:

<u>Rebecca and Ali</u> have opened a new store.
Both <u>Jasodra and Kim</u> enjoy accounting.
Our <u>manager and the team leaders</u> will meet on Wednesday.
<u>Males and females</u> alike appreciate a bonus.

Subjects joined by connectives such as "or"

◆ if both words in the subject are singular, use a singular verb:

Either <u>Franco or his brother</u> is coming tonight.

◆ if both words are plural, use a plural verb:

Not only the <u>store managers</u> but also the <u>clerks</u> came.

◆ If the subject consists of one singular and one plural word, the verb must agree with the noun/pronoun nearer to it:

Neither the <u>teacher nor the students</u> work alone.

NOTE In cases in which sentence construction is awkward because of this rule, rewrite the sentence:

Either Gisele or I am planning to work tomorrow.

Change to:

Either Gisele or I will work tomorrow.

Subjects with intervening phrases or clauses

◆ verb must agree with the subject noun/pronoun, disregarding the intervening words:

The <u>manager</u>, along with two assistants, *is* representing our company at the convention. (singular)

All <u>employees</u>, as well as the president, *are* going on vacation next month. (plural)

<u>No one</u> except your parents <u>knows</u> where we're going. (singular)

C19 Predicate

The predicate is a verb or verb and complement (verb phrase) that says something about the subject. Complements may include a direct object and/or an indirect object.

Verb

◆ an action word (see this unit, C27)
◆ must agree with the subject:

> All people <u>are created</u> equal.

◆ has present, future, and past tenses
◆ can be used in active or passive voice
◆ has indicative, imperative, and subjunctive moods

Verb phrase (two or more verbs—one principal and one auxiliary—used as one)

> Bob <u>will be returning</u> your telephone call tomorrow.

C20 Object

An object is one or more nouns or pronouns. The object receives the action of the verb.

Direct object

◆ follows a transitive verb
◆ answers the question *who* or *what*:

> Our client signed <u>the contract</u>.

Object of a preposition

◆ follows a transitive verb:

> The chief engineer asked about the <u>plans</u> for the <u>new plant</u>.

Indirect object

◆ must appear with a direct object
◆ answers the questions *to what*, *to whom*:

> Our client gave the signed contract to the <u>president</u>.

> *– or –*

> Our client gave the <u>president</u> the signed contract.

Object complement

◆ several words referring to the direct object:

The president signed the contract <u>consisting of seven pages</u>.

C21 Phrases

A group of words without a subject or predicate—an incomplete thought—is a phrase. Phrases can function as nouns, adjectives, or prepositions. When used as subjects, they always take the singular verb form. Phrases do not contain verbs:

<u>Completing the project</u> was a relief. (noun)
The applicant <u>with the best credentials</u> got the job. (adjective)
The meeting <u>in the boardroom</u> was a success. (preposition)

Phrases are used effectively to introduce a sentence or to emphasize a point:

<u>In spite of the snow</u>, the convention proceeded on time.
It was clear, <u>from the voters' reaction</u>, that victory was at hand.

C22 Clauses

A group of words including a subject and a predicate is a clause.

Independent (main) clauses can stand alone because they express a complete thought (i.e., they can be sentences):

Each staff member was given a 6 percent salary increase.

Dependent (subordinate) clauses—not complete thoughts—usually occur in complex sentences in which they are connected to an independent clause:

<u>Because everyone had worked so hard</u>, each staff member was given a 6 percent salary increase.

Verb tenses must match. For example, if the verb in the main clause is in the past tense, the verb in the subordinate clause should be in the past tense also:

Because everyone <u>had worked</u> so hard, each staff member <u>was given</u> a 6 percent salary increase.

If the verb in the main clause expresses necessity, demand, a strong request, or urging, the present tense (without the *s* in the third person singular) should be used in the dependent clause:

They insist that she <u>report</u> to work immediately.

If the verb *to be* is used in the dependent clause, use only *be* with all three persons:

It is essential that I <u>be</u> present at the next meeting.

C

If a sentence begins with a subject and the verb to wish, the subordinate clause should contain a subjunctive verb:

> She wishes she <u>could attend</u> the seminar.
> They wished he <u>were going</u> with them to Ottawa.
> I wished I <u>had been able</u> to stay longer.

▶ C23 Types of sentences

A sentence is the most important part of the structure of language. Its shape may be simple or complicated. The writer's language expertise will determine which type of sentence suits the occasion and the reader.

Simple sentences consist of only one independent clause (a main thought) that may contain numerous words and phrases:

> The stock market rallied at the end of the week.

Complex sentences are made up of one independent clause and one or more dependent (subordinate) clauses:

> Although the stock market rallied at the end of the week, the brokers were not optimistic.
> After the stock market had rallied, the brokers, who had spent many sleepless nights, took a holiday.

Compound sentences contain two or more independent clauses (main thoughts):

> The crisis was over, so the brokers went home.

Compound-complex sentences are composed of two independent clauses and one or more dependent clauses:

> The crisis was over, so the brokers went home after they had finished the paperwork.

▶ C24 Sentence construction hints

Select your words with care. Use words as precisely as possible. Avoid wordiness.

> ***Wordy:*** The customer was angry because when he returned the merchandise the clerk was rude and she refused to give him a refund.

> ***Better:*** When the customer returned the merchandise, he was annoyed at the clerk's rudeness and refusal to refund the money.

Be grammatically consistent. Avoid disagreements in number, tense, or mood.

> ***Inconsistency in number:*** <u>Each person</u> is responsible for <u>their</u> own assignment.

> ***Correction:*** <u>Each person</u> is responsible for <u>his or her</u> own assignment.

> ***Inconsistency in tense:*** The architect <u>designed</u> the city hall, and then the council <u>rejects</u> it.

C

Correction: The architect <u>designed</u> the city hall, and then the council <u>rejected</u> it.

Inconsistency in mood: We <u>would</u> appreciate it if you <u>can</u> come early.

Correction: We <u>would</u> appreciate it if you <u>could</u> come early.

Use parallel (balanced) structure. Make your writing flow smoothly.

Not parallel: Do you think faxing or a courier would be faster?
(Here, <u>faxing</u> is a participle, <u>courier</u> is a noun.)

Correction: Do you think a fax or a courier would be faster?
(Here, <u>fax</u> and <u>courier</u> are both nouns.)

Position modifiers (descriptive expressions) properly. Closely related parts of a sentence should be placed close together to avoid ambiguity.

Improperly placed modifier: Having lost his job after 15 years of service, the company gave him a good separation package.

Correction: The company gave the man whom they "retired" after 15 years a good separation package.

Use the active voice as much as possible. Give your words energy.

Weak: His name will be seen in lights. (passive voice)

Better: He will see his name in lights. (active voice)

Avoid excessive co-ordination (too many "ands" and "buts").

Too many "ands": I attended a meeting and she stood up and took her time and started a long monologue on her new invention.

Correction: I attended a meeting, during which she stood up slowly and began a long monologue on her new invention.

Place the part to be stressed at the beginning.

Stress improperly placed: One of its major disadvantages is high cost, but our busy sales representatives really feel that the time it saves is worth the expense of a cellular phone.

Correction: Cellular phones save so much time that our sales representatives feel the cost is more than offset.

▶ C25   Sentence flaws to avoid

Sentence fragment (incomplete thought):

Although the singer is good.

Correction: The singer is good.

Comma fault (do not separate subject from verb unless a nonrestrictive clause is used):

The woman with the broken leg, could not walk.

Correction: The woman with the broken leg could not walk.
(See also this unit, C54.)

Shifted constructions:

Because of the recession and we are losing money, the plant will have to shut down.

Correction: Because of the recession and a loss of money, the plant will have to shut down.

– or –

Because we are suffering from the recession and are losing money, we will have to shut down.

Pronoun-antecedent non-agreement (pronoun must agree with antecedent in number and gender):

Everyone was given their own office.

Correction: Everyone was given his or her own office.

– or –

All staff members were given their own offices.

Subject-verb non-agreement (in number):

His contribution to the recycling committees were extremely high.

Correction: His contribution to the recycling committees was extremely high.

The president, as well as her staff, have arrived.

Correction: The president, as well as her staff, has arrived.

Incorrect case (nominative, objective, or possessive):

Me and my brother are telecommuters.

Correction: My brother and I are telecommuters.

We do not approve of them arriving late.

Correction: We do not approve of their arriving late.

NOTE A noun or pronoun preceding a gerund (e.g., *arriving*) is written in the possessive case.

Adjective and adverb confusion:

He did a real good job.

Correction: He did a really good job.

Kathy played good yesterday.

Correction: Kathy played a good game yesterday.

– or –

Kathy played well yesterday.

C

C26 THE PARAGRAPH

A paragraph is a series of sentences developing *one central purpose or idea*. The *topic* sentence opens the paragraph and the *transitional* one (linking the paragraph that follows) ends it.

> Golf is a game that many people play. Most of my friends are golf fanatics, and they particularly enjoy competition. (topic)

> The club in town runs four major tournaments each season to test every golfer's skill. (transitional)

Good paragraphing is an essential element of effective writing. It helps writers to progress logically by forcing them to stay on topic, and keeps readers on track by helping them to focus on one idea at a time.

Paragraphing business letters can sometimes be difficult. Most letters should contain at least two paragraphs, but very short letters, memos, faxes, and e-mail messages are acceptable with only one.

C27 PARTS OF SPEECH

Words are classified according to the jobs they do. These categories are called *parts of speech*. Although most words fall into just one classification, many are versatile and perform several functions. The information that follows is by no means complete. The user who requires full details should consult a more complete source.

Part of speech	Function	Example
Noun	Is a person, place, or thing	president, dog
Pronoun	Replaces person, place, or thing	me, it
Verb	Is an action word, state of being	go, talk, is
Adjective	Describes noun or pronoun	fair (referee)
Adverb	Describes verb or adjective	(talk) softly
Preposition	Connects noun or pronoun to make it the object	under (the window)
Conjunction (connective)	Connects words, phrases	(men) and (women)
Interjection	Is an expressive word	Wow!

▶ C28 Nouns

- ◆ names of persons, places, things, animals, actions, or concepts
- ◆ used as the subject or object of a sentence
- ◆ have singular, plural, and possessive forms

Types of nouns
Proper nouns

Person	*Place*
Mother Teresa	Canada
Conrad Black	Mt. Edziza
Pierre Berton	Beijing

Common nouns

Thing	*Animal*	*Action*
apple	bird	game
desk	dog	labour
tree	lion	race

Abstract nouns (concept)

hate, love, sympathy

Collective nouns (groups)

committee, population, team

Usage of noun

A noun can act either as the subject or the object of a sentence.

Forms of nouns

The original form of most nouns is singular (i.e., describing one person, place, etc.). It can be changed to a plural form and to a possessive form.

◆ Plural form of nouns

Most nouns are made plural by adding s to the singular:

apple	apples	committee	committees
boy	boys	Henrik Ibsen	the Ibsens
chair	chairs	valley	valleys

Exceptions to this rule include:

Nouns ending in ch, s, sh, x, *or* z—*add* es:

box	boxes	church	churches
brush	brushes	class	classes
bus	buses	fizz	fizzes
business	businesses	Jones	the Joneses

Nouns ending in y *preceded by a consonant—change* y *to* ies:

city	cities	country	countries	lady	ladies

Nouns ending in y *preceded by a vowel—add* s:

attorney	attorneys	tray	trays

Nouns ending in o *preceded by a consonant—add* es:

cargo	cargoes	potato	potatoes
hero	heroes	tomato	tomatoes

Exceptions include some musical terms, abbreviations, and nouns from foreign languages. Check the dictionary if you are in doubt.

condos	Filipinos	memos	pianos

Most nouns ending in o *preceded by a vowel form plurals by adding* s:

| radio | radios | rodeo | rodeos |
| ratio | ratios | studio | studios |

Most nouns ending in f *or* fe—*change* f *to* v *and add* es:

| knife | knives | loaf | loaves |
| life | lives | shelf | shelves |

Exceptions include: beliefs, chiefs, reefs. Hoof and roof can be either hoofs or hooves and roofs or rooves.

Never *change the* f *to* v *in proper nouns. Simply add* **s**:

Maple Leaf team
The Maple Leafs played at home last night.

Nouns with the same singular and plural forms:

deer	deer	sheep	sheep
fish	fish	trout	trout
series	series		

Nouns always singular in meaning include:

| measles | news | physics | politics |

Nouns always plural in meaning are:

| clothes | earnings | people | proceeds |

Some nouns have irregular plural endings:

| child | children | foot | feet | man | men | mouse | mice |

◆ Compound nouns

Hyphenated and compound words, as a rule, call for pluralizing the principal word:

leave of absence	leaves of absence
officer-in-charge	officers-in-charge
sister-in-law	sisters-in-law

If the compound word is foreign, add s *to the end of it*:

| cul-de-sac | cul-de-sacs |

Unhyphenated words form plurals by adding s to the end:

| cupful | cupfuls | yearbook | yearbooks |

◆ Latin and other foreign nouns

Some terms derived from other languages retain their own plurals; others have been anglicized. The following are the preferred plural forms of some commonly used expressions:

alumna	alumnae
appendix	appendices
campus	campuses
criterion	criteria

datum	data (may be used with a singular verb except in formal or technical usage)
formula	formulas
medium	media
memorandum	memorandums
thesis	theses

◆ Abbreviations, letters, numbers, words

Form the plural by adding *s*:

ands and buts	the 5 Cs	the pros and cons
in twos and threes	the 1900s	YMCAs
the PCs	the 2000s	

If the plural form is not clear with the simple addition of *s*, use *'s* to remove confusion:

37 B.A.'s and 42 B.Sc.'s

There are two a's in my name

◆ Possessive form of nouns

Nouns in the possessive form indicate ownership. To simplify speech and abbreviate writing, the apostrophe is used to replace the words *belonging to* or *of*. For example, instead of saying, "The workstation of Cindy is untidy," we say, "Cindy's workstation is untidy." Possessive nouns refer to living things rather than inanimate objects.

The walls of our office   – *not* –   Our office's walls

Basic rule: To make any noun (singular or plural) possessive, add *'s*:

Jack's car is an antique.

The judge's decision was final.

She spent $1000 on her children's clothes.

For a noun that ends in *s*, add only an apostrophe, for ease of pronunciation:

directors	directors' meeting
fathers	fathers' advice
girls	girls' shoes
secretaries	secretaries' desks
Del Marinas	Del Marinas' cottage

Exception: Add *'s* to one-syllable proper names ending in s: James's business. See also "Apostrophe," C37.

■ Articles

Most languages using an alphabet have a *definite article* and an *indefinite article* preceding nouns. In English, the definite article, which refers to something specific, is *the*; the indefinite article is *a* or *an*:

The weather is perfect today. (definite article)

A sunny day makes everyone happy. (indefinite article)

C

*<u>An</u> apple a day keeps the <u>doctor</u> away.
*They waited for <u>an</u> hour.

* **NOTE**   *An* is used instead of *a* before a noun beginning with a vowel or a vowel pronunciation.

▶ **C29 Pronouns**

◆ substitute for persons, places, things, and other nouns
◆ are used to avoid repetition of nouns/pronouns
◆ have singular and plural forms
◆ are used as the subject or object (direct or indirect)
◆ have three cases:

Nominative (subjective) (initiates action): *I, he, she, we, they, who*:

   <u>Who</u> can write good reports?

Objective (receives action): *me, him, her, us, them, whom*:

   Give <u>them</u> the printout.

Possessive (ownership): *my (mine), your (yours)*, etc.:

   I use <u>my</u> computer every day.

Types of pronouns
Personal pronouns replace persons or things.

Singular		
Subject	*Object*	*Possessive*
I	me	my, mine
you	you	your, yours
he, she, it	him, her, it	his, her, hers, its
Plural		
we	us	our, ours
you	you	your, yours
they	them	their, theirs

Impersonal (indefinite) pronouns have no specific relationship to a noun— they are always singular: *one, one's*.

Relative pronouns refer to nouns or pronouns that appear elsewhere in a sentence, usually as the antecedents.

Subject	Object	Possessive
who	whom	whose
which	which	whose
what	what	what
that	that	that

Please give my donation to the <u>person who</u> needs it most.

NOTE *Who* always refers to people. Additional forms of *who, which,* and *what* are also used to reflect or emphasize a noun. These forms are: *whoever, whomever, whichever, whatever.*

Reflexive pronouns refer to or stress the subject. The word *self* is always part of this pronoun:

The premier herself attended the rally.

Demonstrative pronouns point to specific nouns or pronouns and do not change their form: *this, that, these, those.*

Interrogative pronouns are used when asking a question: *Who? Whom? Whose? Which? What?*

▶ C30 Verbs

- ◆ tell what happens in a sentence
- ◆ are all or part of the predicate
- ◆ are used in first, second, or third person
- ◆ indicate time of action by tenses
- ◆ have active and passive voices
- ◆ have indicative, imperative, and subjunctive moods

Conjugation of verbs

Verbs, which must agree with the nouns that govern them, are conjugated (presented in different forms) in first, second, and third person singular and plural, as follows.

Regular verb (to work)	Singular	Plural
First person	I work	we work
Second person	you work	you work
Third person	he/she/it works	they work

NOTE The form changes only with the third person singular.

C

Irregular verb (to be) (does not follow the pattern of the regular verb)		
First person	I am	we are
Second person	you are	you are
Third person	he/she/it is	they are

Just as words begin with a root, verbs start with the *infinitive*, the basic verb form preceded by *to* (e.g., *to work, to travel*). From this starting point come the other forms of the verb.

Verb tenses

The principal parts of a verb guide you to the time of action (i.e., the *tenses* of verbs).

Infinitive	Present tense	Past tense	Past participle	Present participle
to ask	I ask	asked	(was) asked	(am) asking
to like	I like	liked	(have) liked	(am) liking

The present tense is formed from the infinitive; the progressive present tense, indicating ongoing action, is formed by using the verb *to be* and the present participle (e.g., *I am going; they are planning a trip*, etc.). The past tense of regular verbs adds *ed*, as does the past participle, which is always used in conjunction with the auxiliary verbs *to be* or *to have*. Irregular verbs do not follow this rule. Refer to the dictionary for the principal parts of irregular verbs.

Voice

Verbs can be used in either the active or the passive *voice*. Active voice is used when the subject directs the verb. Passive voice makes the subject the receiver of the action (hence, passive) and thus diminishes the strength of the statement.

James wrote an excellent program. (active)
An excellent program was written by James. (passive)

Mood

The *mood* of a verb conveys the feeling of the subject.

Indicative mood shows the ongoing action of the subject:

Josie is planning a workshop for us.

Imperative mood takes the form of a command:

Leave the room at once!

Subjunctive mood expresses a wish or hope:

If I were younger, I could run the marathon with you.

C

Types of verbs

Regular verbs form their parts according to the basic rule mentioned under "Verb tenses," on the previous page.

Present	Past	Past participle	Present participle
open	open*ed*	open*ed*	open*ing*
sail	sail*ed*	sail*ed*	sail*ing*
work	work*ed*	work*ed*	work*ing*

Irregular verbs do not conform to the basic rule. Some examples of irregular verbs, given in the first person singular, are shown below.

Infinitive	Present	Past	Past participle *(with have or has)*
to be	am	was	been
to begin	begin	began	begun
to bring	bring	brought	brought
to come	come	came	come
to do	do	did	done
to get	get	got	got
to give	give	gave	given
to go	go	went	gone
to have	have	had	had
to know	know	knew	known
to lay	lay	laid	laid
to lie	lie	lay	lain
to ride	ride	rode	ridden
to run	run	ran	run
to see	see	saw	seen
to sing	sing	sang	sung
to speak	speak	spoke	spoken
to take	take	took	taken
to throw	throw	threw	thrown
to write	write	wrote	written

Auxiliary verbs are used in conjunction with other verbs. The auxiliaries are *to be* and *to have* and are used in the following forms, among others: *be, can, could, have, may, might, ought, shall, should, will, would.*

> They <u>should</u> arrive at any minute.
> You <u>can</u> help Jack in records management if you like.

Transitive verbs require a direct object to complete the meaning of the sentence. Some examples are *believe, catch, cook, lay, play, raise, wear.*

> Geese <u>lay</u> large eggs.
> Lu <u>plays</u> the clarinet, trombone, and trumpet.

C

Intransitive verbs do not require a direct object to complete the meaning of the sentence. Some examples are *be, become, grow, lie, rise, seem, stay*.

> My job *is* very stressful.
> In the tropics, many people *lie* down at siesta time.
> Our sales <u>seem</u> to be on target.

Linking verbs (copula verbs) are non-action words that often connect subject and adjective. Some of these verbs are *appear, feel, look, sound, smell, taste*.

> The office <u>feels</u> cool today.

Gerunds are the present forms of verbs with *ing* endings and are used as nouns.

> <u>Getting</u> that report out on time was a challenge.

▶ C31   Adjectives

- ◆ describe a noun or pronoun
- ◆ are classified into three degrees of comparison
- ◆ can answer the questions how many? what kind? which one?

> Ramesh has worked with us for <u>several</u> years.
> If we buy <u>superior</u> equipment, it will last.
> You are invited to our <u>next</u> meeting.

Adjective comparison

Because adjectives modify nouns or pronouns that can be either singular or plural, they must change to match those nouns. Adjectives fall into three categories, called degrees of comparison:

- ◆ The simple form applies to a singular noun.
- ◆ The comparative compares two nouns/pronouns.
- ◆ The superlative compares more than two.

> Our <u>new</u> office is spacious and bright. (simple)
> Your office is <u>newer</u> than ours. (comparative)
> Mr. Black's office is the <u>newest</u> one in the building. (superlative)

Most adjectives change to the comparative form by adding *r* or *er* to the simple form and to the superlative by adding *st* or *est* to the simple form.

Simple	Comparative	Superlative
brave	braver	bravest
busy	busier	busiest
cold	colder	coldest
old	older	oldest

Irregular adjectives do not conform to the regular pattern when changing to comparative and superlative. Most of them are common words; some of them are often misused.

Simple	Comparative	Superlative
bad	worse	worst
good	better	best
little	less	least
many	more	most
much	more	most
well	better	best

Most adjectives of two or more syllables use *more/less* and *most/least* to form comparatives and superlatives.

Simple	Comparative	Superlative
careful	more careful	most careful
descriptive	less descriptive	least descriptive

Compound adjectives are a combination of two or more words used as an adjective to describe a noun. They should be hyphenated if they precede the noun they modify:

Dennis has an <u>old-fashioned</u> printer.
An <u>18-year-old</u> university student joined us.
Thank you for your <u>up-to-date</u> report.

– but –

Please bring your report up to date.

Linking verbs with adjectives
Use an adjective with the verbs *feel, look, smell, sound, taste*:

Most employees feel <u>satisfied</u> on payday.
The buffet you have arranged looks <u>impressive</u>.
Doesn't lobster taste <u>delicious</u>!

▶ **C32 Adverbs**

◆ modify verbs, adjectives, and other adverbs
◆ are used mainly in answer to the question "How?"

The Canadian team played <u>well</u>.

It was <u>extremely</u> hot last summer.

A wise worker evaluates <u>daily</u>.

Christo writes <u>very</u> quickly.

One clue to identifying adverbs is that they often end in *ly*—the ending that is added to an adjective to change it to an adverb.

Adjective	Adverb
real	really
reasonable	reasonably
special	specially
sure	surely

Many common adverbs, however, do not have the *ly* ending. Some examples are *again, everywhere, here, now, soon, there, very, well.*

Adverbs can never be the subject of a sentence:

Here is the doctor. (<u>doctor</u> is the subject)

A number of adverbs have two forms (the first of which is also an adjective), but only one form can be correct in a sentence. Some examples of these words are:

close	closely	loud	loudly
direct	directly	quiet	quietly
fair	fairly	short	shortly
hard	hardly	slow	slowly
late	lately	wide	widely

The train arrived <u>late</u>.
They took the <u>slow</u> train.

Have you read any good books <u>lately</u>?
Please drive <u>slowly</u>.

▶ C33 Prepositions

◆ link a noun/pronoun to show its relationship to another word in a sentence

◆ always make their nouns the objects

Please give this package <u>to</u> Mr. Ho.

That fine illustration was done <u>by</u> Laura.

Some of the most common prepositions are:

about	as	beside	for	near	over
above	at	between	from	of	to
across	before	by	in/into	off	up/upon
among	below	down	like	on	with

▶ C34 Conjunctions

◆ connect words, phrases, or clauses

Co-ordinating conjunctions link similar grammatical parts (i.e., word to word, phrase to phrase, or clause to clause). The most common co-ordinating conjunctions are: *and, but, for, or, nor, yet.*

You <u>and</u> Sylvia share the same workstation.

You enjoy keyboarding <u>but</u> Sylvia does not.

A number of co-ordinating conjunctions are also *conjunctive adverbs*— they connect independent clauses. Some examples are:

accordingly	however	nevertheless
also	moreover	now
furthermore	neither	therefore

The project is incomplete; <u>therefore</u>, we will have to work on Saturday.

We want to win the contest; <u>accordingly</u>, we will have to increase our efforts.

NOTE   A semicolon precedes a conjunctive adverb and a comma follows it.

Correlative conjunctions are used in pairs to relate words, phrases, or clauses to each other. Examples of these are:

both .... and	not only .... but also
either .... or	whether .... or
neither .... nor	

<u>Neither</u> sleet nor snow will hold up the <u>mail</u>.

<u>Not only</u> is the accountant accurate, <u>but</u> he is <u>also</u> conscientious.

Subordinate conjunctions connect dependent clauses to independent clauses. They can also act as adjectives, adverbs, or nouns. Examples are:

after	because	in order that	since	whereas
although	before	otherwise	unless	while
as	if	provided	until	

<u>After</u> the statistics were compiled, the accounting department went home.

You may use our courier service, <u>provided</u> you complete a requisition form.

▶ C35   Interjections

◆ are single, emphatic expressions, usually followed by an exclamation mark:

Oh!	Ouch!	Wow!

C36 PUNCTUATION

Punctuation marks give sentences meaning and expression. Properly used, punctuation makes the reading of sentences easier by showing the relationships among the various parts.

Punctuating should not be a difficult matter. If, however, you do have a problem choosing the appropriate punctuation for a sentence, perhaps your sentence has been improperly constructed. Should this be

C

the case, restructure your sentence into a form that you *know* is correct and one that consequently becomes easy for you to punctuate. The information in this section will acquaint you with all of the punctuation marks that might be used in a sentence.

C37 APOSTROPHE (')

Use the apostrophe to form contractions, to indicate omissions, to form plurals, to form possessives, and as a single quotation mark.

▶ C38 To form contractions

When a letter or number is omitted, use an apostrophe to indicate the omission:

you are	you're	I will	I'll
do not	don't	2008	'08
does not	doesn't	Halloweven	Hallowe'en

NOTE Do not use an apostrophe to form the possessive of personal pronouns: *yours* not your's

theirs not their's

▶ C39 To show omissions

Use the apostrophe where the noun modified is not shown:

We're going to the Sullivans'. (home implied)

▶ C40 In plurals

Although plurals of many single letters or words are formed simply by adding an *s* (see this unit, C28), the apostrophe is used before the *s* in cases where confusion might result with the addition of s only:

Please dot all the i's.

One can never earn too many A's.

– but –

He understood the five Cs.

They ordered five new PCs.

▶ C41 To form possessives

In singular nouns

To form the *singular possessive*, add an apostrophe plus *s* *('s)*.

Singular	Possessive
assistant	assistant's
boy	boy's
witness	witness's
woman	woman's
Charles	Charles's
Joan Haslam	Joan Haslam's

The <u>boy's</u> coat and the <u>woman's</u> shoes were dirty.
<u>Joan Haslam's</u> responsibility is to pay the <u>assistant's</u> salary.
You are invited to <u>Charles's</u> party tonight.

NOTE Where the addition of an apostrophe plus *s* would add a new syllable that would make pronunciation difficult, add the apostrophe only:

goodness   goodness'
For goodness' sake be on time!

Use of *it is* or *it's*

its   is the possessive form
it's   is the abbreviated form of it is

TIP   When is it its?
When it's not, it is
When is it it's?
When it is it is.

With compound words

Add the possessive ending to the last syllable:

She borrowed her <u>father-in-law's</u> car.

In plural nouns

To form the *plural possessive*, add an apostrophe if the plural noun ends in *s*; add an apostrophe plus *s* if it does not.

Plural	Possessive
boys	*boys'
children	children's
men	men's
witnesses	*witnesses'
women	women's

* The *s* after the apostrophe is omitted in most plural words ending in *s* to make pronunciation easier. The words noted above are examples.

<u>Boys'</u> coats and <u>women's</u> shoes are on special this week.
The two <u>witnesses'</u> testimony continued all day.
The <u>children's</u> bulletin board was blank.

NOTE Possessive pronouns are already possessive (see this unit, C29). They do not need the addition of an apostrophe:

According to an old cliché, "You can't judge a book by <u>its</u> cover."

To indicate types of ownership

Individual ownership: To show individual ownership when two or more words or names are involved, use an apostrophe after both words to make the meaning clear. The following example clarifies that both Phil and Maya had high marks, but they did not both get the same mark:

Phil's and Maya's marks were good last term.

Joint ownership: Using an apostrophe only after the final name or word indicates that ownership is shared:

Hulan, Emily, and Nadia's apartment is spacious.

In expressions relating to time or measure

They ordered <u>ten dollars'</u> worth of muffins to go.
Justin will be home in <u>two months'</u> time.
She was released with <u>one week's</u> pay.

With gerunds

When a verb form ending in *ing* is used as a noun (gerund), the noun or pronoun that precedes it takes the possessive form:

We were surprised by <u>John's</u> leaving.

NOTE Inanimate objects (non-living things) do not generally use the possessive form. Restructure your sentence to avoid such problems:

The colour of the wall

– not –

The wall's colour

▶ C42 As single quotation mark

When a quotation occurs within a quotation, use quotation marks for the main quotation and the apostrophe (single quotation mark) to surround the inner one:

Mr. Stefanopoulos said, "They told me this was a 'rush' order."

C43 COLON (:)

▶ C44 With direct quotations

Introduce a quotation of more than three lines with a colon:

When you are feeling downhearted, remember these lines from the poem "Smile":

We know the distance to the sun,
    The size and weight of earth,
But no one's ever told us yet
    How much a smile is worth.

Use the colon to introduce and to separate:

Kelly was asked to order the following: ten dozen pens, six boxes of paper, four toner cartridges, and an up-to-date dictionary.

▶ C45 With introductory statements followed by lists or series

Use a colon to introduce a list (and, sometimes, examples, as has been done in this book):

The agenda is as follows: ...
They brought the following: ...
We still need these dishes for the staff party: stroganoff, rice, salad, and broccoli.

NOTE Use a period rather than a colon if the introductory statement is contained within a preceding sentence:

Participants will find that the following agenda items will provoke a lively meeting. The items have been carefully selected.
Flexible hours
Cash bonuses
Staff holidays

▶ C46 In business letters

Use a colon after the salutation in business letters when mixed (standard) punctuation is being used (see Unit 12, K20):

Dear Ms. Chang:

Use a colon to separate the reference initials:

PHE:PS

▶ C47 In times and ratios

Use a colon to separate hours and minutes:

9:56 a.m.   21:56

Show ratios with a colon:

3:2

▶ C48 In references to publications

Separate the title from the subtitle with a colon:

Canadian Business: Its Nature and Environment

C49 COMMA (,)

The comma is the most common punctuation mark and is often misused and overworked. Apply good sense to your writing by asking yourself if there *is* need for a pause where you have placed the comma. Remember, "When in doubt, leave it out!"

▶ C50 In compound sentences to separate independent clauses linked by a conjunction

Compound sentences contain two or more independent clauses. Independent (main) clauses are complete thoughts that have their own subjects. When these are joined by a conjunction (*and, but, for, or, nor, yet*), use a comma before the conjunction to separate them. An exception is permitted if the sentence is quite short.

C

Subject 1

Our former office manager demanded a very high standard of work,

Subject 2

but the new one is more interested in quantity than in quality.

Exception: The former manager demanded high work standards but the new one does not.

NOTE If a conjunction does not separate the clauses, use a semicolon, not a comma. If one or both of the clauses already has internal punctuation, use a semicolon. (See this unit, C87, for information on semicolon usage.)

▶ C51 After introductory words, phrases, or clauses

Place a comma after an introductory word, phrase, or clause:

Yes, restructuring is essential.

In the circumstances, it was the best decision.

Our journey over, we checked into a motel.

When the convention ended, all of the participants flew home.

▶ C52 To set off parenthetical expressions

Parenthetical words and phrases are ones that are not essential to the meaning of the sentence but give added emphasis. Such expressions can occur at the beginning, within, or at the end of a sentence. They should be set off by commas:

Needless to say, he did not show up.

The matter, as far as I am concerned, is closed.

England is a beautiful country, without a doubt.

Everyone knew, of course, that Adana would win the party leadership.

The most popular version, however, is out of print.

▶ The following words and phrases are common introductory and parenthetical expressions that are usually set off with commas:

accordingly	however	obviously
also	in addition	of course
as a matter of fact	in fact	otherwise
as a result	in my opinion	personally
besides	in other words	secondly
consequently	in the meantime	that is
finally	meanwhile	therefore
first, first of all	moreover	thus
for example	namely	well
fortunately	needless to say	without a doubt
further, furthermore	nevertheless	yet

C

▶ C54   To set off appositives

Appositives are words or phrases that rename or explain something about the subject, and should be set off by commas:

> Telemarketing, an effective sales tool, is gaining in popularity.
> Kieron, a recent immigrant, is an excellent advertising representative.
> Your best friend, Sylvia Harding, won the competition.

NOTE   Restrictive appositives (those that are essential to identification) should not be set off by commas:

> Your employee Yuko Ohga telephoned us.

▶ C54   To set off non-restrictive phrases and clauses

Restrictive phrases and clauses contribute information to the sentence and are *not* set off by commas.

Non-restrictive phrases and clauses do not add essential information to the sentence. The sentence could stand without them, so they are set off by commas:

> Our new computer, which is in constant use, is a major addition to our office. (Commas are used to set off the non-restrictive expression.)
>
> The new computer that we bought last week is much more powerful than our first one. (Commas are not used because that we bought last week is essential to the meaning of the sentence.)
>
> Employees who can operate computers are highly paid. (essential to meaning—restrictive)
>
> Leon, who is a computer operator, obtained a well-paid job. (not essential to meaning—non-restrictive)

NOTE   *That* and *which* are used in very specific ways with restrictive and non-restrictive clauses. *That* introduces restrictive clauses (no comma); *which*, non-restrictive (comma needed).

▶ C55   To set off subordinate clauses

Use a comma to set off a subordinate clause that precedes the main clause:

> Assuming that you will arrive tomorrow, we will schedule the meeting for 2 p.m.

▶ C56   To separate independent adjectives

When two or more adjectives precede a noun or when several adjectives follow the noun they are describing, use a comma:

> He is a punctual, efficient employee.
> That employee, punctual and efficient, deserves a raise.

C

But when the first adjective qualifies the second, omit the comma:

a <u>large, blue</u> binder

a <u>bright blue</u> binder

The test here is to try to use *and* where the comma might be inserted. If *and* would work, use a comma; if it would not, leave the comma out.

▶ **C57   To separate items in a series**

Insert a comma after all words, phrases, and clauses in a series:

> Her favourite colours are green, purple, and orange.
> The visitors were expected to behave politely, to ask questions, and to return to the hotel by noon.

NOTE   When commas are used within the items in a series, separate the items with semicolons. (See this unit, C90, on semicolon usage.)
Commas are not needed when conjunctions are used in a series:

> Her favourite colours are green and purple and orange.

A comma is needed after the final item in the series when *no* conjunction is used:

> Green, purple, orange, are her favourite colours.

If *etc.* ends the series, use a comma before and after the *etc.*, unless the *etc.* occurs at the sentence end.

> Hockey, baseball, lacrosse, etc., are popular sports.

▶ **C58   In dates**

Separate the day from the year, and the year from what follows, by a comma, unless using the international date method:

> September <u>1</u>, 20-- (but 20-- 09 01)
> Thank you for your letter of September <u>1, 20--</u>, in which...
> <u>Monday, September 13</u>, is the day we leave.

– but not when the date is incomplete –

> Mr. Ondaatje retired in June 2000.
> The year 2000 was important to me. (restrictive; no commas needed)

HINT   Use the function key in the software you are using to bring in the current date.
Keep the month and day together (use a hardspace when keying dates in body or text of document), i.e., April[ ]19, 2000.

▶ C59   In addresses

Place commas after the street address and the town or city when they run on in text, but not before the postal code:

130 Franklin Street, Brandon, Manitoba R7A 5P1

In text, set off the city name and/or province, etc., from the rest of the sentence:

Calgary, Alberta, is a large city.
He lives at 136 Bay Street, Toronto, in an apartment.

▶ C60   In names and titles

Separate the name from the title by means of a comma:

T. Ginelli, our sales manager, is retiring.
J.B. McCumber, Ph.D., is our guest speaker.
Mr. J. Barry, Jr.

– but –

Roger Aldrich II

Do not separate initials from names (use hardspace to keep together).

▶ C61   To set off repeated words or numbers coming together

To avoid confusion, use a comma:

What the task is, is unknown.
No, no, that won't do!
In 2004, 4000 more hectares will be sold.

▶ C62   To show omissions

Insert a comma to indicate that one or more words have been omitted:

He travelled the scenic route; she, the most direct one. (Here, travelled is implied after she.)

▶ C63   Between a statement and a question

Insert a comma to separate the two parts:

I think she did a good job, don't you?

▶ C64   In direct address

Use commas to set off the name of the person:

Thank you, Mr. Kormos, for paying your bill so promptly.

▶ C65   With interruptions, contrasting expressions, and afterthoughts

Set off such expressions with commas:

Katalin, rather than Gayle, completed the assignment.
He was, I suppose, guaranteed a refund.

C

▶ C66   With direct quotations

Use commas as illustrated here:

"I hope," Pierre said, "that you can accept our invitation."

▶ C67   Avoiding comma problems

Restrictive clauses and phrases do not require commas because they are essential to the meaning of the sentence:

The man who held the smoking gun was the obvious killer.
The acid rain that fell on the region damaged the crops.

Do not be trapped into using a comma between the subject and the verb unless these are separated by a non-restrictive clause.

Incorrect: The new computer with the high-resolution colour monitor, gave graphics another dimension.
Correct: The new computer with the high-resolution colour monitor gave graphics another dimension.

– or –

The new computer, which had a high-resolution colour monitor, gave graphics another dimension.

C68   DASH (—)

A dash is a separating device that is used to set off certain kinds of parenthetical expressions. Use it to enlarge on a point or to give strong emphasis to a statement. Do not, however, overwork the dash in your writing because you will diminish the special emphasis it provides.

Roger lost a tough battle—and I don't blame him for being disappointed.
The manager—I'm pleased to say—gave them a special commendation.
Keetah plays excellent tennis—she has lost only 1 match out of 20 this month.
Linda was promoted to Branch Manager—a well-earned promotion.

Use the dash to set off parenthetical expressions that are already punctuated:

He went west—Calgary, Edmonton, and Vancouver—on his last sales trip.

NOTE   With some software, you make dashes by using two hyphens without spacing. Other software permits the user to make the full dash that is shown in the preceding examples.
Always position a dash at the end of a line, never at the beginning.

C69   EXCLAMATION MARK (!)

Use an exclamation mark to indicate surprise, enthusiasm, strong emotion, or a command:

Happy birthday, Canada!
Stop, thief!

Use the exclamation mark after the interjections *Ah* and *Oh*:

Ah! What low prices!
Oh! How beautiful!

Use the exclamation mark when a single exclamatory word is used as a sentence:

Help!   Wait!

When exclamations are not strong ones, use a comma or a period rather than an exclamation mark:

No, this is not quite satisfactory.

NOTE   One exclamation mark does the job. *Never* use a string of them in formal writing.

C70   HYPHEN (-)

Use a hyphen to form compound words (e.g., *job-sharing*) and adjectives or to indicate word division (see this unit, C13).

▶ C71 In compound adjectives

When two or more words are used in combination immediately preceding the noun they modify, join them with a hyphen to form a compound adjective:

They went away for a six-day holiday.
My car has a four-cylinder engine.

These are state-of-the-art computers.
The job involves the development of problem-solving skills.

Do not use a hyphen when each adjective separately describes the subject:

Her brother is a big, strong man.

Do not use a hyphen when an expression is used adverbially:

This is the most up-to-date edition I could find. (adjective)
It is time to bring this edition up to date. (adverb)

Do not use a hyphen after words ending in *-ly*:

The beautifully wrapped gift came as a complete surprise

▶ C72 In fractions

When fractions standing alone are spelled out, use a hyphen:

Two-thirds of the residents are employed downtown.

▶ C73 In numbers

Use a hyphen when the spelled-out number consists of two words:

> The band consisted of <u>twenty-nine</u> musicians.

▶ C74 With prefixes and suffixes

Most prefixes and suffixes do not require a hyphen. Use them:

◆ to avoid confusion:

> Co-op *not* coop
> re-cover *not* recover

◆ when the prefix ends and the root word begins with the same letter:

> anti-intellectual   pre-empt

◆ after *self* and *ex*:

> self-control   ex-officio

◆ when followed by a capitalized word:

> mid-Atlantic   pre-Cambrian

◆ with *great* in family relationships (but not with *step* or *grand*):

> great-grandfather   stepbrother

◆ with the suffix elect:

> Mayor-elect

▶ C75 In word division

Use a hyphen to divide words (see this unit, C137).

NOTE   When a series of hyphenated adjectives modifies one noun, use a hyphen to avoid repetition. Leave a space after the first hyphen:

> A *three-* to four-month tour   – *not* –   A *three-month* to *four-month* tour

C76 PARENTHESES (), SQUARE BRACKETS [], AND BRACE BRACKETS {}

▶ C77 Parentheses

These are used with parenthetical expressions (i.e., explanatory or supplemental material) made by the author and incidental to the context. Commas and dashes could be used to perform the same functions, but parentheses tend to *de-emphasize* while other forms of punctuation *emphasize*.

> Grammar (*essential to every student*) is high on the priority list.

Parentheses can also be used to set off expressions that require an abrupt change of direction by the reader:

> I saw an ad for a car (*it was in the* Vancouver Sun, *I think*) and went to look at it.

They are also used to provide references:

Letter styles (Chapter 3) was the next topic covered.

Use parentheses to set off enumerations in narrative form:

The reasons I want to leave are: (a) more pay, (b) shorter hours, (c) better prospects.

Use parentheses to set off money amounts or other figures that have been written in words in formal documents:

Five hundred thousand dollars ($500 000)

NOTE   Any needed punctuation must be placed outside the closing parenthesis (unless an abbreviation occurs):

We are leaving on Wednesday (August 13, I think), but we still have much to do.

▶ C78   Square brackets [] and brace brackets {}

Brackets are used to set off inserted matter that is incidental to the context. The insertion is usually made by someone other than the author (e.g., an editor's comments or explanations):

In 1938, he [Best] was involved in one of Canada's most exciting medical research undertakings.

Brackets are also used to set off parenthetical expressions that occur within parenthetical expressions. Use parentheses for the main expression and brackets for the one that comes within it:

Some fine Elizabethan literature (written by William Shakespeare [sixteenth and seventeenth centuries] and others) is still enjoyed today.

Brace brackets can be used to enclose words or figures in books or medical journals.

C79   PERIOD (.)

Use a period after a sentence, a polite request, or an indirect question:

The sun came up very early that day.
Would you kindly send us your cheque.
He asked whether we were willing to go.

Use a period with abbreviations:

Mr. S. Eby	a.m.	attach. (see Unit 12, K35)
St. Cecelia's Church	Ph.D.	
R.S.V.P.	encl.	

For organizations known by abbreviations, the current trend is to omit periods:

IBM	YMCA	CBC

C

NOTE If an abbreviation closes a sentence, only *one* period is needed at the end of the sentence. If a question mark or exclamation mark closes the sentence, position the mark outside the period:

> The goods must have been shipped C.O.D.
> Were the goods shipped C.O.D.?

Use a period to indicate decimals:

In money amounts	$17.75
In percentages	1.82%
With decimal fractions	6.667

Use periods in a series (ellipses) to indicate omissions. This device is used with quoted material. (See Unit 12, K63.)

> Fowler describes grammar as "...the science of language."

C80   ELLIPSIS MARK

Use the ellipsis mark to indicate omissions within quotations. (See Unit 12, K60.)

The ellipsis mark consists of:

◆ three spaced periods (. . .).

> The author says her novel shows "a pattern. . . of how in these small events and in these small lives the world intrudes."

NOTE Use the ellipsis mark and a period, i.e., four periods, if the omission comes at the end of the sentence:

> "The novel quickly moves back in time to the afternoon of the funeral...."

C81   SLASH OR RIGHT DIAGONAL(/)

Use the slash between options and to separate lines of poetry that are run in to the text:

◆ **options:**   P/N/F (meaning "Please Note and Forward")
                    I do not know why the Spring/Summer rates are different.

◆ **poetry:**   Margaret Avison begins "The Swimmer's Moment" with a
                    statement of her universal theme: "For everyone/The swimmer's
                    moment at the whirlpool comes" (1–2).

C82   QUESTION MARK (?)

▶ **C83   Use a question mark**

◆ at the end of a direct question:

> How much does it cost?

◆ to express doubt. Place the question mark in parentheses and use it after the doubtful term:

> He was born in 1963 (?).

◆ To add emphasis, the question mark *may* be used after each question in a series of questions within one sentence. In this case, do not capitalize the first letters of the questions and leave only one space after the question marks:

> Which do you think is more important for career success: having good qualifications? being well educated? possessing a sparkling personality?

▶ C84 Do not use a question mark

◆ after an indirect question:

> I asked him how much it cost.

◆ after a polite request:

> Will you please find out the cost.

C85 QUOTATION MARKS (" ")

Use these in the following ways.

▶ C86 In direct quotes (the exact wording used by a writer or speaker)

> The man cried, "Stop, thief!" and then called the police.
> He said, "Stop, or I'll call the police."
> Did he say, "Stop, or I'll call the police"? No, he did not.
> "If you don't stop," he said, "I'll call the police."
> "Please lend me ten dollars," said Louise.
> "Steve," said Kelly, "can you help me?"

When a quoted reference contains fewer than three lines, place quotation marks at the beginning and end of the quoted material. When more than one paragraph of quoted material is used, use quotation marks at the beginning of each paragraph and at the end of the final paragraph.

> "
> _____
> _____
> _____
> "
> _____
> _____ "

Long quotations do not need quotation marks because they are indented and set off from the rest of the text. See Unit 12, K60.

NOTE Use single quotation marks for the second quotation when a quotation within a quotation must be indicated:

> She said, "I heard him say, 'Come to dinner'."

Use quotation marks to enclose words used in a particular way:

> Although he was not actually put in jail, he was held in "protective" custody for three days.

C

Frequently, the same key is used for both beginning and ending quotation marks. If your software offers you both beginning and ending quotation marks (smart quotes), use them in preference to the indistinguishable type, especially in desktop-publishing applications.

▶ C87 With titles

Parts of magazines, parts of books, articles, essays, sermons, titles of television and radio programs, songs, speeches, and poems are indicated by quotation marks:

> The poem "Ode on a Grecian Urn," by Keats, is famous.
> When you read Chapter 5, "Punctuation," study the section entitled "Comma."

▶ C88 For special emphasis

If you want your reader to be aware that you are using an expression in an unusual way or are attempting to be humorous, use quotation marks for emphasis. Technical terms used in a non-technical way can be emphasized this way also.

> Unfortunately, we committed a "no-no" on our last statement.
> He used the term "input" eight times in the last four minutes.

▶ C89 Punctuating with quotation marks

Current practice is to place quotation marks outside commas and periods (see the examples in C87, above). When used with colons and semicolons, however, quotation marks are placed inside the punctuation:

> Please learn the following verse from "Wildflowers":

Question marks and exclamation marks go inside the closing quotes when they apply only to the quoted matter (see the third example in C86). They go outside when they apply to the entire sentence:

> "It is the east, and Juliet is the sun!"

C90 SEMICOLON (;)

The semicolon is used in a sentence when a stronger break than that provided by a comma is needed.

▶ C91 In compound sentences

Compound sentences consist of two or more independent, related clauses.

Use a semicolon to separate independent, closely related clauses when the second clause is introduced by a transitional expression. Examples of transitional expressions are: *however, therefore, in fact, in other words*. A more complete list is provided in this unit, C52.

> Sales are down badly this quarter; in fact, they are at a record-breaking low.

Use a semicolon to separate independent clauses that are not connected by a conjunction, as in this example:

Fireplaces bring comfort in winter; pools offer cool relaxation in summer.

Use a semicolon before the conjunction (*and*, *but*, etc.) to separate independent related clauses if one or both already contain punctuation:

They promised a much leaner, meaner, and efficient government; and they produced a perfect government.

▶ **C92 In a series**

Use a semicolon for clarity when a comma has already been used to punctuate items in the series:

Most of the executives were present: Hugh Fine, president, Ottawa; Elisabeth Jacques, treasurer, Trois-Rivières; Todd Taylor, secretary, Edmonton; and James Zabig, vice-president, Halifax.

It should be noted that use of the semicolon is decreasing in favour of the comma in business communications. Of the three rules presented in C91, the first is still commonly used, while the other two apply mainly to formal and literary writing. In business, a good rule of thumb is to ask yourself, "Would a comma serve the same purpose as a semicolon, or should a period replace it?" In common usage, a comma could replace a semicolon in the following example:

The wind was high; the sea was rough.

C93 UNDERSCORE (_)

Use the underscore (underline) in handwritten or keyed material to indicate titles of books, plays, works of art, magazines, newspapers, words that need emphasis, and foreign expressions:

Hard Times is a fine novel by Charles Dickens.
The last issue of Maclean's contained an interesting article.
Have you seen Michelangelo's sculpture, the Pietà?
Please tell Bill that this order is rush.

C94 ITALICS

Italics refers to a printing style as shown in this sentence.

◆ Use italics to give special emphasis:

The enclosed information is *confidential*.
Always key *your initials* at the end of documents.

◆ Use italics to set off figures, letters, and words referred to as figures, letters, and words. Usually the word to be defined is italicized and the definition is quoted to distinguish the two elements.

C

The word *principal* meaning "a sum of money on which interest is paid" is often misspelled.

Remember to spell accommodation with two *c's* and two *m's.*

◆ Use italics to set off foreign words and phrases that have not been absorbed into the English language:

What does *caveat emptor* mean?

◆ Use italics to set off titles of complete works published and bound separately: books, poems, magazines, movies, musicals, newspapers, operas, pamphlets, periodicals, and plays. Names of airplanes, ships, spacecraft, and trains are also italicized. Use quotation marks to set off titles of speeches, articles and chapters within books and periodicals, and works of art.

The motion picture *Gone With the Wind* has become a classic.

Did you read this month's issue of *Maclean's* magazine?

We took a cruise to Alaska on the *Nieuw Amsterdam.*

Mr. Renzella chose "Five Important Steps for Financial Planning Success" as the topic for his presentation.

She was asked to order a copy of the *Pitman Office Handbook.*

◆ When referring to the title of a book and to a chapter in it, use italics **or** underline the title of the book and use quotation marks for the chapter title.

Chapter 2 of *English at Work* is entitled "Writing Styles."

NOTE Another method of keying titles is to use all capitals. This method is often used in correspondence of publishing houses in which titles occur frequently. It is also used in advertising and sales promotion as an eye-catching device. Avoid using this style for general use.

If italic type is available to you, you may use it instead of the underscore for the items listed in C93.

NOTE Punctuation marks are not underlined unless they are an integral part of the expression to be underscored.

Pietà? – *not* – *Pietà?*

C95 STYLE MECHANICS

Style defines the details—the mechanics—of the writer's craft. Writing styles are constantly changing. Today, productivity is key, clarity is paramount, and simplicity is desirable. As a result, rules and conventions that used to apply no longer do. Organizations are moving more toward styles and conventions that suit their particular purposes. For example, desktop publishing has resulted in changes in rules for spacing following punctuation marks, the reduced use of hyphens in compounds, and more sparing use of capitalization. This section

C

provides a set of suggested standards that are generally acceptable, that are consistent with the practices of most organizations, and that have productivity as a major concern.

C96 ABBREVIATIONS

Generally, abbreviations should be avoided if they might be misinterpreted; however, they are acceptable in statistical or tabulated matter.

◆ Use only common abbreviations that cannot be misunderstood.

◆ Use capitals only if the word being abbreviated is capitalized:

etc.   *ibid.*   Mon.   Nov.   vs.   i.e.   e.g.

◆ Use the ampersand (&) *only in company names,* never in text matter:

Braithwaite & Singh   Zimmer & Co., Ltd.

NOTE   Do not change *and* to &. Follow what is printed on the company letterhead.

◆ Pluralize most abbreviations by adding *s*. Where confusion is possible, add *'s*:

The five Cs   Dot all the i's.

▶ C97   Academic degrees

Academic degrees are generally abbreviated. No space follows the periods in the abbreviation:

B.Sc.   Bachelor of Science   Ph.D.   Doctor of Philosophy

Capitalize and abbreviate academic titles after a person's name. No title should precede the name if the degree and title mean the same thing:

June Haskin, Ph.D.   *– or –*   Dr. June Haskin   *– never –*   Dr. June Haskin, Ph.D.

(See the Appendix for a listing of academic degrees.)

▶ C98   Addresses

Abbreviate terms such as boulevard, building, etc., only when essential in inside addresses and envelopes, never in the body of a letter or other text. Permissible abbreviations for provinces and states are given in the Appendix. For acceptable mailing abbreviations, see Unit 12, K8.

▶ C99   Broadcasting stations

Call letters are shown in capitals, without spaces. (These are not, in fact, abbreviations.)

CFRH-TV   CHEX   CHUM

C

▶ **C1OO** **Business terms (see also Appendix, p. 567)**

The following standard abbreviations are frequently used in business communications such as forms and tables.

acct. or a/c	account
ad val. or A/V	ad valorem—according to value
agt.	agent
a.k.a.	also known as
AP	accounts payable
AR	accounts receivable
ASAP	as soon as possible
assoc. or assn.	association
asst.	assistant
ATM or ABM	automated transaction machine or automated banking machine
avg.	average
b.l. or B/L	bill of lading
B/S	bill of sale
C	hundred (roman numeral); Celsius; carbon (science)
c.i.f. or CIF	cost, insurance, freight
c.l. or CL	carload
c.o. or c/o	in care of
Co.	Company
c.o.d. or COD	cash on delivery
Corp.	Corporation
cr.	credit
dept.	department
do.	ditto
dr.	debit
E. and O.E.	errors and omissions excepted
e.g.	for example
e.o.m. or EOM	end of month
et al.	and others
ETA	estimated time of arrival
ETD	estimated time of departure
FAQ	frequently asked questions
FIFO	first-in, first-out
f.o.b. or FOB	free on board
fwd.	forward; forwarded
F.Y.I or FYI	for your information
GST	Goods and Services Tax
HST	Harmonized Sales Tax
i.e.	for instance
Inc.	Incorporated
inv.	invoice
K	thousand (metric); Kelvin (science); karat (also carat)
l.c.l. or LCL	less than carload
LIFO	last-in, first-out
Ltd.	limited
M	thousand (roman numeral)
mdse.	merchandise
mfg.	manufacturing
mgr.	manager
misc.	miscellaneous

(continued...)

C

ms. or MS	manuscript
N.B.	nota bene (note well)
NSF	not sufficient funds
n/c or NC	no charge
No., Nos.	number(s) (use only with numerals)
n/30	net in 30 days
os, O/S	out of stock
pkg.	package
P/N/F	please note and forward
P/N/R	please note and return
P.O.	purchase order
P.O. or PO	Post Office (often with box numbers: P.O. Box 96)
P.S.	postscript
qty.	quantity
PST	Provincial Sales Tax
R.R.	Rural Route or railroad
vol.	volume
W.B.	waybill

▶ **C101 Company and organization names**

For companies, agencies, unions, societies, use only the abbreviations shown in the legally registered titles (i.e., the abbreviations in that organization's letterhead):

Bros.   Co.   Ltd.

Many companies and organizations are commonly known by abbreviated names. Current practice is to use capital letters and no spaces for such names:

IBM   UNICEF   YMHA   YWCA

▶ **C102 Compass points**

Compass points may be abbreviated in addresses and technical material, but not otherwise:

N   NE   NNW   SSE   SW   W

▶ **C103 Dates and times**

Abbreviate months and days of the week only in tables, and only then if space is limited.

If the abbreviations B.C. or A.D. are to be shown, use them only when dates are in numerals. B.C. is positioned after the year; A.D. before it:

A.D. 1936   55 B.C.

Use a.m. and p.m. when hours are shown as numerals (not to be used when the 24-hour clock is used):

11:45 p.m.   13:30

Use capitals and no periods if time zones are abbreviated:

EST (Eastern Standard Time)   PST (Pacific Standard Time)

▶ C104 Metric measurements

For metric measurements, see the Appendix.

▶ C105 Places

Country, province, and state names should never be abbreviated in text. Province and state names may be abbreviated in addresses. (See the Appendix.)

UK   – or –   U.K.
USA   – or –   U.S.A.   – or –   U.S.

Country names (except the two shown here) should not be abbreviated in addresses, except on envelopes. Abbreviations are often used, however, in tables, charts, etc.

▶ C106 Publication terms

Standard abbreviations used in referring to printed materials when a number is included are:

Ch., Chap.	Chapter	p., pp.	page(s)
Div.	Division	Sec.	Section
Fig., Figs.	Figure(s)	v., vs.	verse(s)
l., ll.	line(s)	Vol., Vols.	Volume(s)

▶ C107 Titles

◆ after names:

Jr.   Sr.   Dr. R. Farmer, Jr.

(See this unit, C94, for treatment of academic degrees.)

◆ before names (social titles):

Mr.   Mrs.   Ms.   Messrs.   Mmes

The following professional, military, and civic titles are abbreviated when they precede a family name *and* a given name but not otherwise: *Rev., Hon., Prof., Gen., Col., Capt., Lieut.*

Gen. Lewis MacKenzie – *but* – General MacKenzie   Prof. Morley Lazier

Rev. and *Hon.* must be written in full if preceded by *the*:

Rev. Charles Parnell – *or* – the Reverend Charles Parnell
– *never* – Rev. Parnell

C108 CAPITALIZATION

Although the basic conventions of capitalization are common knowledge, there are many specific uses of capital letters for emphasis or clarification of an idea. The general rule is to capitalize proper nouns and words that begin a sentence. Other uses are illustrated in this section.

NOTE A simple, basic guide to correct capitalization is this: When being specific, capitalize; when being general, do not capitalize.

> Prime Minister Greto led the way. (Referring to a specific person)
> There was a heated discussion among the prime ministers. (No specific prime minister in mind)
> Vancouver City Hall is an example of fine architecture. (Specific building)
> A large city usually has a city hall. (General reference)
> I think Unit 3 is the most interesting. (Specific reference)
> Every unit in this book is long. (General reference)

NOTE Some words that were once proper nouns have become common nouns through usage. These should not be capitalized:

> arabic numerals   roman numerals
> manila envelope   venetian blinds

▶ C109 Abbreviations

Capitalize abbreviations only when the words they represent are normally capitalized:

> a.m.   p.m.   Mon.   Nov.

▶ C110 Academic field

Capitalize as follows:

Specific course titles   Biology 23   Linguistics I   Spanish 307Y

NOTE Language names are always capitalized in this context. Other non-specific course titles are not.

> Carl enjoyed French and Japanese, but he did not like accounting or science.

Degrees   B.A.   LL.B.   M.Sc.   Ph.D.

Titles   Dr. Yvonne Borden   Professor William Chiu

College diplomas are designated as Dipl. with a letter(s) that identifies the area of study.

◆ two-year diploma programs add Dipl. after the name:

> Mary Williamson, Dipl. (Business Diploma)

◆ three-year diploma programs add Dipl. and letter to designate area of study:

> Warren Kimoto, Dipl.B. (Business)
> June Bourne, Dipl.H.Sc. (Nursing)
> Carol Mulholland, Dipl.T. (Technology)
> Jane Marusiak, Dipl.A. (Applied Arts)

C

▶ C111 Addresses

Capitalize all key words in addresses—names of streets, avenues, buildings, roads, towns, cities, provinces, countries.

▶ C112 Advertising trademarks

Capitalize trademarks:

Shake 'n Bake   Tide   Dove

▶ C113 Astronomical bodies

Capitalize astronomical bodies (constellations, planets, and stars):

the Great Bear   the Milky Way   Venus

▶ C114 Dates, seasons, holidays, historical periods

Capitalize days of the week, months, festivals, and holidays:

Civic Holiday	November	St-Jean-Baptiste Day
Monday	Ramadan	Yom Kippur

Names of seasons, decades, and centuries are capitalized only when they are personified or used as special terms:

spring sales   – *but* –   Oh! Spring!
early nineties   – *but* –   Fabulous Fifties
year 2000   – *but* –   Year of the Children

▶ C115 Geographic terms

Compass points should be capitalized only when a specific place is intended. They should not be capitalized when they indicate only a general direction.

The Joneses went out West for their holiday.
He drove west from Kenora.
The golf courses in South Carolina are magnificent.
How far south do you plan to drive?

Geographic localities should be capitalized when the compass points refer to people:

Easterners   Westerners

Names of continents, countries, nationalities, bodies of water, provinces, cities, valleys, mountains, regions, and localities should be capitalized:

the Mackenzie River	Barbados	Lake Athabaska
Mont Tremblant	Canadians	the Okanagan Valley
Lake of the Woods	Essex County	

▶ C116 Government and political references

Capitalize as follows:

Bodies:

Industry Canada
Ministry of the Environment
Royal Canadian Mounted Police

the Saskatchewan Legislature
Supreme Court of Canada

Acts, Treaties:

North American Free Trade Agreement
Canadian Charter of Rights and Freedoms

Family Law Act
Maastricht Treaty

Titles:

Governor General of Canada

– *but* –

N. Greco, minister of Transport Canada

▶ C117 Institutions

Capitalize names of institutions and their divisions:

Beth Tzedec Synagogue
Canadian National Institute for the Blind

Mount Allison University
School of Music

▶ C118 Nationalities, languages, races

Capitalize nationalities, languages, and races of people:

Asian   Cree   Hispanic
Chinese   French   Latin

▶ C119 Organizations

Capitalize names of organizations:

Canadian Broadcasting Corporation

Girl Guides of Canada

NOTE   Minor words (*of, the, and*, etc.) in a name are not capitalized unless they start the name:

The Financial Post

▶ C120 Publications

Capitalize the first and all of the important words in titles of plays, books, articles, newspapers, magazines, operas, songs, poems, reports, works of art:

Canada: A Country to Enjoy
The Importance of Being Earnest
"The Night of the Shower of Stars"
Star Trek

C

▶ C121 Punctuation marks

Capitalize the first letter:

◆ after a *colon* when an independent clause follows:

> Canada is beautiful: Its lakes, mountains, and beaches are popular with tourists.

◆ after a *period, question mark, exclamation mark*:

> Please come. If you insist.
> Are you coming? No, thanks.
> Do come! It is not possible.

◆ after the opening *quotation marks* when a complete sentence is quoted:

> The visiting dignitary said, "It's my pleasure to be here."
>
> – *but* –
>
> The visitor's "pleasure to be here" was somewhat dampened by bad weather.

With hyphenated expressions, capitalize only the part that would normally be capitalized:

> cross-Canada   mid-August   trans-Atlantic

▶ C122 Religious references

Capitalize words with religious significance. Capitalize names of deities, the Bible, names of books of the Bible, all other sacred books, festivals and holy days, and adjectives derived from these terms:

> Buddhism   Good Friday   Protestant
> Catholic   Jewish   the Koran
> God   Judaism   the Nicene Creed

▶ C123 Titles

Capitalize titles of relatives when they precede a name. Do not capitalize when these are preceded by a pronoun:

> His uncle left him a small fortune.
> I have invited Uncle Fred for dinner.
> My mother is an important politician.
>
> – *but* –
>
> I asked Mom to help me with my packing.

Capitalize professional, business, civic, military, and religious titles that precede a person's name:

> the Reverend Jim Battye
> Mayor Frank Scarpitti
> General Janik Fletchor

Do not capitalize titles when they follow a personal name or are used in place of a personal name—except in inside addresses. Titles of high-ranking government officials were an exception to this rule at one time but modern usage generally leans toward minimizing capitalization.

C

Barbara Bertin, vice-president of Allied Capital, is coming for lunch.
Jean Chretien, prime minister of Canada, is campaigning in western Canada.

C124 NUMBERS

The question often arises as to whether figures or words should be used to express numerical values. Figures are usually preferred for most business situations because they are easier to read. If in doubt, follow these general guidelines:

◆ Spell out numbers from one to ten and use figures for numbers above ten. Numbers in the millions or higher, however, may be expressed as:

   1 billion   3.5 million (instead of 3 500 000)

◆ If numbers are mixed within a sentence, use figures for all of them or write all of them out:

   Send 15 television sets, 6 CD players, 4 VCRs.
   Of the 12 cats, 6 were tabbies.

   – or –

   Of the twelve cats, six were tabbies.

◆ Always use figures with symbols and abbreviations:

   6°C   3 km   No. 68   #68

   – but –

   6 percent (use the % symbol only in tables or statistical work)

◆ Make the plural form of figures by adding *s*:

   The 1980s saw the start of the information age.

◆ Hyphenate spelled-out numbers containing two words and any number that is part of a compound adjective:

   Thirty-two people were invited.
   A five-hundred-kilometre journey lies ahead of us.

   – or –

   A 500-km journey lies ahead of us.

◆ Spell out any number that starts a sentence (but avoid this situation if possible by rewriting the sentence):

   Eighteen children came.   (All 18 children came.)

◆ When two numbers are used consecutively, spell out the lower number:

   Buy twelve 43-cent stamps, please.

◆ Use a comma for clarity when two numbers used together could cause confusion:

   By 2004, 99 branch offices will be equipped with this technology.

The following examples will provide further guidelines.

▶ C125 Addresses

For house, building, apartment, post office box, and rural route numbers, use figures. (Exception: Spell out "One" in street addresses.)

15 King Street, Apartment 804   R.R. 1   P.O. Box 120

– *but* –

One Crown Crescent

For street names above ten, use figures. For street names under ten, use words.

402 - 40th Street (insert a space on both sides of the hyphen)

– *but* –

240 Fifth Avenue

▶ C126 Ages and anniversaries

Use figures with very precise ages:

She will be 2 years, 3 months old on Tuesday.

Use words for less precise and approximate ages:

Lou will be thirty tomorrow.
Frankie is three.
Ilse is almost eighteen.

Use figures for ages stated immediately after names:

Shafig, 27, and Suni, 25, were engaged last week.

Use figures for ages expressed in a statistical or technical sense:

The legal age for marrying in Ontario is 16.
People in the 65-plus age group qualify for pensions.

Use words for anniversaries except when three or more words are required:

It's their fifteenth anniversary.

– *but* –

Canada celebrated its 125th birthday in 1992.

▶ C127 Dates

Use figures:

February 29, 20--   – *or* –   20-- 02 29

NOTE   Use of *nd* and *st* and *th* is shown in the examples:

On the 2nd of January, they attended a New Year's luncheon.
On January 2, they attended a New Year's luncheon.
They attended the leap-year party on the 29th of February.
On February 29, they will attend a leap-year party.

C

On the 1st of March, they checked their finances.
They checked their finances on March 1.

In legal or formal documents, however:

November eighth, two thousand...

▶ C128 Decimals

Use figures:

0.50   7.3 million

▶ C129 Document numbers

Use figures:

Invoice No. 2071   Order No. 26   Policy No. 168-2948   Cheque No. 2345

(Use a hard space/non-breaking space to keep number with No.,
i.e., No.[ ]2345.)

▶ C130 Fractions and mixed numbers

Spell out simple fractions when used alone:

Only three-quarters of the group attended.

Use figures for mixed numbers:

His mass increased 1 1/2 times.

▶ C131 Metric symbols

Use figures:

3 kg   2 cm   30 km   22 cm × 27 cm   5 L

– but –

six kilometres   nine litres

▶ C132 Money amounts

As a general rule, use figures for money amounts. Round amounts,
however, can be spelled out in text if desired:

twenty thousand dollars

When expressing a series of round amounts in figures, omit decimals
and zeros:

$25 $43 $82   ¥21 000   Mex $50 000

When expressing a series of amounts that includes cents, use
decimals and zeros in all cases, for consistency:

$23.95 $43.00 $9.50   £50.50   DM89.75

C

Use figures with a series of amounts in cents only (the ¢ symbol may be used in statistical material; the word "cents" is used in text):

17¢   28¢   79¢

– *in text* –

17 cents

In a series in which one of the amounts is in cents only, express it as part of a dollar:

$3.50 $0.85 $14.75

For very large amounts, use figures and words:

6.5 billion $5 million

(Use a hard space/non-breaking space to keep number with word, i.e., 6.5[ ]million.)

In legal documents and very formal communications, use words and confirm the amounts in figures in parentheses (note use of capitals):

Two Thousand Dollars ($2000)

NOTE   In some areas (such as banking and accounting), a comma, rather than a space, is used in dollar amounts to prevent fraud and confusion (e.g., $500 000).

▶ C133 Percentages

Use figures:

We saved 20 percent or 20 per cent (accepted as one or two words). (Remember, use a hard space/non-breaking space to keep number with percent or %. Use % symbol only in tabulations or statistical work.)

▶ C134 Ratios and proportions

Use figures:

5:2 – *or* – 5 to 2

▶ C135 Temperatures

Use figures:

49°C   49 degrees

▶ C136 Times

Use figures with *a.m.* or *p.m.* on the 24-hour clock:

2:30 p.m. – *or* – 14:30
4 p.m. – *not* – 4:00 p.m.

When using the term *o'clock*, either figures or words may be used. In a formal context, use words:

The ceremony will take place at three o'clock.
Let's meet at 2 o'clock.

Use figures with exact units of time:

The trip took 1 year, 7 months, 10 days.

C137 WORD DIVISION

Because word-processing software has default settings and automatic wraparound, most routine documents can be produced without requiring any line-end word divisions (or hyphenation). As well, some software offers automatic hyphenation. For those who need assistance with word division, the following will be useful.

Before you contemplate word division, remember that it is better to avoid it. Divided words are unattractive and make reading more difficult. If you absolutely *must* divide a word, follow these guidelines:

◆ Consult your dictionary if you are in doubt about the correct division. Compact word-division reference guides are also available.

◆ Simplify the reader's task by giving a strong indication of the entire word.

◆ Never divide the last word in the first line or the last word in the last line on a page.

◆ No more than two successive lines should end with a division.

◆ There should be no more than three divided words on any page of a report, and no more than two divided words in a one-page letter or memorandum.

◆ Note that the first part of a divided word must contain at least two characters (discounting the hyphen), and the second part must contain at least three (which may include the punctuation mark):

alphabetic	alpha-betic	*– not –*	alphabet-ic
amazing	amaz-ing	*– not –*	a-mazing

◆ Remember that the hyphen is *always* located at the end of a line, *never* at the beginning.

Never divide
◆ words of one syllable or words pronounced as one syllable:

brought	healed	stopped

◆ proper names:

Jonathan	Micheline	Portugal

◆ short words (fewer than six letters):

after	alone

◆ contractions or abbreviations:

haven't	Ph.D.

C

◆ the last word in a paragraph or on a page
◆ where only one or two characters would be separated:

largely   mounted   oblique   ready

◆ numbers and amounts (unless they are *very* long) and units of measure:

$2147.75   2[ ]million   500[ ]km

◆ numbers from streets

112[ ]Main Street

NOTE   Use the comma as the natural connector for sums of money or large number amounts:

$1,200,375 $350,000

Remember to use the hard space/non-breaking space when keying in metric version:

$1[ ]200[ ]375 $350[ ]000

Where to divide words

Always divide words between syllables. Specifically:
◆ as close to the centre as possible:

communi-cation

◆ after prefixes:

contra-dict

◆ before suffixes:

lov-able

◆ between double consonants when the root word does not contain double consonants:

occur-rence   omit-ted   run-ning

– but –

fill-ing   stall-ing

◆ after the vowel when a one-letter syllable is followed by a consonant:

regu-late   sepa-rate

◆ between the vowels when there are two one-letter syllables:

radi-ator   anxi-ety

◆ only at the existing hyphen when the term is already hyphenated:

self-control   two-fifteenths

Where to divide related expressions

Avoid dividing parts of a related expression (i.e., parts normally read together) but, if division is essential, choose the logical breaking point.

NOTE Use the hard space/non-breaking space to keep related expressions together:

Dates: May[ ]24, 20—,   September[ ]5, 2000

Money (very large amounts only): $2[ ]hundred million
  Break after: $2 hundred
  Do not *break:* 2[ ]hundred

If possible, avoid breaking large sums of money:
  $2 600 975

Names: Professor[ ]B. Cormier
  Break after: Professor B.

Numbers (very long ones only): 24[ ]000[ ]500
  Break after: 24[ ]000

If possible, avoid breaking large number streams.

Phone numbers and fax numbers: Do not divide. Use a hard space/ non-breaking space to keep numbers together:

  Tel.[ ](905)[ ]238-6074 Fax[ ](905)[ ]238-6075

Addresses: 37[ ]Bayview Avenue
  Break after: 37[ ]Bayview

Other: *Do* not *break:* Room[ ]7   Schedule[ ]A   Appendix[ ]I

NOTE. Widow/orphan protection: this software function prevents single lines from being separated from a paragraph. You can keep text together on a page in the following ways:

◆ keep the first or last line of paragraph from being separated from the paragraph across a page break

◆ keep a block of text together on one page (a quotation, tabulation, table, etc.)

◆ keep a heading together with the text that follows by specifying the number of lines to be kept together

C

PART 2

THE EXPRESSION OF LANGUAGE

The most effective communications are well organized, clear, concise, courteous, factually accurate, and positively worded. The purpose of this section is to show you how to produce written and oral communications that meet these criteria.

C138 WRITTEN EXPRESSION

This section offers help in writing business letters, memorandums, press releases, and reports. Guidelines for the following writing situations are presented in other parts of this book:

◆ advertisements, see Unit 8, H6

◆ formal acceptances, see Unit 18, S11

◆ job applications, see Unit 11, J12

◆ minutes, see Unit 14, MC11–14

C139 BUSINESS LETTERS

Despite the increased use of fax, e-mail, etc., letters are a common form of communication in business. They represent the sender's company and should therefore make a good impression. The following suggestions will help in the creation of any business letter.

Get off to the right start
Collect all of the facts and documents you need and do one of these:

◆ Make an outline of the points you wish to cover.

◆ Underline or highlight important facts on a document to which you are replying.

◆ Make notes in the margin about points you wish to cover.

Follow the five Cs
Produce correspondence that is coherent, clear, concise, courteous, and correct.

◆ Coherent: Progresses logically, after starting with a clear statement of purpose

◆ Clear: Is written in simple, easy-to-follow, unambiguous language

◆ Concise: Is short and to the point

◆ Courteous: Uses "you" frequently and is written in a tactful, friendly style that shows concern for the reader

◆ Correct: States all required facts accurately and is always correct in spelling, punctuation, and grammar

C

> Dear Sir or Madam:
>
> Would you please send us a copy of *Wordpro Made Easy*, which was previewed in last month's issue of Office Systems and Technology. Your booklet seems to be exactly what our department needs.
> We would appreciate receiving this by September 17, if possible.
>
> Yours very truly,

A concisely worded business letter

Use a logical development

Introduction
Start in a pleasing way with a clear statement of the purpose of your communication. If you do this, the reader does not have to wonder why you are writing.

Development
◆ Develop the introduction by giving further details (background, anticipated outcome, etc.).

◆ Tailor your language to suit the reader (e.g., do not assume that everyone will be familiar with the specialized vocabulary of your particular business).

◆ Give precise information to avoid confusion.

Ending
◆ Find a friendly way to close the letter.

◆ Ask for action, if this is appropriate.

◆ Do not thank in advance because it is an imposition on the reader to assume that he or she will fulfil your request.

Keep it simple
Brevity is the key to quick and effective communication. Focusing on one point at one time leads to easy understanding by the recipient.

Use the "you" approach
Make your readers feel important. Show your consideration by putting yourself in their place when you write. Do not bore them with numerous "I's" or "we's." Be sincere and friendly.

Mean what you say
Be honest in your writing. Stay away from "urgent," "as soon as possible," and similar terms unless you really mean them.

Handle the negatives positively
When you have bad news to impart (e.g., you must close a client's charge account), precede the negative statement with a positive one to soften the blow.

C

> You have been a valued customer of ours for the past five years. However, your record of slow payment this year has forced us to cancel our credit arrangements with you. We will, of course, be glad to accommodate you with cash purchases.

Take care with appearance

A well-formatted, attractively set-up letter makes a favourable impact. Be a good ambassador for your organization. Follow the formatting instructions provided in Unit 12, K19 to K43.

Proofread carefully

A document with mistakes tells the reader that you are careless. Create a good impression by producing error-free communications.

Use short cuts where feasible

Is a letter really necessary? A short fax or e-mail message might be better.

◆ E-mail messages can replace interpersonal and intercompany communications of all types: correspondence, memos, meeting notices. They can be sent to one or many recipients at the same time and can avoid telephone tag. (See Unit 5, "Electronic Mail," and consider the advantages offered.)

NOTE   All types of correspondence can be sent (via e-mail) as attachments to e-mail messages.

◆ Instead of a formal letter in reply to a routine request, attaching a compliment slip with the sender's name or a business card will often fulfil the same function and save time.

The Sylvia Harding Music Co.	*Compliment slip*

The Sylvia Harding Music Co.
4716 13 Street N.E.
Calgary, AB T2E 6P1

Sylvia Harding
President

(403) 692-9213 Fax. (403) 692-9000
E-mail: sharding@hardingmusic.com
Web site: www.hardingmusic.com

The Sylvia Harding Music Co.
4716 13 Street N.E.
Calgary, AB T2E 6P1

With the compliments of
Sylvia Harding
President

Business card

◆ Consider a telephone call instead of a letter.
◆ If a very brief answer is required, reply on the bottom of the incoming letter, make a photocopy for your files, and return the original to the sender.
◆ Consider using a form letter rather than creating an original. (See Unit 12, K41.)

C

▶ C140 Letter samples

Effective business correspondence demonstrates courtesy, conciseness, clarity, coherence, and correctness. The sample letters in this section are offered as guides to achieving best results. For business etiquette practices regarding salutations and their appropriate complimentary closings, see this unit, C161 and 162.

C141   Acknowledgment letter (in someone's absence)

If your task is to handle someone's correspondence and certain decisions must wait until that person is able to deal with them (e.g., on returning from vacation), the polite thing to do is to write an acknowledgment.

Dear Ms. Belza:

   Thank you for your kind invitation to Mr. Reubens to make the keynote speech at the Kiwanis Club Annual Meeting on May 10, 20--.
   Mr. Reubens is away on a trip at the moment. He will be returning next week and will contact you then.

Yours sincerely,

B. Barrett
Administrative Assistant

C142   Apology letter

If something more formal than a telephone call is appropriate, write a note giving a reason for your regrets.

Dear Mr. Smillie:

   Thank you for inviting me to be a panelist at your forum on "Ergonomics in the Workplace" on November 3.
   Much as I would relish the opportunity to share my views and discuss them with colleagues, I regret that I must decline the offer because of a previous commitment. Please accept my thanks and my apologies.
   I wish you and the Forum success.

Sincerely,

C143   Collection letter

After several statements and reminder notices have been sent without effect, it is time to demand payment for an overdue account by means of letters. Start with a lenient reminder letter.

C

Dear Sir:

We hope you are satisfied with the personal computer you bought from us three months ago.

At the time of purchase you made a down payment of $500, with a promise to pay the balance in 30 days. However, we have not heard from you.

If you are having a problem with the equipment, please let us know; if not, we would appreciate a cheque for the outstanding amount right away.

Yours truly,

If there is no reply in two weeks, send a more demanding note.

Have you overlooked us? According to our records, your balance outstanding is still $1100.

The amount due is, as you know, nearly four months old. Since we also have to meet our financial commitments, we would appreciate your completing your end of our bargain by putting a cheque in the mail today.

If you have already sent your payment, please ignore this reminder. If you have not, please act now to preclude our taking further action.

Yours truly,

If this firmer request brings no response, the following letter may work.

You have not replied to, nor acted on, our two reminder letters about your outstanding account of $1100. We must inform you, therefore, that unless you send us a cheque for the full amount within one week, we will put your account in the hands of a collection agency.

We regret having to take this step, but you have given us no other choice.

Yours truly,

C144   Complaint letter

If a verbal expression of dissatisfaction brings no results, try a firmly worded but courteous letter. Wait until you are calm before writing, because anger works against you.

C

Dear Mr. Boehmer:

Our July shipment of frames arrived on schedule but, unfortunately, 100 of them were badly damaged.

We contacted your shipping department twice last week and were told the matter was under investigation; however, we have heard nothing. Since we want to enter a claim with the carrier for the damage and also need replacement frames as soon as possible, we would appreciate your immediate attention to our problem.

Please telephone or fax Ms. Lopez before Friday so that she can proceed with the necessary paperwork.

Yours sincerely,

Reply to complaint letter

Dear Mrs. Ling:

As requested in your letter of July 15 regarding the damaged frames, I telephoned Ms. Lopez to discuss the problem.

I apologize for the delay, but our shipping department had difficulty reaching the carrier for the details you required. Happily, Ms. Lopez now has the information she needs to enter a claim with the transport company. She has also placed an order for 100 frames to replace the broken ones.

Thank you for your patience and courtesy. I hope our future dealings will be trouble-free and mutually beneficial.

Yours sincerely,

C145   Congratulatory letter

Make it short and sincere.

Dear Marcello:

I was delighted to hear of your promotion to the position of national sales manager of Elliott Galleries. After all of your years of dedication and service, you certainly well deserve this honour.

Congratulations, Marcello! I hope you will be happy in your new post.

Most sincerely,

C

Reply to congratulatory letter
Yes! You need to write one.

Dear Catherine:

How kind of you to write a note about my recent promotion. Your good wishes certainly added to my delight at being promoted at Elliott Galleries. I look forward to a challenging and rewarding future.

Cordially yours,

C146 Donation (response to request for)

Whether your reply is affirmative or negative, be kind.

Affirmative reply

Dear Ms. Blackburn:

In reply to your request for a donation toward prizes for the "Games for the Handicapped," I am pleased to enclose our cheque for $250. On behalf of the manager and staff, I wish you and your organizers every success.

Yours sincerely,

Negative reply

Dear Ms. Blackburn:

Thank you for inviting us to participate in your annual "Games for the Handicapped" by means of a donation toward prizes.

Unfortunately, we cannot assist you because it is our policy to make one major donation yearly to the United Way.

Please accept our regrets and our good wishes for a successful event.

Yours sincerely,

C147 Form letters

When routine correspondence is mailed to a large number of people (e.g., advertising a new product, introducing a new salesperson, announcing a change of location, asking repeatedly for payment of an account), the most efficient method of handling this is by keying and saving a master of the body (primary file) and inserting only the variables (secondary file) (date, inside address, salutation, and other pertinent information) at the time of mailing.

Dear

    Enclosed is our cheque for $, which represents the proceeds of your loan. The attached statement shows the terms of your contract.
    Your monthly payments are $, payable on the   of each month, and the first payment will be due on   . It is wise for you to meet your payments on time in order to maintain your good credit rating.
    Thank you for bringing your financial requirements to our company.

            Very truly yours,

Standard paragraphs can also be created on a computer for assembling in any order. See Unit 12, K42.

C148   Gratitude or thank-you letter

Avoid gushing phrases, but show your genuine appreciation.

For a gift

Dear Armand:

    It was so thoughtful of you to send me the Picasso print for my birthday. I will have it framed to hang in splendour in my office.
Thank you very much. Perhaps the next time you are in town, you will drop in for lunch and let me show you your generous gift in its new setting.

            Kindest regards,

For a favour

Dear Lison:

    Thank you very much for the tickets to the final round of the Canadian Open last week. What an exciting experience it was to see the pros in real life!
    I know that you went out of your way to get the tickets. Your thoughtfulness was very much appreciated.
            Cordially,

To a speaker

Dear Dr. Liontos:

    It was a pleasure to meet you at our annual board meeting and to hear your thoughts on technology in this decade.
    I know I voice the opinion of all of our members when I say a sincere thank you for coming to address our organization. We are all grateful for your interest.

            Sincerely yours,

C149 Inquiry letter

When a telephone inquiry is not possible, send a written request for information. Be specific about the information you require.

Dear Sir or Madam:

Our class is conducting a survey to find out which computer hardware and word-processing and accounting software programs are currently most popular with business firms in our community.

To simplify the process, we have enclosed a form that we believe is straightforward. If you would complete the form and return it to us by August 28, we would be very grateful.

We look forward to hearing from you.

Yours truly,

Reply to inquiry letter

Dear Ms. DiFiore:

Thank you for your letter of August 3.

We are pleased to take part in your hardware/software survey and hope that the completed form enclosed will give you the information you require.

Good luck in your endeavours.

Yours sincerely,

C150 Introduction letter

A letter introducing a person may either be mailed directly to the addressee or delivered to the addressee by the person being introduced. It should clearly state its purpose.

Dear Dr. Shaefer:

Please allow me to introduce my friend, Professor Morley Mazier, whose work in mechanical engineering is probably familiar to you. He is keen to visit your research laboratory and to discuss a matter he believes will interest you greatly.

I hope your meeting will prove mutually beneficial.

Yours sincerely,

– *or* –

> May I introduce to you Max Von Eben, my colleague of the past five years.
> Max and his family have decided to move West for business reasons,
> and it occurred to me that you and he might derive some mutual benefit
> from a meeting. I would be very grateful for any assistance or guidance you
> could offer Max.
>
> > Sincerely,

C151   Job application letter

See Unit 11, J13.

C152   Job recommendation or reference letter

On occasion you may be asked to write a letter of reference for an
employee or co-worker. Keep it short, positive, and honest.

> Dear Miss Wang:
>
> I am very pleased to recommend Glenn Asano to you as a prospective
> office manager.
> Glenn has worked with our organization for four years as an accounting
> assistant, payroll clerk, and finally, office supervisor. He has been a loyal
> and conscientious worker, and his eagerness to improve, combined with his
> friendly personality, has made him very popular.
> Our loss will be your gain. I know Glenn will be an asset to your
> company, and I wish him every success.
>
> > Yours sincerely,

If you do not have an addressee's name, in place of a salutation, use
To Whom It May Concern.

Request for job recommendation/reference letter

If you wish a former employer to recommend you for a new position,
the following letter would be suitable.

> Dear Judge Vanek:
>
> Would you please write a letter of reference on my behalf to Mrs. Ayako
> Okamoto of Computemps (business card enclosed), to whom I have applied
> for the position of legal placements officer.
> Mrs. Okamoto has indicated that my qualifications are satisfactory, but
> I feel sure that your confirmation of my capabilities will give added weight to
> my application.
> I would be most grateful for your assistance.
>
> > Sincerely,

C

C153   Job refusal letter

It is courteous to send a brief note when declining a job offer.

Dear Ms. Conrad-Knight:

Thank you very much for offering me the position of...with your organization. I have accepted another job offer, however, so regret that I must refuse yours.

I enjoyed meeting you and appreciate the time you spent with me.

Yours sincerely,

C154   Job rejection letter

Letters to unsuccessful job applicants should be brief but kind and should be mailed as soon as possible after selection of the successful candidate. The first example below would be suitable for a person who you feel would never be suitable for your organization.

Dear Mr. Hubel:

I regret to inform you that you have not been successful in your application for a position with our organization.

The decision we had to make was extremely difficult, but we believe we have chosen the best candidate of the many who applied.

Thank you for the time and effort you expended for the interview, and good luck in the future.

Sincerely,

The following letter could be sent to an unsuccessful candidate who might be suitable for another position in your company later on.

Dear Mr. Robinette:

I am sorry to inform you that you have not been successful in your application for the position of administrative assistant with our organization.

A number of strong candidates applied and it was difficult to make a decision. We do feel, however, that a position for which you might be a candidate may become available in the future, and we will keep your application on file for that purpose. We will contact you if such an opportunity arises.

Sincerely,

C

Response to unsolicited job application

Try not to discourage the writer. Be straightforward in a gentle way.

Dear Mr. Denobrega:

Thank you for submitting an application to join our organization. Unfortunately, we cannot help you at the moment because there are no openings in our accounting department.

If a position to suit you does become vacant, we will contact you. In the meantime, good luck with your job hunting.

Yours sincerely,

C155   Job resignation letter

It is customary to submit a written intent of resignation as well as a verbal one when you wish to leave an organization. Be prepared to depart on a positive note—for your own benefit.

Dear Mrs. Mammone:

It is with sincere regret that I offer my resignation to Financial Associates Inc., to take effect on October 31, 20--.

The past three years have taught me a great deal, but it is now time for me to move on to a new set of challenges. Thank you for your part in my growth at Financial.

I wish you and your organization continued success.

Yours sincerely,

C156   Order letter

When a preprinted order form is not available, send a simple, detailed letter to make your request.

Dear Sirs:

Would you please send the following items to our branch at 16 Sheppard Avenue, Shubenacadie, NS, immediately.

Qty.	Description	Unit Price	Total
1000	No. 204 T hinges, copper plate	$2.00	$2000.00
500	No. 72 corner braces, copper plate	2.25	1125.00
		Total	$3125.00

An unexpected increase in orders means that our supplies are low. We would, therefore, appreciate your rushing this shipment to us.

Very truly yours,

C

C157   Payment letter

If a letter is required to accompany a payment, give an explanation of the payment.

Dear Sirs:

Enclosed is our cheque in payment of Invoice No. 473.
The amount of $784 on the cheque is equivalent to the invoice total of $800 less your 2% discount if payment is made within 10 days.

Yours truly,

C158   Reservations letter

Although most reservations for convention facilities or hotel accommodation are made by telephone, fax, or e-mail, a letter is sometimes necessary. Remember to give full details and to address the letter to the reservations manager at the hotel.

Dear Sir or Madam:

Please reserve a three-room suite for September 17 and 18, 20--, for our annual conference of sales managers.
One room should be suitable for informal social meetings, one for product displays, and one for formal meetings for 15 to 20 people.
The conference will open with a social gathering at 3 p.m., September 17 and close with a brief business meeting at 10 a.m. on the 18th.
An early confirmation of this booking will be appreciated.

Yours truly,

C159   Sales letter

Since the purpose of a sales letter is to sell a product or service, be positive and use the *you* approach.

Dear Mr. Shkuda:

How would you like to increase the efficiency of your office workers by 10 percent this summer? Tests in 100 offices where Iceberg air conditioners were installed proved that worker efficiency improved 10 percent.

Greater efficiency means larger profits for your organization; thus, the Iceberg pays for itself in a short time. Spread the cost of the air conditioner over one, two, or three years if your wish. The money you spend to improve worker comfort and morale and to increase productivity will be wise investment.

Won't you call us today and let our engineer determine your office air-conditioning needs? Every day without an Iceberg is costing you money.

Yours sincerely,

Covering letter with sales information
Use this letter as a friendly encouragement to a prospective buyer. Make sure you close with a request for action.

Dear Mr. Shkuda:

We are pleased to enclose a catalogue and price list of Iceberg air conditioners as requested by our engineer, Joe Ubelacker, following his visit to your company. Joe has indicated which models are best suited to your office needs.

If you have any questions after you have had an opportunity to look over the catalogue, please give us a call. We know you and your employees will be delighted with the performance of the Iceberg.

We are at your service. Call us now for immediate delivery.

Yours sincerely,

C160   Sympathy or condolence letter

Letters of sympathy should be brief but compassionate.

Dear Miss Jacques:

It was with much regret that I read today about your brother's sudden death. Everyone who knew him will feel the loss.

I realize I cannot offer you much comfort, but please count on me if you need anything in the difficult days ahead.

Most sincerely,

Reply to sympathy letter

Dear Ms. Kordez:

Your thoughtful note and donation to the Cancer Society were very much appreciated by our family.

It is good to be back at the office again, with plenty of work to occupy me. I know that your kind thoughts will help sustain me through the weeks ahead.

Yours sincerely,

C161 FORMS OF ADDRESS

Addresses in business correspondence follow an established pattern (see Unit 12, K6, regarding envelopes). The form of address consists of the addressee plus mailing address (individual's name and title—if known, organization name, address, and postal code), the salutation, and the complimentary closing. The two most common examples are:

C

Mr. B. Machon, President   Eglinton Enterprises Ltd.
Machon, Mortimer, and Oxley   495 Eglinton Avenue East
296 Landy Lane   Toronto, ON M5N 3A2
Saskatoon, SK S7L 2C7

Dear Mr. Machon: Dear Sirs:

    Yours sincerely,   Very truly yours,

In a situation where *the gender of the addressee is unknown* and in cases where *individuals prefer to be addressed without a social title*, use the following:

T. Weazy   Leslie Winger
(address)   (address)

Dear T. Weazy: Dear Leslie Winger:

    Yours truly,   Yours truly,

Where the *name of an addressee is unknown*, choose from the following:

Human Resources Manager
(company name and address)

Sir or Madam

– or –

Dear Sir or Madam

    Yours truly,

Addressing individuals
Female:
Miss   Misses   Ms.   Mrs.
Mademoiselle (Mlle): French for an unmarried woman
Mesdemoiselles (Mlles): French for two or more unmarried women
Madame (Mme): French for a married or mature woman
Mesdames (Mmes): French for two or more married or mature women

Male:
Mr.   Monsieur (M.): French
Messieurs (MM.; Messrs.): French plural; also sometimes used in English when addressing two or more men:

> *Messrs. Smith and Weston*

Addressing organizations
In these situations, the company name appears as the first line of the address. The appropriate salutations are:

Organizations consisting of all women:
◆ Ladies
◆ Mesdames

Organizations consisting of all men:

◆ Gentlemen

Organizations consisting of women and men:

◆ Gentlemen

◆ Ladies and Gentlemen

◆ Gentlemen and Ladies

◆ Dear (organization name)

Although most written communication in business is an exchange between organizations, it is sometimes necessary to contact individuals outside industry or commerce. The correct method of addressing prominent people in all sectors is included in the following section.

FORMS OF ADDRESS CHART

Title	Address	Salutation	Complimentary closing
Armed forces			
Officer			
Lieutenant-General	Lieutenant-General F. Hebert, V.C., O.B.E.	Dear Lieutenant-General Dear General Dear Sir Dear Madam	Yours very truly
Non-commissioned officer			
Sergeant	Sergeant C. Lichten	Dear Sergeant	Yours truly
Diplomatic			
Ambassacor or High Commissioner (Canadian)	C. Ronning, Esq. Canadian Ambassador to...	Dear Sir Dear Mr. Ronning	Very truly yours
Ambassador or High Commissioner (foreign)	Her Excellency D. Raj Ambassador of...	Dear Madam Excellency	Respectfully
Education			
President of university	Joseph L. Billings, LL.D. President, University of...	Dear Sir Dear Dr. Billings Dear Mr. President	Very truly yours
Chancellor of university	Mary L. Billings, Ph.D. Chancellor, University of...	Dear Madam Dear Chancellor	Very truly yours
Dean of college/faculty	Joseph L. Billings, Ph.D. Dean of...	Dear Sir Dear Dean Billings Dear Dr. Billings	Very truly yours
Professor of university	Mary L. Billings, Ph.D. University of...	Dear Madam Dear Professor Billings	Very truly yours

Title	Address	Salutation	Complimentary closing
Government**			
Governor General	The Right Honourable Adrienne Clarkson Governor General of Canada	Your Excellency	Yours sincerely
Lieutenant-Governor	The Honourable Hilary Weston, Lieutenant-Governor of Ontario	Your Honour	Yours sincerely
Prime Minister	The Right Honourable Lesley Billings, P.C., MP* / Prime Minister of Canada	Sir / Madam	I am, Sir, yours very truly / I am, Madam, yours very truly
Premier of province	The Honourable Sir John Billings, MLA* / Premier of the Province of....	Sir	Respectfully yours / Sincerely yours
Minister	The Honourable Mary Billings / Minister of....	Madam / Dear Madam	Respectfully yours / Sincerely yours
Mayor	His/Her Worship, / The Mayor of [name of city]	Dear Sir/Madam / Dear Mr./Ms./Mrs. Mayor	Yours sincerely

*The prime minister and federal cabinet ministers are members of the Privy Council (P.C.).
The Governor General is a Privy councillor (P.C.), as well as a chancellor of the Order of Canada.
All members of the federal Parliament have the designation Member of Parliament (MP) after their names.
Members of provincial and territorial legislatures use the designation Member of the Provincial Parliament (MPP) in Ontario, Member of the National Assembly (MNA) in Quebec, Member of the House of Assembly (MHA) in Newfoundland and Nova Scotia, and Member of the Legislative Assembly (MLA) in the other provinces.

Title	Address	Salutation	Complimentary closing
Judiciary			
Chief Justice, Supreme Court of Canada	The Right Honourable Mary Billings, Chief Justice of Canada	Dear Madam / Madam / Dear Madam Chief Justice	I am, Madam, yours very truly / I am, Madam, yours faithfully / I am, Madam, yours sincerely
Chief Justice, Provincial Supreme Court	The Honourable John Billings, Chief Justice of [name of province]	Dear Sir / Sir / Dear Mr. Justice Billings	Yours sincerely / I am, yours very truly

** To find the name of a member of Provincial Parliament (MPP): www.gov.ontla.on.ca/

Title	Address	Salutation	Complimentary closing
Justice, Supreme Court of Canada	The Honourable Mr. Justice John Billings	Sir Dear Mr. Justice Billings	Yours sincerely I am, yours very truly
Judge (federal and provincial courts)	Her Honour Judge Mary Billings	Madam Dear Judge Billings	Yours sincerely
Judge (district and county courts)	His Honour Judge John Billings	Sir Dear Judge Billings	Yours sincerely
Professional			
Doctor	Dr. B. Borden B. Borden, M.D.	Dear Dr. Borden	Yours sincerely
Lawyer	Mr. N. Jacobi Barrister and Solicitor	Dear Mr. Jacobi	Yours sincerely
(if Queen's Counsel)	N. Jacobi, Esq. N. Jacobi, Q.C.	Dear Mr. Jacobi	Yours sincerely
Religion			
Archbishop (Anglican)	The Most Reverend John Dawes, D.D., Archbishop of...	Most Reverend Sir Your Grace	Respectfully yours
Archbishop (Greek Orthodox)	His Eminence the Archbishop of the Greek Orthodox Church	Your Eminence	I am, Your Eminence, respectfully yours
Archbishop (Roman Catholic)	The Most Reverend John Billings, Archbishop of...	Your Excellency	Respectfully yours
Bishop (Anglican)	The Right Reverend John Billings, D.D., Bishop of...	Right Reverend Sir	Respectfully yours
Bishop (Greek Orthodox)	The Most Reverend Bishop of the Greek Orthodox Church	Right Reverend Bishop	Very respectfully yours
Bishop (Roman Catholic)	The Most Reverend John Billings, Bishop of...	Your Excellency	Respectfully yours

C

Title	Address	Salutation	Complimentary closing
Cardinal (Roman Catholic)	His Eminence John Cardinal Billings Archbishop of...	Your Eminence	Respectfully yours
Moderator	The Right Reverend Carol Dawson, D.D., Moderator of the...Church	Right Reverend Madam Dear Dr. Dawson	Respectfully yours
Mother Superior (Roman Catholic)	The Reverend Mother Superior, The Congregation of...	Dear Madam Reverend Mother Superior Dear Mother Superior	Respectfully yours
Pope (Roman Catholic)	His Holiness The Pope	Your Holiness	I have the honour to be, Your Holiness' obedient servant
Rabbi (Jewish)	The Reverend Rabbi Jacob Abrams	Dear Sir	Respectfully yours

C

▶ **C162   Salutations and complimentary closings**

Consult the following chart to ensure that you use the appropriate salutation and complimentary closing in your business and personal correspondence.

Correspondence	Salutation	Complimentary closing
Formal		
◆ writing to a person of high political, diplomatic, royal, or religious rank	(See the "Forms of Address Chart" in the previous section.)	
◆ writing to a company or organization and addressing no one in particular	Dear Sirs Gentlemen Gentlemen and Ladies Ladies and Gentlemen Dear [company name]	Yours truly
◆ writing to a person whom you have not met but are mentioning specifically in the inside address	Sir Madam Dear Sir Dear Madam	Very truly yours Yours truly Yours very truly
◆ when an attention line is used	Gentlemen Dear Sirs Ladies and Gentlemen Ladies or Mesdames (when the company is totally female)	Very truly yours Yours truly Yours very truly
◆ writing to a person but using only a business title (e.g., Sales Manager)	Dear Sir Dear Madam	Very truly yours Yours truly Yours very truly
Less formal		
◆ writing to a person you know but on a business basis only	Dear Mr. Robinette Dear Miss Jones Dear Ms. Chantrelle Dear Mrs. Kuman	Sincerely Sincerely yours Yours sincerely Cordially yours
◆ writing to a businessperson you do not know and whose gender is unknown	Dear Sir or Madam Dear Madam or Sir Dear C. Kreiner	Yours very truly
◆ writing to an unknown address in a form letter	Dear Friend Dear Customer Dear Homeowner	Very truly yours
Personal		
◆ writing to a friend	Dear Maurice My dear Ginette	Cordially yours Most sincerely Kindest regards Best wishes Regards Sincerely
◆ writing to a friend in a business situation	Dear Mr. Bird	Yours very sincerely
◆ writing to a young person	Dear Jonathan	Yours sincerely

C163 MEMORANDUMS

The interoffice memorandum is designed for sending messages within an organization and therefore does not need an inside address, salutation, or complimentary closing. Designed for short, factual communications, one paragraph is acceptable. See Unit 12, K44, for formatting information.

Memo to: T. Pinchon, Sales Rep.
From: Megan Laurence, Sales Manager
Date: Current Date
Subject: May Sales Meeting

The next monthly sales meeting is scheduled for Thursday, May 13, at 10 a.m. in my office.

A valuable addition to the agenda would be a 15-min presentation by you to the salespeople on the ad campaign you ran so successfully in January. Please let me know by Friday if this will be possible.

phe   M.L.

NOTE It is not necessary to key in sender's initials if his or her name appears in the From:[   ] line.

C164 PRESS RELEASES

When a new product is introduced, a senior managerial appointment announced, or other notable event occurs, the occasion is often publicized in the media by means of a press release. This is a bulletin sent out to newspapers, trade magazines, and other pertinent journals in the hope of free publication. The press release follows this format:

◆ Key on standard-sized company letterhead.

◆ Use wide margins.

◆ Double-space to allow for editing.

◆ Insert the name, title, telephone and fax numbers, and e-mail address of a company contact person.

◆ Key the story headline in block capitals.

Insert FOR RELEASE ON [provide the date on which the announcement becomes official] or FOR IMMEDIATE RELEASE and the date of transmission underneath.

End the release with –30–.

Contents of the press release

Keep the contents to one page if possible and the writing strictly factual. A well-written release enables an editor to do an accurate précis if one is necessary.

C

The first paragraph should tell a brief story that answers the questions of who, what, when, where, why, and how. Subsequent paragraphs amplify or expand on the news. No concluding paragraph is necessary.

PRESS RELEASE

Pitman Office Handbook
Fifth Edition © 2002
Joan I. Campbell
Pat Smith
Pamela Hay-Ellis

FOR IMMEDIATE RELEASE

August 2001
Contact: Barbara Chen, Publicist
Tel: 416-447-5101, ext. 214
Fax: 416-447-7755

Workplaces and work styles are continually changing and presenting new challenges. Full of productivity tips, the *Pitman Office Handbook* helps readers keep up with the times with this fully updated and expanded fifth edition.

SOME FEATURES OF THE FIFTH EDITION

- Alphabetic locator codes and an expanded index make it easy to find information quickly

- Expanded coverage of technology, including computer systems, company intranets, and using the internet to conduct job searches, make travel arrangements, or plan events

- Sound advice about communication, language and presentation skills, such as telephone techniques, *Net*iquette, and conflict resolution in the workplace

- Expanded coverage of marketplace terminology and tips about financial management

-- 30 --

Representing PRENTICE HALL • ALLYN AND BACON • ADDISON WESLEY LONGMAN
26 Prince Andrew Place, Toronto, Ontario M3C 2T8
Tel: (416) 447-5101. Fax: (416) 443-0948
E-mail: phabinfo.pubcanada@pearsoned.com
Visit our web site at: www.pearsoned.ca

A press release

C165 REPORTS

Reports come in two broad categories: the *information* report, which provides data, and the *research* report, which outlines a problem, presents facts and findings after research has been carried out, evaluates the data collected, and recommends a solution. The information report is informal and usually brief; the research report is complex and therefore requires a more structured format. (See Unit 12, K45–K67, for formatting instructions.)

Preparing a report

Research Before you start writing the report, gather all of the facts to be presented. Go to appropriate and, of course, reliable sources for records, figures, dates, and other pertinent information.

Primary research data is information that you gather specifically for the project you are doing. This information can be the result of your own observations or surveys, or can be derived from general reference books or materials.

Secondary research data is information that has been collected and compiled by others on the topic that you are investigating and that exists in printed or electronic form.

> "The report notes should be generous in the use of headings throughout the report."
>
> Lanham, Stewart, Zimmer:
>
> Business English and Communication 3rd Cdn. Ed. McGraw-Hill Ryerson, Toronto, 1987 p. 106
> Advocates
> 1. Closely written text boring.
> 2. Break up text into many sections.
> 3. Make reader's task easy.

Report notes

NOTE Names of magazines, newspapers, books, or periodicals should be in *italics* or underlined.

The Internet as well as libraries, whether company, university, or public, are usually the best source of information on a wide variety of subjects. Each library will have its own system for retrieval of publications and other materials that might be useful. If you encounter any difficulty, a librarian is usually available to provide assistance (see Unit 10, "Information and Reference Resources").

Once you locate the material you need, use an index card or a laptop computer to record each relevant piece of information. Be sure to record in full the bibliographical information for any sources that you might quote in your report, as detailed below.

C

For a book: Name(s) of author(s) and/or editor(s), book title and subtitle (if any), the name and location of the publisher, year of publication, and page number(s). Additional information might be required, such as edition or volume number.

For a magazine, journal, or newspaper article: Author (if known), name of article, name of publication, date of publication, page number. Volume numbers are also sometimes included.

The outline Once you have collected all of the relevant data, prepare an outline for your report, similar to the following illustration.

NOTE Some software packages help in producing outlines. The software automatically assigns section designators (numbers, letters, etc.) and appropriate indents. If you decide to add or delete information, the program will renumber and reorganize the outline, together with accompanying text.

OUTLINE—THE BUSINESS REPORT

I. Locating Information
   A. Company sources
      1. The resource centre
      2. Online databases
   B. Internet
   C. University libraries
   D. Original research

II. Appearance
   A. Advantages and disadvantages of printer types
      1. Laser
      2. Dot matrix
      3. Ink jet
   B. Stationery choices
      1. Recycled
      2. Paper weights
      3. Colour
      4. Finish

III. Production and Distribution
   A. In-house facilities
   B. Outside print sources

A typical outline

Rough draft Build on the outline and add the appropriate substance to the report.

◆ First write an introduction stating the purpose of the report and indicating research methods, background information, and any other pertinent details.

◆ Enlarge on the points made in the introduction by giving details, comparisons, statistics, etc. Organize the body into sections and subsections and try to provide clear headings for each topic or paragraph.

◆ End with a conclusion that summarizes the report findings or research, and offer your recommendations for future action.
To be of greatest benefit to the reader, a report should be:

◆ complete (any questions should be anticipated and answered)

◆ concise (this enables the reader to quickly understand the facts being presented)

◆ clearly written and easy to read (no confusion should be raised in the reader's mind)

◆ more objective than subjective

◆ developed in logical sequence

◆ accurate and contain only verified information

◆ supported by specific and precise evidence that reinforces your arguments

Final report   Edit and polish the rough draft (several times if necessary) until you are satisfied that your words tell an accurate, understandable story.

Obviously, word-processing software is recommended. Editing is easy, production is less time-consuming, and many writers find that their creative abilities are increased because of the ease of making changes. As well:

◆ footnoting can be done automatically

◆ graphics are easily produced to make financial and statistical documents more meaningful

◆ paging and repaging are automatic

◆ reformatting without rekeying can be done

◆ the report can be distributed via e-mail, fax, or hard copy immediately on completion

Read the draft aloud to hear how it flows; ask yourself if every point has been clearly expressed; try to see your work from the reader's perspective. If you have time, put the report away for a couple of days and come back to it with fresh eyes before the final production occurs.

If you plan to mail the report, enclose a *letter of transmittal* that explains the purpose of the report and contains your recommendations.

Parts of the report

Depending on its length, a report usually consists of all or most of the following parts. Refer to Unit 12, K45–K67, for properly formatted examples.

Title page or cover sheet   The title of the report, name and department or company of the originator, name of the recipient (unless intended for broad distribution), and the date are attractively keyed on this first page.

C

Table of contents Each heading and its page number are set up for easy reference on this sheet. When keying the contents page, use dot leaders for easy reference to page numbers. (See Unit 12, K48.) The contents page tells the reader what topics are covered in the report and where to find them quickly. Illustrations may also be listed in the table of contents.

TIP Use the automatic table of contents feature on your word-processing software.

Preface or summary In long reports, a preface or summary enables the reader who does not have enough time to read the whole report to pick out the main points quickly.

Body of the report The main body of the report consists of an introduction, details of the topic under discussion, and a conclusion as described earlier under "Rough draft."

TIP If you use the styles feature of your word-processing software, you can easily update formats and generate automatic table of contents.

Footnotes, endnotes, and textnotes These are numbered references that provide additional information or identify specific sources used in the report. Footnotes appear at the bottom of each page; endnotes appear on a separate page at the end of the report; textnotes are recorded in the appropriate place in the report. (See Unit 12, K61.)

Bibliography The titles of books, periodicals, and other reference sources; their authors; and date, place, and name of publisher comprise this list of sources used in compiling the report. It is always arranged alphabetically by author or editor. (See Unit 12, K66.)

Appendix When a number of graphs, tables, special vocabulary lists, etc., are included in a report, they are compiled in an appendix. The appendix/appendices should be placed before the bibliography.

TIP Use all caps when keying in the word APPENDIX (e.g., APPENDIX A, APPENDIX B, and so on). You may also use the roman numeral designation (e.g., APPENDIX I, APPENDIX II).

NOTE Roman numerals should line up from right to left:
APPENDIX   I
APPENDIX II
APPENDIX III

Number the pages using the same numbering format as the body of the report, and place the appendix pages behind the body of the report.

C166 ORAL EXPRESSION

Most people spend more time speaking (giving instructions, asking questions, selling, etc.) than they do writing. With the spoken word, tone, pitch, volume, rate, enunciation, pronunciation, and language skills are important considerations. Skilful use of the voice and clever choice of language will help you to achieve the desired effect on your audience.

Tone: Indication of attitude and feelings; voice modulation.

Pitch: Degree of highness or lowness of the voice (variations in pitch add interest and indicate meanings).

Volume: Quality that enables you to be heard (volume is influenced by the size and acoustics of a room and use or non-use of a microphone).

Rate: Tempo of your speech (use a rate that ensures each word is intelligible).

Enunciation: The precision with which you express each word (let your audience hear your words: "What did you say?" not "Wojasay?").

Pronunciation: Correct expression of each word (correct pronunciation is the mark of an educated person: film not filum; maintenance not maintainance).

C167 PRESENTATIONS

▶ C168 Introducing a speaker

Keep the introduction short and simple. Include:

- ◆ print or write the speaker's name on the board or flip chart (if available, or if you feel this is necessary); this is helpful for the audience if the name is difficult to pronounce or to spell
- ◆ a warm, welcoming comment
- ◆ a statement of the speaker's topic
- ◆ a very brief summary of the speaker's background or special interests
- ◆ an introduction of the speaker by name (Do this *last*. The speaker knows that at this point he or she takes over.)

▶ C169 Thanking a speaker

Again, say very little. Comment on the importance of the speech and then simply thank the speaker, expressing appreciation on behalf of everyone present.

▶ C170 Making a speech or oral report

Getting started

Establish a purpose. Is your purpose to inform, persuade, or entertain (or a combination of these)?

C

Determine your topic and decide on the key ideas.

Consider your audience age, type, and number.

Collect and organize your reference materials.

Preparing an outline

Prepare an outline by building a "frame" that consists of an introduction (what your presentation is about), the body (which includes the details needed to satisfy the listeners' curiosity and keep them interested), and a conclusion (which reaffirms the opening statement).

Your outline will resemble the one shown for a written report in this unit, C165.

Writing the speech

Enlarge on your outline until you have produced a speech (either in point form or in full) that is the right length.

◆ Have a compelling opening. Use a startling question or a challenging statement, or recount an incident that will grab the audience's interest.

◆ Keep the main points that you want to make to only three or four. Audiences won't remember if you say something once and just move on. Make the point. Say it again differently, illustrate it, and then say it again.

◆ Have a strong closing, also. Use a summary of the points you have made and the conclusions to be drawn, or make some type of appeal for action.

Producing your speaking notes

From the finished speech, produce your speaking notes. These may be in one of three forms:

◆ Cut back your speech to key words or phrases and write these boldly on small cue cards.

◆ Use the outline you prepared earlier, with the key points highlighted or underscored.

◆ Use your entire speech, with the key points highlighted or underscored. This is the least desirable option because you should not get up in front of your audience and *read* a speech. If you must use this method, then type the speech using only the top half of each sheet so that you will be glancing only at the top of the lectern and can keep your head up.

Practising

Even the most experienced speakers practise their presentations. Inexperienced speakers may find it helpful to practise the presentation aloud to a friend or in front of a mirror. Audio- or videotaping your speech and playing it back can also help you to identify any problems.

- Time yourself, allowing time for laughter or audience participation if applicable.
- Practise your opening and your closing until you have memorized them. Do not, however, memorize the rest of the speech. This will restrict your delivery.

Delivering the speech

When it is time for you to speak, walk calmly to the appointed spot, look up, smile, and make your presentation, bearing in mind these tips:

- Make a good first impression. Look as good as you can. Have good posture and maintain this all the way through the presentation.
- Be well prepared. Preparation breeds confidence.
- Don't *read* your speech. It is preferable to use an outline or cue cards. If you insist on the comfort of a full script in front of you, don't turn the pages on the lectern. As you finish a page, slide it face up to your left so that your eyes move easily to the next sheet. If you do this, you will not look down as much.
- Speak slowly, clearly, and loudly enough to be heard by everyone. Keep your head up and be sure that people in the back row can hear you.
- Dress appropriately; business clothing is recommended if you are speaking to a group of business people.
- Speak with enthusiasm and vary the pitch of your voice. Vocal variety is vital.
- Try to be natural, spontaneous, and conversational in your delivery, but avoid using too many words like "uh," "like," "you know," etc.
- Feel your audience's reaction and respond to it.
- Establish a bond with each listener in the audience by making frequent eye contact.
- Body language is important. Use gestures, body movements, and facial expressions as valuable tools. However, avoid irritating mannerisms (too many hand movements, fiddling with buttons, playing with hair, or moving around too much).
- Conceal any nervousness as well as you can. Use a lectern to hold on to, keep taking deep breaths, don't hold on to papers—they rustle!
- Make use of visuals if possible to present difficult concepts or statistical information. Make sure the audience can see them—don't get in the way!

Closing

- Be aware of the time available and don't exceed it.
- Deliver your strong closing and turn the proceedings back to the chair or facilitator.

▶ **C171 Pointers for effective oral presentations**

Physical setting
◆ Make sure everyone can hear and see easily.

Rate of speaking
◆ Speak slowly. This means at a relaxed rate, not unnaturally slowly. Don't overdo it.

Speech plan
◆ Try to create a "road map" to your presentation. Clearly state the purpose of your presentation and how many points you'll make. Try to say "First," "Second," "Next," etc., so that the audience has a sense of the progression as well as a set of expectations about where you're taking them.

Language
◆ Simplify your vocabulary and avoid ambiguities.
◆ Explain essential content vocabulary.
◆ Reduce the use of idioms.
◆ Use active voice and positive sentences where possible.
◆ Monitor sentence length.

Visual cues
◆ Use charts, maps, pictures, or photographs.
◆ Do not put too many items or points on a visual; there should only be six to eight items on a page or screen.
◆ Use a large print font for easy reading.
◆ Take a course on how to use software packages for effective presentations (e.g., PowerPoint).
◆ Today's employees are expected to be knowledgeable in using presentation software.

NOTE Proofread very carefully; errors in visuals or handouts can damage the impact of the presentation.

Handouts
◆ Provide an outline of the presentation.
◆ Provide a list of the key terms used.
◆ Provide copies of important charts or other visuals.

TIP Decide whether you wish the audience to have the handouts *during* or *after* the presentation.

Give handouts *after* the presentation, if they are not needed for reference, to prevent the flipping of pages (noise factor and undivided attention of audience).

C172 DICTATION TECHNIQUES

Whether you dictate to a person or into a recording device, advance preparation is the key to success. For greater efficiency, plan to do all of your dictating in one session, if possible. If you travel on the job and are required to document details, you may be wise to dictate a report (or brief notes to be expanded later) after each call or contact, while the information is still fresh in your mind.

Preparation

♦ Assemble all of the information you need—files, correspondence, calendar, address book.

♦ Organize your thoughts in advance and make notes of the points you want to include.

♦ When you want to reply to incoming correspondence, make notes in the margins.

♦ Set time aside to dictate your material.

♦ Close your office door or post a "DO NOT DISTURB—DICTATION IN PROGRESS" sign; if possible, give the time that you do not wish to be disturbed (e.g., "from 10–11 a.m.").

♦ To avoid interruptions, ask someone to take your phone calls during this scheduled time (ringing phones are a distraction).

♦ Never dictate with a radio playing in the background.

NOTE If you bring dictation home with you, do not let children play with the equipment when you are not in the room (could be embarrassing).

Dictation instructions

♦ Identify the type of message (letter, memo, fax, etc.).

♦ Indicate priority or rush work.

♦ Specify the number of copies to be made and to whom they should go.

♦ Give any special instructions regarding format (spacing, layout) or stationery to be used.

♦ If you are dictating into a recorder, identify yourself by name, title, and location. As well as following the points noted above, if your recorder has the capability, indicate where communications end and if there are any corrections.

Dictation

♦ Remain stationary and do not smoke, chew gum, eat, or play with keys or jewellery while dictating.

♦ If your job necessitates dictating from your car, roll up the car windows and park the car. *Never* dictate and drive. *Never* dictate during a flight unless you are travelling on a company executive jet and it is appropriate to do so.

C

- Hold the microphone or telephone receiver about 10 cm from your mouth.
- Use a natural, conversational voice level and speed.
- Give the name and address of the addressee.
- For memos, indicate the subject.
- Dictate numbers slowly and spell proper names not accessible to the transcriber.
- Spell out troublesome technical terms and other difficult words or names.
- Give as many punctuation and paragraphing instructions as possible.
- Place correspondence being replied to face down on the desk when dictation is finished so that the order of items on the tape is obvious to the transcriber.

UNIT

2 COMPUTERS: HARDWARE AND SOFTWARE

CONTENTS

Computer technology is changing at a mind-boggling rate. The almost daily changes are impossible to keep up with. The basics of the computer should, however, be understood by all office personnel—the processes, the uses, the software and the terms—and that general information is provided in this unit.

Because the topic is so massive, the role of the computer in an integrated environment is dealt with separately in "Information Processing and Integrated Office Automation" (Unit 9), and the place of the computer in desktop publishing (DTP) is provided in "Electronic (Desktop) Publishing" (Unit 4). Where needed, appropriate cross-references are given.

CO

CO1 COMPUTER TYPES

Three main computer types are used in business. The essential differences among them are their storage capacity (memory), processing speed, and cost.

Mainframes These powerful computers are used only by large organizations for their centralized data-processing needs and are generally operated only by experts.

Minicomputers Minicomputers can perform many of the functions of mainframes but are significantly smaller. They can perform a variety of business functions and can also have applications in such fields as science, engineering, and production.

Microcomputers (commonly called personal computers or PCs) These small, desktop computers are now so powerful that in many businesses they have replaced mainframes and minis. They may be used as stand-alones or linked in a network.

Desktop computers come with varying capabilities—from simple data entry and editing to the ability to create multi-dimensional presentations in real time (live video, graphics, and text displayed on the screen in colour, with stereo sound accompaniment).

CO2 PORTABLE COMPUTERS

Several types of portable computers are available that can do virtually everything a desktop model can do.

Portables These are quite small and can be powered by electricity or battery.

Laptops/notebooks/palmtops These are small and extremely convenient.

- ◆ Some can be inserted into a desktop computer in a specially designed "docking station" and provide a wide range of computing power.
- ◆ Most can be used with the monitor and printer of a compatible desktop computer.
- ◆ Some have removable hard drives that can be plugged into a desktop computer.
- ◆ Some can be coupled to a full keyboard.
- ◆ Some have their own in-built printer.
- ◆ "Smart cards" containing microprocessor chips can be inserted into some that can expand the range of their functions.

Hand-held Pen-based, these use the technology of the computer. Users write directly on screens with electronic pens. They are useful in forms applications, scheduling, and tracking.

Personal digital assistant (PDA) This is not quite a computer, but is more than an electronic organizer. Although it does not use a common operating system such as DOS or Windows, it performs many of the tasks normally expected of a desktop or portable computer.

As well as a calendar, scheduler, telephone directory, and calculator, it can contain a mini word processor and a function that allows you to write or draw on the screen and save the image. By means of smart cards containing chips, you can hook up a PDA to a modem, send faxes, receive e-mail and telephone messages, and do spreadsheet and other functions. A communications port means you can share data with other computers or print directly on a laser printer.

CO3 COMPUTER OPERATING SYSTEMS

An operating system is software that manages the basic functions of a computer, such as controlling the application software, copying disks, and storing files. Most computers are sold with the operating system software already installed.

The key operating systems are:

MS/DOS Microsoft Disk Operating System for IBM and IBM clones and compatible computers (Microsoft is the name of the manufacturer).

DOS shell is a simpler version of DOS that makes learning DOS easier.

Finder is the operating system used by Macintosh.

OS/2 permits multi-tasking (working on more than one computer application at a time) and runs on newer, faster, IBM and IBM-compatible machines.

Windows 3-1 was a graphic system that worked on top of DOS and was designed to make DOS easier to use.

Microsoft Windows 95/98/2000 are fully graphical, multi-tasking operating systems that can be loaded directly into computers without the need for DOS.

Microsoft Windows 2000 is a fully graphic, multi-tasking, networking operating system that can be loaded directly into computers without the need for DOS.

Microsoft Windows Millennium Edition is a comprehensive full-task operating system designed for home networking and Web browsing (recommended for home use/small businesses operations).

Windows NT (new technology) is a Microsoft operating system designed for use on high-end workstations and networked computers.

Unix is the operating system of choice for scientific and engineering workstations. There are many versions of UNIX; e.g., Linux.

NOTE Computers are available that allow users to run standard Macintosh programs as well as Windows/DOS programs. The technology that permits this is known as RISC (Reduced Instruction Set Computing).

Graphical user interface (GUI)

To interface in computer language means to communicate. A GUI (pronounced "gooey") refers to the way in which icons (small pictures) are used on the screen to represent desktop tools such as file folders. Instead of keying words, the user simply clicks a mouse onto an icon to carry out an operation. Examples of such operations are opening and closing applications and files and moving items around the screen.

CO4 COMPUTER COMPONENTS

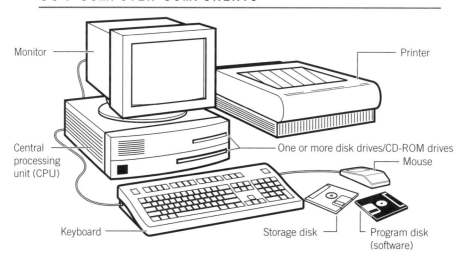

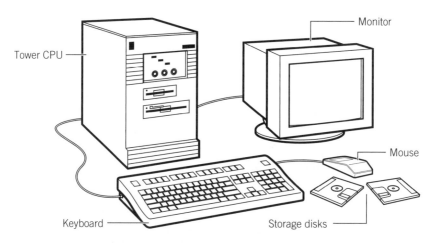

Components of a typical desktop microcomputer (PC) workstation

Computer hardware is all of the electronic and mechanical parts—printers, disk drives, keyboards, video displays.

Workstations with no intelligence are referred to as *dumb*.

Workstations with intelligence are referred to as *smart*.

Computer software is all of the instructions that tell the computer to perform certain operations.

CO

C05 CENTRAL PROCESSING UNITS (CPUs)

The CPU, also referred to as the microprocessor, is a silicon chip consisting of thousands of electronic circuits and transistors. This is the "brain" of the computer.

A computer follows the instructions it receives from a program. The program is fed into the computer memory as is also the data to be processed. The program and data are accessed (located and read) by the CPU, and whatever action is required is carried out. The CPU has three parts:

Primary storage unit (memory) This unit provides for the temporary storage of data. All data and instructions must be received here before the computer can start its work. All calculations performed are also stored here until further processing or output is required.

Arithmetic/logic unit This unit processes the data. It can do calculations and take logical action (compare possible courses of action and decide between alternatives). It might, for example, compare two figures, decide which is the larger, and put them in order.

Control unit This unit maintains order and controls the entire system (input, output, and CPU), ensuring that everything is working in accordance with the program it has received.

CPUs vary as to processing power, memory, and storage space.

Pentium II or III Expanded central processing units: Pentium II, III, and Celeron CPUs are modular and plug into a slot on the motherboard.

▶ C06 Processing power

Processing power is a major consideration in computer choice. It is determined by the kind of microprocessor chip installed. The benefits of higher-powered machines are faster opening and saving of files, deleting blocks, running spell checks, or, say, processing changes in calculations in a spreadsheet.

▶ C07 Memory

Although low memory is less expensive, you should consider future needs and the quantity of memory needed for each program you may want to run. A computer has two types of internal memory:

Random access memory (RAM)

◆ Also known as *working memory*, stores data and programs and can be accessed or altered by the user.
◆ Memory measurements normally refer to RAM. The size of the program and amount of data with which you are working are limited by the amount of RAM installed in your computer.

CO

Read-only memory (ROM)

◆ Is used by the manufacturer to store preprogrammed instructions.
◆ Can be read and used by the user but not accessed or altered.
◆ Is used when you turn on your microcomputer:
  • It checks RAM and loads the operating system.
  • When the computer is turned off, anything in RAM is lost if not already saved. ROM contents are kept.

▶ **CO8   Storage space**

RAM is where the CPU does its work. With more storage space (larger RAM), the computer can work faster and handle more complex tasks.

Many programs require a great deal of memory. Current versions of Windows, for example, require at least 16 megabytes (MB) of RAM; however, 32 MB is recommended, and 64 MB preferred. Newer versions, still to be released, will require 64 MB, or even more.

The hard drive is the device used most frequently to store software and data. Again, because programs require considerable disk space, the larger the capacity the better. At the time of writing, 4 GB would be the minimum; 60 GB would provide flexibility for future expansion capabilities. (Currently, the average is 10 to 15 GB.)

For additional data storage devices, see CO32.

CO9 MONITORS

Monitors are rated on their ability to use dots (pixels) to create patterns—the more pixels, the better looking the picture. The quality of display is referred to as *resolution.*

Colour is an important consideration. Quality, however, is not necessarily associated with colour.

Monitors vary in size, shape, type, and quality of resolution and the amount of text or data they can display. They come in 10-, 14-, 15-, 17-, 19-, and 21-inch sizes, and for graphics, computer-aided design (CAD), and desktop publishing (DTP) applications with one-page and two-page screens. Terms used include:

CGA	320 × 200 pixels	colour graphics adapter
EGA	640 × 360 pixels	enhanced graphics adapter
VGA	720 × 400 pixels	video graphics adapter
Super VGA	800 × 600 pixels	super video graphics adapter

CO10 INPUT DEVICES

Before data can be read (loaded) into the computer, it must be changed into a format acceptable to the computer (i.e., it must be digitized). By far the most commonly used direct input device is the keyboard.

▶ **C011   Keyboard**

When a key is pressed, an electrical pulse is emitted that is converted into a digital code. Most keyboards contain some or all of the following:

Function keys These programmable keys perform whole functions such as save, print, delete.

Cursor control keys These position the marker (cursor) that indicates the working point on the screen. They are usually labelled with arrows.

Designated-purpose keys (ctrl, alt, etc.) The use of these is determined by the software used.

Some keyboards provide a *numeric keypad* and some a *trackball* that functions like a mouse.

See Unit 3, page 156 for information on newer, ergonomically designed keyboards.

▶ **C012   Non-keyboard input devices and methods**

Bar code The computer reads information contained in specially imprinted codes. The universal product code (UPC) used in retail stores is a major example of the use of this system. Other uses are in inventory control and records.

Digital cameras Digital cameras offer high-quality image enhancement technology: images can be instantly printed out, sent through e-mail, or viewed on TV with a video cable. You can choose which pictures to print and/or store. You can use software to organize and record pictures, and to correct colour-casts and contrast problems. You can choose to share or delete the images in record mode before storing them on the memory card.

The *memory card* is an electronic storage device that stores each picture until it is unloaded to the computer. You can use these images for presentations, printed publications, Internet pages, and other applications.

NOTE PC System Requirements: 50 MB of available hard disk space
VGA Monitor with at last 256 colours
Pentium processor or higher

Graphics tablet This allows the user to draw anything—images, graphics, schematics—on-screen. It is popular in DTP, CAD, and presentation graphics applications. The user employs a graphics pen to draw on a special pad attached to the computer.

Handwriting recognition This is a device that records handwriting electronically for processing.

Light pen The light pen enables the user to write or draw directly onto the screen (monitor).

Magnetic disk or tape For large processing tasks such as payroll or accounting, it is faster to encode data onto a magnetic disk or tape and then feed it into the computer.

CO

Magnetic Ink Character Recognition (MICR) A special ink containing a trace of iron is used to imprint the MICR code on documents. The iron is magnetized, and the computer senses it and interprets the data it contains. This method is used by financial institutions for processing cheques.

Mouse New: 2-Wheel Scroll Mouse, Wheel Mouse optical, and Trackman Marble Wheel. This is an electronic pointing device used to move the cursor around the screen and to help in making selections. The type of mouse used will vary with the operating system of the computer. Most have two buttons and some have three. They are available in mechanical, optical, cordless radio, or high-resolution versions.

High-tech mouse This mouse has no track ball and uses an optical sense called IntelliEye. It scans the surface under the mouse 1500 times a second to track the smallest motion, and a mouse pad is not required. It also, has two programmable side buttons that allow the user to go back and forth between Web pages.

NOTE Other pointing devices are joysticks and trackballs.

Optical Mark Reading (OMR) In this system, marks on cards or sheets are scanned and interpreted by the computer. Market research surveys are examples of the use of OMR.

Point-of-sale terminals These are used, for example, in stores to track inventory and pricing when goods are sold.

Scanner Images of all kinds (text, numbers, graphics) can be scanned and converted by the computer into digital information for processing (known as image processing). The images can be manipulated into new shapes and sizes. This is particularly useful in page composition and page layout as in desktop publishing, for example.

You can also use scanners to convert a black-and-white or colour printer into a copying machine or fax, and/or to scan images into installed e-mail applications. There are two types of scanners for general use: the *flatbed*, which looks like a photocopier; and the *sheet-fed*, which can accept single sheets or paper documents. The *photo-scanner*, a small sheet-fed machine, is used for photographs. *Handheld* scanners have a span of 2" to 5".

All scanners work in essentially the same way; a light-sensitive device called a CCD (charged-coupled device), similar to what a camcorder uses to "see" images, converts light reflected from the original into an electronic signal. The signal is then digitized and stored on the computer's hard drive.

The *flatbed* scanner moves its CCD past the original, which sits on a fixed, transparent surface; *sheet-fed* and *photo scanners* use rollers to move the original past a fixed CCD.

Scanners typically come with three basic types of software: one to control the scanning, one to adjust an image's appearance after it has been scanned, and one to recognize text.

Touch-sensitive screen The touch of a finger will cause the computer to respond. Menu selection is the most frequent use of touch technology.

Video input Images can be captured from a video camera, stored electronically, and processed by the computer for incorporation into any type of document.

Voice recognition This system is based on the unique quality of each person's voice and permits direct input by means of the spoken word. A microphone attached to the computer records the voice electronically, processes it as text, and provides a soft copy on-screen for editing. The voice can be used to activate certain computer commands also, as in forms completion, for example.

CO13 SOFTWARE (PROGRAMS)

The computer must be told how to solve a problem by means of a *program*, a series of instructions written in computer language that guides the computer step by step through a process. Programs are written by computer manufacturers, by software marketing companies (vendors), or by an organization's own programmers.

Popular software today consists of office suites made up of word processing, spreadsheet, database, presentation, personal information manager, and Web browser.

CO14 BUSINESS-RELATED SOFTWARE

Because there is such an immense variety and diversity of software available, most businesses purchase software packages rather than write their own. These packages are updated regularly and updates can usually be bought for a reasonable price. The most popular software types (known as *applications software*) for business use include:

▶ CO15   Accounting and financial management

Many are available covering report-generating, job-costing, order-processing, accounts receivable and payable, general ledger, collections, inventory control, cheque-writing, and payroll. Some packages offer most or all of these functions; some handle just one task.

▶ CO16   Communications software

These programs allow you to connect computers so that they can "talk" to each other. You can transfer files or send messages across the room or across the country. As well, they allow you to take advantage of online information services and connect with electronic bulletin boards.

Communication among computers is possible because of communications software and modems (see this unit, CO41).

CO

Many integrated software packages feature communications as part of the package. Most incorporate a telephone book feature that allows you to store and automatically dial frequently called numbers.

▶ CO17 Databases

These electronic records management programs are designed to help organize, record, track, access, and analyse information. You can input millions of records (customers' names, inventory records, for example), sort them in any order, quickly select any information, and display and print your needs.

- ◆ After data is entered, you can access it easily. You can sort, search, and arrange the data in any way you wish without any rekeying.
- ◆ Sorts can be alphabetic or numeric in ascending or descending order.
- ◆ Printing can be in many forms: reports, lists, labels, envelopes, for example.
- ◆ Searches can be as specific as you wish.

Databases are created on electronic forms that you design to meet your own needs. Each form consists of *fields* (as many as you need), which are separate information items such as name, address, telephone number. A separate form is keyed for each client (or whatever). The completed form is known as a *record*. A set of records is referred to as a *file*.

Databases are of two types—flat and relational:

Flat Stores, organizes, and retrieves data from one file at a time. Each record contains all of the data related to a particular topic.

Relational Allows linking between databases so that, for example, an inventory database could be linked to a database of manufacturers so that as stock gets low you could contact the manufacturer to reorder.

Additional features of databases

- ◆ They permit integration with word processing so that merging can occur (e.g., name and address information can be combined with text to generate business letters, envelopes, or labels).
- ◆ Some permit the user to change font, size, style, and colour.

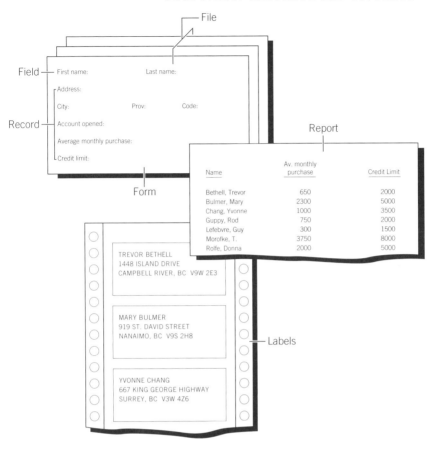

Databases can be printed as lists (reports) or as labels.

▶ CO18   Desktop accessory packages

These combine some or all of word processing (notepad), appointment calendar, electronic filing (database), electronic mail, and a calculator. Some provide an alarm clock to remind you of time, events, etc.

▶ CO19   Desktop publishing

Complete details are provided in Unit 4.

▶ CO20   Forms software

This is available to assist in the design of requisitions, invoices, telephone messages, timesheets, etc.

- ◆ includes logos and graphics, text and database functions, and design tools
- ◆ contains a library of sample forms

CO

◆ permits automatic calculations

◆ provides indexing and sorting capabilities

See Unit 7, "Forms and Forms Design," for more details.

▶ CO21   Graphics software

There are essentially four types:

◆ Paint programs   ◆ Presentation graphics

◆ Draw programs   ◆ CAD programs

Paint programs provide access to a variety of tools, colours, and patterns that allow the user to "paint" the screen.

◆ can be used to create colourful pictures and images for documents, brochures, newsletters

Draw programs are used by designers, engineers, and architects to create sophisticated graphic art illustrations.

Presentation graphics software, in its simplest form, allows for the attractive displaying of information—charts, graphs, etc. In its most complex form, it refers to highly sophisticated multi-media presentations that include live video, graphics, animation, text, and stereo sound.

CAD programs are computer-aided design programs created to replace the drafting table and drafting tools.

◆ used for sophisticated engineering and architectural work

◆ one drawing can be presented from several perspectives and on-screen objects can be rotated

▶ CO22   Groupware

This is software designed for use in a network. The software programs used are basically the same as those used for any computer application. It is their ability to be shared that makes them different.

◆ Some are for small groups only, e.g., as few as 5 on a local area network (LAN). Others can accommodate up to 100 000 on a wide area network (WAN) through "gateways." See Unit 9 for more information on networks.

◆ They can handle all internal business operations and communications electronically (meetings, appointments, tasks, paperwork), with automatic reminders of upcoming events.

◆ Participants can accept, reject, or delegate meeting requests. Personal calendars across any number of networks—even in dissimilar operating systems—can be checked for conflicts.

◆ They can control how information reaches staff, where it is filed, and where it is routed.

◆ Incoming mail can be automatically sorted and forwarded to others in a user's absence or it can be handled from a laptop at a remote location (see Unit 5, "Electronic Mail").

Users can check the status of any message or project as well as retract and rethink any unopened message.

▶ CO23   Integrated software

This combines programs such as word processing, spreadsheet, database, and communications. Some packages also include graphics, electronic scheduler, calculator, telephone dialler, and utilities programs. While not always quite as sophisticated as programs that are available separately, integrated software offers these advantages:

- ◆ data easily merged between applications (e.g., a spreadsheet can be integrated into a memo)
- ◆ easy to learn—some commands can be used for several applications
- ◆ less time spent on loading and in opening and closing files
- ◆ most allow data to be exchanged among other programs
- ◆ cheaper than buying the separate applications
- ◆ take up less disk space and are therefore ideal for notebook computers and less powerful machines

NOTE   Office suites are sets of software sold as a package that permit easy integration of data via importing, exporting, and linking. Content varies, and the choice is usually determined by the word-processing package included. Such packages are less expensive than separate components. Office suites can be loaded with standard, custom, or laptop configurations.

▶ CO24   Shareware

These are programs that can be distributed and copied at little or no cost without breaking copyright laws. They are distributed through the Internet, electronic bulletin boards, online information services, user groups, and mail-order services.

NOTE   See Unit 10 for more information on freeware/shareware.

▶ CO25   Spreadsheets

These are electronic worksheets designed to assist those involved in calculations and financial analysis (number-crunching) of any kind—from balancing a chequebook to running a large organization.

The worksheet resembles accounting paper and consists of multiple columns and rows, the number depending on the program purchased. The intersection of each row and column is known as a *cell*, into which you enter data (values or labels) and formulas. Complex calculations can be performed instantly and the results presented in a clear, organized format. If you change one value or formula, the effect is reflected immediately and automatically throughout the entire spreadsheet. As well, spreadsheets:

CO

- ◆ allow formulas to be saved with the spreadsheet
- ◆ permit sorting and moving columns and rows with formulas intact
- ◆ can copy existing values (replicate) or can increase or decrease incrementally by a specified value
- ◆ can be printed in a variety of formats
- ◆ provide "what-if" scenarios (i.e., testing of important decisions)
- ◆ permit the user to control the way numbers are displayed (dollar signs, decimal places, negative numbers, etc.)
- ◆ allow users to start with a result and work backwards in some cases
- ◆ offer macros that perform repetitive functions

Maximum size of spreadsheet

Cell

A cell is where a row and column intersect.

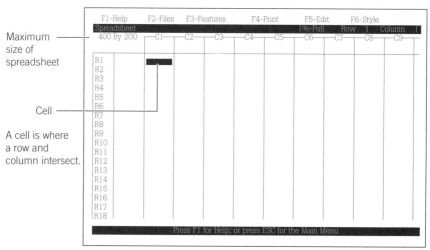

Typical spreadsheet screen

Spreadsheets can be printed as reports or graphics.

CO26 Spreadsheet formulas

While extensive mathematical skill is not needed to operate a spreadsheet, an understanding of the basics of formula creation and symbols is needed. Formulas tell software how to calculate the value in a cell, using the following symbols:

+	addition	/	division
−	subtraction	^ or **	exponentiation
*	multiplication	=	equal to

Each software program has its own method of building a formula; however, common starting symbols are = and @.

Operations are performed in a specific order. That order is ^; − (when used for a negative number, not a minus sign); + (positive); * and / (evaluated from left to right if both appear); + and − (evaluated from left to right if both appear).

You can change the order of calculation by using parentheses. If you enclose a calculation in parentheses, the software does the calculation within the parentheses first. The following examples show how parentheses change the order of calculations:

◆ 5 + (5 * 3) − 12
The answer will be 8.
(Multiply 5 by 3, then add 5, then subtract 12.)

◆ (5 + 5) * 3 − 12
The answer will be 18.
(Add 5 and 5, then multiply by 3, then subtract 12.)

◆ (5 + 5) * (3 − 12)
The answer will be −90.
(Add 5 and 5, then subtract 3 from 12, then multiply the results.)

To save time, spreadsheet software provides many in-built mathematical, trigonometric, and statistical formulas for use in calculations. Consult your manual for a full listing. The most-used business formulas generally provided include average, round to, total, depreciation allowance, and interest.

CO27 Spreadsheet graphics

Spreadsheet information can be presented automatically in graphs and charts of various kinds. The user chooses the type of graphic, indicates the titles, labels, and legends to be shown, and the software does the rest.

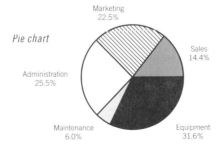

Pie chart

Marketing 22.5%
Sales 14.4%
Administration 25.5%
Maintenance 6.0%
Equipment 31.6%

CO

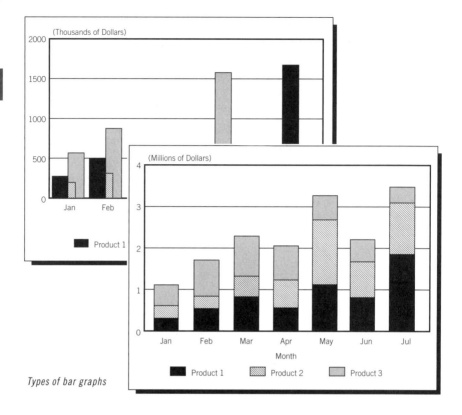

Types of bar graphs

► C028   Utilities

These are useful packages designed to assist with disk management. They help organize files and will come to the rescue when things go wrong (e.g., if data is lost).

► C029   Virus protection

This will help eliminate problems of viruses (i.e., disks or files that have been contaminated).

Important (for students)

◆ Always keep backup disk copies of your work.

◆ Use a working disk for the lab you are working in, and keep another for open access or home use.

◆ Do not keep bad/unusable disks.

◆ If virus protection is not on your system/network, please report any "virus message" to the instructor or monitor in the lab you are working in—write down the screen message regarding the virus.

◆ Anti-virus programs should be upgraded regularly.

▶ **C030   Word processing**

Additional information on word-processing software is provided in Unit 21, "Word Processing."

C031 CHOOSING SOFTWARE

Observe the following points if you are buying software for business or private use (for help in selecting word-processing software, see Unit 21):

1. Carefully establish your needs first.

2. Be sure the software is compatible with your system in terms of memory and hardware. For example, is it compatible with:
   • the kind and version of operating system you have?
   • the kind of monitor and video adapter available?
   • the amount of RAM available?
   • your particular printer?

3. Make sure reference manuals (documentation) and instructions are clear.

4. Check into service. Does your vendor represent a reliable, well-established business? Is training offered? Is a hotline service provided? Can you try the software before you buy it?

5. Can the program be custom-tailored to your needs if necessary?

6. What will be the situation in the event of updates or the discovery of errors?

7. Must the program be compatible with other programs already owned?

8. Consider the skill level of the people who are likely to use the program. How difficult will it be to learn?

9. Consider the future. Will this package be appropriate for some time? Don't risk outgrowing this one in a few months.

C032 STORAGE AND RETRIEVAL

The CPU stores data for processing and instructions as well as data that has been processed. However, since the amount of internal memory is limited, external (or auxiliary) storage is needed when processed data is to be stored for future use. Depending on the equipment used, storage may be on any of the following media.

CO

C033 MAGNETIC DISKS

Magnetic disks are available in formatted or unformatted versions and in two densities:

* 3.5"-720 KB (double density) or 1.44 MB (high density)

NOTE A disk drive with a higher capacity can read from and write to a lower-capacity disk. However, the reverse is not possible.

◆ *Floptical disks* are 3.5" disks capable of holding up to 21 MB of memory. This is more than 14 times the capacity of the most commonly used micro-floppy.
  * The disk and drive look like the familiar floppy ones; however, a special floptical drive is needed, but this can also read conventional floppy disks.
  * The disk combines flexible magnetic media with optical positioning. It achieves its massive storage-capacity increase by putting more tracks of data on each side of the disk, using the same magnetic recording found in conventional devices but with an optical tracking system.
  * Flopticals cut seek time by more than half that of floppies. Floptical disks may, in time, become standard in the computer world.

◆ *Hard disks* are rigid, random-access, high-capacity magnetic storage devices, and are much faster and more convenient than floppies. Hard drives may be internal or external. All computers today come with hard drives built right into the system.
  * They store both programs and data.
  * Today, capacities range from about 4.3 up to 60 GB.
  * Optical disks—used with CD-ROM drives, holdup to 650 MB of information

C034 MAGNETIC TAPE

This may be in reel, cassette, or cartridge format that holds large amounts of data. Magnetic tape, a very inexpensive medium, tends to be used only in very large systems; however, tape backup is a viable option on PCs.

C035 MICROFILM DEVICES (MICROFORMS)

These are used to microfilm information directly from the computer. The process is known as COM (computer output microfilm) and is described in Unit 16, "Records Management."

C036 OPTICAL DISKS

For archival and backup purposes, the trend is toward cost-effective optically stored data. One 650-MB CD-ROM optical disk can replace 250 000 sheets of paper documents, for example. Optical disks offer these advantages:

- are not affected by the same problems as magnetic disks
- mean no misplacements because software does the filing and retrieval
- allow data to be accessed by several users at the same time
- enable images to be retrieved to a screen or to be printed
- are particularly attractive because of their non-volatile nature (retain data with or without power, like a hard disk) and long shelf life (30 years or more)
- are impervious to damage by magnetic or electrical spikes or surges
Optical mass storage is available in these general forms:
- CD-ROM (compact disc, read-only memory); this means that it cannot be resaved or erased by the user. However, text can be edited and saved by another name.
- M-O (magneto-optical), which come in two versions:
  - WORM (write once, read many)
  - rewriteable (known also as erasable)

CD-ROM These are 4.75" optical disks that look like the compact discs used in the music industry. These are useful for storing archival data.

- CD-ROMs are available in read-only or rewriteable formats.
- CD-ROM drives can be internal or external. A CD-ROM drive uses a laser that projects a tiny beam of light onto the disk to read the data.

The technology offers wide, multi-functional capabilities, including the ability to store text, graphics, video, and sound on the same disk.

Massive volumes of information are now available on CD-ROM including encyclopedias, huge medical databases, manufacturers' parts lists and manuals, applications software packages, computer operating system manuals, multi-media training courses on everything from the Japanese language to electronic publishing, libraries of clip art, and digitized images of photos.

A CD-ROM disc is created using a laser beam, which alters the surface of the disk creating bumpy and flat "pit" areas on the bottom of the disk. These areas represent data.

WORM (write once, read many):

- WORM disks are more flexible than CD-ROM because data can be added.
- Data cannot be changed, however.
- WORM disks come as blank disks on which an organization can etch its own data for storage.
- They are capable of storing images and sound as well as text.

Rewriteable (erasable) These are rewriteable, allowing the user to write data, erase data, and write over it again.

C037 DISK-MANAGEMENT TECHNIQUES

This topic is covered in depth in Unit 21, "Word Processing," and in the interests of space is not repeated here.

C038 PRINTERS AND PLOTTERS

C039 PRINTER TYPES

Printers may be impact or non-impact. For information on printer types, see the chart on the following page. In selecting the appropriate printer, consider production speed and the print quality desired. If space is limited, consider a laser *bookshelf printer*. These are not much taller than a hardcover book and produce high quality work.

In a networked environment, costly printers may be shared. This is possible also in a non-networked environment through switch boxes, which are available for both dot matrix and laser printers. From 2 to 16 people can share.

A *photo printer* is a digital camera that can be connected to the printer for top-quality pictures. It prints photos directly from the camera and only prints in colour, but an identical picture or photo is printed. See Unit 17, Reprographics, for more about digital cameras.

C040 PLOTTERS

These output devices are used for producing graphics. A movable arm holds coloured pens that draw images on a page. They are used in engineering, architecture, and construction, and are good for printing blueprints and electrical diagrams.

C041 COMMUNICATIONS

Computers and some peripherals do not need to be in the same room or even in the same geographic area. They can be connected in a network. Networks are described in detail in Unit 9, "Information Processing and Integrated Office Automation."

Stand-alone computers not connected to any other computer can also have data communications capability through the use of a modem.

Type	Characteristics	Used for
Impact		
Dot matrix	• hammer-driven pins create a character by building up a composite of dots • several fonts possible from one head • near-letter-quality is produced when head is passed several times over same line • top-line model has 24 pins and produces good quality. This does not need a second pass • can print graphics and in condensed mode	• where print volume and speed needed • rough draft, graphics, and near-letter-quality work • colour work
Non-Impact		
Bubble jet	• inexpensive	• good for home/personal use
Ink jet*	• controlled jet of quick-drying ink forms dot patterns on page • faster and noiseless	• high-quality reproduction superior to dot matrix • draft and letter-quality possible • colour work and graphics
Laser	• printing is by laser beam • quiet and fast • flexible font/typeface selection • enables users to scale fonts	• photographic or offset repro-duction • high-quality, high-resolution work • colour work and graphics
PostScript laser	• all the features of lasers • provides a wide range of scaleable fonts	• high-resolution graphics • used in DTP
Thermal transfer	• melts wax-based ink off the printer ribbon and onto paper • higher quality than dot matrix • low noise	• very high quality text • high quality colour work

*Ink jet printers require either black or colour cartridges or both. High-resolution print cartridges are expensive; therefore, set print for draft copy if possible.

C042 MODEM

A modem (MOdulator-DEModulator) sends and receives information between computers over telephone lines. The modem converts the analog (wavelike) signals of telephone lines into the digital (on/off) signals needed by computers.

Speed of data transmission is known as its *baud* rate. Most modems used in offices today communicate at 56 K up to 128 K (bits per second). The faster the modem, the cheaper the transmission cost.

CO

Communications software, as discussed earlier, is needed with modems.

C043 FAX

Faxes can be sent directly from some PCs. A mix of hardware and software permits the computer to function as a fax and allows you to send and receive files directly without the need for a separate fax machine (see Unit 5, "Electronic Mail").

C044 VIDEO CONFERENCING

This capability can be added to a desktop computer (see Unit 14, "Meetings, Conferences, and Teleconferences"). A video camera, a board to fit in a desktop computer and software, and network communications enable people at considerable distances to see each other while holding a telephone conversation. Screen-sharing is permitted so that users can jointly edit documents.

C045 VOICE-MESSAGING

A desktop computer can be used to provide all of the functions of a regular answering machine. It can play greetings, take messages, retrieve messages from a touch-tone telephone, forward messages, and prioritize messages.

C046 CARING FOR YOUR COMPUTER

◆ Use screen-saver software so that images do not get burned into the screen (older PCs only).

◆ Don't move machines with hard drives without securing the heads first (older PCs only).

◆ Install anti-virus software.

◆ Disks used elsewhere should be scanned for viruses.

◆ Keep your monitor dust-free (cover when not in use).

◆ Cover keyboard when not in use; do not put anything heavy on top of the keyboard.

◆ Never have food or drink around your computer workstation.

C047 INFORMATION SECURITY

Information is a valuable commodity and keeping information confidential is a major issue in the business world. Most organizations implement a program that uses some or all of the following:

- user identification such as an access password, fingerprint or retina scans; change passwords on a regular basis
- activity logs
- anti-theft software
- appointment of a security official to:
  - investigate violations
  - audit activity logs
  - monitor hard copies to guard against equipment misuse
  - supervise secure storage of sensitive data

CO48 COMPUTERS AND OFFICE PERSONNEL

It has become essential for every office worker to have an understanding of basic computer operations. If you are not already "computer literate," try the following:

- Take a keyboarding course. Keyboarding skills are invaluable for computer use; it is recommended that you achieve a minimum of 30 wpm.
- Take a computer course—many short, introductory ones are available. One-day workshops are useful for an overview of a particular software package.
- Don't be afraid of computers. A simple word-processing package would get you started easily.
- Watch and talk to computer users; ask as many questions as you can.
- Read as much as you can.
- Check TV guides for regular computer updates or program tutorials.
- Subscribe to computer magazines. Some magazines focus on particular hardware and software applications and upgrades.
- Join a user group or local association. Groups consist of keen users who favour particular hardware, software, and industry trends. They can be contacted through telephone directories, vendors, bulletin board services, and the Internet.
- Attend business expos and seminars for new product and software information.
- Hire a tutor for more in-depth or reinforcement training.
- Access the Internet to keep abreast of industry changes and technological advances.

CO49 COMPUTER TERMS

Access: The operation of seeking, reading, or writing data on a storage unit

CO

AGP: Accelerated Graphics Port; the latest in technology for high-end graphics card support.

Artificial intelligence: Software that will permit a computer to perform such human-like functions as reasoning and learning

ASCII: American Standard Code for Information Interchange; pronounced "askee"; an 8-bit code developed to ensure compatibility among equipment produced by different manufacturers

Baud: A unit for signalling speed. Frequency of signal that carries data is referred to as *baud rate*

BIOS: Basic Input/Output System. The interface between the system hardware and the operating system

Bit: The smallest measurement of data; taken from the term *binary digit*, a bit is an electrical representation that is either 0 or 1

Bit streams: Processors (32 bits to 64 bits) with the capability of processing information at extremely high speeds

Bitmap: Graphics that consist of an arrangement of small dots

Boards: Used to house computer chips. *Motherboard* holds the microprocessor chip of the computer

Boot process: The process of starting the computer, either by turning on the power, pressing the reset switch, or pressing the < CTRL + ALT + DEL > keys simultaneously

Buffer: A storage device used to compensate for a difference in rate of data flow when transmitting from one device to another. It is a temporary location for the transmitted data to occupy

Bug: An error in a computer program. *Debugging:* A procedure to identify and correct any mistakes found during the testing of a program

Byte: A measurement of computer memory or disk space. It represents roughly one character or eight bits

Cache: High-speed memory for temporary information storage, usually used between a slow storage device (e.g., a disk) and a fast central processing unit

CAD/CAM: Indicates the relationship between computers and manufacturing. CAD is computer-aided design. CAM is computer-aided manufacturing. CAD increases the productivity of draftspeople, designers, and engineers. On-screen designs can be translated into tapes that are then fed into a computer that operates the equipment

Cascade: A window arrangement that layers open windows and fully displays the active window and the title bars of all other open windows behind it

CO

Click: The process of using the mouse pointer to select an icon or menu item

Client server: Mainframe use is gradually diminishing in favour of more economical and efficient client-server networks, in which computing tasks are split up and distributed among various desktop computers and file servers

Clipboard: A memory area that temporarily stores or translates information to be copied or moved within files and applications

Compatibility: This term describes the ability of some hardware and/or software to work harmoniously with other hardware and/or software

Configuration: Description of a computer hardware setup, such as amount of memory and number and types of accessible drives

Crash: Refers to a failure of a computer's hardware or software, which prevents the system from functioning

DDE: Dynamic Data Exchange—a process that allows the linking of information between applications

Dialog box: A window that provides information needed to complete a command

DIMM: Dual Inline Memory Module—a 72- or 76-pin memory module. DIMMs can be used singly, unlike SIMMs, which must be used in pairs. Different speed CPUs require that the DIMMs operational speed must match the CPU's bus speed:
CPUs 350 MHz and above—use PC100 DIMMs
CPUs 333 MHz and below—use PC66 DIMMs

Downloading: Capturing information from the Internet, bulletin boards, or online services and importing to a software package for processing

Downtime: Time that is lost due to computer breakdown

Dump: To copy the contents of all or part of a storage device, usually from a central processing unit, into an external storage unit

Electronic Data Interchange (EDI): A technology developed to allow interbusiness communication without the use of paper.

Embedded object: An object that is stored in the destination document and can be edited using the server application

Expansion slot: A connector on the system motherboard into which an adapter card can be inserted, i.e., ISA, PCI, and AGP slots

Expert systems: Systems programmed to organize knowledge according to given rules, conditions, or situations. They can call up information relevant to a problem and discriminate which data to select

CO

in certain circumstances. Expert systems are based on *artificial intelligence* (see above)

Explorer: A Windows application that helps organize or view files on disk

Field: A unit of information on a database record

File: A collection of information (records) stored in a database

File server: *See* Client server

Gigabyte (GB): Approximately one billion bytes

Graphical user interface: The capability to communicate with a computer by selecting graphic objects on the screen

Hard copy: A printed copy

Hierarchy: A tree-like representation of the organization of files and folders on disk

Icon: A graphic object that represents elements of Windows (e.g., a document that can be opened or a program that can be run)

Interactive processing (online or real time): Terminals can access the computer and get results immediately. Banks, airlines, and hotels use interactive processing constantly

Interface: The connection between the system board and a peripheral

ISA: Industry Standard Architecture; a type of expansion slot that operates at 8.33 MHz bus speed

Kilobyte (KB): 1024 bytes of information

MHz (megahertz): Millions of cycles per second; the measurement used in the speed of processing data

Megabyte (MB): One million bytes of information

Motherboard: Main circuit board inside your computer with most or all of the RAM and the microprocessor

Multi-tasking: Running more than one application program at a time (e.g., sort an accounts receivable file, print out some word processing, and work on a spreadsheet). Operator can move from one program to the other without interrupting them

Multi-user: Several terminals connected to a single computer with different users working simultaneously, or several computers connected to each other, actively sharing programs and information

NT: New technology

OLE: Object Linking and Embedding—a process that allows the creation of an embedded object

CO

Online: Terminals hooked up to the computer using its processing capabilities in real time

Open Database Connectivity (ODBC): A subsystem to Windows that allows the user to open or connect to databases created by different database programs

Operating system: Controls all input to and from the disk drives, keyboard, display, printer, and other peripherals, and the running of other programs

Parallel port: Also called printer port, or LPT 1; the parallel port is used to attach a printer or other peripheral using a centronics parallel cable

Peripherals: Add-on equipment such as printers, scanners, screens, etc. that can be externally connected to a computer

Printer ports: The ways in which a printer transmits data to and from the system unit. They are either *serial* or *parallel*. (Be sure you know which one is appropriate for your printer)

Properties: The attributes and settings associated with all items on the screen

Protocols: Sets of rules governing the way in which devices communicate; *protocol converters* exist to help compatibility problems

RISC (reduced instruction set computing): RISC computers are able to run any software under any operating system, with no hardware or software additions

Robots: Computer-controlled arms or manipulators used in the manufacturing industry

Scroll arrows: The arrows on the scroll bar that move information in the direction of the arrows and that allow new information to be viewed on screen

Scroll bar: A bar window located on the bottom or right window border that displays text not currently visible in the window; it contains scroll arrows and a scroll box

Scroll box: A box on the scroll bar that indicates the position within the area of available information; this box can be moved to a general location within the area of information by dragging it up/down the scroll bar

Serial port: A communication port used by the computer to communicate with the outside world, i.e., mouse, modems, serial printers, plotters, and other serial devices. An IBM PC-compatible normally recognizes four standard serial ports: COM 1, COM 2, COM 3, and COM 4

CO

Shading/fill: A feature that changes background from black and white to various shades or densities of black

Sleep mode: A "hot key" on the newer keyboards, such as Internet keyboards, which suspends the PC and lets you resume work later (an energy saver)

Soft copy (readout): The processed information displayed on a screen. Printers can be linked with computer terminals if a permanent record of the readout is required

Source file: The document where an object was created

Status bar: At the bottom of a window; displays information about current program settings (e.g., tasks being performed)

Subfolder: A folder that is created beneath another folder

Taskbar: A Windows 95/98 desktop element that contains the start button, buttons that represent active applications, the clock, and other indicators

Toolbar: A bar of icons displayed below the menu bar and used for shortcuts for many of the common menu commands

Toolbox: A toolbar of icons provided for the most common drawing commands; used with Paint

Tooltip: A description or help message displayed when pointing at the taskbar or toolbar icons

Turnaround time: Time between submission of a job to the computer centre and the return of the results

USB: Universal serial bus; a new standard for attaching peripherals to PCs.

User-friendly: A system designed for ease of operation

Windowing: Several documents can be displayed on the screen side by side or overlaid

3 EFFICIENCY, TIME MANAGEMENT, AND ERGONOMICS

E

CONTENTS

Accomplishing all that is required of you in a day—keeping your sanity, accepting the challenges of an increasingly technological workplace, and maintaining a high efficiency level—is a difficult juggling act. In this unit you will find ideas on how to become a successful "juggler"—how to manage time well, how to make good use of software and technology, how to avoid stress, and how to get more out of your day without the day taking too much out of you.

E1 TIME MANAGEMENT AND EFFICIENCY

To make the best possible use of your time, you will need to plan carefully and use efficient methods.

E2 THE STARTING POINT

◆ Find out what you are currently doing with your time by keeping a record of each day's activities over a period of several weeks.

◆ Analyse your findings and try to determine which time periods were most productive in a typical day and which were least productive.

◆ Rank all of the types of jobs you must do in order of their importance and compare this with the actual time spent on each job.

◆ Make up a revised schedule showing how much time you should spend on each job, according to its importance.

◆ Keep a record of estimated time to complete a job versus the actual time to complete the job. Write this information on the file or hard copy or key in "document comments section" on disk.

◆ Now start to plan your days for the most efficient use of your time.

E3 PLANNING YOUR DAY

◆ Make a daily work schedule for yourself—list exactly what you must accomplish that day.

◆ Assess each task, assign priorities (A, B, C), and establish deadlines.

◆ If possible, delegate all C jobs (and as many others as you can). For example, you could delegate:
  • opening and sorting mail, and faxing
  • photocopying
  • annotating magazine articles

THINGS TO DO LIST

1. Call Sylvia re Monday's meeting.

2. Order more disks.

3. Set up appointment with M. Nehru re phones.

4. Start collecting figures for August sales report for keying into spreadsheet.

5. Start on checklist for January sales conference.

E

- Do unwelcome jobs first, when you are freshest.
- Check each job off the list as you complete it (this is a positive act and very satisfying).
- Finish one job before you start another if the jobs are reasonably small.
- If you are faced with a large task that cannot be handled at one time, do it in small chunks. Work on the assignment by doing small parts of it in any 10- or 15-minute spare-time segments that occur during the day.
- Maintain a long-term calendar as well as a daily one, and note on it routine dates (regular meetings, report due dates, etc.) and other commitments for several months ahead.
- At the end of the day, analyse why each unchecked job was not completed. Incorporate these incomplete jobs into your "to do" list for the next day.
- Incorporate into your daily plan as many of the following time-saving tips as you can.

E4   TIME-SAVING TIPS

Office Management

- Try to get everything done in the shortest time with the fewest wasted motions. Think out an activity and reduce it to a series of mechanical routines.
- Avoid interruptions. The stop-start approach to a job wastes time. Avoid an "open door" policy. Don't position your desk so that you appear to welcome casual socializers; sit with your back or side to the door.
- Surround yourself with useful reference sources (e.g., telephone directories for all provinces, fax directories, software manuals, office procedural manuals, an atlas, and an excellent office handbook).
- Pace yourself. Allow sufficient time to complete a job so that you are not under unnecessary stress (see this unit, E26).
- Refer to notes on previous documents where you recorded the time it took to complete large tasks, e.g., monthly or annual reports, and then plan accordingly.
- Keep your desk tidy. You waste trying to find documents buried under other paper. Set up a separate folder for each job.
- At times, working away from the office may be advantageous.
- Set firm and realistic deadlines.
- Learn to say "no" if you are overloaded.
- If you know you cannot accomplish everything, be realistic and request outside help, whether from another department or from a temporary employment agency.
- Set up a records management system that is easy to use and clean it out frequently (see Unit 16). Do not file records and forms that no one needs.

E

- Develop good reminder and follow-up systems (see Unit 16).
- Don't file paper documents if filing electronically would do, but make sure you have a good computer backup system.
- Maintain an up-to-date database of customers and suppliers that you contact frequently so that you have available in one source all of the information you will need for a number of purposes, such as fax numbers, invoices, form letters, invitations, announcements, greeting cards.
- Learn to compose at the keyboard. Keying is faster than writing.
- Guard against schedule disruptions due to the absenteeism of key personnel by training backup staff to fill in or by having detailed procedures manuals available (see this unit, E7).

Computer Software/E-Mail/Telephone

Remember to empty computer trash or e-mail messages regularly. Clean up your disk directories; delete information not needed and back up important documents.

NOTE Some database software packages have a communications feature that allows you to dial anyone on the list automatically.

- Create a database of factual information you may use again on your own or a supervisor's behalf (e.g., equipment repair services, conference and accommodation facilities, restaurants).
- Read instruction manuals (e.g., fax, software, printer) to get the best use out of your equipment and software.
- Maintain equipment to maximum efficiency by scheduling annual maintenance checks.
- Guard against downtime on major equipment by:
  - becoming fully familiar with manufacturers' instruction manuals; make sure the updates to equipment problems are placed in manuals on a regular basis
  - arranging for guaranteed fast and efficient service from vendors or other service organizations
  - arranging for emergency backup with another department or at vendors' offices
- Use professional consultants and/or services to help you maximize office potential (e.g., records management).
- Do not put everything into writing.
- Send notes to co-workers by e-mail so that you don't interrupt them or run the risk of long conversations. (Make sure they are available so they can respond)
- Prepare and save form letters, form paragraphs, and frequently used formats.

◆ Create a tip sheet on shortcuts for software functions that are not used by all employees on a regular basis (e.g., merge function, graphics, etc.).

◆ If necessary, post IMPORTANT INFORMATION regarding printing, printers, procedures, etc.

◆ Create templates or macros for such things as frequently used headings, letter parts, or expressions peculiar to your organization.

◆ Manage your telephone time efficiently. Make all of your calls in a block of time set aside for this purpose. Have questions prepared in advance, with files, calendar, pen and note pad handy (see Unit 19 for more hints).

◆ Block time to access your e-mail and voice mail each day.

◆ Have an easy-to-read telephone number and record system that is well cross-referenced.

◆ If you are working on a difficult or rush project, activate your e-mail or answering machine to avoid disrupting telephone calls. Store messages until you can deal with them.

◆ Obtain the telephone company services that will allow you to become more efficient (see Unit 19).

◆ Investigate personal call-management software. Thousands of names and numbers can be stored and then auto-dialled. Each entry allows for a notes section, maps, or photographs. It also identifies callers and their telephone numbers whenever the telephone rings and allows prioritizing of incoming calls to alert you to the most urgent ones.

◆ If you must leave the office frequently, make yourself fully productive by acquiring equipment that will allow you to continue your work wherever you are (e.g., portable or cellular telephones, laptop or hand-held computers, portable fax machines, portable photocopiers).

◆ Or, consider renting or leasing computer equipment as well as collators, power staplers, paper shredders, postage machines, etc.

◆ Use outside print shops for large printing, collating, and binding jobs. If you produce pamphlets and other textual material, explore the possibilities of desktop publishing software (see Unit 4).

◆ Investigate a type of software known as groupware (see Unit 2). This allows people on a network to work together and speed up document processing and group communications such as meeting planning and multi-use calendars.

◆ Time-management software (also known as electronic organizers) can be invaluable. Depending on the make purchased, these feature appointment scheduling (i.e., can be used to notify potential meeting participants and then confirm attendance; set up appointments and inquire into co-workers' availability without having to personally contact them), project and task management (i.e., an automated "to do" list), a database of basic reference material, expense tracking, note-making, and a database of telephone numbers that can be auto-dialled.

◆ Pocket electronic organizers allow you to record appointments, store telephone numbers, record notes, and do calculations. Many can be linked to PCs, allowing notes to be edited and printed later.

E5   DEALING WITH CORRESPONDENCE

◆ Schedule a specific time of day for dealing with correspondence and discourage all interruptions during this time.

◆ Don't write unless it's absolutely necessary. Use the telephone and e-mail as much as possible. If it is easier, walk over and talk to people in the office.

◆ Use word-processing equipment. Changes are easily made and rekeying is avoided.

◆ Don't procrastinate. Handle each document only once and make decisions immediately, if possible. Often you will know nothing more about the subject three days later.

◆ Learn to dictate efficiently and avoid writing by hand material that can be keyed.

◆ Use a pocket-sized dictating machine for use when you are out of the office. Ensure that the recording medium is compatible with the transcribing units in the office.

◆ Use preprinted slips for repetitive information such as distribution lists. The stick-on type is best.

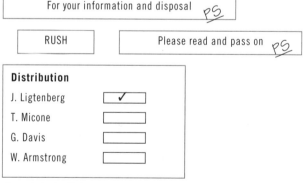

Preprinted stickers

◆ For some routine requests, consider simply writing on incoming letters or memos, photocopying them for your file, and sending the original back to the writer.

◆ Follow up on unpaid bills by photocopying them and writing or keying a reminder on them.

◆ Use rubber stamps (see Unit 7, "Forms and Form Design").

E6   MAINTAINING AN APPOINTMENT SCHEDULE

◆ Use a pencil to write in your diary or calendar all relevant information about appointments (including telephone numbers) in case changes are needed.

◆ Keep all diaries and calendars used in the office up to date with each other.

◆ In particular, the assistant should maintain a diary or calendar that matches the supervisor's.

◆ Note appointments for the following year at the back of your calendar and enter next year's appointments in the new calendar as soon as you receive it.

◆ Use calendaring software if possible (see this unit, E4).

E7   PROCEDURES MANUALS

Manuals that outline the standard procedures of an organization are excellent guides for avoiding wasted time. They are efficient handbooks for new employees, eliminate the need for verbal instructions from one employee to another, and are invaluable reference sources. To be truly effective, they must be updated regularly.

Ideally, procedures manuals are keyed and maintained in a database that all employees can access. This eliminates the need for printing and binding, saves shelf and desk space, and makes updating a simple task. If a computer network is not available, the manuals should be keyed, saved, and issued in a loose-leaf format that can easily be updated. Examples of effective procedures manuals are:

◆ a manual for your records management system that describes the types of equipment used; explains indexing, coding, cross-referencing, and charge-out procedures; and outlines your records retention policy

◆ job descriptions to aid takeovers when a person leaves

◆ job procedures for reports, etc., that are not done frequently or that are not done by one person all of the time. The instructions must be clear enough that anyone can follow them and do the job

◆ a company style manual so that all employees follow the same writing style rules and have available an instant reference source

◆ a manual for form paragraphs or form letters appropriate for most routine situations

Remember:

◆ Keep procedures manuals up to date.

◆ Add new formats.

◆ Create instruction manuals for software applications and for training purposes.

Well-written procedures manuals contain easy-to-follow instructions and readily understood terminology, are liberally illustrated, and use

E

many headings and subheadings to make items easy to find. (See also Unit 8, H15, for help with creating a staff manual.)

E8 DECISION MAKING

Making responsible and reasonable decisions is an important part of efficiency. The office worker should understand the decision-making process and must never make a fast decision without considering the consequences. All decision making should involve common sense, logic, previous similar experience, and intuition or creativity. The following systematic approach will assist in decision making:

◆ Define the problem and write it down. Try to state the problem broadly and express it as a question.

◆ Gather the facts.

◇ Develop a list of alternative solutions to the problem.

◆ Examine the advantages and disadvantages of each possible solution.

◆ Select the best solution and review the possible consequences.

◆ Implement your decision.

◆ Evaluate the results.

E9 OFFICE TECHNOLOGY

To work efficiently, staff members must have the best possible equipment. Today, that usually means electronic equipment, which is now quite affordable or can usually be rented or leased. For cost-effectiveness, of course, consideration must be given to the capability of the equipment and the best return possible on the investment. Constant updating and upgrading of office equipment is mandatory. For further information on electronic equipment and processes that can improve office efficiency, see Unit 5, "Electronic Mail" and Unit 9, "Information Processing and Integrated Office Automation."

E10 IMPROVING YOUR READING SKILLS

Research has shown that the faster you read, the more you concentrate and the more you retain what you have read. Most people read material of average difficulty at approximately 250 words per minute (wpm). The most efficient reader can get as high as 1000 wpm, with 500 wpm being attainable by most people after some effort.

Efficient readers do not read every word, pause, skip back, or silently mouth the words; they skim the pages while focusing on key words. To encourage efficient reading, find your present rate and then be determined to increase it.

Finding your reading rate
◆ Start a stopwatch.

◆ Read a two-page, non-fiction article.

E

◆ Stop the watch. Calculate the amount of time (in seconds) that it took you to read the two pages.
◆ Count the number of words in the article by adding up the number of words in one line and multiplying this by the total number of lines in the article.
◆ Divide the total number of words by the number of seconds that it took you to read the article.
◆ Now multiply the answer by 60 to obtain your score in minutes.

There is no such thing as a uniform reading rate; the difficulty of a passage will determine your rate. Your goal is to attain the fastest possible rate, adjusted to the purpose and nature of the material, without sacrificing comprehension.

Tips to increase your reading rate

◆ Always try to read as fast as you can.
◆ Increase the size of the image your eyes send to your mind. In other words, instead of reading one word at a time, stretch your vision to include three or four words at one time. Remember, you don't need to look at every letter of every word to absorb the sense of a group of words.
◆ Look for topic sentences (main ideas) and don't get bogged down with details.
◆ Don't worry about unfamiliar words. The meaning of these usually becomes clear as you continue to read, and rarely does the sense of a paragraph depend on them. Keep reading, so that you don't lose the main idea.
◆ Work at building a wider vocabulary.
◆ Skim to find particular pieces of information.
◆ For the best results, take a speed-reading course and practise faithfully in short, daily sessions, or buy a good self-instruction manual, master the techniques, and follow a consistent training schedule.

Tips to increase your reading efficiency

To increase your reading efficiency, follow these steps:
◆ Decide why you are reading before beginning to read a book or article in earnest. Ask yourself:
  • What do I want to find out?
  • What do I already know?
  • Is this new material?
  • Should I read all of this?
◆ Preview the material:
  • If it is a book, read any information on the jacket.
  • Review the table of contents.

E

- Read the first paragraph or first sentence of several chapters to get a feel for the author's style and purpose.
- Survey the subheadings and take a look at the illustrations and graphics.
- Determine what level of concentration will be needed.
- Ask yourself whether the article or book is worth reading at all.

E11 BECOMING A BETTER LISTENER

Employers often complain that many of their employees have poor listening skills. Do not allow yourself to be open to this criticism. More effective listening leads to greater understanding and, therefore, to greater personal efficiency. Force yourself to concentrate on what is being said, so that you comprehend the intended meaning. The process of listening requires an active mind.

The roadblocks to effective listening are that we can think much faster than a person can speak and so sometimes our minds wander or we are busy planning a reply rather than truly listening. At other times, our emotions get in the way and cloud our understanding. To overcome these roadblocks and improve your listening skills, do the following:

- Keep quiet and focus on what is being said.
- Review the speaker's statements in your mind as you listen.
- Use non-verbal actions (nods, smiles, frowns) to encourage the speaker. This also ensures that you must actively listen.
- Judge the words, not the speaker. Don't be affected by distractions.
- Have a notepad handy. Listen and then write down the main points. Don't trust your memory.
- Give the speaker your undivided attention. Try not to permit interruptions (e.g., telephone calls) while someone is speaking to you.
- If the speaker's message is not clear, ask for clarification or repetition.

E12 ERGONOMICS AND SPACE MANAGEMENT

E13 ERGONOMICS

Ergonomics is the study of the compatibility of people, equipment, and surroundings. This is a vitally important concept in efficiency because comfort and productivity are closely related. Poor terminal design, bad lighting, high noise levels, poor ventilation, uncomfortable chairs, improperly designed workstations, and unsuitable colour schemes all contribute to occupational stress.

Repetitive motion injuries, or repetitive strain injuries—painful disorders of muscles, tendons, and nerves, e.g., carpal tunnel syndrome, tendonitis, thoracic outlet syndrome, and tension neck syndrome—are caused by awkward postures resulting from badly designed work areas and work activities that are frequent and repetitive. Obviously these must be guarded against.

Some authorities say that many work injury problems can be diminished or eliminated by changing tasks often to help alleviate the muscular stress that causes injuries. Take rest breaks to ease muscle aches, eyestrain, and stress. Stand up. Move around. Do stretching exercises, shoulder rolls, leg lifts.

Change your *body position frequently* when working at a computer.

Use document holder to reduce the number, pattern, and extent of neck movements, thus reducing muscular strain to your neck, shoulders, and back.

Eyes

If you wear glasses or contact lenses, ask your doctor for *your* focal length and adjust the screen and copyholder distances accordingly.

If your job involves a lot of keyboarding and you wear contact lenses, be aware that lenses can dry out. Staring at the screen creates a non-blinking situation in which lenses dry out.

If you wear bifocals, the variety of neck adjustments needed to read the different copy surfaces may cause strain. Have your eyes checked regularly.

The National Institute for Occupational Safety and Health (NIOSH) recommends that if your job involves many hours of keyboarding, you should take a 15-minute break after two hours of continuous keyboarding. After two hours the eyes are fine, but the tense body takes longer to de-stress; therefore, when the job is stressful take a break after one hour.

Reducing the risk

IFS — Information Fatigue Syndrome
CPI — Carpal Tunnel Syndrome
RSI — Repetitive Stress Injury

Keyboarders can reduce the risk of developing IFS/CPI/RSI by following some helpful guidelines.

Workstation

◆ Position the keyboard directly in front of the chair.
◆ Place the keyboard at elbow height.
◆ Situate the front edge of the keyboard even with the edge of the desk; wrists should not be restricted while keying.
◆ Place the monitor about 45 to 60 cm from your eyes; the top edge of screen should be at eye level.
◆ Locate the mouse next to and at the same height as the keyboard.

Chair and sitting position

◆ Adjust your chair regularly.

◆ Keep your feet flat on the floor while keying.

◆ Sit erect and keep your shoulders back (do not slump).

Arm and wrist movement

◆ Keep your forearms parallel to the floor and level with the keyboard; your wrists should be in a flat, neutral position rather than flexed upward or downward.

◆ Keep your elbows in, near the side of your body, in a relaxed position.

Keyboarding techniques

◆ Keep your fingers curved and arched over the home-row keys.

◆ DO NOT rest your wrists on any surface while keying.

◆ Strike keys lightly; do not "pound" the keyboard.

◆ When using a keyboard or mouse, take short breaks.

◆ Exercise your neck, shoulders, arms, and fingers regularly.

▶ **E14   Computer considerations**

E15   Monitors

◆ Characters on the monitor should be sharply focused and flicker-free to reduce eyestrain while doing on-screen activities.

◆ Monitor stands should permit tilting and swivelling so that the screen position can be adjusted. The top of the screen should be at eye level and the monitor should be tilted backwards a little so that the centre of the screen can be viewed with a slight downward gaze.

◆ Adjustable contrast and brightness controls are important features that allow the user to choose levels that alleviate eyestrain.

◆ Use a filter or anti-glare spray to eliminate glare.

◆ Clean the screen regularly.

◆ Have any flicker or screen noise problems attended to promptly.

◆ Look away from the monitor often to rest your eyes.

◆ Vary work tasks to include non-computer tasks as well as computer assignments.

◆ Use an adjustable document holder and alternate it from one side of the computer to the other to prevent neck muscle strain.

E16   Keyboards

◆ Ideally, the keyboard should be separate and adjustable to provide the greatest flexibility. The keys should be gently contoured to the fingers and matte-finished to prevent fingers from slipping on the keys.

E

◆ The type of keyboard selected should be geared to the needs of the user. The professional word processor should choose one that offers the most comfortable arrangement of alphabetic and function (or service) keys. The person using the keyboard for numeric applications such as spreadsheets and accounting should select one that provides an easy-to-use number pad and a separate cursor key pad in addition to the standard alphabetic keys.

◆ Forearm and upper arm should form an angle of 80° to 100°, with wrists relaxed, not bent. Wrist rests are available to help ease the strain on wrist muscles.

◆ Move the keyboard occasionally to change arm and shoulder positions.

Keyboards are available that are designed to put the wrist in a neutral position, level with the forearm and perpendicular to the upper arm. These include keyboards that:

◆ are divided and support wrists while fingers rest in cups containing keys

◆ are split in half (see below), each hand resting at shoulder width to strike the keys

◆ incorporate wrist rests

◆ have a hinged pan that allows the keyboard to move up and down or be pushed out of the way when not in use

Internet Keyboard   The enhanced keyboard provides 10 "hot keys" that can be programmed for quick online access to frequently used programs or Web sites, such as e-mail and favourite or frequently used programs (a 486 Pentium computer is required for this keyboard).

Detachable palm rest This ergonomically designed palm rest can be attached to the keyboard to reduce wrist strain.

Split keyboard

The mouse

The mouse should be contoured to fit the hand and support the palm. Ideally it should suit the size of the user's hand and have some type of wrist support.

▶ E17 Lighting

Good lighting means a sufficient quantity of light, sufficient brightness, proper contrast, and minimal glare. Light fixtures should not emit noise of any type.

◆ Lighting should be uniform and suited to easy reading of handwritten and printed material.

◆ Ambient (deflected) and task lighting (e.g., a desk lamp) are better, more flexible sources than overhead (direct) lighting because they help eliminate problems of glare (light reflected from a desk top, wall, or screen directly into one's eyes). Hoods and anti-glare filters are available, however, to shield monitor screens from reflection.

◆ Lighting should be adjustable to permit change from computer tasks to paperwork jobs.

◆ Drapes, window blinds, and partitions should be used where glare is a problem.

◆ Use grid or parabolic filters on fluorescent lights to evenly disperse light.

◆ Use non-glare finishes and neutral colours on walls, furniture, and equipment.

◆ Windows should be located at right angles to the screen.

▶ E18 Noise

Sounds from office equipment bounce off walls, ceilings, and other surfaces and cause noise disturbance. Ceiling insulation, carpeting, drapes, and room-dividing panels are invaluable sound-absorbing materials. Some companies use non-distracting background sound ("white noise") to solve the problems created by unavoidable noise.

▶ E19 Heating, ventilation, and air-conditioning (HVAC)

For greatest efficiency, people and equipment must perform in comfortable temperature and humidity ranges. Too much heat induces sleepiness, and equipment will not function well in high heat or low humidity. A humidity level of 50 percent and a temperature level of about 22°C is comfortable for most people.

▶ E20 Chairs

Lower back pain can reduce productivity. Improper seating is often the cause of such discomfort. A chair with adjustable backrest and height features and a stable base is best. A five-caster (star) design ensures stability.

The seat of an office chair should have a woven fabric that "breathes" and a contoured front edge. If chairs have arms, they must not interfere with use of the work surface or with keyboarding action.

◆ The highest point of the seat should be just below the kneecap.

◆ The seat must not press against the underside of thighs.

◆ The backrest of the chair should support the hollow in the lower back.

◆ Readjust your chair and/or the height of your work surface throughout the day to vary body position. Adjust the chair, then adjust the work surface. The work surface should be regulated so that it is at elbow level when your arms are hanging straight down. When you are sitting at a keyboard, your elbows should be level with the middle row of keys.

◆ Don't share chairs. We are all unique.

◆ An adjustable footrest should be used if your feet do not rest flat on the floor.

▶ E21   Workstations

Desks and work surfaces

Furniture-purchasing decisions should be based on what tasks users perform, what tools they use, amount and type of office space available, and how tasks are organized.

◆ The angles and heights of work surfaces and shelving in desks and tables should adjust to match placement of equipment to each worker's particular physical needs. This flexibility also means that changes can be made during a working day to permit a worker to avoid fatigue by changing posture.

◆ Colour is an important consideration in work surface choice. Light colours are easier on the eyes than are dark ones.

◆ Desks should allow the neat and safe installation of equipment cables.

Workstation design

For computer use, the standard office desk is not appropriate. The typical workstation in an electronic office should have provision for most of the following:

◆ computer terminal

◆ file cabinet(s) and/or drawers and disk and stationery storage

◆ telephone

◆ reference materials

◆ space for secure storage of personal items

NOTE   CPUs are available in tower systems that sit vertically—on a desktop or, more usually, on the floor—creating more desk space and keeping the system away from hazards such as coffee spills.

E

A well-designed systems workstation

Systems workstations have a number of advantages:

◆ They permit greater concentration because their acoustic panelling reduces noise levels.

◆ They produce enough room to work yet do not take up a great deal of floor space. This is achieved by means of cabinets and shelves suspended on the acoustic panels.

◆ They help to eliminate visual distractions because of the privacy they afford.

◆ They offer well-planned lighting, come in a variety of colours, and provide an attractive working environment.

▶ E22 Colour

The influence of colour in wall, floor, and window coverings on comfort, mood, and productivity is significant. The colours at the warm end of the spectrum (red, yellow, orange) are exciting, vital, and stimulating. Blue, green, and purple—the colours at the cool end of the spectrum—induce a muted, comfortable, soothing response. Office colour(s) should be geared to the nature of the business being conducted.

E23 SPACE MANAGEMENT

▶ E24 Office layout and landscaping

Office layout has considerable influence on efficiency and productivity levels. Work areas must be set up with the performance of tasks in mind as well as with consideration for the individual's need for privacy, quiet, and security.

E

- Consider an open-plan office concept. Its flexibility means that 80 percent of available space can be used, whereas the conventional plan permits use of only 40 percent.
- Provide enough space for people to move around freely.
- Match the positioning of desks and workstations to the information flow. Paperwork must flow smoothly, with a minimum of interruptions and backtracking.
- Choose records storage cabinets or shelves to suit the amount of space available and the types of records to be stored (see Unit 16). Locate these near the people who will use them most.
- Position shared equipment (e.g., fax machines, copiers) so that the area does not serve as the office socializing spot.
- People who have frequent outside visitors should be located close to the office entrance.
- Group together employees using the same equipment or records.
- Locate service sections (e.g., mailing departments) near the departments that use them most.
- L-shaped desks provide 80 percent more workspace than conventional ones. Choose light or medium colours for desk tops because this is less tiring on the eyes than dark colours.
- Systems or modular furniture creates the most efficient workstations as far as space and employee productivity are concerned. Modular furniture consists of pre-wired movable panels of varying heights plus added components such as work surfaces, files, and individual lighting in whatever configuration is best suited to the tasks performed by the occupant.
- Use colour, wall coverings, art, plants, and music to help create a pleasant working atmosphere. Flowers and plants do more than provide eye appeal—they take in pollutants and stale air and produce oxygen.

E25   HEALTH IN THE WORKPLACE

- Avoid eyestrain by taking frequent breaks from intense keyboarding tasks.
- Take assigned breaks for stress/work relief; occasional breaks are helpful when working on complicated or long assignments.
- Do not regularly skip breaks, lunch, or dinner because of work.
- Wash your hands regularly, especially after using the washroom.
- Report any unclean eating areas and washrooms to your office manager or supervisor.
- Clean your telephone on a regular basis, especially the mouthpiece if you share a telephone.
- Avoid using a co-worker's phone if he or she has a cold or the flu.
- Get flu shots before the flu season.

E

- Clean earphones regularly to avoid ear infections and germs.
- Clean coffee cups thoroughly; do not share cups or water glasses.
- Clean your work area once a week (desk tops, keyboards, monitors, mouse, etc.)
- Eat healthfully; maintain a well-balanced diet.
- Exercise regularly.
- Use "sick days" when you are ill to avoid spreading germs to co-workers; a sick day can sometimes prevent a more prolonged illness.
- Dress appropriately for office/workplace temperatures (air conditioning in summer/dry heat in winter months).
- Avoid injury by bending, lifting, and shifting properly when moving boxes or office equipment.
- Schedule regular medical checkups.

E26 STRESS MANAGEMENT

Stress is often a result of poor time management. An inability to handle stressful situations well results in loss of efficiency. The main stress management tip is to pace yourself throughout the day so that you avoid periods of stress and fatigue. Other tips are:

- Prepare for the morning the night before.
- Plan the toughest or least pleasant jobs or appointments for the start of the day.
- Don't cram too many activities into a short time span. Plan for breathing space between appointments and tasks.
- If you must leave the office or building, allow sufficient time to arrive at your destination without rushing.
- Allow for rest periods when planning long business trips. Jet lag is a serious stress problem.
- Delegate as many routine tasks as possible.
- Keep breaks short, but take them. A break will keep your energy level up.
- Don't rely on your memory. Record appointment times and other important details.
- Avoid procrastination. Whatever you want to do tomorrow, do today if you can; whatever you want to do today, do it now.
- Ask questions. Taking a few moments to confirm directions or to restate what someone expects of you can save hours.
- Organize your work space so that you always know exactly where things are. Put things where they belong.
- Check your breathing throughout the day and before, during, and after high-pressure situations. If you find that your stomach muscles are tied in knots and your breathing is shallow, relax all of your muscles and take several deep, slow breaths.

- Get up and stretch periodically if you have to sit for extended periods.
- Take a lunch break every day. Try to get away from your desk or work area in body and mind, even if it's just for 15 or 20 minutes. Avoid lunch and evening business appointments.
- Maintain a proper diet and exercise program. Non-rigorous exercise—stretching plus deep breathing—can be done in the office. Out of the office setting, rigorous, non-competitive exercise is excellent.
- Colour, art, plants, shape, and contour all have an impact on stress control in the workplace (see this unit, "Ergonomics, " E14).
- Use your weekend time for a change of pace.
- Attend stress management seminars/workshops.

E27   OFFICE SAFETY

Unsafe practices are inefficient practices. Bear the following safety pointers in mind:

- Do not leave desk drawers and filing cabinets open.
- Do not stand on swivel chairs.
- Repair tears in carpeting immediately.
- Wipe up spills as soon as they happen.
- Be careful when lifting or moving equipment.
- Do not permit obstructions in aisles.
- Use separate power outlets for each machine.
- Avoid use of extension cords.
- Deal with defective cords, wires, and cables immediately.
- Do not trail cords, wires, or cables across walkways.
- Cover up loose wires and cables.
- Know where fire exits and extinguishers are located, and understand the procedures to follow in the event of an emergency.
- Display emergency numbers in a prominent place.
- Be able to locate the first-aid kit.
- Know where to obtain first-aid assistance.
- Know the rules for handling any dangerous substances that might be present in the workplace.

E28   WHMIS—WORKPLACE HAZARDOUS MATERIALS INFORMATION SYSTEM

This is a Canada-wide system that provides employers and employees with information about the hazardous materials they work with on the job. The system has three purposes:

- to apply labelling and other information requirements of WHMIS to suppliers of hazardous materials and to establish rules for deciding what substances are considered "hazardous" materials

E

◆ to allow manufacturers to protect their legitimate trade secrets without endangering employee health and safety

◆ to apply WHMIS under the federal labour jurisdiction by amending the health and safety section of the *Canada Labour Code*

The *Occupational Health and Safety Act* (OHSA) requires employees to identify hazardous materials in the workplace by:

◆ preparing a workplace inventory

◆ performing assessments on hazardous materials produced and used in the workplace

The "Workplace Inventory" is a list of all hazardous materials present in the workplace—including all hazardous physical agents. The employer must prepare and maintain this inventory after consultation with the joint health and safety committee in the workplace or with the worker health and safety representative, if any. In a workplace without a committee or a representative, employees may select one of their number to represent them. Copies of the inventory must be given to the joint health and safety committee or employee representative and must also be made available to employees. WHMIS gets this information to employees by:

◆ labels
  • supplier label: the label placed on a container or enclosed with the shipment of hazardous material by the supplier before shipping
  • workplace label: these labels must be placed on hazardous materials in the workplace or on material decanted from its original container into another container at the workplace

◆ Material Safety Data Sheets (MSDS)

Federal law requires the supplier of a controlled product to provide a MSDS for that product. The data sheet must be in English and in other main working languages of the workplace if required. The MSDS contains nine different kinds of information (plus any other relevant information that the employer should be aware of):

  • hazardous ingredients: names, concentrations, and other details of known hazardous ingredients, and of other ingredients that the employer or supplier suspects may be hazardous, or whose dangers to the body are unknown
  • preparation information: name and telephone number of the person who prepared the MSDS and the date of preparation
  • product information: name and address of the producer and/or supplier; must be the same as shown on the supplier label
  • physical data: properties of the material, such as physical state (gas, solid, or liquid), smell, and appearance
  • fire or explosion hazard: flashpoint of the material and other similar data
  • reactivity data: details of stability and reactions to conditions such as light, heat, moisture, vibration, etc.

- toxicological properties: adverse health effects from exposure
- preventive measures: instructions for safe use, handling, and storage
- first-aid measures: instructions for initial treatment of those exposed to the material

Every MSDS must be current (less than three years old). It must be revised within 90 days of any new hazard information becoming known about the material.

◆ employee training

Employers have the duty under the law to deliver employee training. The *Health and Safety Act* directs employers to instruct employees and acquaint them with workplace hazards. With the addition of WHMIS, employers must instruct and train employees who are likely to be exposed to hazardous materials and/or hazardous physical agents.

E

UNIT

4 DESKTOP PUBLISHING

DP

CONTENTS

The term *electronic publishing* covers two important activities—desktop publishing and multi-media document production.

In desktop publishing (DTP), most or all of the production of business-related documents (brochures, catalogues, advertisements, forms) within the organization are produced on a desktop computer. The skilled desktop publisher can electronically blend text and graphics (drawings, photographs, etc.) into a professional-looking printed product, thus combining the specialized skills of designers, copywriters, artists, typographers, and printers in one operation.

In multi-media document production, computer-generated slide or overhead presentations and electronic documents that combine elements of sound, video, animation, text, and graphics are created. For example, entire catalogues might be created and distributed on disk that allow the customer to see a product, perhaps even to see the product in use, and to hear that product being described.

This unit will focus on DTP, the print form of electronic publishing.

DP1 WHO USES DTP?

- Many organizations and businesses use DTP for document production. Such documents might be in-house or external reports, announcements, advertisements, newsletters, brochures, office stationery, catalogues, forms, manuals, or flyers.
- In the printing industry, DTP is used for magazine and newspaper layouts and for advertising layout and design.
- Advertising and marketing firms use it extensively to produce high-quality communications of all kinds.
- Educational institutions use it for announcements, instructional materials, calendars, and yearbooks.
- Community organizations such as religious organizations and service clubs use it for newsletters, bulletins, etc.

DP

DP2 ADVANTAGES AND DISADVANTAGES OF DTP

Advantages

Cost Production and printing times are shortened and operator costs are lessened.

Flexibility Changes can be made easily and at any stage at a lower cost.

Control Each phase of the process can be easily overseen.

Time Production and printing time is saved when there is no need to wait for the outside production of copy and graphics.

Security and confidentiality Because all or most phases of production stay within the organization, outsiders do not see the document.

Professionalism DTP allows even small businesses to create professional-looking forms, stationery, etc.

Disadvantages

- Documents that show lack of design knowledge, lack of writing expertise, or lack of skill with typography.
- Too many people having access to DTP and producing documents that are not unified (i.e., that can damage a firm's image).
- Too many unco-ordinated mailings and promotions.

DP3 SKILLS NEEDED IN DTP

Some companies install their own DTP shop and employ specialists. Many companies assume that because an office worker already has keyboarding and word-processing skills, DTP is a natural extension of

DP

those skills. In organizations like these, *anyone* may be expected to do it. However, because DTP combines the skills of many specialists, considerable knowledge is needed. This knowledge includes:

◆ Expertise with the software used

◆ Knowledge of design and layout principles

◆ Skill with typography

◆ Awareness of the publishing process

◆ Familiarity with the vocabulary of DTP

This unit will attempt to provide a summary of that essential knowledge.

DP4 DTP HARDWARE

The following hardware and peripherals are needed, regardless of the type of computer used:

◆ A powerful microprocessor, or central processing unit (CPU), that can handle the work efficiently. At least a 16-GB hard disk is recommended for professional-looking documents. Graphics require a considerable amount of disk storage space, as do completed pages of text and graphics.

◆ A networked system is not essential but is valuable if files are to be shared.

◆ A monitor that can display graphics well is vital. The best choice is a full-page, high-resolution graphics monitor.

◆ Most printer types can be used but laser-printer quality is optimal. There are two kinds of laser printers: laser and PostScript. The difference is in how they handle fonts (a specific size and style of typeface). PostScript allows lasers to change (scale) font sizes as desired.

◆ A mouse or trackball. The keyboard is used for many operations but cannot be used on its own.

◆ A scanner (image digitizer) allows for text, illustrations of all types, and handwriting to be digitized (i.e., changed to a form a computer can store) and manipulated (i.e., edited, moved, rotated) so that they can be included in your document.

DP5 DTP SOFTWARE

A wide range of DTP software is available. High-end, professional software offers the features needed for producing sophisticated documents. Low-end packages are appropriate for less sophisticated documents and for home and community use.

◆ All DTP software allows the user to integrate graphics and text on a page and to design, lay out, and produce attractive, effective documents.

◆ DTP packages all have text-editing capability but this is usually appropriate only for short passages and headings. Lengthy text is normally produced with word-processing software and then copied (imported) into the DTP application.

◆ DTP packages usually offer simple graphics-creation ability such as line drawing and creating circles and boxes. When more complex graphics are needed, they are usually produced in a separate graphics program or digitized by a scanner and imported.

DP

Word-processing software

Any word-processing software capable of being saved in ASCII can be used for DTP. Some word-processing software packages allow limited DTP on their own. For example, they allow columns, permit type size and style changes, contain their own clip art, and permit line drawing. Clip art can also be downloaded from the Internet.

Illustration software

This software allows users to create original drawings, or work with the many clip-art images and fonts provided, or edit scanned images. The high-quality results can then be imported into DTP applications.

Some illustration software permits the user to work with photographs—cropping, rotating, resizing, or creating special effects—and some provides animation possibilities.

DP6 PRODUCING A DOCUMENT

To produce an effective document, use a systematic approach such as the following:

1. Plan the publication.
2. Prepare preliminary page designs.
3. Prepare the text.
4. Prepare the artwork and graphics.
5. Finalize the design and page layout.
6. Print and finish (collate, bind) the final version.

DP7 PLANNING THE PUBLICATION

To effectively plan the publication, you might try answering the following questions:

What is the purpose? To inform? To persuade? To amuse? To obtain a reaction?

Who is the audience? What age group? To what social and cultural group do they belong? How much are they likely to know already about the subject matter?

What image should be projected? Contemporary, classic, dynamic? Solid, dependable, well informed? Creative, aggressive, avant-garde? Scholarly, reliable, authoritative? Exciting, adventurous, entrepreneurial?

How long should it be?

How much money is available?

How is the document to be produced? In-house printing or not?

When is it needed?

Who will do what? Who in-house will be involved? Will freelance personnel be needed? Who will do the writing? Who will do the designing? What tasks can be performed simultaneously?

How will it be distributed? Mailed? Self-mailer?

DP8 PREPARING PRELIMINARY PAGE DESIGNS

Thumbnail sketches are usually produced to indicate page layout and design. Text is represented with solid lines and graphic areas with the shape of the graphic. Stock (paper) (see this unit, DP33) and colours to be used (see this unit, DP22) are often determined at this stage and samples included with the thumbnail sketches.

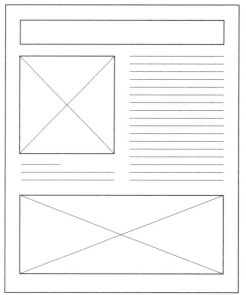

Thumbnail sketch

DP9 PREPARING THE TEXT

▶ DP10 Body text

This refers to the main copy (paragraphs, etc.) of a publication.

DP11 Text content

The amount of text and the approach taken will vary with each document. The following considerations, however, apply to any publication:

◆ Write clearly and concisely.

◆ Avoid gender, race, age, ethnic background, religion, physical ability.

◆ Check spelling, grammar, and punctuation.

◆ Proofreading and use the spell-check and grammar-check features of the software.

◆ Use consistent style.

◆ Ensure that content is accurate.

DP12 Body text format

Text can be produced in four formats: flush left, ragged right; justified; ragged left, flush right; or centred. Each may be used to add to the appearance of your document. Some, however, are harder to read than others. Justified is better for longer publications; ragged right is better for short documents.

Paragraphs may be indented or blocked. Most DTP software provides a *style sheet*. The user can decide on, for example, the indents and heading styles to be used. The style sheet will automatically make them consistent throughout the document.

DP13 Display text

This refers to headings and is normally created in the DTP package. Keep headings short and in capitals or have just the first letter of the first word capitalized. The latter is preferred.

DP14 Working with typefaces (fonts) and type styles

DTP allows you to work with many different typefaces (fonts) and styles. The software provides many, laser printers provide additional ones, and you can buy even more as cartridges or on disk if you need more variety.

DP15 The language of typography

Font   A typeface in one specific size and style and all of the characters and symbols available in that typeface (e.g., 10-point Times Roman is a font). People involved in DTP tend to use *typeface* and *font* as interchangeable terms.

Font style   The choices available of roman (upright), italic (slanted), outline, bold, shadow, reverse, etc., that exist within the typeface (or font) selected.

Kerning   The amount of space between adjacent letters on a page; usually affects only type of 12 points or more. In some cases, the space between characters may appear to be too large. By using the kerning

DP

feature you can remove some of this space and create a consistent spacing that improves appearance and readability. All DTP software provides a kerning feature. The high-end type allows for automatic kerning.

Leading The spacing in points, measured from the baseline of one line to the baseline of the next, between horizontal lines of type. Leading adds to the readability of text. The body text of this book is printed in 9.5-point type with 12-point leading, which would be described as "9.5/12" and read as "nine-point-five on twelve." The page would have looked crowded and would have been difficult to read if 9.5/9.5 had been used.

◆ DTP usually has a default leading of two points, which is fine for most publications:
  • extra leading increases readability
  • type set on its own body size without additional spacing (leading) is "set solid"

Points Point size is measured by the vertical height of an uppercase character, i.e, from the baseline to the top of the capital letter—72 points equal one inch. Most letters, memos, newsletters, and reports are created in 12 point. Point size is used with proportional spacing, i.e., an uppercase W takes more space than a lowercase i. Typefaces of the same point size can have different horizontal measurements. Consider this if space is an issue. For advertisements, flyers, and headings, larger point sizes are needed.

Sans-serif A typeface without short lines, or feet, attached to the bottoms of characters. Characters are perfectly plain, with lines of uniform thickness. Sans-serif type is generally used only for headings and very short blocks of text because it is harder to read than serif type. The main heads in this text are in a sans-serif typeface.

Serif A typeface with short, light lines or feet projecting from the top or bottom of the main stroke of the character. Serif type is generally used for body text. The body of this book is in a serif typeface.

Type size (points) The measurement from the top of an ascender (d, for example) to the bottom of a descender (y). Approximately 72 points equal one inch. This text is printed in 9.5-point type, which is fairly standard for most body text in, for example, newsletters and reports. For advertisements, flyers, and headings, larger point sizes would be needed. Typefaces of the same point size can have different horizontal measurements. Consider this if space is an issue.

Typeface A particular style of type. Typefaces come in three general classes: serif, sans-serif, and script (which resembles handwriting).

DP16 Commonly used typefaces

Fonts	Fonts	Font style
Script	*Brush Script*	Decorative type font
Times New Roman	*Garamond*	Serif font
Century Schoolbook	Neuva	
Arial	Futura	Sans-serif font
Univers	Modern	

Typeface examples

DP17 Type selection

Remember these points as you choose typefaces and styles for your document:

◆ Try to use only two fonts in a document but make them different enough that the difference shows. Also, take advantage of the many styles (italic, bold, outline) that exist in those particular fonts.

◆ Some typefaces are more appropriate for some situations and audiences than others. Try to match your choice to the job (e.g., an informal invitation might be attractive in script whereas a business form would be better in Times Roman).

◆ Use upper case (capitals) for single words and very short headings, but not otherwise. Too much emphasis kills the purpose!

◆ Ornate typefaces are hard to read; use a large point size (18 point or larger) so that the text is easily read.

◆ Consider your audience. Young and old like large type. Busy people like to quickly scan; therefore, something easy to read is helpful to them.

◆ Do not use text lines that are too long for the eye to follow.

◆ Consider reading distance (e.g., billboard posters).

DP18   PREPARING THE ARTWORK AND GRAPHICS

Artwork may be drawings, sketches, photographs, or anything that has not been produced on a computer. *Graphics* are illustrations of any kind produced on a computer.

You can add artwork to a document in a number of ways. For example:

◆ Original line drawings can be pasted into the final layout.

◆ Photographs can be professionally converted into film and stripped into film of the layout.

◆ Any artwork can be scanned and imported into the DTP file.

▶ **DP19   Creating graphics**

The following methods are possible:

◆ scanning and digitizing artwork and then importing it into your DTP file; the result can be sized and cropped (trimmed) to the desired shape

◆ creating graphic images using a graphics software program

◆ using commercially prepared graphics known as *clip art*. These are available in a great variety and are easy to use. You can also edit and change parts.
  • Some DTP packages contain their own clip art; others can be purchased.
  • Clip art is copyright-free.

◆ using the symbol and ornamental typefaces (dingbats) available in your DTP software (some word-processing packages refer to these as *character sets*)

◆ creating line graphs, bar graphs, and pie charts in the DTP program, in charting software, or in a spreadsheet, and then importing them

▶ **DP20   Web graphics**

Web graphics is the process of creating pictures to use on a Web site by using a software graphics package, which allows you to optimize pictures for print or online use using the default or customize settings.
Most graphics files are either GIF or JPEG. These picture file formats can be used for printing, but if you are manually saving Web graphics, you can choose the appropriate format as discussed below.

GIF—Graphic Interchange/Internet Format (pronounced "jiff")
The GIF format is a picture format commonly used on the Internet to store non-photo pictures, such as drawings, cartoons and icons and can display a maximum of 256 colours. It is best used for black-and-white line drawings, colour clip art, and pictures that use large blocks of solid colours, such as cartoon characters.
    Unlike pictures saved in JPEG, pictures saved in GIF format will not degrade in quality, even though the file is compressed.

NOTE   To reduce download time, an animated GIF should contain only a few frames.

JPEG–Joint Photographic Experts Group
The JPEG format contains thousands or even millions of colours and can be used to display high-quality photographs, scanned pictures, photographs from a digital camera, or smooth colour gradations.
    JPEG format was designed as an image storage format; therefore, it can efficiently compress large, high-quality photos into compact file sizes. The more reduction of the picture's file size, the more image information is omitted, decreasing the quality of the picture.

TIP Keep backup copies of all your pictures to revert to the originals if necessary.

JPEG does not support *transparency* or *animation*. When a picture is saved in a .jpg file, the transparent areas in the picture are converted to the nearest solid colour.

▶ DP21   Hints on using artwork and graphics

◆ Uses them to help explain text and to support instructions.

◆ Use them only if they add to the message.

◆ Keep them with the relevant text.

◆ Mix them with text; don't isolate them.

◆ Keep them simple.

◆ Use captions to explain them unless they merely decorate.

◆ Change shapes and sizes to add interest to the layout.

◆ Hard-hitting charts and graphs are attention-grabbers, but using too many can reduce their impact.

◆ Refer to the source of the artwork and graphics in the caption.

▶ DP22   Colour

Colour is an important aspect of document production.

◆ Colour can be used as background tint, as decoration, for emphasis. Functionally, it:
  • helps to get ideas across
  • speeds comprehension
  • clarifies relationships
  • creates moods (dark colours, for example, are prestigious)
  • focuses attention

Consider your colour scheme in advance of production and be aware of the printing process capabilities. Colour separations can be expensive!

DP23   FINALIZING THE DESIGN AND PAGE LAYOUT

Graphic design describes the process of selecting the individual elements (text, illustrations, and headings) that will make up the finished page. The selection includes choices of typefaces, styles, and point sizes, as well as margins and column widths. *Layout* refers to positioning the various elements on a page.

▶ DP24   The DTP layout screen

The screen displayed by DTP software resembles a designer's layout page. This is the working screen on which text and graphics are manipulated and arranged. Menu commands and tools needed to create the publication are shown on the screen.

◆ The user creates a master page (a grid or skeleton of a finished page) for each document, showing top, bottom, and side margins, column widths, and paper size. This helps to determine graphics sizes. Once designed, the page can be saved as a template for future use.

◆ A single page or two facing pages may be displayed at any one time.

DP

◆ DTP elements can be placed temporarily on the pasteboard while page layout is under way.

◆ Horizontal and vertical rulers help with positioning the elements.

◆ The tools permit text and graphics to be displayed in a variety of ways. Typically, they allow you to draw squares and rectangles with and without corners, circles and ovals, straight lines at any angle, horizontal and vertical lines, and lines at 45° angles, and to crop (trim) the edges of graphics.

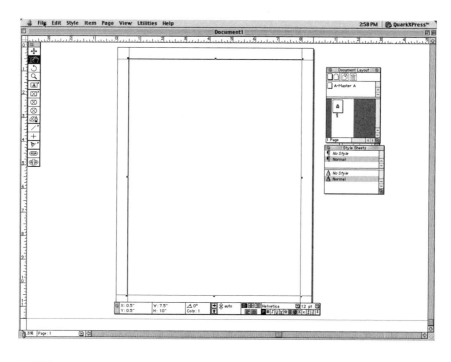

A DTP layout screen

▶ **DP25   Horizontal and graphic lines**

Use graphic lines to:

◆ separate information on the page

◆ divide a heading from the body of a page

- break up a page into columns
- design customized forms
- create borders and unify page elements

Lines can be enhanced by a number of DTP features, including:

- shading (also known as fill), or screening, which permits blocks of shading or fill from 10 percent to 100 percent to be inserted over ruled sections
- patterns that permit backgrounds of various types (such as cross-hatching) to be shown in graphic shapes

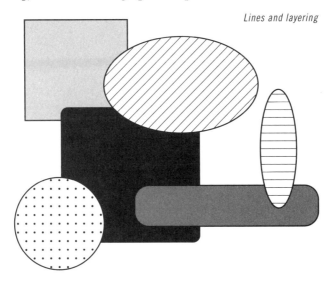

Lines and layering

- layering, which permits shapes to overlap each other
- drop shadows, which create a three-dimensional effect by layering two identical shapes

▶ DP26   The principles of design

The principles of design—proportion, balance, rhythm, contrast, harmony, and unity—should be followed to achieve an effective page layout.

Proportion   The golden rule of proportion states that rectangles with a ratio of approximately 1:6:1 are the most pleasing to the reader. "Golden rectangles" (placed vertically or horizontally), comfortable margins, and appropriate white space create proportion.

Balance   This is achieved through an appropriate symmetry of elements, white space, and the weighting of text and graphics on the page. If a page is in balance, everything above, below, to the left, and to the right of the optical centre will be symmetrical.

Balance aids in sending a formal, conservative, and precise message. An informal, asymmetrical design sends the opposite message—a less formal, more energetic one.

Contrast This attracts and keeps the reader's attention. Contrast is achieved by the use of boldface, reverse type, or graphics, for example.

Rhythm This is created by arranging elements so that the flow is smooth. Repeated elements such as horizontal, vertical, or diagonal units help create a sense of rhythm.

Unity This means that the design elements blend with each other and complement one another. Rules should match line drawings, typefaces should be weighted to rules, etc.

▶ DP27   Design hints

There are no absolute rules in this area, but the following hints will be useful in achieving good design:

- ◆ Consider the eye movement of your reader and be aware that, typically, the reader is attracted to a point close to the centre of the page (the optical centre) and will scan in a Z-pattern, with the eyes coming to rest toward the bottom right-hand corner.
- ◆ The optical centre and the Z-pattern both help to grab your reader's attention with the careful positioning of headings and text.
- ◆ Too much balance can be bland.
- ◆ Unify, co-ordinate, and organize each page around a single, dominant, visual element.

▶ DP28   Placement of text

Working with columns:

- ◆ Vary the widths to attract the reader's eye.
- ◆ Don't leave too much space between columns. Two picas is standard.
- ◆ Try to keep columns the same length.
- ◆ Avoid widows and orphans.

▶ DP29   Placement of graphics

One-column format Place graphics that are less than a third of a page deep at the top of a page. Those more than a third of a page deep should go at the bottom.

Two-column format Place graphics within a column, overlapping columns, or at the top or bottom, bearing in mind the size of the graphic, placement of the text to which it relates, and the design principles described earlier.

Text can be wrapped around a graphic for increased eye appeal if desired.

DP30   PRINTING AND FINISHING THE FINAL VERSION

The considerations here will vary with the size of the job. Very small jobs may be printed and finished in-house, some may best be handled by a service bureau (check the Yellow Pages), and larger and more complex ones may be completed by a commercial printer.

▶ DP31   Working with commercial printers

The following hints can prevent costly errors:

◆ Write out your printing specifications very clearly.

◆ Obtain written quotations from several printers and be sure these match your specifications before you make your selection.

◆ Inform the selected printer of the production schedule.

◆ Stay in touch with your printer through all of the production stages.

◆ Ensure that your printer orders the required paper stock early enough.

◆ Make sure that your camera-ready art or disk(s) is acceptable.

◆ If colour is involved, try to arrange to approve a press proof. If possible, go to the printing plant to approve the colour on site.

▶ DP32   In-house printing

Printing will generally be by laser, photocopier, or offset printer and will depend on the size and sophistication of the job and the equipment available within the organization. New developments in in-house printing may include:

Intelligent printer/copiers that combine the technology of the microprocessor, laser, and photocopier and have features of both printers and copiers. They can accept text, graphics, and instructions from computers or magnetic media. They produce hard copy directly from the digitized information received.

Colour printers that work on regular paper, provide colour close to that on the computer screen, can be shared on a network, and can accept input from different types of computers.

Direct imaging that merges the high quality of offset printing with the speed and convenience of a photocopier. The page layout (image data) is converted to high-resolution digital masters that can be sent directly from the computer to the printing press without the typical intermediary film and plate stages. The entire document production process—printing, folding, cutting, collating, stitching, binding, stacking, etc.—can be done in-house in minutes. The masters can also be archived digitally for repeats.

See Unit 2, p. 124 for information on scanners.

▶ DP33 Stock (paper)

The type of paper selected and its finish will contribute to the effectiveness of your document. Therefore make your choice carefully, based on:

- ◆ budget available
- ◆ purpose of the document and image to be projected to the reader
- ◆ printing process to be used (in-house photocopier or commercial printer)
- ◆ size and number of pages

Standard paper sizes exist to save waste. To save money, create a dummy of your document and make it fit one of the standard sizes.

Paper types

Groundwood (newsprint)   Inexpensive and useful for documents with a short life span such as flyers, newspapers, and inexpensive catalogues.

Bond   A high-quality paper used for most office-related documents.

Book (also known as offset)   Used mainly for book and magazine production.

Cover   Heavyweight stock used, as the name implies, for covers of pamphlets and journals.

Paper finishes

Your decision will be related to the image you wish to create. You may select from among gloss, dull, matte, vellum, textured, smooth, linen, and rippled finishes.

▶ DP34 Finishing

Finishing refers essentially to collating and binding. Commercial printers will arrange this as part of their service. In-house possibilities include easy-to-use mechanical binders that connect pages of documents such as reports by means of plastic strips, or binders that may be purchased from a stationery store and customized with your own cover page.

DP35 A FINAL WORD

If you are new to DTP, consider these ideas:

- ◆ Seek the help of experts when a difficult job is involved.
- ◆ Keep a file of ideas you like.
- ◆ Look at all the junk mail that arrives and consider it for ideas, "how-to's" and "how-not-to's."
- ◆ Study your DTP manual. The software can do amazing things.

- Keep abreast of new technology and software by subscribing to current magazines.
- Focus on the design element in everything you read. Many aspects of design can be learned, but it is experience that really helps.
- Register for a course.
- Observe, and ask questions of, experts.

DP36 DTP TERMS

Ascender: The proportion of the lower-case letter that rises above the x-height, as in the letters *b, d, f, h, k, l,* and *t*

Banners: Large headlines or titles extending the width of the page

Crop: To choose a section of a graphic, illustration, or photograph and size it to fill a specific area on a page

Descender: The part of a lower-case letter that drops below the x-height, as in the letters, *g, j, p, q,* and *y*

Display type: Type larger than 14-point; commonly used for headlines and advertising copy

DPI (dots per inch): Describes the resolution of a printer. Over 1000 DPI is considered to be typesetting quality; about 300 DPI is desktop laser quality

Drop capital: A capital that hangs below the top line and takes the vertical space of more than one line at the beginning of a paragraph

Em dash: A long dash used to indicate a sudden break in thought. Originally, the length of an em dash was the portion of a line occupied by the letter *m*. Now it refers to the square of any size of type

Em space: A square of a given point size. A 12-point em space would be a square of 12×12 points

En dash: Half the length of an em dash but longer than a hyphen. Used mainly to indicate continuing or inclusive numbers (e.g., 2003–12; pages 56–99)

En space: Half the width of an em space. Most commonly it is the width of the character *0* (zero)

Halftone: The process by which a continuous tone is simulated by a pattern of dots of varying size. This is used, for example, when photographs must be changed to a format of dots so that a printer can reproduce them. Specify lines per inch (lpi) for the printer. All halftones in one document must be the same lpi screen

Hanging Indent: The first line of a paragraph begins at the left margin and the following lines are indented one-half inch

Mastheads: Similar to banners but located at the top of the first page or cover and usually containing the name of the bulletin, newsletter, or company

Process colour separation: To reproduce full-colour documents using offset lithography, colour pages must be broken down into the four-process separation plates—cyan, magenta, yellow, and black

DP

Resolution: The accuracy of reproduction and distinctness of visual elements. For printer output and computer screens, resolution is defined in dots per inch. The more dots per inch, the better the output quality

Run-around/wraparound: A feature that automatically causes text to flow around a box, picture, or line

Scale: To reduce or enlarge text or pictures according to a fixed ratio

Style sheet: Allows user to save character styles, tabs, and margins. Once created, style-sheet format information can be applied to any paragraph

Template: An electronic prototype of a document that provides the layout grid and style sheet for similar publications. DTP operators can create and save their templates

Text wrap: Lets you specify the relationship of text to graphic. Can go around, through, or over a graphic

TIFF files (Tag image file format): An electronic format for storing and transmitting scanned images between applications

WYSIWYG (What You See Is What You Get): The representation on a computer screen of text and graphic elements as they will look on the printed page

x-height: The size of the lower-case x in a typeface; considered the main element of the character, excluding ascenders and descenders

5 ELECTRONIC MAIL

CONTENTS

In today's fast-paced global business world, instant communication and high-speed information transfer are essential. Electronic mail (e-mail) makes immediate intercommunication possible through telephone and computer link-ups, cables, microwaves, light beams, and transcontinental satellites. At one time, separate equipment was needed for the electronic transmission of data, text, graphics, voice, and video. Now, advances in technology permit the integration of such telecommunications.

♦ Many companies have their own private (in-house) networks (Intranets) and can exchange electronic mail from person(s) to person(s) through the use of computers, cables, and modems.

♦ Smaller companies with some electronic equipment can send and receive electronic mail through their own systems linked to telecommunications services provided by various organizations.

♦ Companies or individuals without their own electronic mail facilities can use the e-mail services offered by organizations such as Canada Post.

This unit briefly describes the scope of electronic mail systems. The unit opens with a chart that highlights the commonly used e-mail services and then moves into a discussion of computer-based message systems (in-house Electronic mail/Intranet).

EM

System	For sending	Service	Delivery time
Computer-based message systems (LANs, WANs, and modems)	correspondence and documents of all types	in-house system (Intranet), communications companies	instantaneous
Dialcom	correspondence, documents	Unitel Communications	same day
Fax	exact copies (contracts, plans)	telephone companies	within minutes
Internet	correspondence and documents of all types, e.g., Web graphics	global communication	instantaneous

EM1 COMPUTER-BASED MESSAGE SYSTEMS (IN-HOUSE/INTRANET))

Workers are linked through the computer network and can receive, send, and manage correspondence with other users. Appointments can be scheduled and calendars kept up-to-date using the software. Most electronic mail passes to employees as brief messages, reports, and statistical data. Computer-based message systems save time. For example, instead of making several phone calls to arrange a meeting, the caller uses a terminal just once to transmit the details to all participants. Rather than send a report in hard copy to several colleagues for their comments, the author keys in the text and data, which are then displayed on the recipients' screens for reading and editing.

Although this communication tool is important in today's office, if it is not used properly productivity can be affected and the disadvantages can outweigh the advantages.

Advantages
◆ can save time by eliminating telephone tag
◆ sender can distribute one or more messages to several people
◆ sender can add attachment/s to message
◆ receiver can read messages at his or her convenience
◆ receiver can print hard copy if needed

- messages can be circulated, deleted, stored
- messages can be sent/received on a 24-hour basis
- costs less than sending paper letters and faxes or than making long-distance telephone calls

NOTE Grammar/spelling/communication skills are apparent through e-mail use; employers can use e-mail as an evaluation tool for employee assessment for career advancement.

Disadvantages
- time wasted if abused or used for personal interoffice messaging; do not send chain letters or graphic jokes (workplace time abuse)
- time lost if receiver does not access messages regularly or if receiver/sender absent due to illness, leave of absence, etc.
- e-mail designed for short messages; if long reports input, forwarded, or stored, uses memory and can clog the network
- outbox or trash must be emptied on a regular basis, otherwise more network memory needed
- deleting an e-mail message doesn't guarantee it will be permanently erased because all e-mail is tracked on the mail servers (be very careful of what you input and send)
- unethical users may try to intercept e-mail; protect e-mail by storing mail messages in a file that only you can access
- computer viruses can be transmitted over the Internet via e-mail

Important
- See Unit 10 for additional information on the Intranet.
- The user list should be updated on a regular basis. Add new employee names and delete names of employees no longer on the network.
- Passwords should be changed on a regular basis if you are handling high priority or confidential files.
- Passwords should be left with superiors or assistants who may need access in case of your absence (check company policy).
- See Unit 10 for more information on the Intranet.

EM2   E-MAIL/VOICE-MAIL PLANNING

Communicating by e-mail and voice mail is so easy that sometimes people use them without planning properly. This can leave people and their messages open to all kinds of misinterpretation.

Remember:
- Think through your message before you respond.
- E-mail may not be private. Many unfortunate rumours have been started this way.

♦ Use e-mail as a business communications tool only.

Follow the basic rules of writing when you use this medium: keep your messages short and businesslike but not so brief that they can be construed as being abrupt and hostile. (See Unit 5, EM14, for more information.

EM3 COMMUNICATING (NETWORKED) COMPUTERS/E-MAIL

Electronically networked computers can send and/or receive messages instantaneously. This most popular electronic mail service operates within a department, a corporation, a country, or globally. Communicating computers have a built-in "mailbox" at each terminal.

♦ The sending operator keys in the receiver's number to make a connection and then keys in the message.

♦ The "send message" command puts the message into the recipient's mailbox.

♦ The receiver reads the mail on his or her monitor when convenient.

♦ The recipient can add to, then print or forward the message.

♦ The recipient can circulate an incoming message by using the "forward message" command.

♦ The "group" command permits message distribution to several boxes.

♦ The "store and forward" capability enables the sending computer to store the message for future delivery.

♦ A "timed message delivery" command can be used as a reminder to transmit.

♦ The receiving box can accept messages as they are transmitted or store them for retrieval on a 24-hour basis.

♦ Messages can be transferred to be combined with other electronic files for storage, or thcy can be deleted.

EM4 INTERNET/E-MAIL

E-mail messaging is universal and is now one of the accepted methods for sending and receiving mail within and outside companies (Intranet) and for global communication.

The letter 'e' in front of mail means electronic. Just as your street address is where your everyday mail is sent, an e-mail address identifies where your electronic mail should be sent, e.g., cam123@aol.com or cam123@netcom.ca

NOTE Do not use spaces. Periods are called *dots* and they separate the elements of an address but are not placed at the end of the address.

An Internet e-mail address must have a Domain Name System (**DNS**), which consists of a name or identifier, followed by @ (the symbol for *at*), followed by the domain name.

Domain name—Computers connect to each site using a series of numbers for identification; however, because it would be very difficult to remember numbers, most sites have a name that allow users to access a site without having to know the numerical address. Domain names always have two or more parts separated by dots.

dot.com refers to business on the Internet. Most commercial sites end with *dot com* (which stands for "commercial"). Many Canadian businesses end in *dot ca* (Canada) and other countries use their own endings/zone names.

EM

Examples: .edu – education   mcgill.edu (McGill University)
.gov – government   can.gov.com (Canadian government)
.org – other organizations   isoc.org (the Internet Society)

Within are provincial sub-domains, e.g., .ns for Nova Scotia, .ab for Alberta, .on for Ontario, .bc for British Columbia, etc.

Internet E-mail format:
The format of an e-mail is similar to the simplified office memo with the following guide words:

Send to: Copy to: Subject: Sender:

The date and sender's name and e-mail address are automatically inserted.

Salutations and complimentary closings may be omitted.

If you are sending a message to more than one person, use a comma to separate the names, and add each recipient's e-mail and address.

NOTE   Some software programs display additional information, i.e., routing data to show all the relays/computer links required to forward an e-mail message.

See illustration below.

E-mail format

EM

EM5 COMPUTER TELECONFERENCING

Just as teleconferencing enables more than two people to conduct a meeting without face-to-face communication, computer teleconferencing permits immediate information exchange and discussion without the need for people to travel. Computer teleconferencing takes place as follows:

◆ The meeting is conducted through computer keyboards and monitors operated by the participants.

◆ The material to be discussed (which all members can access) has been entered and stored in a computer.

◆ Each member at a computer terminal can call up these documents, as well as exchange information by keying in text that other participants can share and react to immediately.

Some of the features of computer teleconferencing are:

Personal notepad and file Electronic "desk" containing files of current memos, correspondence, and plans. These can be sent to other participants or to the "discussion" file.

Bulletin board The equivalent of the traditional bulletin board for policy changes, notices, job postings, etc.

Status and tracking functions An electronic means of catching up on how a project is proceeding.

Online search operations A reminder, if needed, of the names of conference members, points of discussion, and participants' personal notepads.

EM6 FACSIMILE TRANSMISSION

Facsimile transmission (fax) is common for both large and small businesses. It is the virtually instant sending of a document over telephone lines to a remote location where it appears as an exact copy of the original (statistical information, graphics, photographs, or documents with signatures). The sender simply dials a number (as with a telephone call) and is connected to the receiver's fax machine.

Operation of a standard fax machine

A photocell or laser beam scans the document to be sent and converts the text, graphics, etc., into analog signals, which are received at another fax machine or computer. The receiving machine reconverts the signal and prints a replica of the transmitted document.

▶ EM7 Types of fax machines

The standard fax units suitable for transmission of text, image, and data are:

◆ Simple fax attached to telephone

◆ Fax with telephone and memory built in

◆ PC-fax: A microcomputer with a faxboard, modem, scanner, and printer enable a PC to double as a fax machine. This allows you to send and receive soft copy directly from the computer without the need for printing.

For transmission of text, image, data, and voice, as well as for video and audio conferencing, subscription to one of the public carriers is needed.

▶ EM8 Fax features

Fax units come in desktop size or stand-alone models; as portable units for travel and home use; with colour-transmission capability; compatible with cellular phones; as a combination of fax, copier, personal computer, telephone, and answering machine; or as voice-to-fax, where the caller leaves a voice message that the machine converts into a printout. As well, numerous additions to fax machines are available to increase their capability.

Constantly evolving technology is bringing even greater variety for fax users. To make the best choice, check with vendors before purchasing a fax unit.

▶ EM9 Costs of fax transmissions

Fax to fax Charge is based on the time taken to transmit. One fax page can be transmitted in as little as six seconds, depending on the speed capability of the sending unit.

Computer to fax Charge is for message only, on the basis of the number of characters per half page.

Courier to fax for courier or postal delivery Charge is for message only and is based on the number of characters in the message.

NOTE Fax service is also available through commercial outlets. The sender simply presents the hard copy to be transmitted and pays when the communication is sent.

When sending a fax, use a cover sheet. Make sure all pertinent information is given, i.e., sender's name, address (company or home if necessary), phone and fax numbers, receiver's name and phone and fax numbers, date, and number of pages being sent.

EM10 VOICE MAIL

This is in fact a sophisticated telephone-answering service that combines telephone, computer, and recording devices. Organizations are installing voice-mail systems (which can be purchased or leased) to speed up the handling of incoming calls and routine inquiries. Telephone companies also offer voice-mail services to their subscribers. The caller leaves a message with a voice-storage device that converts the voice into digital format and stores it in the absent or busy recipient's mailbox (terminal equipped with necessary software) to be retrieved when convenient. Features of voice mail are:

◆ operates in the same way as telephone-answering system

◆ is good for short messages

◆ is convenient, especially for evenings, weekends, and when an organization operates on shifts

▶ **EM11   Incoming messages**

You can:

◆ Check the sender's number, date, time, and length of message.

◆ Play urgent messages first.

◆ Dial in from remote locations to collect your voice mail.

◆ Forward messages to other mailboxes.

◆ Designate how many days to archive your messages.

▶ **EM12   Outgoing messages**

You can:

◆ Identify messages as "private" to ensure confidentiality.

◆ Identify urgent messages.

◆ Send one message to several clients without dialling each number directly.

◆ Acknowledge receipt (or non-receipt within two days) of your message.

◆ Postdate several messages to different destinations and send up to one month in advance.

NOTE   Once you have sent a voice-mail message, you cannot recall it.

With the more advanced, completely automated voice-response telephone systems, a caller can simply push a button to:

◆ switch to several extensions and leave messages or hear pre-recorded announcements of often-requested information

◆ choose between two languages

◆ contact pagers or mobile telephones

The same system offers fax-response capabilities:

• The caller hears a pre-recorded message, enters a fax number, and sends a fax, or enters a fax number and can receive a fax.

• Faxes are stored until accessed or can be forwarded to remote machines.

• Documents from a PC or fax can be entered into memory; the voice-response system tells callers which numbers to press on touch-tone telephones to receive any of those documents.

- The system provides an automated attendant function that works if the required extension is busy. A voice tells the caller this, the number of callers waiting, and offers a choice of: wait, leave a message, or switch to another extension.

NOTE   Remember to change your voice message for incoming calls on a regular basis (e.g., when on vacation or not available—give dates).

TIP   E-mail, telephone answering devices/answering machines/voice mail are not always appropriate and should not substitute personal contact. In many cases, people prefer to interact with co-workers, management, and especially clients.

EM

EM13 USING E-MAIL SERVICES

- Most of these services are now less expensive than telephone calls. Don't just reach for the phone—especially when expensive day-time rates prevail.
- Use the least expensive service possible. Some offer time advantages; some, speed.
- The ease of communicating computer services makes it tempting to abuse the system with "conversations" that are not always necessary. Avoid this trap.
- Check your electronic mailbox several times a day—set a schedule and read the urgent messages first.
- File message(s), remembering to give it (them) a document name(s) for future access.
- Delete messages once handled to avoid unnecessary clutter.

EM14 E-MAIL ETIQUETTE/NETIQUETTE

Give special attention to preparing messages, because voice intonation is lost with e-mail. Choose words carefully and reread and rewrite the message if necessary. These points will be useful:

- Double-check e-mail addresses before sending messages.
- Use one message for one subject.
- Make paragraphs concise.
- Remain professional.
- Key e-mail text in lower- and uppercase, not all in capitals
- Do not send chain letters, jokes, or material unrelated to your workplace; this is a form of workplace time-theft, and only clogs the network.
- Check time-zone differences and holidays in other countries.

- Follow the usual hierarchical lines of communication.
- Take care with the use of humour, sarcasm, etc.
- Keep your return address details to a maximum of four lines at the end of the message.
- Respond promptly to e-mail messages received.
- Proofread carefully for grammar and spelling errors.
- Do not overload network with large attachments, i.e., reports.
- Empty outboxes and trash on a daily or weekly basis.
- Advise co-workers or clients of availability, i.e., vacation dates or extended absences.

EM

NOTE Do not open unfamiliar e-mail messages, especially those with attachments, to avoid infection of unwanted viruses. Caution: Be careful about redirecting personal e-mail messages received from others; they may contain viruses.

EM15 INTERNET PROTOCOLS/SERVERS

Various protocols are used between clients/customers and servers to communicate within the Internet mail system. Some of these are:

- **FTP (File Transfer Protocol).** The Internet protocol that permits you to copy files from one computer to another.
  - **FTP client:** A program used to copy files to or from a FTP receiver.
  - **FTP server:** A server to which or from which files can be copied using FTP.
- **HTTP (Hypertext Transfer Protocol):** The protocol used to transfer data/information between Web clients/customers (browsers) and Web servers.
- **IP (Internet Protocol).** The protocol used with TCP to send data over the Internet. The IP sends the data blocks.
- **IMAP (Internet Message Access Protocol.** A protocol used by a mail client/customer program to receive incoming messages from a mail server. Messages will remain on the server until they are deleted by the user.
- **IMAP server.** A server that a mail client/customer program can access to receive incoming mail via the **IMAP** protocol.
- **POP (Post Office Protocol).** A protocol used by a mail client/customer program to receive incoming messages from a mail server. Messages are deleted from the server as soon as they are sent to the client/customer.
- **POP,** also known as "point of presence" or an access point provided by an ISP; usually accessed by dialling a telephone number.
- **POP server.** A server that a mail client/customer program can connect to to receive incoming mail via the POP protocol.

- **Private Communication Technology (PCT):** A protocol developed by Microsoft, used to provide secure connections over the Internet.
- **SMTP (Simple Mail/Transfer Protocol:** This protocol is used to send messages to a mail server.
- **TCP (Transmission Control Protocol).** This protocol, along with IP, sends data over the Internet. IP sends the data blocks and TCP manages the data flow and ensures that the data arrive intact, without errors.
- **TCP/IP.** A family of protocols used to run the Internet.

NOTE   See Unit 10 for information on searching/surfing the Net.

EM

6 FINANCIAL MANAGEMENT

FM

CONTENTS

All organizations, regardless of size—from local corner stores to giant corporations—must keep financial records. Most office workers are involved to some degree in financial record-keeping, depending on the size of the organization and the degree of automation used.

The efficient office worker must be able to carry out, or at least understand, the routine tasks associated with money management. The valuable employee understands the work of the organization's accounting department; can read and understand financial statements; knows how to use the business services provided by financial institutions; understands payroll procedures, and, if required, can prepare a simple one; can use and operate a petty-cash fund; and is familiar with terms and processes related to money and banking.

FM1 ACCOUNTING

Accounting involves the recording of all financial transactions (purchases, sales, returns, money received, and money paid out), summarizing the recorded data into meaningful reports that indicate the firm's operating position, and interpreting the data to help management in the decision-making process. Although the accounting function in most large organizations is automated and is the concern of specialists in the field, every office worker should at least be familiar with the terms and processes involved.

FM2 ACCOUNTING RECORDS

▶ FM3 Source documents (forms)

The accounting process (cycle) starts with a basic business record or form known as a *source document*, which establishes that a transaction has taken place. Invoices, credit invoices, cheques, purchase orders, cash register tapes, and time cards are all examples of source documents. If an automated accounting system is used, the source document information must be translated onto a medium that can be used by the system (e.g., magnetic tape or disk). It may be keyed into a computer or it may be electronically scanned.

▶ FM4 Journals

Information from a source document is recorded in a journal (a daily record of transactions). For very small manual or mechanical accounting systems, journals may be in loose-leaf, book, or card form. On computer-based systems, a printout may be produced. The journal entry shows the accounts affected by the transaction and provides a brief explanation. Very small businesses may use only one (general) journal; larger ones may use some or all of the following special journals:

Cash receipts journal Used to record cash received in currency, cheques, money orders, or other cash substitutes.

Cash payments (or disbursements) journal Used to record payments made by cash or cheque (other than payroll).

Purchases journal Used to record purchases made on account.

Sales journal Used to record sales made on account.

General journal Used to record transactions not already recorded in one of the other journals.

Payroll journal (See this unit, FM59.)

Some very small businesses integrate these journals into one multi-column combination journal.

▶ **FM5   Ledger accounts**

General journal

GENERAL JOURNAL				Page 12
Date 2002	Description	Post Ref.	Debit	Credit
June 5	Cash	100	14 980	
	Service Fee Revenues			14 000
	GST Payable	201		980
	To record services performed for cash			
10	Office Equipment	157	62 000	
	Cash	100		22 000
	Notes Payable	263		40 000
	Purchased equipment for cash and issued short-term note			

Account – Cash					Account No. 100
Date 2002	Item	Post Ref.	Debit	Credit	Balance
June 1		J1	60 000		60 000
2		J1		12 000	48 000
3		J1		960	47 040
5		J12	14 980		62 020
6		J1		120	61 900

Ledger account

The information recorded in a journal is posted to (transferred to or recorded in) separate, individual accounts. An account is set up for each of the company's individual assets, liabilities, owners' equity items, revenues, and expenses. These are used for recording the effects of changes (transactions).

Each account has three columns—debit, credit, and balance—and a system known as *double entry* is used. This means that for every debit recorded, there must be a matching credit. Increases in assets, expenses, and purchases of merchandise for resale are recorded in the debit column; decreases are recorded in the credit column. Increases in liability, revenue, and owners' equity accounts are recorded in the credit column; decreases are recorded in the debit column. The difference between the total debits and total credits is known as the *account balance*. (In a computerized system, posting takes place automatically once the journalizing has been completed.)

▶ **FM6   A ledger**

A group of related accounts is referred to as a *ledger*. In a small organization, all of the accounts may be referred to as "the ledger."

When accounts that *could* be part of a general ledger are grouped together for ease of handling, these are referred to as *subsidiary ledgers*. For example, you might have a subsidiary ledger for accounts receivable, another for accounts payable, and others for large numbers of similar accounts.

▶ **FM7   Statement of account**

Monthly statements of account are sent to customers as a record of the transactions that have taken place and a reminder of the balance owing. The statement shows the opening balance, purchases, returns, payments, and the closing balance for the month (see Unit 7, F22, for an illustration). The statement of account is, in fact, a copy of the relevant part of the customer's ledger account. In computerized accounting systems, statements are generated automatically; in manual ones, they must be specially prepared.

▶ **FM8   Trial balance**

A trial balance is prepared regularly to check on the mathematical accuracy of the ledger. The trial balance lists balances of all of the separate accounts under the debit or credit headings. The totals of the two columns must be identical. The information provided in the trial balance is used to prepare the financial statements.

FM9   FINANCIAL STATEMENTS

The operating results and financial standing of a business are reported to shareholders, investors, management, and others by means of financial statements. The two key statements are the income statement and the balance sheet.

▶ **FM10   The income statement**

This is a summary of the revenue, expenses, and net profit or net loss over a given period.

For a merchandising business (one that buys at one price and sells at another) or manufacturing business, the typical income statement will have three sections: income, cost of goods sold, and expenses.

Gross sales is the total amount of sales made.

Net sales represents gross sales minus any returns or discounts given.

Cost of goods sold is arrived at by adding the beginning inventory and purchases made during the period and then deducting the ending inventory.

FM

Gross profit is found by deducting cost of goods sold from net sales. The figure should be large enough to cover the expenses of the business and provide a reasonable profit. If gross profit is not large enough to cover expenses, an overall loss will result.

Expenses are the costs incurred in operating the business (e.g., salaries, heat, light, telephone, etc.).

Net income is the gross profit less the expenses.

In comparative income statements, comparisons are usually related to net sales. Net sales are established at 100 percent and all other items are expressed as a percentage of that figure.

```
                          J. Savage Services
                           Income Statement
                   For the Month Ended December 31, 20--

                                        Current Year          Previous Year
Income
Gross Sales...........................  $963 000
     Less Returns ....................    13 000
Net Sales ............................             $950 000  (100%)   $750 000  (100%)

Cost of Goods Sold
Opening Inventory, Dec. 1.......  $100 000
Purchases...........................    450 000
Cost of Goods for Sale ...........    550 000
     Less Ending Inv., Dec. 31...     50 000
Cost of Goods Sold.................               500 000
Gross Profit .........................            450 000 (47.36%)   $300 750 (40.1%)

Expenses
Salaries Expense ...................  $200 000
Advertising Expense ...............     35 000
Depreciation Expense .............      20 000
Miscellaneous Expense ...........       15 000
     Total Operating Expenses....                 270 000

Net Income...........................            $180 000 (18.94%)   $105 750 (14.1%)
```

Comparative income statement

▶ FM11   The balance sheet

The balance sheet provides information about how much a business is worth at a specific time. It summarizes the assets (owned items of value), liabilities (amounts owed by the business), and the owner's equity (capital), which is the owner's claim against the assets. The "balance" in the title of the statement means that the total of the assets must balance with (equal) the total of the liabilities plus the owner's equity:

assets = liabilities + owner's equity

This formula is the underlying foundation of any accounting system, and is referred to as the *fundamental accounting equation.*

Current assets are assets likely to be sold, used up, or converted into cash within one year.

```
                        J. Savage Services
                         Balance Sheet
                       as at December 31, 20--

                            ASSETS

Current Assets
Cash.........................................    $      25 000
Accounts Receivable .........................          95 000
Notes Receivable.............................          10 000
Inventory....................................          50 000
                                                              $   180 000

Fixed Assets
Land ........................................    $1 450 000
Buildings ...................    $500 000
    Less Depreciation .......      50 000
                                                     450 000
                                                                1 900 000

Total Assets.................................                 $2 080 000


                          LIABILITIES

Current Liabilities
Accounts Payable ............................    $   152 000

Long-Term Liabilities
Mortgage Payable ............................        200 000
Total Liabilities............................                 $   352 000


                        OWNER'S EQUITY

J. Savage, Capital...........................    $1 548 000
Net Income ..................................        180 000
                                                                1 728 000

Total Liabilities and Owner's Equity.........                 $2 080 000
```

Balance sheet

Accounts receivable is the amount owed to the company by customers supplied with goods or services on credit.

Notes receivable are outstanding promissory notes, which are written promises to repay a debt.

Fixed assets are the virtually permanent assets of the firm.

Current liabilities are debts that will normally be paid within one year.

Accounts payable refers to the amount of money to be paid by the business to its creditors.

Long-term liabilities are debts that are not likely to be paid off within one year.

Owner's equity (or shareholder's equity) represents the claim of the owner(s) or shareholder(s) on the assets.

▶ FM12 Financial statement analysis

Information in financial statements can be converted into percentages, ratios, and averages to provide information for business owners and managers, investors, creditors, and others, on which well-informed business decisions can be based. Such information can also be used to provide comparisons with company performance in previous years, to highlight trends, and to provide comparison with the performance of similar businesses.

Percentages, ratios, and averages provide clues only. They are useful indicators but do not give a full picture. The key ratios and relationships include those that show liquidity, performance, and profitability. A few examples are provided below.

Liquidity

Liquidity tests indicate a firm's ability to pay its debts and can be determined by examining the current ratio, working capital available, and the acid-test ratio.

The *current ratio* is a measure of a firm's short-term debt-paying ability. It is calculated by dividing total current assets by total current liabilities. To have meaning, the resulting figures must be compared with the company's ratio on previous dates or with the current-ratio average that exists for the industry to which the company belongs. The type of business must also be considered. A ratio of two to one is usually thought to be satisfactory.

Working capital is represented by the amount by which current assets exceed current liabilities, the amount that would be left free and clear if all current debts were paid off. This amount shows in monetary terms the company's debt-paying ability that is represented by the current ratio.

The *acid-test ratio* (or *quick ratio*) is found by dividing the total of cash and accounts receivable (liquid assets) by total current liabilities. A one-to-one ratio is considered satisfactory.

Performance

The *inventory turnover* ratio shows how much sales revenue is being earned with a given amount of capital invested in stock (i.e., how fast the inventory is being turned over). This is a useful device for comparing present performance with past performance or for assessing the efficiency of firms in the same type of business.

Profitability

Gross profit margin shows how much profit exists after the cost of goods has been deducted:

$$\text{gross profit margin} = \frac{\text{total sales} - \text{cost of goods sold}}{\text{sales}}$$

This is expressed as a percentage.

Net profit margin shows the profit remaining after all expenses have been paid. The formula is:

$$\frac{\text{net profit after taxes}}{\text{sales}}$$

It is important to remember that each ratio is meaningless on its own. Ratios, etc., should be used to measure the firm's performance in relation to its own past activities, the firm's close competition, and the firm's performance within that particular industry.

FM13   ACCOUNTING SYSTEMS

Accounting systems vary with the size of the company. Only very small organizations now keep records by hand. Such organizations often use a one-write system, in which several records are created as entries made on forms attached to a specially designed board. Computerized forms of one-write systems are now available. They are much more simplified than most accounting systems. In most organizations, a computer is used for all record-keeping and financial statement preparation.

FM

▶ FM14   Computer accounting systems

Computer accounting systems range from those used by individuals to produce cheques and reconcile bank accounts, to multi-user systems that take the data input by many operators and process it through all of the required steps to produce financial statements.

FM15 Accounting software

Software packages are available that parallel the traditional manual systems and use the same language, or programs may be written especially for an organization. Such software can range from relatively simple types to highly sophisticated, integrated ones. The simpler programs provide modules covering all or some of the fundamental operations of journalizing, posting, trial balance, financial statement generation, payroll, job costing, inventory control, and sales order entry. The more sophisticated ones offer total integration of all of the key aspects of an organization's finances—sales, inventory control, purchasing, billing, accounts receivable, accounts payable, payroll, budget control, and financial reporting.

   Accounting experts analyse the data contained in source documents and data-entry staff input it into the accounting databases. Once transactions have been input, software automatically produces journals, updates ledgers, prepares trial balances and financial statements, and can manipulate data in other ways. Some, for example, can produce aged accounts receivable reports that show which accounts are 30, 60, and 90 days overdue. For security, administrators can allow or deny access to various accounting modules and functions within any or all of the accounting modules.

   A spreadsheet also has wide applications in accounting. Spreadsheets can be used for totalling and balancing journals, calculating sales taxes and discounts, creating bad-debts schedules, and estimating profits and prices, for example. For more information see Unit 2, CO25.

FM

NOTE For more information on the accounting process, see Unit 7, where billing and purchasing are fully described in the context of the forms used in the processes.

FM16 BUDGETS

The preparation of budgets is an accounting-related activity. A budget is a financial plan for a period—usually a year—that projects expected income and expenditures. There are several types, but the two key types are:

- operating budgets, related to such activities as sales, advertising, salaries, production, maintenance, etc.
- capital expense budgets, which project long-range expenditures on major items (new equipment, replacements, etc.)

The companywide budgets determine division and departmental budgets and contain both capital and operating items. Budget information must be constantly updated so that those responsible for control of finances can track actual performance and make appropriate changes to ensure that budget requirements are met. Budgets may also be drawn up for projects. In this case, records of all costs associated with that project must be kept.

Spreadsheets are the best tool to facilitate budget record-keeping because:

- calculations are done automatically (less room for error)
- changes can be reflected without the need for recalculating
- graphs and charts needed for reports can easily be produced

Expense reports

These may be a feature of the operating expense budget (see Unit 20, "Travel Arrangements," for information). Some software allows the two to be combined so that an expense report update automatically adjusts the budget.

FM17 BANKING

The banking transactions most commonly handled by general office workers include making deposits and withdrawals, preparing cheques, endorsing cheques, and reconciling the account balance with the chequebook balance. However, office workers should also be aware of the special services offered by financial institutions because this information may be useful for handling their personal finances and those of their employers, if necessary.

FM18   FINANCIAL INSTITUTIONS*

Legally, only chartered banks operating under the Bank Act can call themselves "banks." However, other financial institutions such as trust companies, provincial savings banks, credit unions, and caisses populaires offer services similar to those provided by banks. The information that follows is relevant to all types of financial institutions.

▶ FM19   Types of accounts

The accounts described here are available at most financial institutions; their names and terms might vary somewhat.

FM20 Current account (business chequing account)

This account is used by businesses for making deposits and payments:
◆ No interest is paid.
◆ An unlimited number of cheques may be written.
◆ Regular account statements, plus cancelled cheques and debit or credit memorandums (explanations of special transactions), are returned to the account holder.
◆ Monthly service charges are calculated according to the number of transactions and the balance in the account.

FM21 Business interest account

This account is suitable for businesses that maintain a fairly large daily balance:
◆ Interest is calculated daily and paid monthly if a minimum daily balance is maintained.
◆ An annual bonus interest is paid on the minimum monthly balance.
◆ Cheques may be written on it.
◆ Two free debits are permitted each month.
◆ Some restrictions may be placed on types of deposits accepted.

FM22 Personal chequing account

This account is used by individuals for making deposits and payments:
◆ No interest is paid.
◆ Service charges depend on the number of cheques written. Some institutions waive service charges if a specified monthly balance is maintained.
◆ Account statement and cancelled cheques are provided monthly.

NOTE   Some financial institutions also offer a daily interest chequing account, a personal chequing account on which a low interest rate is paid.

*To register any concerns or complaints in the banking industry, call 1-888-451-4519 or contact the Canadian Banking Ombudsman at www.mail@bankingombudsman.com

FM23 Savings accounts

Chequing savings account

This is used by individuals who want to earn interest on their account balances and who write few cheques:

◆ Interest is paid but is lower than that paid on a non-chequing savings account.

◆ Interest is usually calculated on the minimum half-yearly balance and is paid each April 30 and October 31. Interest is paid only on sums on deposit for complete calendar months.

◆ Cheques may be written on these accounts but the cancelled cheques are not returned.

◆ A service charge is usually made for cheques processed but certain financial institutions permit some free cheques, depending on the account balance maintained.

◆ A savings passbook is issued that can be updated to provide a record of all transactions.

Daily interest savings account

Generally, this is used by individuals who want to earn interest on deposits made too late to earn the full month's interest payable on other savings accounts. Because the interest rate is calculated daily, the rate may be lower than that paid on regular savings accounts.

◆ A charge is made for withdrawals if the daily balance falls below a minimum figure.

◆ A passbook is issued in which all transactions are recorded.

FM24 Investment account

This account offers depositors the convenience and flexibility of a savings account, yet provides a higher interest rate—comparable to mortgage or government treasury bill interest rates:

◆ A high minimum balance is required.

◆ Interest is calculated daily.

◆ Two free cheques or withdrawals are permitted each month, with a charge for additional cheques.

◆ Passbook or monthly statement is provided.

FM25 U.S. dollar account

A selection of accounts is available to clients who want to keep funds in U.S. dollars. Inquire at your financial institution for details.

FM26 Joint account

A joint account is one that is shared by two or more people. Any type of account can be made into a joint account. Each person may use the account on his or her own signature, unless arrangements with the financial institution specify that two or more signatures are necessary for each transaction.

► FM27   Making deposits

NOTE   This section on making deposits and the following one on making withdrawals do not apply to transactions carried out at an automated banking machine (ABM), which is discussed in this unit, FM37.

Deposit slips for all accounts are similar in format and are designed to indicate to the financial institution which account should be credited, date of deposit, who is making the deposit, the amount of the deposit, and if some of the money is to be retained by the depositor. If a deposit is to be made to a savings account, provide the teller with the account passbook.

FM

Current account deposit slips come in book form and consist of deposit slips with copy paper behind each one. When a deposit is made, the financial institution retains the original and stamps the copy, which remains in the book as the customer's record.

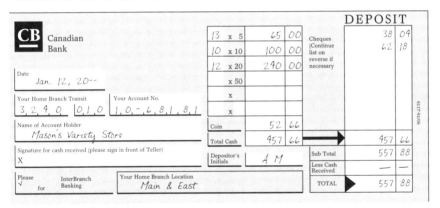

Completed current account deposit slip

To speed up the processing of your deposit:

◆ Fill out the deposit slip carefully.

◆ Arrange bills with the smallest denomination on top and place a rubber band around them.

◆ If there are enough of each coin denomination, roll them in coin wrappers.

◆ Endorse each cheque properly (see this unit, FM31).

► FM28   Making withdrawals

Where withdrawals are to be made from, for example, a chequing savings account, use the withdrawal slip provided by the financial institution. Where withdrawals are to be made from current or personal chequing accounts, a cheque or the withdrawal slip may be used.

▶ FM29   Preparing cheques

Cheques can be written for any amount up to the amount on deposit in the account. They can be prepared by hand, cheque protector machine, or computer.

◆ Complete the cheque stub or account record book first.

◆ Use ink if you prepare the cheque by hand.

◆ Insert the correct date.

◆ Correctly spell the full name of the payee. Titles such as Mr., Ms., Dr., Rev. are unnecessary. Fill in any unused part with a line so that no other name can be added.

◆ Write the amount in figures close enough to the printed $ sign so that the amount cannot be altered.

◆ Write the amount in words, making sure it is the same amount as the figures indicate. (Express cents as fractions of a dollar.) Begin at the extreme left and fill in any unused part with a line so that there is no space for changes.

◆ Do not erase or use liquid paper. Either prepare a new cheque or properly correct and initial the correction on the original cheque. Do not destroy an unused business cheque: write "Void" in large letters across the face of it and the stub, and keep the cheque in the files.

◆ Ensure that the cheque is properly signed in ink.

Completed personal cheque

Voucher cheques, which are commonly used in business, consist of a cheque portion and a voucher (stub) portion that contains the document number relating to the amount of the cheque and other explanatory details.

Pearson Education Canada, Inc.
P.O. Box 580 – 26 Prince Andrew Place
Don Mills, Ontario
M3C 2T8

Pearson Education, Inc.

VENDOR No.	VENDOR NAME	CHECK NUMBER	CHECK DATE
0083	SPEEDY PRINTING	15353	10/08/2001

PEARSON EDUCATION CANADA INC.   THE ROYAL BANK OF CANADA   15352
P.O. BOX 580- 26 PRINCE ANDREW PLACE   33 CITY DRIVE BRANCH   CHECK NUMBER
DON MILLS, ONTARIO, M3C 2T8   MISSISSAUGA, ONT. L5B 2N6

Pay $ Four hundred & fifty dollars   450.36

to the order of : Speedy Printing

⑂ 03│32   │││   003.│   │03│││ 802│││ 5││

Voucher cheque

FM30 Cheque clearing

Once a cheque has been cashed or deposited, the payee's financial institution submits the document to a clearing house to receive payment from the drawer's institution. Technology now enables this process to be completed electronically on the day of the transaction. The issuer of a cheque must ensure that sufficient funds are in the account to cover the cheque being written.

▶ FM31   Endorsing cheques

Before a cheque can be cashed or deposited, it must be properly endorsed. This means that the payee signs his or her name on the back of the cheque or, in the case of a company, uses a rubber stamp. The endorsement does three things:

◆ relieves the financial institution of responsibility should the cheque be dishonoured

◆ acts as a receipt for the cash

◆ serves as identification of the payee

There are three types of endorsements:

Blank endorsement

This is used if the payee cashes or deposits a cheque:

◆ Endorse the cheque exactly as the name appears on the face of the cheque.

◆ Endorse the cheque only at the financial institution, just before cashing or depositing it, because the blank endorsement enables anyone presenting the cheque to cash it.

NOTE   If the payee's name is incorrectly spelled on the face of the cheque, endorse the cheque twice—once as shown on the cheque and then correctly. This is called a *double endorsement*.

Full endorsement

This is used if the payee wants to transfer ownership of the cheque to another person. Endorse the cheque with the wording "Pay to the order of [new payee]" and sign it as shown on the face. The new payee may then cash, deposit, or transfer ownership of the cheque again.

Restrictive endorsement

This limits what can be done with the cheque. For example, if the words "For deposit only to the account of..." are written on the back of the cheque, it is not possible for even the payee to cash it. It must be deposited. This provides protection against loss or theft of a cheque. The endorsement may either be written or rubber-stamped in the manner shown in the illustration on page 208.

FM

Blank endorsement	Full endorsement	Restrictive endorsement
Mike Belza	*Pay to the order of*	*For deposit only to*
Double endorsement	*A. Frendinette*	*Ac. 04-0167*
Mike Belza	*Mike Belza*	*for Mike Belza*
Mike Belza		*Mike Belza*

Endorsement styles

▶ **FM32   Special types of cheques**

Certified cheques

These are used when a personal cheque is not acceptable:

◆ Prepare a cheque in the regular way and present it to the teller for certification.

◆ The teller will stamp "Certified" on the face of the cheque and return it to you.

◆ The amount of the cheque will be deducted from your account by the financial institution and transferred to a special account to ensure payment when the cheque is presented.

Stopped cheques

For a fee, cheques can be stopped by a financial institution when for some reason—theft, loss, error in preparation—you do not want the institution to make payment on a cheque you have issued:

◆ Phone the financial institution immediately and ask for stop payment of the cheque, giving complete details of the cheque.

◆ Send a confirming fax or letter to the institution or go in person and fill in a stop-payment form.

◆ Do not issue a replacement cheque until the financial institution confirms that payment has been stopped on the first one.

Post-dated cheques

These are issued for a date in the future. Financial institutions recommend that they not be used because the issuer can easily forget them and the money may not be available in the account when they are actually presented.

Stale-dated cheques

In the eyes of financial institutions, cheques have a life span of six months. Stale-dated cheques are over six months old and will not be accepted.

NSF cheques

"NSF" means "not sufficient funds." Cheques stamped with these letters are returned to the payee when the maker's account lacks enough money to meet the amount. It is up to the payee, not the financial institution, to follow up on the problem.

Cancelled cheques

These are cheques on which all transactions have been completed. With certain types of accounts, they are returned to the maker with the regular statement.

Dishonoured (irregular) cheques

This term is used when a cheque is not accepted by the financial institution for some reason (e.g., amounts in words and figures do not agree; the cheque is undated and/or unsigned).

▶ FM33   Service charges

Several types of accounts are eligible for operating service charges. Charges are made for almost all services provided by financial institutions, but special packages that remove service charges are available. For example, for a monthly fee, some financial institutions will allow an unlimited number of free cheques (see this unit, FM19).

▶ FM34   Reconciling the account statement

The balance on the monthly statement sent to you by your financial institution will usually differ from the balance shown in your records. There may be several reasons for this difference:

- ◆ All of the deposits you have made may not have been recorded.
- ◆ All cheques issued have not yet been cleared for payment (outstanding cheques).
- ◆ Interest or other credits (credit memos) may have been added.
- ◆ Service charges (debit memos) or NSF cheques may have been deducted.
- ◆ An error has been made.

Reconciliation procedure

Follow these steps to reconcile the discrepancy between the statement balance and yours:

- ◆ Compare the amounts on cancelled cheques and other documents with the amounts shown on the statement and in your records. Call the financial institution immediately if there are any statement discrepancies.
- ◆ List the numbers and amounts of all outstanding cheques. Include any from previous reconciliation statements that still have not been cleared.
- ◆ Compare the deposits shown on the statement against those in your records.

FM

- List any deposits not shown on the statement (late deposits).
- Write down the statement balance, then add the total of late deposits and subtract the total of the outstanding cheques. This balance will be the *adjusted statement balance.*
- Write down the balance in your cheque record book (or cash account) for the end of the month.

  Add any credit memos shown on the statement.

  Subtract the bank service charge and any debit memos or NSF cheques shown on the statement. The balance will be the adjusted amount of your records (*adjusted chequebook balance*).

  The adjusted statement balance and the adjusted chequebook balance should now be the same. If they differ, repeat the above steps. If they still differ, contact your financial institution.
- Finally, produce for your permanent records a formal account reconciliation statement as illustrated here.

J. Young Landscaping Company
Account Reconciliation Statement
October 31, 20--

Account Statement Balance		$2542.00
Plus Late Deposit		350.00
		2892.00
Less Outstanding Cheques		
Cheque 102	$ 51.00	
Cheque 107	214.00	
Cheque 110	110.46	
Cheque 116	151.07	
		526.53
Adjusted Account Balance		$2365.47
Chequebook Balance		$2116.22
Plus Credit Memo—Bond Interest		47.00
		2163.22
Less Outstanding Charges		
NSF Cheque—Daley Co.	$132.50	
Service Charges	13.75	
Loan Interest	56.00	
		202.25
Adjusted Chequebook Balance		$2365.47

Account reconciliation statement

NOTE You may need to amend your chequebook balance or cash account to include the new information reported to you on the statement. Interest earned and service charges represent amounts that you often do not know until you receive the statement. Remember to record all bank service charges, debit memos, and credit memos in your accounting system.

▶ FM35   Other key banking services

FM36 Accounting

Various types of accounting services are provided by some financial institutions, including payroll preparation and account statement reconciliation for customers who issue a large number of cheques. Large-volume customers can also receive daily updates of their accounts, if required.

FM37 Automated banking machines

An automated banking machine (ABM), sometimes called an automated teller machine (ATM), allows 24-hour access to a wide range of banking services such as deposits, cash withdrawals, automatic updating of accounts, payment of bills, or transfer of funds. Users receive a special card and a confidential code number (PIN: personal identification number).

The ABM network allows people to use their banking machine cards to withdraw cash from ABMs at any participating financial institution. A service charge is applied. Other banking transactions must still be carried out at an ABM operated by a customer's own financial institution.

The three main shared ABM networks in Canada are currently Interac, Cirrus, and Plus, of which the Canadian system, Interac, is the largest. Many Interac member institutions are also linked with Cirrus and Plus, international ABM networks that allow cardholders to withdraw cash both in and outside Canada.

Electronic funds transfer at point of sale (debit cards)

Presently, only Interac offers debit card service in Canada. Called Interac Direct Payment, it allows cardholders to use their current ABM cards to pay retailers directly from their accounts. The service is expected to grow.

Service charges vary among financial institutions. Additional charges may also apply when using banking machines provided by some retailers, such as at gas stations or convenience stores. These machines will inform you of any extra charges, and you can choose to cancel the transaction. Out-of-country service charges are higher for banking machine transactions.

FM38 Automatic bill payment

Many financial institutions now permit bill payments across Canada and in certain states via a computer connection or the telephone. When customers apply for this "link" service, they register with the bank a list of the companies they wish to pay. A monthly fee is charged.

Credit unions do not charge fees if your pay is automatically deposited by your employer.

The types of bills that can be paid on a monthly basis are:
- automobile club memberships
- cable
- car payments
- insurance (car, home, and life)
- mortgage
- subscriptions
- taxes (business/property)
- utilities (hydro, telephone, and gas)

You can also choose to have weekly/monthly payroll deductions for bonds and RRSPs (if offered) at your place of work.

FM39 Banking by telephone

Many financial institutions now offer a telephone service through which customers can carry out routine transactions such as paying bills, transferring funds, buying and selling mutual funds, and obtaining account and loan balances and information on interest rates and foreign exchange rates. These services vary from institution to institution, but many offer virtually worldwide 24-hour-a-day service through toll-free numbers in North America and paid calls from elsewhere.

NOTE The same services are available using a computer terminal and modem.

FM40 Collection

Financial institutions offer collection services for businesses, including collection on commercial drafts and discounting of promissory notes.

Commercial drafts Once the buyer and seller have come to a financial agreement, the creditor originates a commercial draft, indicating that presentation of the draft will be made on a particular date. On that date, collection is made from the debtor's financial institution by the creditor's and the amount (less collection charges) is added to the creditor's account.

Discounted notes If the holder of a promissory note needs the funds before the date specified on the note, the institution may discount the note (i.e., give the creditor the value of the note, less a discount that the institution charges for redeeming the note earlier than the due date). The institution then collects the proceeds of the promissory note from the debtor on the basis of the note's original terms.

FM41 Credit cards

Participating financial institutions issue credit cards such as Visa and MasterCard to approved customers. These cards can be used to purchase goods and services, to withdraw cash, or to obtain cash advances.

Accounts can be paid in full or in part each month. If only partial payment is made, the unpaid balance is automatically carried to the next statement and interest is charged.

Interest: If payment in full is not received by the payment due date, interest charges are assessed from the date when purchases are posted to the account. Interest is calculated and accrued daily (compounded); therefore, it is advisable to pay off balances in full to avoid high interest charges (17.9%–21.0%). Interest rates for cash advances are higher than for purchases (18.75%–22.0%).

Foreign transactions: Transactions made outside of Canada are converted to U.S. currency and then to Canadian currency, both at the exchange rates in effect at the time of posting. These rates may differ from the rates in effect on the date of the transaction.

Cheques for these credit card accounts are also available to holders for use in cases where the credit card is not accepted. These cheques are treated as cash advances. All cash advances are treated as loans on which daily interest is charged.

Cardholders usually pay a flat annual service fee.

NOTE *Convenience cards* are issued to customers by financial institutions for withdrawing cash, transferring funds, paying bills, or checking balances. They cannot be used for purchasing goods or services, however.

Caution: Be very careful when using credit cards on the Internet.

FM42 Drafts

These are documents issued by one financial institution that instruct another to pay a specified sum to the person or company named on the draft.

Commercial draft See this unit, FM40.

Domestic draft For use in Canada only and can be obtained for unlimited amounts.

International draft For use outside Canada and can be obtained in domestic or foreign currency.

FM43 Electronic funds transfer (Online banking)

This service permits the transfer of funds directly rather than by cash, cheque, or other means. For example, an account holder can instruct the financial institution to electronically credit a supplier's account and debit his or her own account in payment of a bill. The transfer is immediate. Instruction to the bank to transfer funds in this way can be by computer and modem, by telephone, or by personal visit. For security reasons, pre-arranged identification is needed before transactions are completed. The service is international in scope and enables funds to be moved between countries and cleared in a few days.

FM44 The Mondex Smart Card

This is a new product presently being introduced to the financial marketplace. This card has an approximate $20 limit and its purpose is to eliminate the need to carry coins. The Smart Card is designed for use in parking meters, payphones, vending machines, etc. When the limit is depleted, the card can be replenished by using any Interac machine.

FM45 Financial advice

Officers of financial institutions offer advice on savings and investment programs, pension and annuity plans, home ownership plans, trust fund arrangements, etc.

FM

FM46 Foreign currency

This may be bought and sold at most branches of any financial institution. Some, however, deal only in U.S. dollars. Call your financial institution to order special currencies.

FM47 Investments

Customers can use a financial institution's services to invest in foreign exchange, foreign and domestic export trading, gold and silver bullion, bonds, and money market securities.

FM48 Letters of credit

A letter of credit gives instructions from one financial institution to another to pay up to a specified amount of money to the holder. Satisfactory identification is needed. Letters of credit may be used in Canada and internationally.

FM49 Loans

These are available for many business and personal purposes. The contractual agreement to repay the loan is a *promissory note* (loan agreement), which shows the date of the agreement, amount borrowed, the interest rate charged, any other loan terms, and the due date.

FM50 Money orders

Domestic money orders are issued in Canadian dollars for amounts up to $1000. These may be purchased and redeemed at any Canadian financial institution.

International money orders are issued in U.S. funds up to $1000, pounds sterling to any amount, and unlimited Canadian dollars, for transmission to overseas destinations.

FM51 Mortgages

Approved clients may obtain mortgages for real estate purchases.

FM52 Overdraft protection

Businesses and individuals requiring protection against being overdrawn may apply for overdraft protection on certain types of accounts (e.g., current account, personal chequing account).

FM53 Package services

These are designed for people who use a variety of banking services frequently. For one fixed service charge each month, the customer is provided with personalized cheques; has free, unlimited chequing privileges; buys drafts, money orders, and traveller's cheques without a service charge; receives a discount on a safe deposit box rental if that facility is available; and often is provided with other services.

FM

FM54 Payroll servicing

Some financial institutions will calculate, distribute, and record payroll transactions for an organization. The client provides the institution (frequently through a computer link-up) with the necessary information. The institution then produces a payroll register, payroll cheques, statement of earnings showing tax calculation, unemployment insurance payment, etc. It then deposits the appropriate salary in each employee's account, no matter what other financial institutions are involved. In addition, the institution will make up T4 slips, cost analyses, and any other payroll-related information the company requires. At month-end, the institution simply debits that company's account for the amount of payroll and charges.

FM55 Retirement savings plans

Some financial institutions will open and administer retirement accounts and retirement income funds. (For more information see this unit, FM68.)

FM56 Safety deposit boxes

These are available for rental by customers on the premises of some financial institutions for the safekeeping of valuables.

FM57 Term deposits

A term deposit is a savings plan that can be used when a sum is left on deposit for a preset period of time. Such deposits will earn a higher interest rate than in an account that can be accessed at the customer's convenience.

FM58 Traveller's cheques

Traveller's cheques are a safe method of carrying money for vacations or business trips, and are available in many currencies. If they are lost or stolen, your money will be replaced. The purchaser signs each traveller's cheque at the time of purchase and countersigns it when the cheque is used.

The fee for buying traveller's cheques is one percent of their value, unless the purchaser has an account that includes this service.

NOTE Bank cards are the preferred method of many overseas travellers.

FM59 PAYROLL

Every business has a payroll—a listing of all employees being paid and the amounts they are to be paid. In larger organizations, the payroll is usually an automated function handled by a specialized department. In a smaller firm, the work may be performed as part of an office worker's other duties. As well, many companies use commercial payroll service organizations or their financial institution payroll service (see this unit, FM54).

Regardless of the number of employees and the extent of automation, the fundamentals of successful payroll operation are the same:

◆ Every employee should be paid on time.
◆ Payment must be accompanied by a statement explaining gross earnings, deductions, and net payment.
◆ Federal and provincial laws concerning payroll records and payment of collected funds to the appropriate government agency must be followed.
◆ All payroll information must be kept confidential.

It should be noted that all provinces have employment standards legislation that covers minimum wages, hours of work, statutory holidays, vacation pay, overtime, and other employment practices that must be followed.

FM60 CALCULATION OF GROSS EARNINGS

Earnings are usually calculated in one of the following ways:

Commissions Paid as a percentage of the dollar amount of sales. Employees may receive straight commission or a combination of salary and commission.

Piecework rates Earnings based on the number of units produced.

Salaries Incomes quoted for a specific period of time (weekly, biweekly, monthly, or yearly) with equal payments being made each pay period.

Wages Earnings based on an hourly rate.

In an hourly wage system, employers are required by law to keep a record of the hours worked by employees. In most cases, this work attendance record is some form of time card or time sheet. This provides a record of the employee's arrival and departure times, or the time spent on a particular job. The employee's gross earnings are based on the total hours shown on the time card. Overtime rates may be established by company policy, government regulations, or union contracts. In addition, most companies have a lateness policy and impose a penalty. Lateness is usually counted in 15-minute segments, as the time card illustration shows.

Time Card

Week Ended   September 14   20--
            Social Insurance No. 603 456 667
Name   Burns, Joseph

Day	Morning In	Morning Out	Afternoon In	Afternoon Out	Extra In	Extra Out	Total Hours
M	7:58	12:01	12:59	5:01			8
T	7:56	12:01	12:58	5:02			8
W	8:03	12:00	12:58	5:01			$7\,{}^{3}/_{4}$
T	7:58	12:01	12:59	5:01			8
F	7:59	12:01	12:57	5:00	5:57	7:02	8 / 1
S	7:59	12:02					/ 4
S							

	Hours	Rate	Earnings
Regular Time	$39\,{}^{3}/_{4}$	13.00	516.75
Overtime	5	19.75	98.75
Gross Pay			615.50

Time card

FM61   PREPARING THE PAYROLL

The payroll journal (summary or register) is kept as a permanent record of all employees' gross earnings, deductions, and net earnings. This journal must be complete for each pay period. In the payroll journal:

◆ The sum of the regular plus overtime earnings columns must equal the sum of the gross earnings column (i.e., the time card totals will match this column).

◆ The sum of the total deductions column must equal the total of all of the separate deductions columns.

◆ The sum of the net earnings column must equal the sum of the gross earnings column minus the total deductions column.

COMPANY NAME _____

PAY PERIOD ENDING _____

PAYROLL JOURNAL

PAGE 19

EMP. NO.	NAME OF EMPLOYEE	NET CLAIM CODE	GROSS EARNINGS	NONTAXABLES RPP	UNION DUES	TAXABLE EARNINGS	INCOME TAX	CPP	EI	HEALTH INS.	GROUP INS.	TOTAL DEDUC- TIONS	NET EARN- INGS
1618	Brown, W.	7	900.00			900.00	201.85	20.86	22.35			245.06	654.94
1619	Hughes, M.	2	600.00			600.00	118.50	13.41	18.00			149.91	450.09
1620	Lumis, M.	1	600.00			600.00	122.60	13.41	18.00			154.01	445.99
1621	Kahn, S.	1	400.00			400.00	68.35	8.41	12.00			88.76	311.24
1622	Manga, K.	7	450.00			450.00	36.60	9.66	13.50			59.76	390.24
1623	Rinka, P.	8	500.00			500.00	41.15	10.91	15.00			67.06	432.94
			3450.00			3450.00	589.05	76.66	98.85 764.56			2685.44	

Proof

Gross Earnings	$3450.00
Less: Total Deductions	764.56
Net Earnings	$2685.44

Payroll journal (summary or register) page

An employee earnings record must also be kept for each employee. This is a cumulative record of the employee's earnings and deductions for the whole year.

EMPLOYEE EARNINGS RECORD FOR THE YEAR 20--

NAME Lumis, M.
ADDRESS 29 Queens Street
Halifax, NS B3P 2L5
TELEPHONE 829-6712

DEPARTMENT Word Processing
POSITION Operator
SOCIAL INS. NO. 425-839-925
SALARY $600/week

DATE EMPLOYED 09/03/--
TERMINATION DATE
NO. OF DEPENDANTS 00
NET CLAIM CODE 1

EMP. NO.	REGULAR	OVERTIME	GROSS EARNINGS	CPP	EI	INC. TAX	HEALTH INS.	GR. INS.	OTHER	TOTAL DEDUC- TIONS	NET EARNINGS	TOTAL CPP TO DATE	CH. NO.	PAY PERIOD ENDING
1620	8400.00		8400.00	187.74	252.00	1716.40				2156.14	6243.86	187.74		Jan./Apr. 2
	600.00		600.00	13.41	18.00	122.60				154.01	445.99	201.15		Apr. 9
	600.00		600.00	13.41	18.00	122.60				154.01	445.99	214.56		Apr. 16
	600.00		600.00	13.41	18.00	122.60				154.01	445.99	227.97		Apr. 23
	600.00		600.00	13.41	18.00	122.60				154.01	445.99	241.38		Apr. 30
	600.00		600.00	13.41	18.00	122.60				154.01	445.99	254.79		May 7

Employee earnings record

FM62 PAYROLL DEDUCTIONS

The employer withholds a portion of an employee's pay because of compulsory government and union regulations and for fringe benefit schemes.

Compulsory deductions

Government pension Employees between ages 18 and 60 in all provinces except Quebec must contribute to the Canada Pension Plan. Employees may elect for early retirement at age 60 and receive a reduced pension, they may work and continue to contribute until retirement at 65 on full pension, or they may work and contribute until 70, at which time they receive an increased pension. Quebec employees must contribute to the Quebec Pension Plan, which is administered by that province. The amount of the Canada Pension Plan or Quebec Pension Plan contribution is shown in tables available from Canada Customs and Revenue Agency (CCRA).

Employment insurance Deductions for employment insurance are compulsory for employees under 65 who are employed for more than a prescribed number of hours or paid a specific weekly sum. (The currently prescribed number of hours or weekly sum may be obtained by contacting the Employment Insurance Commission.) Deductions are made according to a schedule issued annually by CCRA. The employer records payments made, weeks worked, and employment insurance contributions.

Income tax Deductions for income tax must be made for all employees except those whose yearly taxable income falls below the minimum taxable income. These deductions must be made in accordance with tables issued annually for each province by CCRA. New employees must complete an Employee's Tax Deduction Declaration (TD1), a claim for personal exemptions that provides the employer with a net claim code for the employee.

FM

Provincial health insurance In some provinces, it is compulsory for employers to deduct health insurance premiums. Sometimes the employer pays part or all of the premium as a taxable fringe benefit.

Voluntary deductions
The following is a list of other deductions that might be made. Such deductions may be made only with the employee's permission:

Private pension plan contributions	Professional association fees or union dues	Bond purchases
Extended health care plan contributions	Group life insurance premiums	Charitable contributions
Dental plan contributions		Stock purchases

These amounts are collected and then remitted by the company to the agency concerned.

FM63   VACATION PAY

In most provinces, it is mandatory for certain classes of workers to receive vacation pay. This is usually handled by issuing the regular pay cheque for the vacation period on the payday before the holiday commences. The employee is paid for the most recent pay period worked as well as for the earned holiday period.

If an employee who has not earned the full year's vacation entitlement leaves a job without having taken the earned holiday time, that employee is entitled to vacation pay for a percentage of the annual salary. Provincial legislation determines the percentage.

FM64   SEVERANCE PAY

If an employee is to be discharged, the employer should give prior notice in writing. The discharged person may be entitled to receive severance pay according to his or her length of service. The severance pay entitlement is dictated by the employment standards legislation of each province.

FM65   MAKING PAYROLL PAYMENT

If payroll payment is not handled by a financial institution, employers pay employees by cheque, by transferring the funds to the employee's financial institution, or by cash.

Payment by cheque or transfer of funds eliminates handling large sums of cash and cuts down on the danger of theft. Payroll cheques are usually issued on a separate account. To transfer funds to this account, a regular cheque for the amount of the total payroll is issued and deposited in the special payroll account. This account is easy to reconcile because when all the cheques are cashed, the balance will be zero.

Attached to each employee's cheque is a voucher (earnings statement) that shows gross earnings, deductions, and net earnings. If funds are transferred to the employee's account, a statement showing the same information is forwarded to the employee.

STATEMENT OF EMPLOYEE EARNINGS AND PAYROLL DEDUCTIONS														
1620	600.00		600.00	13.41	18.00	122.60					154.01	445.99	187.74	3821	May 7, 20--
EMP. NO.	REGULAR	OVERTIME	TOTAL GROSS EARN.	CPP	EI	INC. TAX	HLTH	GR. INS.	OTHER		TOTAL DEDUC- TIONS	NET EARNINGS	TOTAL CPP TO DATE	CH. NO.	PAY PERIOD ENDING
	GROSS EARNINGS					DEDUCTIONS									

Earnings statement

FM66   EMPLOYER'S LEGAL FINANCIAL OBLIGATIONS

Remittance of collected funds to
Canada Customs and Revenue Agency
Each month, a remittance must be made to the Receiver General that includes the combined employee deductions for income tax, Canada or Quebec Pension Plan, and employment insurance, as well as the company's share of Canada or Quebec Pension Plan and employment insurance payments.

Workers' compensation
All provinces require employers to contribute to a workers' compensation fund. The amount is based on the annual payroll amount, the type of industry, and the company's safety record. Details of amounts payable and payment dates may be obtained from the Workers' Compensation Board.

T4 (withholding statement)
By February 28 of each year, employers must provide each employee with a T4 form, which shows the employee's gross earnings and the

value of any taxable benefits (such as an employer-provided automobile) for the preceding year, and contributions withheld for Canada or Quebec Pension Plan, employment insurance, income tax, and any other deductions (such as union dues and charitable donations). One copy of the form must be sent to CCRA as part of the annual T4-T4A employer's summary and two copies to the employee.

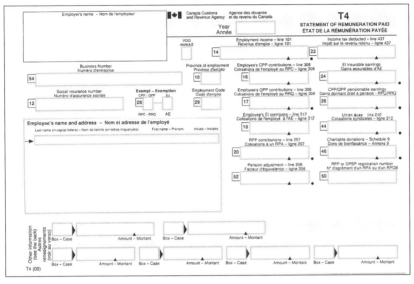

T4 form

Separation certificate

An employee leaving employment must be given a separation certificate (record of employment form). The person named must present this document to the local Canada Employment Centre in order to collect unemployment insurance benefits.

FM67 PETTY CASH

Petty cash is the amount of cash kept in the office to pay for small purchases or expenses such as taxi fares, stationery items, and mailing costs. The following are basic guidelines for administering a petty cash fund:

- Decide on a starting sum for the fund (usually enough to cover miscellaneous expenses for approximately one month).
- Give one person responsibility for operating the fund.
- Keep the cash and supporting records in a locked cash box or drawer during the day and in the vault or safe overnight.
- Fill out a petty cash voucher (showing amount paid, date, purpose of expenditure, and signature of spender) for each amount paid out of

the fund. Obtain receipts (invoices, sales slips) whenever possible and attach them to the voucher.

◆ Record each transaction. Use a spreadsheet, petty cash book, or sheets of two- or three-column accounting paper kept in a binder.

◆ Replenish your fund before it becomes too low. (The amount required to restore the fund to its original amount should be the sum of the vouchers.)

◆ Prepare a petty cash replenishment request that summarizes by account name the information contained in the petty cash book, and pass this to the accounts department.

◆ Record the cash received in the petty cash book.

◆ The cash box should always contain cash and/or vouchers totalling the exact amount of the fund.

PETTY CASH VOUCHER

Date: _March 16, 20--_

Amount: _$5.12_

Account to be charged: _Postage Expense_ Acct. No. _170_

Paid to: _Drew Young_

For: _Mailing a registered letter_

Received payment: _D. Young_
(signature)

Petty cash voucher

Petty Cash Book for March, 20--

Date		Receipts	Payments
March 1	Balance	100.00	
March 2	Postage		9.00
March 5	Taxi Fare		6.50
March 6	Owner's Drawings		25.00
March 8	Meals		15.85
March 16	Postage		5.12
March 21	Stationery		5.00
March 27	Donations		10.00
		100.00	76.47
Apr. 1	Cash on hand	23.53	
Apr. 1	Cheque No. 171	76.47	

Petty cash book page

LAURA LARNEY COSMETICS
Petty Cash Replenishment Request

Petty cash summary
Period March 1 through March 31, 20--

Postage	14.12
L. Larney, Drawings	25.00
Meals	15.85
Donations	10;00
Misc. expenses	11.50
Total disbursements	76.47
Cash on hand	23.53
Amount of petty cash fund	100.00

B. Farrar

Petty Cash Clerk

Petty cash replenishment request

FM68 An Overview of the Financial Marketplace

Some basic products and services available for investment purposes in the financial marketplace are:

◆ short- and long-term deposits/Guaranteed Investment Certificates (GICs)
◆ Registered Education Savings Plans (RESPs)
◆ RRSPs (Registered Retirement Savings Plans)
◆ RRIFs (Registered Retirement Income Funds)
◆ mutual funds
◆ stocks and bonds

FM

FM69 SHORT- AND LONG-TERM DEPOSITS/GUARANTEED INVESTMENT CERTIFICATES (GICs)

These deposit plans are good for people who have extra income for saving or investment purposes.

◆ Deposits can be short term (30 to 364 days) or long term (1 to 5 years).
◆ The primary objective is to improve investment income.
◆ The minimum/maximum deposit requirements vary within financial institutions.
◆ They are a higher-interest alternative to keeping funds in a savings or chequing account.
◆ They provide various interest incentives for larger deposits.

FM70 REGISTERED EDUCATION SAVINGS PLANS (RESPs)

These are contracts between an individual (subscriber) and a financial institution where contributions are made to a plan for educational assistance in later years, such as when the student enrolls in college or university.

◆ RESPs are tax-sheltered investments (savings are exempt from taxation until the student withdraws funds from the plan).
◆ The contribution limit is $4000 per year, for a lifetime maximum of $42 000.
◆ The student assumes the taxes of the RESP while attending college or university and therefore is taxed at a lower rate because of his or her income bracket.

FM71 REGISTERED RETIREMENT SAVINGS PLANS (RRSPs)

These are federal government–approved plans that encourage people to save money during their income-earning years to provide a source of income during their retirement years.

◆ They are tax-sheltered investments (i.e., savings are exempt from taxation until funds are withdrawn from the plans).

◆ Contributions to the plans are tax deductible and can be made at any time during the year; contributions made within the first 60 days of the current calendar year can be used as contributions for the current or previous tax year.

◆ A holder can have any number of different plans providing the total yearly contributions do not exceed the maximum amount allotted for that person's income range as defined in the *Income Tax Act*.

◆ RRSPs can be purchased from credit unions, banks, trust companies, life insurance companies, investment dealers, and mutual fund companies, or can be self-directed.

◆ RRSPs can be used to participate in the RRSP Home Buyer's Plan.

FM72   RRSP HOME BUYER'S PLAN

The Home Buyer's Plan could originally only be used by first-time home buyers. As of 1999, individuals are permitted to utilize the plan agian if they have repaid all previous amounts received. A total of $20 000 can be withdrawn from an RRSP for the purchase of a residence located in Canada, without immediate deduction of withholding tax. The plan holder must repay (to any RRSP) the amount that was withdrawn, without interest and in equal payments, over a

15-year period commencing in the first calendar year following the year of the withdrawal. All withdrawals must be made within the same calendar year.

FM73   REGISTERED RETIREMENT INCOME FUNDS (RRIFs)

These funds are RRSP termination options that allow the investor to retain the same investments as were held in the RRSPs. RRIFs are designed to provide a source of income during retirement years.

◆ The present RRIF age is 69 (i.e., the plan holder must convert an RRSP plan to a RRIF plan by age 69).

◆ The funds are registered with CCRA.

◆ The funds are designed to provide payments to the holder (subject to an annual minimum amount).

◆ RRIFs can be purchased from credit unions, banks, trust companies, life insurance companies, investment dealers, and mutual fund companies.

FM74   MUTUAL FUNDS

A mutual fund is an investment where a group of people pool their money in order to have greater investment flexibility with the potential for higher rates of return.

- Mutual funds offer improved potential returns (the firms selling the funds hire investment managers who research the funds carefully).
- There is reduced volatility because investments are diversified over many types of securities, countries, industries, and issuers.
- There is access to top-quality investments in markets anywhere in the world.
- Costs are lower and service is better because of simple administration and information.

Mutual funds are designed for investors who have a diverse range of investment amounts, time frames and experience; for example, a program can be started for as little as $500. As well, mutual funds are well suited for experienced investors with substantial portfolios.

The risk factor   The value of any mutual fund fluctuates day by day. Generally, the higher the opportunity for growth—such as funds invested in the stock market—the greater the fluctuation in price. Investors can lower potential risk, however, through diversification among various funds in the same family.

Mutual funds can only be sold by a licensed representative and are available through banks, trust companies, credit unions, life insurance companies, and independent brokers.

NOTE   Mutual fund investments are not insured or guaranteed.

FM75   STOCKS AND BONDS

Stocks and bonds are other investment alternatives for investment planning.

Stocks (common shares versus preferred shares)

Common stocks   Common shares represent residual ownership in the issuing company and entitle the holder to vote at shareholder meetings. Common shares are issued by corporations that need capital for long-term purposes. Interest is paid to investors through dividends and capital gains.

Preferred stocks   Preferred shares are issued by corporations to raise capital for investment projects, and they represent a less important source of financing than either bonds or common shares. Preferred shareholders receive dividends before common shareholders, at the discretion of the corporation's management.

Stocks must be purchased through licensed stockbrokers.

Bonds

Bonds are fixed income securities and are like loans that investors make to governments and corporations. The borrower agrees to pay interest regularly and to pay back the principal or par value at maturity. There are various types of bonds available, for example, government bonds (Treasury bills), corporate bonds, etc.

Bonds can be purchased through financial institutions or independent brokers.

INVESTMENT TERMS

Actively managed funds: Mutual funds in the investment portfolio, in which the manager can use his or her discretion to buy, sell, or hold. Most funds are actively managed.

Balanced funds: Sometimes called "hybrid" funds, balanced portfolios are a type of mutual fund that invests in a combination of stocks and bonds.

B2B funds: "Business-to-business" funds are a specialized form of technology sector funds that seek Net companies investing in business-to-business solutions.

Blue chips: A name given to large established companies.

Canadian Venture Exchange (CDNX): Market for Canadian small capitalization stocks.

Certified Financial Planner (CFP): A person licensed to advise and handle funds for investment purposes for clients.

Deferred sales charge (DSC): A commission paid to a financial advisor or institution.

Diversified funds: Mutual funds that invest in a wide variety of different types of stocks in the Dow Jones industrial average.

Dividend: A share of profit distributed among stockholders.

Equity-income funds: Conservative stock funds that seek dividend income as well as capital appreciation.

Growth funds: Stock mutual funds that seek out shares of companies with rapidly expanding earnings and/or revenue.

Index fund: Passively managed portfolios that track an existing market benchmark, i.e., Standard & Poor's 500 Index of blue-chip stocks.

Management expense ratio (MER): Expenses incurred for the managing and marketing of a mutual fund portfolio.

NASDAQ (National Association of Securities Dealers Automated Quotations): Over the counter market where smaller capitalization stocks are bought and sold.

Pre-authorized contribution plan (PAC): Authorized permission to deduct monies from a bank account for various plan contributions, such as RRSPs.

New York Stock Exchange (NYSE): The location where U.S. stocks are bought and sold.

Toronto Stock Exchange (TSE): A financial facility where stocks of Canadian companies are bought, sold, and traded daily. The price of the stock is reported as the high, low, and closing price, as well as the number of shares traded for each day.

World Equity Benchmark Shares (WEBS): Stock exchange-traded index funds that reflect the stock market of a single country.

7 FORMS AND FORM DESIGN

CONTENTS

F

Regardless of size, nature of business, or type of ownership, organizations tend to operate along similar lines because they must all deal efficiently with certain basic activities. These activities are purchasing, receiving, inventory control, producing, selling, shipping, billing, and keeping records of money received and paid out. These interdependent activities are linked by means of forms, each designed for a particular purpose.

More and more, activities related to forms are being automated. However, the basic activities do not change. Familiarity with an organization's activities helps office workers to understand the business, the roles people play in it, and the best way of serving customers.

The illustrations on pages 228 and 229 describe the flow of activity around purchasing and sales, the two systems that constitute the lifeblood of any business organization. The illustrations show the interdependence of the departments involved and identify the types of forms used at each stage of activity.

F1 WHAT ARE FORMS?

Forms are used to record the details of business transactions. A form can be used to create or cancel a transaction, request action, confirm a request, give instructions, report facts, summarize information, and serve as a base for work flow.

Forms can be in hard copy (i.e., to be completed by computer input or by longhand), or by soft copy (electronic forms) to be displayed on a computer screen and filled in by keying in the information. Some must be completed entirely; with others, considerable amounts of information can be inserted automatically, simply by, say, inserting an account or telephone number.

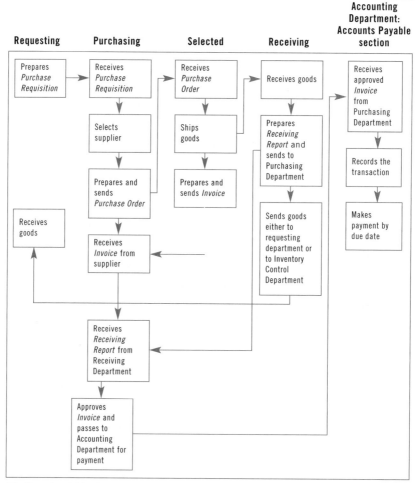

The flow of activities in a typical purchasing system

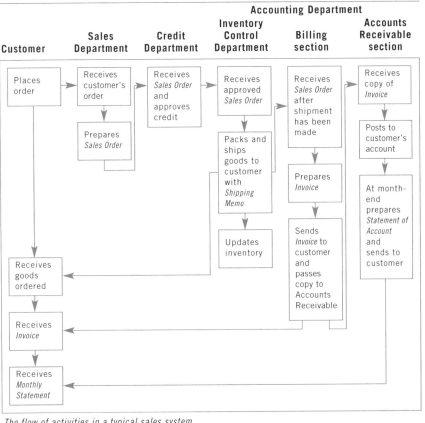

The flow of activities in a typical sales system

Regardless of their type or appearance, forms always serve the same purpose—to ease the flow of information.

F2   FORMS USED IN BASIC BUSINESS ACTIVITIES

In some small organizations, hard-copy forms are used exclusively to implement the various business activities, with each department creating forms that meet its particular needs. To carry out the procedures illustrated in the preceding diagrams, the appropriate form would be sent from one department to another in the order shown.

In electronic systems, however, the supplier (in the case of a purchase) and the customer (in the case of a sale) might be the only people in the chain who receive a hard-copy form. All of the intercompany departments are linked electronically, so that as each department completes its required action, the information is fed into a database that informs the next department of the action required of it, until the procedure has been completed. Electronic systems vary, depending on the type of programs used.

In the following sections, each of the common activities carried out regularly by most companies is discussed and the usual required number of hard copies of each form is indicated. In the case of an electronic system, of course, the information is automatically transmitted to the appropriate departments and the necessary action is taken.

F3   PURCHASING

Purchasing means buying everything an organization needs in its operation, from paper clips to delivery trucks. In a small company, buying may be done quite informally (by e-mail, fax, letter, or telephone, for example), but a large company needs forms to control and record purchasing functions. In most organizations, buying is handled by a purchasing department, which acts only on receipt of an approved purchase requisition.

Today, many small and large companies are using online buying of goods and services, also known as e-business (electronic business) or e-commerce.

▶ F4   Purchase requisition

◆ issued by a company department and, if approved by a designated person in that department, sent to the purchasing department for action

◆ usually, only one copy for the purchasing department and one for the requesting department

REQUISITION (NOT A PURCHASE ORDER)			007266		
TO _Purchasing Dept._		DATE _Aug. 20_ 20 --			
ADDRESS		FOR			
SHIP TO _Production Dept._		DATE REQ'D. _Sept. 17_			
QUANTITY		PLEASE SUPPLY	PRICE	AMOUNT	
1	50	oak frames, 50 cm x 35 cm			
2	25	mahogany frames, 70 cm x 60 cm			
3	50	panes non-glare glass, 50 cm x 35 cm			
4	25	panes non-glare glass, 70 cm x 60 cm			
5	3	rolls canvas, 80 cm wide			
6					
7					
8					
9					
JOB NO. _1602_	SALES TAX (CHARGEABLE) NOT CHARGEABLE		ORDERED BY _W. Stanley_	APPROVED BY _E. Chin_	

Purchase requisition

▶ F5   Purchase order

◆ prepared by the purchasing department from the information provided in the purchase requisition and sent to the vendor (supplier) who offers the best price and delivery terms

◆ copies for the supplier, receiving department, and purchasing department

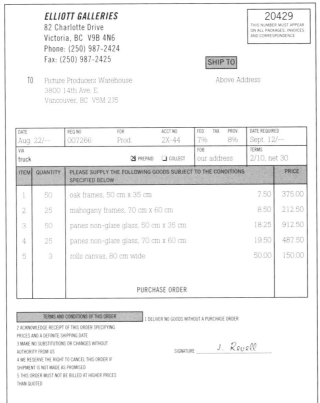

Purchase order

F6   RECEIVING

Goods received must be matched against the original purchase order for accuracy in quantity and type. The goods must also be checked for condition. The receiving department is responsible for checking the goods and completing a receiving report.

▶ F7   Receiving report

◆ prepared after incoming goods have been checked against the purchase order

◆ copies for accounts payable, purchasing, inventory control, and receiving

Receiving report

F8 INVENTORY CONTROL

Inventory control is responsible for the storage, care, and distribution of supplies and raw materials required for operations, and of finished goods to be sold.

▶ F9 Inventory record

An inventory record can vary in format, but the following is one example.

- kept for each product; shows quantity received and distributed either within the company or to customers, and the amount of each item presently on hand
- only one copy usually required for inventory control

NOTE In many businesses, inventory control is automated. Additions and deletions to inventory are handled automatically as customer invoices are issued and supplier invoices are paid. Periodic computer printouts provide a hard-copy inventory record, if required.

▶ F10   Stock requisition

- sent to the purchasing department by the inventory control department when it is necessary to replenish supplies that have reached minimum-quantity levels
- purchasing department handles a stock requisition in the same manner as it does a purchase requisition from the other company departments
- one copy usually needed for the purchasing department and one for inventory control

NOTE In some automated systems, the computer is programmed to notify inventory control when minimum quantities of supplies or raw materials have been reached and more must be ordered.

F11   PRODUCING

In manufacturing firms or in some service businesses (such as garages or equipment repairers), an authorization form known as a *production order* or *work order* is required before the actual production of goods or servicing of equipment can begin.

▶ F12   Production order (work order)

- given to the person, division, or section within the production department that will do the job
- usually one copy for the worker, division, or section doing the job and one for the requesting department

F

ELLIOTT GALLERIES
82 Charlotte Drive
Victoria, BC V9B 4N6
Phone: (250) 987-2424
Fax: (250) 987-2425

PRODUCTION WORK ORDER	
Work Order No.	F276
Customer P.O. No.	AE99
Date	-- 09 16
Job done by	

Customer
Scotts Art Stores
739 Appian Way
Coquitlam, BC V3J 2A9

Ship to:
same address

Billing Instructions
Prepaid ☐   Collect ☐
          Invoice ☑
Date Required   -- 09 30

Shipping Instructions
Phone when ready.
Customer will pick up.

Job Description	Unit Price	Total Cost
30 B.C. Scenic prints No. 10-160 to be framed in oak frames with non-glare glass. 50 cm x 35 cm	50.00	1500.00

Date Completed_____

Inspected by _____

Date Shipped _____

Production order

F13   SELLING

A customer who wants to buy goods or services places an order with a firm, activating the sales procedure.

▶ F14   Sales order

◆ made up by a sales representative after taking an order in person, by telephone, through the mail, by fax, or by e-mail, for example
◆ copies usually required by the credit department, customer, and the inventory control, shipping, accounts receivable, and sales departments

NOTE   In retail sales, a sales slip is issued at the time of a sale and given to the customer with the goods purchased.

◆ copies usually required for the customer, the accounts receivable section (when the sale is on credit), and the sales department

Picture Producers Warehouse   0179

3800 14th Avenue E.
Vancouver, BC V5M 2J5
Phone: (604) 521-6307
Fax: (604) 521-6322

SOLD TO   *Elliott Galleries*
       S   *same*
       82 Charlotte Drive   H / I / P
       Victoria, BC   V9B 4N6   T / O

DATE	SHIP VIA	CUSTOMER ORDER NO.	SALES REP.
Sept. 8/--	*truck*	*20429*	*Kenneth Ramsey*

QUANTITY ORDERED	DESCRIPTION	UNIT PRICE
50	*oak frames, 50 cm x 35 cm*	*7.50*
25	*mahogany frames, 70 cm x 60 cm*	*8.50*
50	*panes non-glare glass, 50 cm x 35 cm*	*18.25*
25	*panes non-glare glass, 70 cm x 60 cm*	*19.50*
3	*rolls canvas, 80 cm wide*	*50.00*

Sales order

F15   SHIPPING

When goods are shipped, acknowledgment of their receipt by the addressee is often necessary. Many companies use a specially prepared shipping memo.

                                 040573

FROM	*Picture Producers Warehouse*		DATE	*Sept. 11/--*
TO	*Elliott Galleries*		YOUR ORDER	*20429*
ADDRESS	*82 Charlotte Drive*	CITY	*Victoria*	

PACKAGES	RECEIVED IN APPARENT GOOD ORDER	WEIGHT
9	*Contents - frames*	
	- glass	
	- canvas rolls	

RECEIVED BY	TOTAL PACKAGES	*9*	TOTAL WEIGHT	
A. McLaughlin	C.O.D. CHARGE		DELIVERY CHARGE	

Shipping memo or delivery receipt

▶ F16 Shipping memo (delivery receipt)

◆ signed by the customer and returned to the carrier on receipt of merchandise

◆ two signed copies usually required: one for the customer, and one for the shipper

▶ F17 Bill of lading

◆ the standard shipping document that serves as a contract between the consignor (the supplier) and the carrier of the goods

◆ used for all forms of transportation (rail, water, air, or road transportation) (see Unit 15, P63)

F18 BILLING

After the supplier has shipped the articles ordered or provided the service requested, the customer is billed. This is done by sending the top copy of the invoice described below.

▶ F19 Invoice

◆ sent by the billing section of the accounting department to the customer

◆ shows details of the goods ordered or services provided, cost, shipping charges, terms of payment, discount applicable, taxes, and total amount due

◆ three copies usually required: one for the customer, one for accounts receivable, and one for the billing section

◆ additional copies of the invoice may also be required by the credit, accounts receivable, sales (to acknowledge an order or to indicate that shipment was made), inventory control, and shipping (as a packing slip to accompany the goods) departments

If the total order cannot be shipped, the invoice will show that fact. For example, if a quantity of 100 was ordered and only 80 were available for shipment, 20 would be entered in the "Back Ordered" column and 80 in the "Quantity" column. The outstanding 20 would be shipped and invoiced at a later date.

In most electronic systems, when invoices are issued, automatic updating of inventory, accounts receivable, and general ledger accounts occurs.

Picture Producers Warehouse   101001

3800 14th Avenue E.
Vancouver, BC V5M 2J5
Phone: (604) 521-6307
Fax: (604) 521-6322

SOLD TO Elliott Galleries   SHIP TO   SAME
         82 Charlotte Dr.
         Victoria, BC V9B 4N6

DATE	SHIPPED VIA	FED. LICENCE NO.	PROV. LICENCE NO.	YOUR ORDER NO.	PROV. SALES TAX	TERMS	SALES REP.
Sept. 8/--	our truck	Z276	BC0490	20429	316592	2/10 n30	

BACK ORDERED	QTY. ORDERED	DESCRIPTION	QTY. SHIPPED	UNIT PRICE	AMOUNT
	50	oak frames, 50 cm x 35 cm	50	7.50	375.00
	25	mahogany frames, 70 cm x 60 cm	25	8.50	212.50
15	50	panes non-glare glass, 50 cm x 35 cm	35	18.25	638.75
	25	panes non-glare glass, 70 cm x 60 cm	25	19.50	487.50
	3	rolls canvas, 80 cm wide	3	50.00	150.00
					1863.75
		Trade discount 20%			372.75
		Sales Tax Exempt			1491.00
		7% GST			104.37
		TOTAL			1595.37

	DATE SHIPPED	B/O FROM	B/O TO
INVOICE	Sept. 8/--		

Invoice

▶ **F20   Credit invoice**

◆ issued by the billing section of the accounting department in cases of returned or damaged goods or an overcharge

◆ informs the customer that his or her account is reduced (credited) by the amount shown

◆ copies usually needed: one each for the customer, accounts receivable, and billing

F21   COLLECTING

Customers who do not pay for each order as it is invoiced are sent a monthly statement.

▶ **F22   Statement of account**

◆ sent by accounts receivable section of the accounting department to the customer

◆ itemizes purchases, returns, payments made, and any interest charges for the month and shows total balance due

◆ three copies are usually necessary—for the customer, accounting, and accounts receivable

F

Picture Producers Warehouse
3800 14th Avenue E.
Vancouver, BC V5M 2J5
Phone: (604) 521-6307
Fax: (604) 521-6322

TO ▶ Elliott Galleries

82 Charlotte Dr.

Victoria, BC V9B 4N6

MONTH OF September 20--	CUSTOMER ACCOUNT 2X-44	AMOUNT OF REMITTANCE

PLEASE RETURN THIS PART WITH YOUR REMITTANCE   DETACH HERE ▼

- -

Picture Producers Warehouse
3800 14th Avenue E.
IN ACCOUNT   Vancouver, BC V5M 2J5
WITH   Phone: (604) 521-6307   Fax: (604) 521-6322

KEEP THIS PART

STATEMENT DATE: Sept. 31/20--   ACCOUNT NO.: 2X-44   AMOUNT PAID:

DATE		PARTICULARS	DEBIT		CREDIT		BALANCE	
		PREVIOUS BALANCE FORWARD					735	28
Sept.	5	Payment received			735	28	nil	
Sept.	8	Invoice No. 101001	1714	65			1714	65
Sept.	21	Invoice No. 101036	46	33			1760	98

STATEMENT   Please pay last amount...   IN THIS COLUMN ▲

Monthly statement of account

F23   DISBURSING

Payment of a company's costs and expenses is most frequently made by cheque by the accounts payable section of the accounting department. Salaries and wages are handled by the payroll section (see Unit 6, "Financial Management").

F24 PREPRINTED BASIC BUSINESS FORMS

If a business is small and the expense of custom-printed forms is not felt to be justified, preprinted forms may be purchased at stationery or office supply stores. These forms may then be keyed or rubber-stamped with the company name and a form identification number if necessary. Preprinted forms include:

billing forms
customer statements
expense accounts
invoices
ledger sheets, accounting paper
petty cash vouchers

purchase orders
receipts
requisitions
sales representatives' order books
shipping memos
time and payroll forms

Preprinted business forms are also available for specialized business purposes, including:

- Legal forms for mortgages, leases, wills, etc. They are available from major stationery and office supply houses.
- Tax forms are available through the local Canada Customs and Revenue Agency.
- Banking forms of various types can be obtained from financial institutions.

F25   RUBBER STAMPS, DIE STAMPS, AND PREPRINTED STICKERS

In some situations, rubber stamps can replace forms. You can stamp information directly onto documents to indicate date of receipt, date of shipment, priority in handling, department routing of documents, filing information, etc.

In addition, rubber stamps can be imprinted with an organization's name and address or any other required information. These are useful with preprinted forms.

Self-inking die plate stamps may also be purchased. You can use these to show such variables as time, date, and year, and they are also available as self-inking sequential numbering devices.

Carefully worded stickers may do the job of forms in certain circumstances. For example, routing of documents, message taking, and payment reminders can be dealt with in this way.

```
          ROUTING REQUEST
Please
❑ READ
❑ HANDLE          To _____
❑ APPROVE            _____
and                  _____
❑ FORWARD            _____
❑ RETURN             _____
❑ KEEP OR DISCARD _____
❑ REVIEW WITH ME  _____
Date _____   From _____

                            File No. _____
```

Stickers

F26 DESIGNING BUSINESS FORMS

Forms must be well designed so that they are effective working tools, economical to produce, and a favourable reflection of the company image. Business forms should be designed with the primary goal of speeding the flow of information. Poorly designed forms that are difficult to understand will waste employees' time.

Business forms producers and the larger stationery and office supply houses will assist you with forms design. Keep the following points in mind.

F27 APPEARANCE

◆ Aim to achieve a sense of balance and neatness.

◆ Conform to company style and standards.

◆ Use white space, screens (tints), rules, colour, reverse captions (white on black), highlighting, and boxes for emphasis, clarity, and readability.

◆ Use different typeface styles and boldfacing or italics to add variety.

F28 WORDING, INSTRUCTIONS, AND USEFULNESS

◆ Show a short, clear title or heading at the top of each form (e.g., "Invoice," "Purchase Order").

◆ Use simple language and avoid abbreviations that might be confusing (e.g., not everyone might know that "DOB" means date of birth).

◆ Preprint as much information as possible (e.g., if your company's payment terms are always net 30 days, print it on the form).

◆ Include clear, simple completion instructions at the top of the form or in the sections to which they apply.

◆ Include routing instructions at the bottom of multi-part forms.

◆ Use box design for variable data and place boxes to the left of text if possible. (Box design ensures that information will be inserted in the proper place.)

Not recommended—too vague   Recommended—specific

◆ Keep similar information together (e.g., "Quantity," "Description," "Prices," and "Amount" columns) and co-ordinate the design of forms (e.g., purchase orders, invoices) that are related and contain the same details.

◆ Consider a form number-coding system for forms control.

◆ Prenumber in sequence most forms dealing with money as an aid to records management and accounting control (e.g., purchase orders, invoices).

◆ Carefully position address information so that window envelopes can be used. The mailing address must show through the window when the form is folded.

◆ Update forms/formats regularly for efficiency and productivity in the workplace.

F29 PAPER TYPE AND SIZE

- Consider whether forms are for inside or outside use; choose paper weight and quality on the basis of the form's purpose, its expected life, and the amount of handling it will receive.
- Use standard-sized stationery because envelopes, file folders, paper, and equipment sizes are standardized.
- Use interleaved carbon or, better yet, carbonless paper for forms in sets if an impact printer is to be used.
- Forms for machine applications require special attention to the needs of those machines.
- Forms to be stored in special containers must be designed and sized for that equipment.
- Comply with size limits such as those imposed by postal regulations.
- Colour-coding of paper in sets is useful for routing purposes.
- Use recycled paper where possible.

F30 SPACING CONSIDERATIONS

Allow sufficient space for filling in information and for any signatures needed. Take into account whether the form will be completed by computer (online) or in handwriting. More space would be required for handwriting.

F31 Forms Designed for Computer Use

Many business forms are produced for computer use. Such forms may be designed specifically for an organization or may be standard ones personalized with an organization's identification. Forms for computer use must be compatible with the software used so that lines, boxes, etc., are in the right place for the printed output.

These types of forms are available in multi-copy sets, carbon paper interleaved, or carbonless, and in various colours. Parts of the form may be blocked out if desired. For example, the last part of an invoice might have the price column blocked out so that it could be used as a shipping memo (delivery receipt).

F32 MAILING SETS

Suppliers also offer a one-part, self-contained mailer (mailing set) in continuous form for key business activities. This speeds mailing by presealing one or more inserts (including even a return envelope) into one outgoing mailing piece. Folding, stuffing, sealing, and postal metering are eliminated. Most self-contained mailers are for impact printers, but some are available for laser printers.

In the case of the monthly statement mailing set shown here, the external part of the mailing set provides a file copy. The mailer set is the envelope, a statement (which may include a remittance stub if desired), and a return envelope for payment.

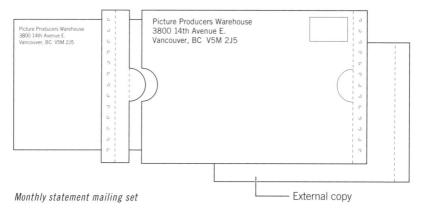

Monthly statement mailing set　　　　　　　└────── External copy

F33 COMPUTER-DESIGNED FORMS

You can reduce the time to design forms if the design is done on a computer, either with forms-design software or with desktop publishing software. Forms designed this way can be reproduced by a forms manufacturer, printed on an in-house laser, or used as electronic forms (forms filled in on-screen).

Electronic forms offer the advantages of increased productivity, greater accuracy (because some forms are practically self-completing), reduced costs, and improved forms control. They also relieve you of the burden of purchasing and storing paper forms that can take up office space and become outdated. Forms-design software offers two services: design tools and automation tools.

Design tools
- tools to create and maintain elaborate electronic and printed forms that can support all types of output—laser printers, dot matrix, etc.
- considerable numbers of templates of ready-made, customizable forms to help in forms design

Automation tools
- Electronic forms can be saved for access by others on a network.
- Completed forms can be saved directly into a database.
- Taxes, discounts, totals, etc., can be calculated automatically and totals categorized by type and time period if desired.
- Forms can be completed automatically with information from databases. For example, a purchase order form can be completed automatically with blocks of information saved from previous, similar purchases.

- Forms can be distributed by e-mail to decrease the need for paper and avoid the traditional mailing process.
- Forms can be re-routed and their progress tracked.

F34 OTHER FORMS-RELATED TECHNOLOGIES

Bar codes

A quick pass with a portable laser gun can replace several manual procedures. For example, it can replace a bulky invoice pack to show the contents of a shipment, what has to be done with it, where it has come from, where it has to go next, and when.

Electronic data interchange

It takes time and costs money to manually generate a paper form, duplicate it, process it, store it, and eventually destroy it. Therefore, completing business transactions electronically is recommended to save both time and money (see Unit 9).

Imaging and forms

Scanners with optical character recognition (OCR) software can automatically translate information from forms into data and store the image in a readily retrievable manner. Any type or size of form can be handled.

The system scans and converts forms as they are fed in. It produces an electronic image of the form, strips away all of the rules, lines, and preprinted information, and converts the remainder into computer data. Images of zones that cannot be read (e.g., handwritten information) are displayed on-screen so that an operator can enter and verify manually.

The image of each form can be held in optical storage and indexed so that fast retrieval is possible in the event of queries. Hard copies can be made as needed.

Pen-based computers

These small, hand-held computers allow the user to print directly onto a screen with an electronic pen. The form is displayed on-screen and the operator fills in information as check marks, letters, and numbers. The computer translates this into data to process immediately and transfers it to a larger computer for further processing. A customer signature can be captured on-screen for authorization of the transaction.

Voice-activated forms

A slow, well-modulated voice, speaking directly to a screen, can be used to complete forms without the need for keying. For example, a lawyer can fill in a standard legal form (e.g., a will) by calling the standard form onto the screen and speaking the details out loud.

Voice macros can be created to complete information known. For example, a code word could result in the completion of name, address, telephone number, and account number.

F35 Forms Control

Forms control is the planned and orderly management of all phases of a form—its authorship, design, specifications, ordering and reordering, storage and distribution, numerical control, and its function.

All of these phases must be managed to guarantee that the business form will perform the function for which it was intended within the business system. The goals of an efficient forms control program are to:

- maintain aesthetic design technique standards
- eliminate forms that perform the same functions
- ensure that forms are designed for economy, whether purchased from a supplier or produced internally
- provide well-designed forms that are effective working tools
- eliminate unauthorized forms
- review all forms to determine their usefulness and efficiency

F36 Government Forms

Government forms are always needed in the workplace for various government/workplace situations, i.e., applications for tax deductions, child tax benefits, claims for moving expenses, etc.

Frequently requested forms fall into two categories: Customs and Tax Forms. Some examples include:

Customs
AG1   General Declaration Form
B3   Canada Customs Coding Form
B4   Personal Effects Accounting Document Form

Tax forms
RC1   Request for a Business Number
RC66   Canada Child Tax Benefit Application
T1-M   Claim for Moving Expenses Form
T4   Statement of Remuneration Paid or Employment Income and Deductions Form

You can access these forms at the Government Forms Web site: www.ccra-adrc.gc.ca

8 HUMAN RESOURCES MANAGEMENT

CONTENTS

H

The success of any business organization depends on the effective management of its human resources (staff). Company policy must be fair and consistent in recruiting, training, motivating, paying, and caring for employees, and supervisors must have the skills and personal qualities to administer it. This unit looks at sound human resources management policies suitable for most firms, large or small, and outlines the supervisory techniques and qualities necessary for success.

Human resources management must be flexible, because it must meet the challenges of the changing workplace:

- ◆ changes in employment practices, with increases in contract work and employees working from home
- ◆ changes in the work force in gender and ethnicity
- ◆ focus on self-management and teamwork rather than traditional hierarchical or authoritarian approaches
- ◆ breaking down of traditional roles and decreased emphasis on status
- ◆ integration of many activities due to technology

H1   HUMAN RESOURCES PLANNING

In human resources planning, the first questions to assess are: What are the firm's needs for staff? How are these needs to be met? Most organizations favour the following systematic procedure in arriving at answers to such questions:

1. Study existing use of staff to see if greater efficiency can be achieved.
2. Predict future volume of work, based on the firm's long-range plans.
3. Forecast future numbers and types of employees needed to deal with the anticipated volume and types of work.
4. Seek input from existing staff about how work is currently done and how it might be done in the future.
5. Consider the present human resources inventory so that the anticipated contribution of the present staff to future needs is known.
6. Decide if full-time or contract workers would be best.
7. Plan the recruitment of the right numbers of appropriately qualified staff.

H2   RECRUITMENT OF STAFF

H3   JOB ANALYSIS

People involved in recruiting must be properly prepared and know the details of any job to be filled. The position must be clearly defined (usually by a department manager or other executive) and a job description drawn up. A typical job description shows: title, location, responsibilities, hours of work, equipment used, skills and other qualifications needed (including education and experience), salary, and opportunities for promotion.

Job descriptions are useful in other ways. They can be used in advertising for staff and for acquainting new employees with their responsibilities.

```
                        JOB DESCRIPTION

  Title:        Administrative Assistant

  Department:   Sales

  Supervisor:   Jason Hayward

  Hours:        8:30–4:30              Salary:   $25 000–$30 000
```

Skills and Training

The position demands excellent written and oral communication skills. Ability to compose responses to routine communications is essential. A knowledge of all basic business procedures is required. Exceptional interpersonal and public relations skills are mandatory. This tends to be a high-pressure job at times. Flexibility and the ability to prioritize tasks are needed. Skill in word processing and spreadsheet preparation is required. Excellent English language skills are essential. Promotion to sales staff is possible after one year.

Education and Experience

Must be post-secondary business graduate. Business experience desirable (preferably gained full-time but could have been acquired through co-op or part-time employment).

Duties

1. Responding to routine sales inquiries.
2. Dealing with customer queries in writing, by telephone, and in person.
3. Maintaining department records management system.
4. Planning meetings and making travel arrangements for department executives.
5. Conducting research as needed.

Typical job description

H4   RECRUITMENT PROCEDURE

Human rights legislation (Section 15 of the *Canadian Charter of Rights and Freedoms*) affects the staff selection procedures (wording of advertisements, information required on application forms, and questions that can be asked during interviews) and precludes discrimination in hiring practices, levels of salary, and conditions of employment. This legislation varies with each province but, essentially, discrimination is not allowed on the basis of race, colour, national or ethnic origin, age, gender, religion, marital status, conviction for an offence that has been pardoned, and physical disability. Check the legislation that applies in your province.

Employment equity plans also exist in many organizations. Known also as affirmative action, employment equity involves taking note of past cases of possible discrimination and setting up procedures to ensure that such situations are remedied and that new ones do not occur. This could involve people with physical or intellectual disabilities, native peoples, women, men, and people of all races and religions.

H5   SOURCES OF APPLICANTS

- ♦ personnel already employed (promotion from within or lateral transfers)
- ♦ advertisements placed in local or national newspapers or on the organization's home page on the Internet
- ♦ student services or placement offices of schools, colleges, and universities
- ♦ employment agencies and human resources consultants
- ♦ applications already on file
- ♦ recommendations of other employees
- ♦ walk-in applicants
- ♦ professional associations
- ♦ local Canada Employment Centres
- ♦ local union offices

▶ H6   Advertisements

The job description can serve as the advertisement for most of the sources of applications shown here. Advertisements placed in local or national newspapers or professional journals will require special treatment. A well-written advertisement gives a complete, clear description of the job and strikes a suitable balance between over- and underselling the position.

Hints for effective advertising
- ♦ Be specific. Avoid vague expressions such as "good wages," "pleasant working conditions," "good personality needed," "large," "progressive," "expanding," or "leading" company.
- ♦ Limit each advertisement to one job.
- ♦ Aim to attract the most suitable applicants for the job, not just to obtain a large response.
- ♦ Choose newspapers with care. Some are best for management positions, others for clerical positions.
- ♦ Advertise in newspapers toward the end of the week, as there is a larger readership then.
- ♦ Remember that mention of salary can be a natural screening device.
- ♦ Gear the size of the advertisement to the importance of the position.
- ♦ Follow the provisions of federal and provincial human rights codes.
- ♦ Be truthful. If the job has many routine aspects, say so. Applicants do not want to waste their time applying for the types of jobs they do not want, and employers do not want to screen unsuitable candidates.

H

JR. ADMIN. ASST.

Admin. asst. required for busy sales dept. to respond to sales inquiries. Excellent language skills essential. Other duties include making travel/meeting plans, maintaining records management system. Word processing, spreadsheet skills needed. Post-sec. business grad with some experience. Excellent promotion prospects. Salary range $22 000–$26 000. 3 weeks' annual vacation. Dental plan. Send written application with résumé to B & G Specialty Products Ltd., 1349 Portage Ave., Winnipeg, MB R8A 2N9 or fax to (204) 837-0191.

Concisely worded advertisement

H7 THE APPLICATION FORM

The application form must provide a detailed yet pertinent description of the candidate. Care must be paid to its design so that the form:

◆ gathers sufficient relevant information

◆ provides enough writing space for full responses

◆ meets federal and provincial legislative requirements

◆ is clearly worded

The form should be divided into five sections: *personal, education, work experience, interests,* and space for any *additional information* the candidate may wish to provide. Since the form may be the only source of information on some applicants, provide enough space to write in starting and finishing dates with other employers so gaps that may require explanation are apparent.

NOTE Review the design and wording of the application form from time to time to make sure it is still effective. An electronic master will make updating easy.

H8 SCREENING

Screening is the process of narrowing down applicants so that only the most appropriate candidates are interviewed. Applications are sorted on the basis of how well applicants match the job specifications (close, possible, unsuitable). Interview appointments are made with suitable applicants and letters of regret (see Unit 1, C154) are sent to the others. If the organization intends to reply only to those selected for interview, state this in the advertisement as a courtesy.

NOTE Keep application forms of possible future candidates on file and reactivate them when job openings occur.

H9   THE INTERVIEW

The interview:

- helps the employer assess details that are not apparent in the application form or résumé—appearance, attitudes, ambitions, skills
- gives the applicant a chance to discuss details not present in the advertisement—salary, working conditions, promotion possibilities, fringe benefits

▶ H10   How to conduct an interview

Be properly prepared

- Prepare a list of the desired applicant characteristics, such as qualifications and experience, personality and attitudes, general intelligence, special aptitudes, interests, and career goals.
- Be familiar with the details of the job being applied for and the special skills needed, as set out in the job description.
- Review the applicant information already on hand—covering letter, résumé, application form.
- Have questions ready. Be objective—ask the same carefully thought-out questions of all candidates. (In wording questions, consider the provisions of your provincial Human Rights Commission.) Questions should, of course, be designed so that they capture information appropriate to the job description.
- Create a chart that allows you to evaluate on a scale each candidate's response to set questions. This is especially useful when more than one company representative is involved in the interview.
- Where two or more people form an interview team, decide on the areas to be covered by each person and the procedure to be followed.

Make the applicant comfortable

- Do not keep the applicant waiting.
- Be the first to offer a handshake.
- Indicate clearly where the applicant is to sit.
- Provide a comfortable chair and be sure not to put the candidate at a disadvantage (e.g., ensure that the applicant's chair height is not lower than that of the interviewer's or that the sun is not shining in the applicant's eyes).
- If possible, sit on the same side of the desk as the candidate so that there are no artificial barriers between you.
- Applicants are likely to be nervous, so make them feel comfortable enough to present a fair picture. You must therefore lead the interview and the discussion at first.
- Use a language level appropriate to the candidate.

H

- Be warm and friendly and give your full attention to establish a good rapport.
- Avoid interruptions such as telephone calls.
- Avoid making long notes during an interview; take brief notes about each candidate.

Give the applicant an opportunity to respond

- Be a good listener.
- Word questions so that they encourage a full response, not just a "yes" or "no" answer.
- Allow sufficient response time so that you can determine each applicant's ability to think and to express him- or herself quickly and clearly. Time taken to respond will also indicate a great deal about the candidate's confidence and attitudes.
- Ask applicants to explain their specific interests and goals and why they feel suited to the position.
- Gently probe any vague answers, gaps, tendencies to change jobs, or personality conflicts.
- Invite questions.

Provide all details of the job

- Offer a full description of the position.
- Outline company policy, fringe benefits, promotion possibilities, etc.

Closure

- End on time.
- If a person is obviously unsuitable, try to indicate this gently at the interview. Giving false hope is not kind.
- If a person is a likely candidate, try to give a definite date by which you will be in touch again. He or she may be considering other jobs.
- Find out when the applicant could start if chosen for the job.

Record your reactions

- Before you go on to the next interview, write up a full impression of the applicant who has just left. It may be a few days before you refer to this application again and you might confuse candidates.
- Complete the interview chart if you prepared one.

▶ H11 Tests

- Don't test for the sake of it. Tests are not necessarily good indicators of a candidate's probable performance on the job. An applicant's portfolio of job samples might serve just as well.
- Allow for nervousness.

◆ Provide a comfortable test setting and adequate equipment and supplies.

◆ Make your testing relevant (e.g., ask an administrative assistant to produce a finished letter from a rough draft rather than to take a five-minute speed test).

◆ Use testing material that does not contain unusual terms peculiar to your firm.

▶ **H12   Follow-up to the interview**

◆ Create a short list of possible candidates, ensuring that those listed closely match the job description.

◆ Depending on the firm's policy:
  • check references
  • arrange for a medical examination
  • set up a second interview that involves the candidate's prospective supervisor

◆ Offer the position to the best candidate and confirm all details in writing.

◆ Contact the unsuccessful candidates as soon as possible.

◆ Keep on file the records of candidates who might be suitable for future job openings.

H13   ORIENTATION

A careful orientation and initial training program is necessary for all new employees. This can be a difficult time for them. As soon as they begin work—or shortly after—they should be properly informed about the company's products or services, facilities, policies, structure, and senior management. Acquaint them with their supervisors and with company work standards; explain their jobs and the roles their jobs play within the organization. Let staff know of the arrival of new employees, and ask one person to be responsible for a newcomer's orientation for at least the first few days.

The supervisor should check periodically to identify problems early and deal with them quickly.

H14   TRAINING AND RETRAINING

New employees may require training if applicants without the necessary skills are hired (e.g., someone with word-processing knowledge but without experience on the particular software used).

Training of existing employees (retraining) may be required because of changes in office technology, a lack of trained personnel in certain fields, the need for trained backup staff for some specialized positions, or because of company restructuring.

Training programs are available from several sources, including the following.

Equipment manufacturers or vendors

Programs offered by equipment manufacturers or vendors are usually short and do not permit effective monitoring to ensure that each student has understood every step. Supervisors should not, therefore, expect total proficiency immediately. Follow-up sessions may be necessary.

In-house

If employees need in-house training on new equipment or software, manufacturers frequently offer self-instructional materials. These materials include audiotapes, videotapes, interactive video instruction (where the learner can see, hear, and do), or computer-aided instruction provided on computer software or CD-ROMs.

Allow time for the employee to complete the self-instructional program and then gradually to become involved in actual applications. A knowledgeable person (a trainer) should be available at all times or employees should have access to the problem "hotline" service provided by many manufacturers and vendors.

The person selected as a trainer must:

◆ have considerable knowledge of the equipment or process being taught

◆ want to do the training (the best qualified operator may not always be the best teacher)

Schools and colleges (public and private)

Public and private educational institutions provide adult training and retraining programs. Contact local boards of education and community colleges for details. Private colleges are listed in the Yellow Pages of the telephone book.

Seminars, workshops

Professional consultants offer training programs on a wide range of business procedures, philosophies, and systems.

H15   STAFF MANUAL

A well-prepared and well-maintained staff manual is invaluable. An up-to-date manual provides useful background information for new employees and for temporary and contract workers, and it facilitates job-sharing and flextime situations.

Ideally, the staff manual should be keyed on a computer and saved. If the company is served by a computer network, all employees can access parts of the manual as needed; there is no need to print it and it can be updated easily. Or, the manual should be prepared in loose-leaf format, so that only single pages will require revision. Keep the manual current so that it maintains its usefulness. The staff manual should contain all or most of the following:

◆ company history and current information
◆ mission statements, detailing the company's goals
◆ general rules and procedures
◆ health and safety procedures
◆ organization chart of the company
◆ names and company positions of key personnel
◆ job descriptions
◆ telephone extension and electronic mailbox numbers

H16 EMPLOYEE EVALUATION

H17 REGULAR PERFORMANCE REVIEW

Job performance reviews are designed to identify dissatisfied employees; unsuitable employees; employees in need of assistance, another job elsewhere within the company, or transfer to another department or branch; employees ready for promotion; employees eligible for salary increases or bonuses. To keep the employee evaluation unbiased, use a carefully designed rating form.

The employee evaluation might be based on quality of work, productivity, initiative, interpersonal skills, attitude and co-operativeness, punctuality, and attendance. Two approaches that might be used in the evaluation process are:

◆ The supervisor might complete a performance appraisal form, then discuss it with the employee and invite reaction.
◆ The employee might be invited to fill out the evaluation form for discussion with the supervisor.

The firm's human resources policy should provide for a follow-up interview with a new employee after the first few days and then for a regular review either at annual or semi-annual intervals, depending on the job.

PERFORMANCE APPRAISAL FORM

Name

Job

Department   Supervisor

Date of last review   Present salary

Each of the skills listed below is to be rated as follows:
A - Strength   B - Meets requirements   C - Needs improvement   D - Not applicable

KNOWS THE JOB		COMMUNICATIONS	
Understands job requirements, skills, and procedures		Listens and demonstrates understanding of information	
Keeps current in job-related knowledge		Writes clearly and convincingly	
Knows our industry and products		Speaks clearly and convincingly	
WORKS WITH OTHERS		**GETS THE JOB DONE**	
Works effectively as a member of a team		Follows up on all required aspects of jobs/projects	
Helps others with work-related problems		Meets deadlines	
Gains the co-operation of others		Produces quality work	
Keeps supervisor and others informed		Pays attention to accuracy and detail	
MANAGES THE WORK		**Produces required quantity of work**	
Identifies and analyses problems and recommends solutions		Exercises good judgment	
Sets demanding but realistic goals		Finds innovative approaches	
Establishes sound priorities		**ADDITIONAL SKILLS**	
Keeps on top of all jobs/projects			
Monitors and operates within budget			
Manages time effectively			

Supervisor's comments and recommendations

SIGNATURE

Employee's comments

Date of review   SIGNATURE

Employee rating form

▶ H18 How to conduct a review

The supervisor should:

◆ use an employee rating form
◆ evaluate frequently and regularly so that the appraisal contains no surprises
◆ allow sufficient time for a full discussion with the employee
◆ be familiar with the job being evaluated (reviewing the job description ahead of time is useful)

- listen carefully
- be as objective as possible
- avoid personal discussion
- give credit where it is due and do not permit the review to be for negative criticism only
- establish reasonable objectives with the employee so that a campaign for improvement can be set up
- criticize the work, not the person

H19 TRANSFER POLICY

Transfer means to move from one job to another in the organization usually without a change in responsibilities or salary (known also as a *lateral move*). Not all employees want to change jobs; some are content to stay put and will decline transfer or promotion possibilities. Employees may initiate transfer requests or management may seek them when:

- an employee is unsuited to his or her present job
- a staff member has personality conflicts with colleagues
- changes in technology and company restructuring have caused changes in the nature of the work
- work in a particular department has decreased
- change is necessary because of unpleasant or routine jobs
- there is concern for older or disabled workers
- an employee's interests and skills change

When management initiates the transfer, the employee should be informed of the reason for the move. An unexplained transfer can cause concern not only to the employee but also to colleagues.

When the employee initiates the request, he or she should give a reason and the request should be carefully considered. Flimsy or "heat of the moment" reasons should never be the basis for a transfer request.

H20 PROMOTION POLICY

Promotion means advancement of an employee to a more responsible and better-paid job. A firm's promotion policy should be to promote someone already on staff (promotion from within) and might be based on: *equality of opportunity* (any suitably qualified employee is invited to apply); *merit* (the ability to do a job well); and *seniority* (length of service). Separately, merit and seniority as the only bases for promotion have definite disadvantages:

- Merit alone may unfavourably affect the morale of very experienced senior but less able employees.

- Seniority alone, although impartial, could prevent the best candidate from getting the job and could be discouraging to new, ambitious, and able staff members.

A fair promotion policy, therefore, mixes merit and seniority.

H21 DISMISSAL AND RESIGNATION

▶ H22 Dismissal

The dismissal of an employee may be unavoidable because of loss of business or company reorganization, takeover, merger, or closure. It may also arise because of employee incompetence, personality conflicts, dishonesty, or failure to comply with company policy. Whatever the cause, dismissal is a very serious matter and should be the subject of a clearly defined policy.

- All dismissals should be based on careful documentation. Employees should first be warned and given an opportunity to change.
- Care should be taken not to influence negatively a person's chances for employment elsewhere.

Except in rare cases (e.g., being discovered in a criminal act), notice of dismissal must be given in writing. The length of notice will depend on the nature of the job, the length of employment, and the contractual agreement with the company. Check with your provincial department of labour to clarify the legal requirements in your province.

In a legal sense, there are two ways to dismiss or terminate an employee: "with cause" and "without cause." In Ontario, the onus is on the employer to prove cause for dismissal, rather than for the employee to prove there is no cause for dismissal; i.e., the employee is presumed innocent until proven guilty. Economic downturns, corporate restructurings, angry disagreements, and the like do not constitute "cause" in a legal sense. If the employer decides that an employee must be terminated and the employer knows or is advised by a lawyer that there is no cause, an agreement will have to be reached with the employee. A list of what should be considered when determining cause follows.

Rules to prove cause for termination

1. Give the employee written warning.
2. Advise the employee of the standard of competence required.
3. Inform the employee that her or his job is in jeopardy.
4. Tell the employee *exactly* what must be done to improve job performance.
5. Give a reasonable time or opportunity to improve job performance.
6. If possible, show the employee how her or his job performance compares to others in the same job category.

7. Demonstrate that the employee has had reasonable opportunity to learn the requirements of the position.

8. Show access to adequate training.

9. Prove that what the employee did, or did not do, damaged the organization.

10. Advise the employee at the time of termination that it was a result of incompetence.

11. Show that the company did not contribute materially to the employee's incompetence.

12. Show that the incompetence is not due to temporary factors.

13. Do not give positive evaluation/letters, salary increases, or merit bonuses prior to termination.

14. Ensure that incompetence is balanced against previous evaluations, years of service, and pressures of age, long service, and change.

For more information, obtain a copy of the *Employment Standards Act* for the province or territory involved. See additional information regarding the *Canadian Human Rights Act* at the end of this unit.

► H23 Resignation

Treat resignations with the greatest seriousness. Obtain a reason for every resignation so that you might:

♦ encourage a valued employee to stay

♦ resolve the underlying problem

H24 EMPLOYEE RECORDS

Keep a file or computer record on each employee in a system that assures confidentiality. The file might contain:

♦ application form and correspondence (including references from previous employers, if appropriate)

♦ current personal particulars

♦ periodic evaluation reports

♦ attendance record

♦ salary record

♦ courses and additional training taken

♦ job description of the position presently held

♦ an indication of career potential and interests

Consult the file or computer record for promotion opportunities. Therefore, in the employee's best interests, records must be complete and up to date.

H25 PAYMENT POLICY

A firm's payment policy will be based on:

◆ legal minimum rates
◆ the need to attract and keep the right kind of employee
◆ the need to keep employees motivated and satisfied

A payment policy must be competitive with that of other firms in the area and in similar businesses, and provide for regular pay increases to cover:

◆ increases in cost of living
◆ rewards for length of service
◆ merit

When a labour union is involved, payments will also be influenced by the union contract.

▶ H26 Establishing pay scales

The decision as to how much to pay one employee in relation to another is best determined by an accurate and fair evaluation of each job. This might be achieved by classifying jobs in order of importance or difficulty and establishing a pay scale for each category.

▶ H27 Fringe benefits

Fringe benefits are supplements to income. They are designed to encourage more and better work and to keep employees contented. Benefits vary with the size and success of the business. Paid annual vacations and some insurance benefit payments are required by law (see Unit 6, FM62, FM63). Other benefits might include paid sick leave, profit-sharing plans, bonuses, flexible working hours, supplementary pension plans, supplementary health insurance and dental plans, group life insurance, staff discounts, payment of education fees, subsidized recreational facilities, seasonal gifts, subsidized meals, child care facilities, and other employee assistance services.

NOTE Fringe benefits are not usually available to temporary or contract workers.

H28 WORKING ENVIRONMENT (ERGONOMICS)

Ergonomics is the term used to describe the compatibility of workers with their machines and surroundings. Supervisory staff should be concerned that the physical and psychological needs of employees are met in their working environment. Office design, lighting, acoustics, heating and ventilation, colour, office landscaping, furniture, and safety are critical factors to an employee's well-being and productivity. More detailed information on ergonomics is provided in Unit 3.

H29 SUPERVISING THE STAFF

H30   MOTIVATING

High employee morale leads to greater productivity. Lateness, absenteeism, poor work, and carelessness are minimized when employees are satisfied with their working conditions. Although outside influences over which the firm has no control may affect employee morale, supervisors can regulate the following on-the-job factors.

Nature of the work   The job should be interesting and worthwhile, with clearly defined objectives, responsibilities, and lines of authority. Recognition for a job well done should be given, and promotion should be a possibility.

Working conditions   These should be safe, pleasant, ergonomically sound, and should include rest and eating areas.

Pay and fringe benefits   These should be competitive with those paid in the same locality and/or industry for similar skills, education, and experience. Regular review is required.

Treatment by others   Employees must understand that their opinions and their problems will be considered.

Security   Employees need to be in an atmosphere where they feel that they are important to the organization and that the organization has genuine concern for their well-being, safety, and future.

Communications   Employees need to have a sense that they know what is going on. Keeping people informed fosters self-esteem and is an important motivator.

H31   QUALITIES OF A GOOD SUPERVISOR

Different management techniques can be used, depending on the culture, administrative structure, and management philosophy of the organization. Most companies today favour a team approach: Managers and supervisors do not make decisions in isolation—they encourage employee input in the form of ideas and concerns, and use this information in final decision making. Today's supervisors need to provide motivation to win worker commitment, not to try for absolute control.

Good supervisors support management in achieving the firm's objectives, know how to recruit the best people, and strive to help employees to realize their full potential. The following suggestions will help you to be a good supervisor:

- Be an excellent role model.
- Demonstrate effective interpersonal and public relations skills.
- Look for better and cheaper ways of performing tasks.
- Set achievable guidelines and objectives as to quantity and quality of work expected.
- Provide clear instructions and easy-to-follow procedures.
- Create a motivating atmosphere (see previous section).
- Foster team spirit.
- Let people know they matter and that their jobs are important.
- Resolve conflicts.
- Give recognition when due.
- Listen to people and encourage them to share ideas and views.
- Know when training, retraining, change, and job enrichment are needed.
- Be concerned about continuing professional growth and development of yourself and your staff.
- Delegate responsibilities to enable employees to develop skills.
- Be a creative problem solver and a capable decision maker.
- Welcome change and be prepared to lead the way.
- Encourage protection of the environment, for example, through recycling of paper, coffee cups, bottles, etc.
- Know how to deal with emergencies:
  - Fire: Know where the firefighting equipment is kept and know the escape routes.
  - Accidents: Know where the first-aid supplies are kept and who on staff has first-aid training.
- Be conscious of the need for safe practices in the office and in handling and transporting dangerous substances.

H32   TAKING A TEAM APPROACH

Many of today's companies are downsizing and reorganizing due to economic pressures, increased competition, and advancing technology. A team approach is therefore increasingly necessary within and among company departments and divisions. Effective teams have a common purpose that the group understands and pursues. A team approach has these advantages:

- It encourages equity and efficiency.
- It creates energy as the team works toward a common goal.
- It has a flexible structure but an orderly organization.
- It permits staff to develop multiple skills.
- It allows staff to set up the most appropriate local system.
- It makes best sense in a computer environment.

◆ It encourages innovation.

◆ It fosters team spirit.

◆ It creates a sense of belonging and trust.

◆ It encourages learning, as teams pursue new ideas together and engage in joint problem solving.

◆ It ensures that team players understand the objective and have a sense of direction.

◆ It encourages team members to focus on the objective and communicate well with each other.

H33 CONFLICT RESOLUTION

Conflicts resolution is an important leadership skill. Conflict need not be thought of as totally negative. Properly managed, it may bring about creative solutions that can improve the workplace atmosphere and result in increased productivity. Reaching toward a situation in which both sides become winners—a win-win approach—is the most desirable. In handling conflicts:

◆ Give both sides a hearing.

◆ Persuade each side to state the problem from its viewpoint.

◆ Persuade each side to see the problem from the other's point of view.

◆ Encourage each side to work with the other to find a solution that both can live with and that allows the self-esteem of each to remain intact.

Negative feedback and counselling

Positive feedback that is sincere and appropriate helps to create a productive and contented work force. However, there are times when negative feedback is required, such as for unnecessary absenteeism, poor punctuality, or other forms of cheating. The supervisor must deal with these promptly so that the employee can be turned around. The following are useful guidelines:

◆ Stay calm.

◆ Arrange a private interview.

◆ Give very specific details of the behaviour being discussed, stating days, times, etc. Criticize actions or behaviour, not the person.

◆ Explain the effect of this behaviour on other team members.

◆ Ask the employee to explain the behaviour.

◆ Listen carefully and encourage a full account.

NOTE   Some problems may not be work-related, but due to home difficulties, illness, drugs, or alcohol.

◆ Encourage the employee to suggest how to change the behaviour.

◆ Agree on a plan that includes time lines for change. Be positive and supportive; do not threaten.

◆ Arrange for or suggest professional counselling if necessary.

◆ Arrange a follow-up or series of follow-ups to monitor improvement.

NOTE Arrange the interview for early in the day so that there is time later to speak to that person in a friendly way.

◆ Resolve a conflict as soon as possible; positive resolutions contribute to a healthy work force and workplace.

◆ Identify the following workplace irritants: the office gossip, negativity in the office, jealousy among employees, and the "martyr (poor me) syndrome." If an employee identifies with any of these, meet with him or her to discuss the situation and the importance of a positive work ethic.

H34 TEMPORARY HELP

H35 FINDING TEMPORARY HELP

If you need additional help for short periods of time (to cover vacations, inventory-taking, etc.), temporary workers are available from a number of sources:

◆ agencies that specialize in providing skilled help of all kinds; the employer pays the agency and the agency pays the temporary employee. Investigate more than one agency (check the Yellow Pages for a list of local agencies). Find out how each agency operates:
  • Are employees bonded (insured as to their honesty)?
  • Have employees been tested?
  • Does the agency handle all payment details?
  • Is satisfaction or a fast replacement guaranteed?
  • Can the agency handle requests at short notice?

◆ advertisements

◆ Canada Employment Centres

◆ former employees

H36 MAKING THE BEST USE OF TEMPORARY HELP

To obtain the best value for your temporary-help dollar, organize the temporary helper's work in advance and:

◆ Provide a properly equipped work space.

◆ Have all necessary supplies available.

◆ Supply as many written instructions as possible (e.g., a style manual or job models).

◆ Have reasonable expectations.

◆ Be available to answer questions.

NOTE See Unit 21 for hints on using word-processing temporary help.

H37 WORKING IN A UNIONIZED ENVIRONMENT

Many companies in Canada are unionized, and employees perform their daily tasks through job description guides, workplace conditions, and for wages that have been agreed upon by management and the union.

A union consists of members (employees/workers) in a company or organization. Elected representatives, known as a union committee or the local executive board, represent the workers and meet with management at regularly scheduled meetings (usually monthly) to discuss benefits, wages, and working conditions.

Union members pay dues, usually monthly through payroll deductions, to support union activities (day-to-day expenses, strike fund, etc.)

Issues that are not resolved at the local level are handled through a grievance procedure. A grievance report is filed and both sides address the issues outlined in the grievance. If agreement cannot be reached in a designated period, the grievance proceeds to arbitration. At this level all issues are resolved.

Members vote on contracts by secret ballot. Contracts are finalized when the majority of workers approve the acceptance of the agreement. Working contracts must be signed by both parties before they are implemented in the workplace.

Union dues are tax-deductible.

H38 THE *CANADIAN HUMAN RIGHTS ACT*

The *Canadian Human Rights Act* sets out clear guidelines regarding discrimination, and these must be considered in human resources management: "Every individual should have an equal opportunity with other individuals to make for himself or herself the life that he or she is able and wishes to have, consistent with his or her duties and obligations as a member of society."

The *Canadian Human Rights Act* (Section 2): Discrimination
Discrimination means treating people differently, negatively, or adversely without a good reason. As used in human rights laws, discrimination means making a distinction between certain individuals or groups based on a prohibited ground.

Under the *Canadian Human Rights Act*, it is against the law for any employer or provider of service that falls within federal jurisdiction to make unlawful distinctions based on the following prohibited grounds:

◆ race
◆ national or ethnic origin
◆ colour

- religion
- age
- sex (including pregnancy and childbirth)
- marital status
- family status
- pardoned conviction
- physical or mental disability (including dependence on alcohol or drugs)
- sexual orientation

Everyone is protected by the *Canadian Human Rights Act* in dealings with the following employers and service providers:

- federal departments, agencies, and Crown corporations
- Canada Post
- chartered banks
- national airlines
- interprovincial communications and telephone companies
- interprovincial transportation companies
- other federally regulated industries, such as certain mining operations

All provinces and territories have similar laws forbidding discrimination in their areas of jurisdiction.

The *Canadian Human Rights Act* deals with discriminatory behaviour in its various forms:

- differential treatment of an individual or a group of individuals based on a prohibited ground
- all forms of harassment
- systemic discrimination—a seemingly neutral policy or practice that in fact is discriminatory

Employment A person cannot be denied a job because of a disability that does not affect job performance or that can be reasonably accommodated.

Employment applications and advertisements Federally regulated employees cannot include requirements that are not clearly related to the job, such as previous Canadian experience.

Equal pay A job performed mostly by women cannot be paid less than a job of equal value done mostly by men. Examples of jobs that might be of equal value are nursing assistants and electricians or secretaries and maintenance staff.

Employee organizations Because of provisions in certain collective agreements, some unions enjoy a monopoly on referring job applications to employers. It is discriminatory for such unions to exclude designated group candidates as referrals.

Provision of goods and services   A bank cannot ask a married woman for her spouse's signature when applying for a loan.

Reasonable accommodation   An individual unable to work certain days for religious reasons may not be denied employment if reasonable accommodation is possible.

Discriminatory notices   A poster that encourages discrimination is illegal.

Hate messages   Pre-recorded telephone hate messages are forbidden.

Harassment   Making demeaning comments because of the person's colour, ethnic origin, age, disability, sex, or any of the grounds in an employment or service situation is prohibited under the Act.

Harassment includes, but is not limited to:

- inappropriate or insulting remarks, gestures, jokes, innuendoes or taunting about a person's race, ancestry, place of origin, colour, ethnicity, citizenship, creed, sex (gender), sexual orientation, handicap (disability), age, or record of offences
- unwanted questions or comments about an employee's private life
- posting or display of materials, articles, or graffiti, etc., which may cause humiliation, offence, or embarrassment on Code prohibited grounds.

Sexual harassment

Sexual harassment is one or a series of comments or conduct of a gender-related or sexual nature that is know or ought reasonably be known to be unwelcome or unwanted, offensive, intimidating, hostile, or inappropriate.

Employees and students have the right to be free from:

- sexual solicitation or advance made by a person in a position to confer, grant, or deny a benefit or advancement
- reprisal or threat of reprisal for the rejection of a sexual solicitation or advance where the reprisal is made by a person in a position to grant, confer, or deny a benefit or advancement

Sexual harassment includes, but is not limited to:

- unwelcome remarks, jokes, innuendoes, or taunting about a person's body, attire, gender, or sexual orientation
- unwanted and inappropriate physical contact, such as touching, kissing, patting, hugging, or pinching
- unwelcome enquiries or comments about a person's sex life or sexual preference
- leering, whistling, or other suggestive or insulting sounds
- inappropriate comments about clothing, physical characteristics, or activities

- posting, keeping, or displaying materials, articles, or graffiti, etc., that are sexually oriented, including electronic publishing of same
- requests or demands for sexual favours that include, or strongly imply, promises of rewards for complying (e.g., job advancement opportunities, improved academic grades) and/or threats of punishment for refusal (e.g., denial of job advancement or job advancement or job opportunities, diminished academic grades)

All or part of these grounds may create a negative environment for individuals or groups and may "poison" the work environment. It includes conduct or comment that creates and maintains an offensive, hostile, or intimidating climate.

Exceptions

The Act provides for exceptions such as:

Bona fide occupational requirement   A job may be refused to a person who cannot perform it safely, efficiently, and reliably.

Bona fide justification   A service may be refused to a person when it cannot be offered without undue costs.

Equal pay guidelines   A difference in wages between men and women performing work of equal value in an establishment may be justified by different performance ratings, seniority, red-circling, training and rehabilitation assignments, internal labour shortages and surpluses, and regional wage rates.

Maternity and child care   An employer can grant workers special leave or benefits in connection with pregnancy or childbirth, or for the care of their children.

Mandatory retirement   A worker can be retired at the age that is "normal" for the kind of work involved.

Age guidelines   Lower transportation fares are permitted for children and senior citizens.

The Canadian Human Rights Commission

The Canadian Human Rights Commission administers the *Canadian Human Rights* Act and ensures that the principles of equal opportunity and non-discrimination are followed in all areas of federal jurisdiction. The commission, composed of two full-time and up to six part-time commissioners, meets regularly to decide on individual complaints and to approve commission policies.

Complaints

When the Canadian Human Rights Commission receives a complaint, it follows the following process:

- It determines if the commission is the right agency to handle the complaint. If yes, the complaint is accepted for investigation. If no, it is referred to another agency that might help.

- An investigation begins; sometimes it results in an early settlement to which both parties agree.
- If the complaint cannot be settled, a report is prepared for commission review.
- The commission may dismiss the complaint, appoint a conciliator, or send the complaint to a Human Rights Tribunal.
- The conciliator tries to settle the complaint by reaching an agreement acceptable to the two parties. If conciliation does not result in a settlement, the case is returned to the commission for a decision. The case may either be dismissed or sent to a tribunal.
- At the tribunal, a hearing takes place where a written decision is given. Unless appealed, tribunal decisions are binding on the parties.

Appeals

Tribunal decisions can be appealed to a review tribunal or to the courts, by the complainant, the respondent, or the commission, depending on the circumstances. Review tribunal decisions can be appealed to the Federal Court or in some cases to the Supreme Court of Canada.

Right to protection

The *Canadian Human Rights Act* provides for fines up to $50 000 for threatening, intimidating, or discriminating against an individual who has filed a complaint, or for hampering the investigating process.

- For more information, contact the Canadian Human Rights Commission:

National Office

Telephone:	(613) 995-1151
Fax:	(613) 996-9661
DD/TDY:	(613) 996-5211 (Deaf and Hearing Impaired)
E-mail address:	http://www.info.com@chrc-ccdp.ca or call 1-800-999-6899 to contact the following regional offices: Atlantic Provinces, Ontario, Quebec, Prairie Provinces, Alberta, B.C., and Northwest Territories.

9

INFORMATION PROCESSING AND INTEGRATED OFFICE AUTOMATION/NEW TECHNOLOGY (NT)

CONTENTS

IP

Advancements in technology that have improved information processing—in processing words and data, in storage, and in communications—are individually enormously impressive. However, the *integration* of these functions is where the major excitement lies and where the greatest impact on office life and information management is felt.

In the past, information was processed in a one-step-at-a-time fashion. Now, information processing is increasingly automated and performed as a single operation.

The extent to which organizations are using office automation technologies varies with size and need. This unit will introduce the separate components and build toward the ultimate—electronic business, where integrated technologies in one organization are meshed with the integrated technologies of trading partners so that entire trading operations can occur with very little human intervention.

This unit describes the excitement, challenge, and possibilities of integrated office automation technologies (OA/NT).

NOTE More detailed information on the separate components of information processing can be found in Unit 2, "Computers: Hardware and Software"; Unit 4, "Desktop Publishing"; Unit 5, "Electronic Mail"; Unit 14, "Meetings, Conferences, and Teleconferences"; Unit 16, "Records Management"; Unit 19, "Telephone Techniques and Services"; and Unit 21, "Word Processing."

IP1 INFORMATION PROCESSING

Information processing is the term used to describe the manipulation of all forms of knowledge expressed in words, numbers, graphics, and images, and by the human voice.

Information processing in the automated office is achieved through the integration of people, systems, procedures, and technology. For example, under one linkage, data and word processing, financial management, electronic mail/messaging, database management, document distribution, and information storage and retrieval can be achieved and communicated in a highly efficient and cost-effective way.

In today's world, information is needed fast. Technology is constantly being redesigned and improved to meet this need. More and more, the business world is taking advantage of the time savings and cost-efficiencies that technology makes possible in information processing functions and tasks.

IP2 INFORMATION PROCESSING TECHNOLOGIES

The following table shows the types of information that might be processed, kinds of information processing systems, and the communications links available for transmitting processed information to those who need it.

Information Processing Systems and Communications Links		
Types of information to be processed	**Information processing systems**	**Communications links**
words	word processing	e-mail
data (numbers and symbols)	data processing	facsimile
	reprographics	linked computers
graphics (drawings and illustrations)	records management	local-area networks
voice (the spoken word)	voice processing	modems
	image processing	teleconferencing
images (e.g., photographs, videos, microforms)		wide-area networks

IP

Word processing describes the equipment, people, and methods used in the production of a document.

Data processing means changing raw facts (letters, numbers, symbols) into usable information.

Reprographics covers methods of reproducing or duplicating information.

Records management describes the control of a firm's records. With some procedures, some records never appear on paper.

Voice processing means that the human voice originates and/or edits information.

Image processing means converting images into a digital form acceptable to a computer. Material for imaging can even include photos and handwritten notes, typed invoices or preprinted forms, and newspaper clippings.

Communications links are the electronic means of moving information over a distance.

In some organizations, these information processing technologies are operated independently as their own departments (e.g., word processing, records management). In others a co-ordinated plan links the technologies and creates an integrated automated office.

IP

IP3 TYPICAL INTEGRATED OA APPLICATIONS

Many tasks can benefit from integrated office automation, ranging from the relatively straightforward production of a document for a mass mailing or a report produced collaboratively (as described in the following examples) to the highly complex electronic data interchange (EDI) described in the next section.

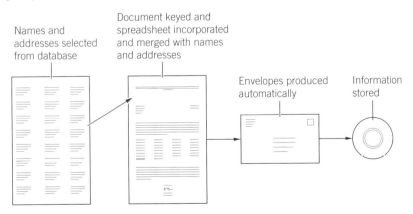

Names and addresses selected from database

Document keyed and spreadsheet incorporated and merged with names and addresses

Envelopes produced automatically

Information stored

Automated letter production for mass mailing

Examples of integrated activities

1. An administrative assistant keys in a letter to all shareholders and incorporates a spreadsheet report produced earlier in the accounting department. The letter is automatically merged with names and addresses selected from a database that contains all of the company's contracts.

2. A report is to be produced for distribution to members of the board and to department heads at remote locations. Several staff members are involved. During production, the network allows them all to work on the report at the same time and send it back and forth instantly for editing and polishing. When completed, the report can be printed by laser as camera-ready copy. Advanced reprographic technology means the copier used to produce the report can automatically collate, insert dividers, staple, bind, and provide a cover. Soft copies of the report can be distributed to the staff at remote locations through the network for printing and binding there if needed.

3. Where an organization has taken advantage of image processing technology, dealing with a customer's inquiries is very straightforward and speedy, as the following example illustrates.

   • All of the records related to a particular customer are scanned and saved electronically on optical disk. An employee dealing with a customer inquiry can instantly call up on a computer screen every document related to that customer (relevant correspondence, records of telephone conversations, etc.) and satisfy the client without delay. When image processing is not used, each of these records would be kept in a separate records management system and several time-consuming searches would be needed to assemble all of the relevant information.

IP

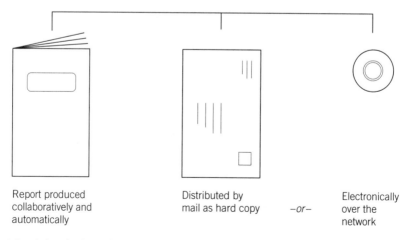

Report produced collaboratively and automatically

Distributed by mail as hard copy

–or–

Electronically over the network

Automated production and distribution of a business report

4. Communication software packages permit travelling business people, newscasters, sportscasters, and others to keep in touch with the home office. These integrated communication packages (also referred to as groupware) are used for:
   - checking calendars and scheduling appointments, meetings, etc.
   - decision making through information transfer
   - electronic messaging: retrieving and sending e-mail
   - image and graphic transfer
   - information sharing with corporate databases (e.g., spreadsheet updates, etc.)

IP4 ELECTRONIC BUSINESS

Electronic business (e-business) is the online buying and selling of products or services. The sale may be consumer to consumer or business to business, and should involve Internet protocols beyond mere voice transmission (voice over Internet protocol). The information processing technologies used in one company are meshed with technologies in others so that computers exchange documents with minimal human intervention. It means that employees can be freed from the grind of data re-entry and assume more creative roles in *exception processing* (dealing with orders that are in some way unusual). Electronic data interchange (EDI) is one type of electronic business that demonstrates the workings of the process.

IP

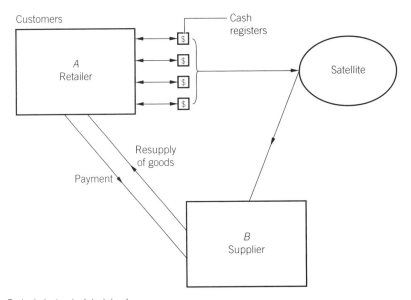

Typical electronic data interchange process

IP5 EXAMPLE OF EDI IN OPERATION

A large retailing giant (A) in dealing with a major supplier (B) does not place orders. A connects its point-of-sale terminals (cash registers) directly to B's computers. Bar codes on the products let A's computers know how many of which B products are sold and this information moves to B by direct satellite transmission. That, in turn, activates a re-supply command for the number of items required to keep A in stock. A pays when the goods leave the shelves—but not by cheque: funds are deposited electronically in B's account and arrive with enough information to make clear the reason for the remittance. No purchase order, no shipping notice, no invoice, no cheques, are involved. This reduces inventory-control problems, increases profits, decreases paper use, and virtually eliminates keying errors.

Governments and banks are already substantial users and will become bigger users, and transportation companies are turning increasingly to EDI.

Security of information is not a problem because of the security codes built into the process.

.IP

IP6 ADVANTAGES OF INTEGRATED OFFICE AUTOMATION/NEW TECHNOLOGIES

Increases productivity and efficiency
◆ Eliminates many tedious tasks.
◆ All users on a network can access and share data and processing capability.
◆ Letters, reports, and other communications can be composed, edited, formatted, distributed, stored, and printed in one process.
◆ Forces rethinking of outmoded methods (e.g., the need for certain forms).
◆ Standardization is promoted because the same software can be used throughout an organization.
◆ People can better understand the operation of the entire organization.
◆ Practically eliminates human error.
◆ Access to outside (subscriber) databases and the Internet (see Unit 10, "Information/Reference Sources and the Internet") can provide a wealth of information on any subject to any terminal.

Speeds up information interchange
◆ Information can be electronically communicated instantly within the same building, across the country, or across the world in an immediately usable form.
◆ Voice and other messages can be stored and forwarded to reduce telephone interruptions and "telephone tag."

Maximizes equipment use

◆ One person can perform a variety of complex tasks working at a single PC.

◆ Expensive equipment such as laser printers can be shared.

Minimizes software costs

◆ A licence for using expensive software in a network can be cheaper than buying separate pieces of software for stand-alone workstations.

Improves competitiveness

◆ Because of fast communications, customer service can be improved.

◆ Twenty-four-hour global communication is readily available.

◆ Interbranch information exchange—credit checks, approval of copy for advertisements, confirmation of large orders, agreement of contract terms—can be instant.

◆ Electronic commerce is made possible (see this unit, IP4).

Decreases duplication of effort

◆ Duplication of effort among departments is lessened because communication and sharing are possible.

IP

Increases storage and retrieval speed

◆ Information stored electronically on magnetic disk or tape, on optical disk, or on microfilm can be rapidly retrieved by many users.

◆ Databases make possible storage and retrieval of many kinds of information that can be cross-referenced and retrieved by several users in various formats.

Improves management effectiveness

◆ Administration, management, professional, and technical personnel can deal with information and ideas still being worked on. For example, spreadsheets allow instant calculation and recalculation; communications links permit transmission of this data for the reaction of others.

◆ Rapid receipt of information and faster decision making increase efficiency and competitiveness.

◆ Managers responsible for productivity can monitor staff performance through computers.

◆ Those involved in writing tasks have access to word-processing capability, can draw on information sources instantly, and can rapidly produce statistical information in attractive formats with ease.

◆ Staff is provided with an easy way to schedule and co-ordinate appointments and meetings through software and the communications network.

IP7 NETWORKING AND COMMUNICATIONS

IP8 NETWORKS

A computer network links expensive hardware, software, and peripherals in the same building or building complex by telecommunications. Computers within a networked system can share files and send messages and documents back and forth. Terminals can access software and information from a central source, process information in a variety of ways, use peripherals in the network, and communicate with other workstations.

Networking may be achieved in a number of ways. The two basic methods are:

Shared-logic system   Several dumb terminals (ones without processing ability) and peripherals share the storage and processing power of one central, or host, computer.

Shared-resource system   Intelligent terminals (ones with their own processing power) are linked so that they share printers and other peripherals.

▶ IP9 LANs and WANs

Networking may be over a local area (LAN) or a wide area (WAN). Connection is by transmission lines that can be of several types.

LANs are privately owned. They connect small groups in a small area—a building or group of buildings.

◆ Usually, they connect PCs to one another.

◆ They can connect microcomputers to a PC or mainframe.

◆ Some systems are multi-tasking, allowing several users access to large amounts of data at the same time. They can also handle numerous transactions from multiple users at the same time.

When communication is required over a larger geographic area than that provided by LANs, a communications server (a "gateway" or bridge) can link LANs and non-networked devices into WANs for long-distance interaction (across the country or around the world).

WANs are publicly owned and use satellites, telephone lines, microwaves, and dedicated communications channels to transfer data.

◆ They can connect to mainframes, minicomputers, and PCs.

◆ Online information services are available through WANs.

◆ WANs can provide access to remote banking, home shopping, and to electronic home bulletin boards.

NOTE   Many portable computers are "network ready," needing only a telephone jack to access data from an office computer or to send messages to anyone on the office network.

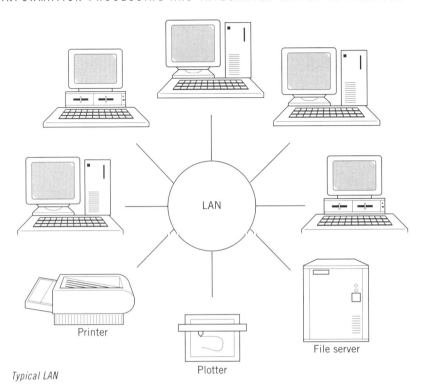

Printer

File server

Plotter

Typical LAN

IP

▶ IP10 Network configurations

In networks, equipment may be linked in various patterns (topologies or network configurations). The most frequently used are shown here.

Ring
Information is communicated by being relayed around the circle in sequence through each device.

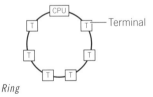

Ring

Peer to peer
Like ring, except that every desktop in this network has equal prominence, which is made possible by software known as *groupware* (see Unit 2, "Computers: Hardware and Software").

Star
◆ Each device has direct contact with the central controller. Terminals (nodes) do not depend on the operations of each other.

IP

• All communications pass through the central computer. Terminals cannot talk directly to each other.

• The file server is usually dedicated.

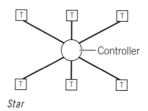

Star

Totally connected (point to point)

• Direct contact is made between each node.

• Because of cabling difficulties, only a few devices can be accommodated.

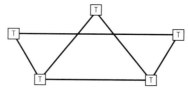

Totally connected

Hierarchical (or tree)

• This type is useful when all information does not have to be shared with the entire network on a regular basis.

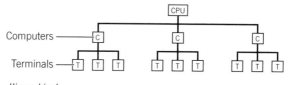

Hierarchical

Bus

• This offers an open communications channel.

• It can move around the organization, joining equipment as needed.

• No central computer is necessary.

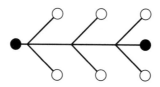

Bus

NOTE LANs may also be *wireless* (i.e., they allow computers within small areas to communicate with one another without the need for cables).

IP11 RE-ENGINEERING FOR INTEGRATED OA/NT

Today, more than ever, workers are faced with information overload; the amount of information available is growing through the use of the Internet/Intranet and the increased range and connectivity of communication media. It is essential that the data available be organized, analyzed, interpreted, and turned into useful information.

Some organizations move gradually into integrated office automation, in stages. As their needs change, they increase the degree of sophistication. However, the results of simply layering technology on top of current work practices may prove disappointing, because this may produce only localized, individual task-level improvements.

A productive environment comes through careful management of people, productivity, and time, and working toward clearly identified goals. To achieve this may lead to the redesign of entire processes, not just to automating some of them. This redesign is known as *business process re-engineering*. The four stages involved in re-engineering are:

IP

* Recognizing that change is necessary
* Analysing the present processes and environment and understanding the shortcomings
* Designing a new and harmonious work environment that ensures optimum productivity
* Implementing (i.e., making the transition from the old to the new)

To achieve a successful and effective re-engineering, certain criteria must be established:

* Equipment and software must be fully compatible and networkable. Purchases must be carefully controlled so that both immediate and future needs are considered.
* Staff must be accepting of, and involved in, the change-over process; they must be provided with suitable training or retraining and they must receive support as they make the adjustment to new procedures and equipment.

IP12 WORK MANAGEMENT

Improving performance is a major challenge for every organization. At the executive level, supervisors must identify what knowledge is needed, which employees can handle specific tasks, and how this knowledge can be used to improve products, services, and client/customer relationships. Most importantly, employees must be part of an ongoing cross-training process, and feel secure in the new technologies (NT) as they are introduced in the workplace.

Work management ensures that *all* participants in the work process have *all* of the information needed to do the job, and access to the required knowledge to complete the job successfully.

Three basic principles of successful work management:

◆ *Performance* — the effective application of technologies to contribute to the design and performance of business objectives

◆ *Potential* — work management technologies that complement and maximize existing basic business technologies

◆ *Productivity* — a business/organization is more efficient when its processes are specifically designed to produce a desired result

IP13   RETURN ON INVESTMENT (ROI)

IP

Businesses are always looking at the bottom line or for a good **return on investment**. This can be achieved through the following:

◆ customer response time — keep up-to-date information about the customer and product to reduce call-backs and unnecessary paperwork

◆ inventory control — maintain an up-to-date filing system to avoid lost and misplaced documents

◆ reduction in errors — provide proper training to eliminate the need to redo a job due to lack of training or outdated technologies

IP14   IMPACT OF INTEGRATED OA/NT ON PEOPLE

The impact of integrated OA/NT on office organization structures, on personnel, on job qualifications required, on procedures, on training, and even on job locations is significant.

◆ More fulfilling jobs are emerging and more routine ones are being eliminated as technology deals with routine activities.

◆ All office staff must be computer literate (understand computer capabilities and the terms involved) and all office workers should have keyboarding skills.

◆ As staff spend increased hours at computers, ergonomic and work environment concerns are important (see Unit 3, "Efficiency, Time Management, and Ergonomics").

◆ New skills and attitudes are needed. Employees will require strong interpersonal skills and will need to view themselves as team players.

◆ People must be flexible and accepting of change. As technology and software advance and improve, we will need to welcome it and reap its benefits.

♦ Office staffs must appreciate that new skills will be needed continuously and be ready to accept retraining as.

IP15 CAREERS IN INFORMATION PROCESSING

Information processing is creating new career possibilities. In particular, opportunities exist in:

- communications management
- equipment use
- consulting
- network designers or service and systems analysis
- equipment sales
- equipment and software training

Careers also exist in

♦ troubleshooting/problem solving

♦ help-desk advisors

IP16 NEW TECHNOLOGIES (NT)

Information processing is a field of enormous growth and never-ending advancement. Just a few of the important emerging technologies include the following.

Open systems This technology enables something that runs on one computer operating system to run on another (i.e., computers are able to "talk" more easily), resulting in a totally flexible, networked computing environment. For example, companies can connect directly online with customers, suppliers, business partners, and others.

Convergence (The Information Highway) Made possible by digitization, convergence is the coming together of computers, broadcast telecommunications, entertainment technology, and media via a single fibre-optic wire.

♦ Interactive telecomputers will be capable of displaying everything you will ever need.

♦ Computer screen and TV set will become one, and a mouse will be able to summon anything you want.

♦ Electronic shopping, banking, medicine, education, news, and politics will be available without your leaving the home.

Personal digital assistants Advances in wireless technology mean voice, data, and video can be merged and picked up on new pocket-sized terminals known as *personal digital assistants* (PDAs). They fit a fax machine, database, and notepad into one hand-held device that provides almost an office desktop.

Bar-coding Bar codes are a pattern of stripes that contain a wealth of data. Light and dark areas are read by a laser scanner and translated into data. Some can be read in two dimensions—width and height. One quick pass with a laser gun replaces several manual procedures. Barcoding is useful in integrated systems:

♦ for indexing purposes

♦ to replace some paper documents

♦ for labelling with detailed warnings or detailed histories

Data Warehouse Traditional operational systems involve the keying of information into a database. This information must be analysed and managed efficiently and safely. Today, many companies are establishing decision support systems built around a data warehouse.

The process of "data warehousing" is the means of getting information from business transactions, storing it, making it accessible for designated employees, and providing users with the tools to analyse the data and make better business decisions. The data warehouse also consolidates data from a wide variety of existing analytical systems in organizations.

Features of a data warehouse system:

♦ provides accurate, high-quality data pertinent to the decision-making process

♦ offers an ongoing and integrated view of data

♦ enables easy access to the data

♦ provides timely access to data through efficient automated data gathering and delivery processes

♦ offers effective access interface technologies

♦ affords flexibility to grow and adapt to changing business requirements

Smart cards A large memory on a small chip makes the smart card ideal for portable storage of data that is constantly changing.

Smart cards look like credit cards but are entire microprocessors with memory chips embedded in them and can change a piece of plastic into a fully functioning computer. They can, for example:

♦ be used to pay highway tolls without the driver needing to stop

♦ be used for building or individual office entry, cafeteria lunch payment, or vending machine purchases

♦ permit access to computers or other equipment

♦ carry complete medical records

♦ contain pictures, fingerprints, or retinal scans for user identification

10 INFORMATION/ REFERENCE SOURCES AND THE INTERNET

CONTENTS

IR

IR

The volume of business-related information available is staggering and ever-increasing. To keep pace with it is impossible for the human mind. Therefore, the secret to success in this area is not *knowing everything* but *knowing where and how to find information*. This unit will provide useful guidelines to help in your search.

First, we will examine the most authoritative printed sources of information as consulted most often by businesspeople and in the categories they use most frequently. Next, we will review comprehensive coverage of electronic information retrieval, today's computer-based way of obtaining information and doing research. Finally, we will outline the many services provided by libraries and the Internet.

IR1 PRINT INFORMATION SOURCES

IR2 ALMANACS AND YEARBOOKS

Almanacs may be most usefully described as "grab bags" of assorted information. This information includes weights and measures, government addresses, proper forms of names for visiting dignitaries, radio and TV listings, obscure facts, or perpetual calendars—all can be found in a general almanac.

Specialized almanacs focus on national information for their country of publication. For example, the front cover of the *Canadian Almanac and Directory* notes that it includes information on abbreviations, honours and titles, associations and societies, broadcasting and communications, religious organizations, commerce and finance, electoral districts, geography, foreign and international contacts, health and hospitals, general and historical facts, the postal service, and tourism and transportation, as well as a cultural directory, an education directory, a government directory including reference contacts, and a legal directory. There are also business, sports, and weather almanacs, which cover a particular subject field in the same comprehensive way.

Yearbooks provide an overview of the past year's events. Specialized yearbooks deal specifically with a defined type of information (e.g., statistics) or with the information of a particular subject field (e.g., articles in *The Modern Plastics Yearbook* detail some of the technological advances made over the year in this field, combining advertisements, specifications, and reference tables with a directory-type buyer's guide).

- *Canada Year Book*. Ottawa: Statistics Canada.
- *Canadian Almanac and Directory*. Toronto: Canadian Almanac & Directory Publishing Co. Ltd.
- *Canadian Annual Review of Politics and Public Affairs*. Toronto: University of Toronto Press.
- *Canadian World Almanac*. Toronto: Global Press.
- *The Broadcasting Yearbook*. Ed. Donald V. West. Washington, DC: Broadcasting Publications.
- *The Europa World Year Book*. London, England: Europa Publications.
- *Statesman's Yearbook*. Ed. John Paxton. London, England: Macmillan Press.
- *The World Almanac and Book of Facts*. New York: Newspaper Enterprise Association.

IR3 ATLASES

Atlases contain detailed maps, as well as statistical and descriptive data about regions and countries of the world.

- *The National Atlas of Canada*. Toronto: Macmillan, in association with the Department of Mines and Resources, Ottawa.
- *The New International Atlas*. Chicago: Rand McNally.
- *The Times Atlas of the World*. New York: Times Books, a division of the New York Times Book Co. Inc.

IR4 BIOGRAPHICAL REFERENCES

These supply data about famous people in the present and past. Biographical dictionaries such as *The Macmillan Dictionary of Canadian Biography*, *Who's Who in Canada*, and *Canadian Who's Who* provide information about individuals in a dictionary format, i.e., individuals are listed alphabetically by surnames. The information is concise and factual, somewhat like a résumé, without analysis or commentary on the data. Each entry includes such elements as family information, date of birth, education, marital status, business background, important positions held, achievements, and any honours received.

◆ *Canadian Who's Who*. Toronto: University of Toronto Press.

◆ *Current Biography*. New York: H.W. Wilson.

◆ *International Businessmen's Who's Who*. London, England: Burke's Peerage Ltd.

◆ *Who's Who in Canada*. Toronto: Global Press.

◆ *Who's Who in Canadian Business*. Toronto: Trans-Canada Press.

◆ *Who's Who in Canadian Finance*. Toronto: Trans-Canada Press.

◆ *Who's Who in Canadian Law*. Toronto: Trans-Canada Press.

◆ *International Who's Who*. London, England: Europa Publications.

◆ *Who's Who in America*. Chicago: Marquis Who's Who Inc.

◆ *Who's Who in the World*. Chicago: Marquis Who's Who Inc.

NOTE For information about notable people no longer alive, refer to encyclopedias or to the *Dictionary of National Biography* of the relevant countries.

IR

IR5 DICTIONARIES

Dictionaries contain words that are listed alphabetically, usually with the following information:

◆ *definitions*

◆ *preferred form of spelling* if more than one is acceptable

◆ *syllabic division* shown by a heavy accent, light accent, centred period, or hyphen

◆ *correct pronunciation* indicated by accent marks—a heavy one ($\bar{e}$) shows special emphasis; a lighter mark ($\breve{e}$) denotes less stress

◆ *part of speech*: if more than one is indicated, any change in pronunciation will also be shown

◆ *derivations of words* (their origins) in square brackets at the end of an entry

◆ *synonyms and antonyms* indicated by *syn* and *ant* at the end of an entry

◆ *usage examples* in phrases and clauses to complement the common definition and clarify usage

◆ *prefixes and suffixes*, with their definitions

Consult the front of the dictionary for detailed information on etymology (word origins), pronunciation, and abbreviations used in the dictionary. The alphabetical list of words is sometimes followed by an addendum of words not listed in the body of the dictionary and further senses and constructions of words already treated, plus a section on abbreviations and foreign words and phrases. Some dictionaries also supply information on international currencies, scientific and technical terms, titles of address, and weights and measures.

- *Gage Canadian Dictionary*. Toronto: Gage Publishing Ltd.
- *The Concise Oxford Dictionary of Current English*. Oxford, England: Clarendon Press.
- *Webster's Ninth New Collegiate Dictionary*. Springfield, MA: Merriam-Webster Inc.

Specialized dictionaries are available for most professions as well as for scientific, technical, and trade specializations. Examples include:

- *Terminology for Accountants*. Toronto: Canadian Institute of Chartered Accountants.
- *The Business Dictionary*. Englewood Cliffs, NJ: Prentice-Hall Inc.
- *Dictionary of Computing*. New York: Oxford University Press.
- *Black's Law Dictionary*. St. Paul's, MN: West Publishing Co.
- *Black's Medical Dictionary*. London: A. & C. Black.
- *Blakiston's Gould Medical Dictionary*. New York: McGraw-Hill.
- *Dictionary of Scientific and Technical Terms*. New York: McGraw-Hill.

IR6   DIRECTORIES

▶ IR7   Business

IR

This section identifies several business, trade, and professional sources that list names and addresses of organizations, corporations, and chief executive officers, as well as products, services, and brand names.

Directories are lists of persons or organizations, arranged in some logical order, usually alphabetical. The telephone book is, of course, the directory format with which we are most familiar. Specialized directories provide information for a defined clientele, and are valuable tools for reference in the workplace.

- *Associations Canada: An Encyclopedic Directory*. Toronto: Canadian Almanac & Directory Publishing Co. Ltd.

  Annual publication that contains a list of Canadian and international associations in Canada, plus dates and locations of major conferences, shows, and meetings scheduled for the current year.

- *Blue Book of Canadian Business*. Toronto: Canadian Newspaper Services International.

  Information on and business rankings of major Canadian corporations.

- *Canadian Advertising Rates and Data*. Ed. Wayne Ibsen. Toronto: Maclean Hunter.

- *Canadian Key Business Directory/Répertoire des principales entreprises Canadiennes*. Toronto: Dun & Bradstreet Canada Ltd.

  Names and addresses of more than 20 000 companies by geographical location and type of business, plus names of key executives.

◆ *Canadian Trade Index*. Toronto: Canadian Manufacturers' Association. Alphabetical list of manufacturers, plus classified list of products.

◆ *Directory of Associations in Canada*. Ed. Lynn Fraser. Toronto: University of Toronto Press.

◆ *Fraser's Canadian Trade Directory*. Toronto: Maclean Hunter. Alphabetical list of manufacturers, plus a list of products by trade names and their manufacturers.

◆ *KWIC Index to Services*. Toronto: Ontario Ministry of Government Services.

◆ *National List of Advertisers*. Toronto: Maclean Hunter.

◆ *Scott's Directories, Ontario* Manufacturers. Ed. Cynthia D. Gardiner. Oakville, ON: Scott's Directories.

◆ *Standard and Poor's Register of Corporations, Directors and Executives*. New York: Standard and Poor's Corp.

◆ *The Financial Post Directory of Directors*. Toronto: The Financial Post.

◆ *The Fortune Directory*. Chicago: Fortune Magazine. Information on and rankings of the 500 largest industrial companies in the United States.

IR

▶ **IR8 City**

City directories provide information on local residents and companies. They usually contain the following sections:

Classified business directory Similar to the Yellow Pages of the telephone directory, with companies and services listed alphabetically.

Alphabetical directory Shows adult residents, their addresses, occupations, and marital status. Also included are business and professional organizations with the address, type of business, and official personnel of each.

Postal code directory Provides postal codes in alphabetical street order.

Street directory Lists each street alphabetically and indicates where intersections occur. The numbers of the residences and business organizations are arranged numerically under each street, and the names of householders and companies and their telephone numbers are placed opposite them.

Telephone number directory Contains a numerical listing with names and addresses of the subscribers beside each number.

Publishers of such directories include:

Halifax:	Might Directories
Toronto:	Bowers Metropolitan Cross Reference Directory Limited
Southern Ontario:	Vernon's Directory
Vancouver:	Henderson, Division of Polk Canada Limited

IR9 ENCYCLOPEDIAS

For historical facts and general information across all disciplines, people, and places of note, these sources are among the most common:

- *The Canadian Encyclopedia.* Edmonton: Hurtig Publishers.
- *Columbia Encyclopedia.* New York: Columbia University Press.
- *Encyclopedia America.* Danbury, CT: Grolier Inc.
- *New Encyclopedia Britannica.* Chicago: Encyclopedia Britannica Inc.
- *New Encyclopedia Britannica.* Chicago: Encyclopedia Britannica Inc.
- *Encyclopedia Canadiana.* Toronto: Grolier of Canada.

NOTE *Encyclopedia Britannica* is now available online without an access fee. (*Britannica.com* is a partner of *Washington Post/* www.washington-post.com).

IR10 ENGLISH LANGUAGE USAGE AND STYLE

The following selections contain information on the fundamental rules of grammar, punctuation, style, famous quotations, and synonyms and antonyms:

- *The Canadian Style: A Guide to Writing and Editing.* Toronto: The Department of the Secretary of State of Canada.
- *The Canadian Writer's Handbook.* Toronto: Prentice-Hall, Inc.
- *A Dictionary of Modern English Usage* (H.W. Fowler). Oxford: Clarendon Press.
- *Bartlett's Familiar Quotations.* Toronto: Little, Brown & Co.
- *Colombo's Canadian Quotations.* Edmonton: Hurtig Publishers.
- *Roget's Thesaurus of English Words and Phrases.* London, England: Longman.
- *The New Roget's Thesaurus in Dictionary Form.* New York: G.P. Putnam's Sons.

IR

IR11 FINANCIAL REFERENCES

Two of the publications issued by the major financial reporting organizations are:

- *Financial Reporting in Canada.* Toronto: Canadian Institute of Chartered Accountants.
- *Dun & Bradstreet Reference Book.* Toronto: Dun & Bradstreet Canada Ltd.

  Dun & Bradstreet will provide credit information and individual credit reports to subscribers.

  Members may also contact the local credit bureau for credit information.

IR12 GOVERNMENT REFERENCES

Federal

The publisher for the federal government is:

Canada Communication Group - Publishing,
Ottawa, ON K1A 0S9

This group is responsible for co-ordinating, publishing, distributing, and marketing priced federal publications, each of which is either produced or sponsored by a government department or agency.

- Topics include aeronautics, agriculture, art, communications, education, energy and natural resources, environment, fauna, fisheries, forestry, geography, geology, government and legislation, health and nutrition, history and archeology, labour, linguistics, marine, science and technology, sociology, trade, transportation, and weather.
- Priced publications may be ordered direct or through local booksellers.
- An annual catalogue of several hundred publications is available.
- Free publications are available from the departments that produce and publish them.

IR

Statistics Canada, a federal government agency, is responsible for publication of all statistical reporting.

The *Statistics Canada Catalogue* contains a list of publications that provide data on the primary industries, manufacturing, transportation, travel, commerce, education, health and welfare, and many other subjects.

Provincial

Provincial government publications on a variety of subjects are available from government bookstores. Each provincial government department produces its own publications. Contact local elected provincial representatives for government information as well.

IR13 OFFICE HANDBOOKS

For guidance on document formatting, business practices and etiquette, and English language conventions, refer to this handbook or to others that are available, including:

- *The Canadian Office.* Toronto: Addison Wesley Longman Ltd.
- *The Canadian Office Management Manual.* Vancouver: Self-Counsel Press.
- *The Gregg Reference Manual.* Westerville, OH: Macmillan, McGraw-Hill School of Publishing.
- *Robert's Rules of Order* (revised). Glenview, IL: Scott, Foresman and Company.
- *Emily Post's Etiquette.* New York: Harper & Row.

NOTE Maintain and update the following:

♦ reference manuals on the hardware and equipment used in your office

♦ reference manuals on the software used in your office (some of these are now available on CD-ROM)

♦ reference manuals related specifically to your organization (e.g., company policies and procedures)

IR14 PERIODICAL INDEXES

Titles of articles from magazines, newspapers, and journals are collected and organized for easy access in periodical indexes, most of which are now in electronic format. For example, *Canadian Business and Current Affairs* (*CBCA*) is a periodical index in CD-ROM format. It indexes articles from more than 500 Canadian sources including magazines, business journals, and newspapers, and is the best source to consult for Canadian information, data, and perspective.

Electronic formats allow fast and sophisticated searches of large information databases such as the *CBCA*, which allows searching by a variety of single and combined access points. The power of today's computers enhances the speed of information retrieval.

IR15 CLIPPING SERVICES

Rather than subscribe to periodicals, companies or individuals can pay for a clipping service, provided by firms such as the following:

♦ Canadian Press Clipping Service. Toronto: M.H. Media Monitoring (Maclean Hunter Ltd.).

Newspaper clipping and electronic clipping service for Canada and the United States:

♦ Electronic Clipping Services. Toronto: Southam Electronic Publishing.

IR16 POSTAL INFORMATION

Canada's Postal Code Directory provides a postal code for every address in Canada. Use the appropriate provincial section to ensure correct addressing of envelopes and faster mail delivery. Copies of this directory are usually available at post offices and postal outlets or can be ordered at the address shown below.

The *Canada Postal Guide* provides complete information on Canada Post services. For complex or unusual mailing situations, consult this guide or contact a Canada Post representative.

Copies of the directory and the guide can be obtained by writing to:

National Philatelic Centre
Canada Post Corporation
Station 1, 75 St. Ninian St.
Antigonish NS B2G 2R8

IR

For more information, call:
Canada Post Corporation (in the White Pages)
Customer Service Information   1-900-565-2633
www.canadapost.ca

IR17   TELEPHONE DIRECTORIES

These are issued by the telephone company. The Customer Guide in
the introductory pages at the front of the directory lists the following:

- emergency numbers
- home and business customer needs
- repair services
- local bell world stores
- local 10-digit dialling
- payment choices
- phone services for people with special needs
- Bell SmartTouch™ Services, which include: call answer/call
  waiting/call forwarding, universal messaging, etc.
- privacy issues, e.g., obscene or harassing calls, telephone solicitation,
  etc.
- exchanges and communities in the directory
- directory assistance
- special calls and services, e.g., mobile and marine calls, conference
  calls, etc.
- local calls
- long distance calls
- area codes, e.g., area codes for Canada, the United States, and the
  Caribbean
- area codes time-zone map of Canada and the United States
- overseas calls, country codes, and dialling instructions
- billing information
- *quality of service standards and tariffs as regulated by the Canadian
  Radio-television and Telecommunications Commission (CRTC)
- terms of service
  *For independent telephone company customers, contact the
  company for standards.

The White Pages list individuals, businesses, and organizations
alphabetically.

The Blue Pages/blue-bordered pages list the three levels of government
alphabetically and by department, e.g., federal, provincial, and
municipal governments.

The Quick Finder Index is helpful for locating a specific product or
service.

IR

The Subject Index is a reference section of general categories to help find a product or service.

The Yellow Pages include an alphabetic and subject index of goods and services and, in many cases, give the Web site address of the company.

The Advertiser Guide is helpful for businesses that wish to advertise in the Yellow Pages. This section includes local and surrounding area guide maps.

For more information, call:

Customer Service Information   1-800-668-6878 or

www.bell.ca or E-mail: bell.direct@bell.ca

IR18   ELECTRONIC INFORMATION SOURCES

IR19   ELECTRONIC REFERENCE SOURCES

◆ Most word-processing software includes a dictionary to assist with spelling and many include thesauruses to provide alternatives to words.

NOTE   You can add new words or terms to existing spell-check packages (e.g., medical or legal terms).

◆ Grammar and style-checkers are also available in software to assist in the writing process.

◆ Dictionaries may also be purchased in electronic (small notebook) form.

◆ Some electronic translators contain two to five languages.

IR20   DATABASES

A database is a large volume of information stored in electronic format. Organizations may maintain databases of information relevant to their own organizations or they may use commercial ones.

▶ IR21   Commercial databases

Many hundreds of commercial databases cover most fields of knowledge. Some provide fast-changing (time-sensitive) information such as stock and commodity prices. Others provide information on business activities, the professions, education, industry, science, technology, political activities, issues, people, places, international news, airline schedules, weather, and sports. Most of the world's newspapers are available online, as are some books, reports, research documents, scholarly papers, encyclopedias, and periodicals. In fact, almost all information imaginable is available through a commercial database of some type. Many databases now use the Internet as a delivery mechanism.

IR

Databases can be used for keeping abreast of current events and for research purposes. For research purposes, two types of online text (or searching) services are available:

Bibliographic Searches in this type of online text database lead you to documents but do not provide the documents themselves (i.e., you obtain a *list* of published reference sources on the topic being researched).

Full text This type of service provides *all* of the article or paper being sought.

In the past few years, magazine publishers have become more comfortable with the concept of electronic access to the full text (often including images) of their articles. Many are licensing this data to electronic publishers for inclusion in reference databases. An advantage of a full-text database is the capability to perform a keyword search on the full text of an article, which can significantly increase the chances of retrieving information on a hard-to-find topic.

▶ **IR22 Major database services**

IR

Only a few of the major services and the types of information they provide are listed here. Fuller listings are provided in the directories listed in the next section. Most libraries offer free or chargeback access to databases. Consult the librarian to find the best database for information needs.

▶ **IR23 Database directories**

Among the large number of database directories available are:

◆ *CD-ROM Yearbook*. Redmond, WA: Microsoft Press.

◆ *CD-ROMs in Print—An International Guide* (annual). Westport, CT: Meckler.

◆ *Directory of Online Databases*. Detroit: Gale Research.

▶ **IR24 Using commercial database services**

Depending on the database being accessed, computer search requests can be made by author, title, subject, or key word(s). In searching, the computer looks for a match between words selected to describe the subject of the search and words used by the database service to index its collection of references. You "log on" (are connected) to the database by keying in a user number or password. Next, using specific commands or key words, define the parameters (framework) of the information sought (e.g., in researching women in Canadian business, you might indicate the time period from 1975 to today and specify the advertising industry). You then interact with the electronic files by responding to questions and eventually obtain a printout of the information. With some services, the printout is sent by fax, mail, or courier service to save online costs.

Deciding on the key words that will lead you to specific information is a highly specialized skill. Trained librarians can be very helpful since they are generally familiar with each service and can save online time.

▶ IR25   Cost

Charges for database use vary. Some are available on a flat fee subscription basis; others are charged on a pay-per-use basis. Although commercial database use may be expensive, users find the cost is generally offset by savings in time. In addition, some databases are an economical alternative to buying magazines and books.

▶ IR26   Advantages

While database services may be costly, the advantages are considerable:

- In-depth searches can be made quickly.
- The user is an active participant and can amend requests by interacting with the computer, if necessary, as searches progress.
- Re-searching using new key words or topics is possible. Manual searches would be too time-consuming to permit such re-searching.
- A far wider range of information sources is available than is possible through local library sources.
- The indexing provided by the database service offers more access to information than the indexing normally available for print media.
- Note-taking is unnecessary; results may be printed, downloaded, and even sent to an e-mail address.
- Costs of searching are specific and can be directly allocated to a project. Manual searches are indirect and difficult to cost.

IR

IR27   USING LIBRARIES

IR28   BOOK RETRIEVAL

All libraries, regardless of size or specialization, provide catalogues of the books and other materials they own. Catalogued materials are usually listed on a computer database easily accessible by clients. Many catalogues are now on the World Wide Web (WWW or the Web). You can search library catalogues in electronic format in a number of ways including by author, keyword, and format.

Classification systems

All libraries use a classification system to catalogue their holdings. The two most widely used are the Dewey decimal and the Library of

Congress systems. The Dewey decimal system is generally used in school libraries and public libraries. This system provides 10 major categories that are further divided into subcategories. The major Dewey decimal categories are:

000–099	General
100–199	Philosophy
200–299	Religion
*300–399	Social Sciences
400–499	Language
500–599	Science and Mathematics
*600–699	Applied Sciences and Industries
700–799	Fine Arts and Recreation
800–899	Literature
900–999	History, Travel, and Biography

*Most business information is contained in these sections.

The Library of Congress system is generally used in college and university libraries. This system provides 21 major categories, based on the alphabet, to classify the principal areas of knowledge.

IR

---

24 JAN 2002	MARKHAM COMMUNITY BRANCH CIRCULATION MODULE	02:22 pm

Call Number	ADULT NON-FICTION COLLECTION 651.30202 SMI 1999	Status : CHECKED IN
AUTHOR	Campbell, Joan I.	
TITLE	Pitman office handbook /	
EDITION	5th ed.	
PUBLISHER	Don Mills, ON. : Pearson Education Canada / 2002	
DESCRIP	vi, 603 p. : ill.	
SUBJECT(S)	1) Office practice -- Handbooks, manuals, etc.	

- - - - More on Next Screen - - - -

Press «Return» to see next screen :
Commands: SO = Start Over, B = Back, RW = Related Works, C = Copy status,S = Select, «Return» = Next Screen, ? = Help

Computer library reference

IR29 NON-PRINT MEDIA RETRIEVAL

Non-print media, such as films, records, and tapes, may also be sources of information and are available in or through most libraries. Although these may be stored separately from the books and periodicals, the cataloguing system is the same as that described for books.

IR30   ELECTRONIC INFORMATION RETRIEVAL (DATABASES)

Most libraries subscribe to commercial database services. Some libraries own CD-ROMs of encyclopedias and certain periodicals. Consult your librarian as to the electronic information retrieval services available to you.

NOTE   If the publication or item is not available at your particular library, most libraries offer rapid interlibrary communication. Consult the librarian, who can probably help with telephone, fax, or communicating computer service.

Since CD-ROM databases are usually purchased on an annual subscription basis, libraries can allow their users to spend as much time as needed in searching for the information they require.

Library Web site: www.lib.berkeley.edu/TeachingLib/Guides/Internet/
Tutorial Web site: www.albany.edu./library/internet/

IR

IR31   THE INTERNET

The Internet (the Net) was developed by the U.S. Department of Defense in the 1960s and was made available to the general public in 1984. The Internet is a communications network where a registered user can sign on to a huge worldwide "network of networks" to obtain information in a multi-media format that includes animation, graphics, text, video clips, and sound.

NOTE   No one owns the Internet.

The World Wide Web (WWW or the Web) is a user-friendly mechanism of the Internet. Anyone can publish information, then list it by subject matter, and users can easily gain access to this information. The Web is very popular for business, academic, and home use. Messages can be sent at any time of the day or night to connected users anywhere in the world.

IR32   HOME/SMALL BUSINESS USE

You will need a computer running Windows 98, with at least 64 MB of RAM. To get the most out of the Internet, your PC should have a fast processor, a V.90 56K modem, speakers and a microphone.

◆ Internet access—you must purchase Internet time from an Internet service provider (ISP) and arrange to connect your computer to the ISP's host computer.

IR33 INTERNET SERVICE PROVIDERS (ISPs)

The ISP maintains the host computer, provides a gateway or entrance to the Internet, and sets up electronic "mail boxes" with facilities for receiving and sending e-mail. The ISP charges a fee for access to the Internet and e-mail services. Each time you want to access the Net, you must log on. You will have to arrange to connect your PC to the ISP. There are four choices for the home computer:

Ways to Connection to An ISP		
Name	Speed	Connection
Dial-up	Slow	Regular telephone line*
ISDN (Integrated Services Integrated Network)	Medium	ISDN telephone line*
DSL (Digital Subscriber Line)	Fast	Regular telephone line*
Cable	Fast	TV cable

* The first three methods use a telephone line, therefore the telephone is inaccessible when someone is on the Net. Use a dedicated cable to avoid this problem. There is an additional monthly charge for cable.

Obtain the fastest Internet connection you can afford. DSL and cable are better than ISDN, and ISDN is better than a regular dial-up connection.

IR34 HOW TO CHOOSE A NET PROVIDER

◆ Reputation (word of mouth)—ask people who are connected; are they pleased with the service? Is online help available?

◆ Charges—get a flat monthly rate that is suitable for your needs, such as 10 hours or unlimited access for a higher rate. Some ISPs will offer the first month or two free. Use this free time to chart your use to enable you to select a suitable billing plan.

◆ E-mail sharing—will others (such as family members or roommates) be using the connection? If so, set up different e-mail addresses to avoid sorting mail. This is also recommended for a home-run business (keeps personal mail separate from business mail). Find out how many mail addresses are provided by the ISP.

◆ Technical support—is help available? 24-hour assistance? Is there a 1-800 number that can be called if needed? Do they provide help on their Web site?

◆ Local phone access—whenever you use the Net, your modem must dial the phone number of the ISP and connect to a modem at the other end of the line. Do you have a local access phone number?

◆ Waiting time for access—ask about the number of phone lines. You don't want to be kept waiting for long periods.

- Does the ISP provide software to new customers? Do you download the software yourself from the Internet? Is the software provided on disk? Do you need an Internet browser, such as Internet Explorer or Netscape, as well as e-mail and setup software?
- Does the ISP charge a fee to set up a personal Web page? (Most ISPs do not.)
- Does the ISP anticipate making any infrastructure repairs or improvements that could interrupt service?
- Are refunds available for customers who cancel the contract?
- How long has the company been in business?

IR35   INTERNET ADDRESSES

Searching the Net is a learned skill that is valuable for researching information, and when used properly, can save time and money and increase productivity in the workplace. This skill is also important for personal use, such as when researching topics for presentations, reports, etc.

Today's knowledge worker should be proficient in "surfing the Net" for accurate information.

Every host computer on the Internet is identified by a unique descriptive address. The address specifies the individual computer in the levels of organization or domain on the Internet. An e-mail address consists of a user name, the "at" symbol @, and the descriptive host name (e.g., jsmith@aol.com).

See Unit 5 for more information on electronic mail.

IR

TIP   Remember to keep an updated reference index of frequently used e-mail addresses/Web sites.

IR36   TIPS FOR SEARCHING THE NET OR WEB BROWSING

- Become familiar with the different search engines and tools on the Web, and use a variety to locate exactly what you are searching for.
- Only search the database of Web pages that a search engine or search directory has previously accessed and stored; do not search the entire Web.
- Bookmark favourite Web sites.
- Update Web sites; dead sites or sites that are no longer accessible are indicated by (error message 404).
- Beware of search engines with heavy advertising.
- Use the Find feature of your Web browser.
- Learn how to string together queries with search terms using search terms of **AND, OR, NEAR** and **NOT**.

  Search with the keyword **NEAR**, rather than **AND**, for words close to each other. For example, both of these queries **bank AND**

administrator and **bank NEAR administrator**, look for the words *bank* and *administrator* on the same page. But, with **NEAR**, the returned pages are ranked in order of proximity—the closer together the words, the higher the rank of that page.

◆ Use quotation marks around keywords if you want them to be taken literally, e.g., if you key "bank near administrator," the search engine will literally look for the complete phrase. However, if you key the same query without the quotation marks, the search engine searches all documents for the words *bank* and *administrator*.

◆ When you find the page(s) that meets your needs, go back to the search results page to find another page. Before you leave the first site, make a note of the links page; the links page usually leads to other similar sites that the search engine may not have found.

IR37   SEARCH ENGINES

With the creation of Web browsers several years ago, computer users are now spending hours surfing the Net. Remember that you are not searching the entire Web; you are only searching the database of Web pages that a search engine or search directory has previously sought out and stored.

A **search engine** is a program that can search a huge database for specific information, i.e., allows users to search for sites that contain the keyword(s) entered by the user.

Reputable editors seek out useful Web pages and information and collect directories of worthwhile sites. See the chart below.

How to Effectively Use a Search Engine

◆ Become familiar with the different search engines and tools on the Web and their characteristics and strengths.

◆ If the first two or three pages of Web sites do not provide the information needed, do not proceed with the remaining pages. Net search experts advise that it will be a waste of time. Try a different search engine or vary the search terms with similar words.

◆ Insert quotation marks around words that must be together, i.e., a name, "campbelljoan."

◆ Specify a list of words, then narrow it down, i.e., use a plus (+) sign to indicate only Web pages that contain a specific word; use a minus (-) sign to indicate only Web pages that do not contain a specific word.

◆ Remember that you can locate specific details by using the "Find" feature of the Web browser.

◆ Access online tutorials, take a course, or borrow one of the many books or magazines on this subject available at your local library.

Examples of Internet Resource Search Engines:
www.altavista.com/
www.google.ca
www.lycos.com/
www.webcrawler.com/
www.yahoo.com/

Another popular Web site that has an index of magazine articles is Northern Light (www.northernlight.com). This site charges a fee for access to periodicals.

NOTE To learn more about search engines and their characteristics: Librarians Index to the Internet: www.lii.org—open the folder: "Searching the Internet."

IR38   COMMON FILE EXTENSIONS USED ON THE WEB

Extension	Meaning
asp	Web page generated in a specific way
exe	Executable program
gif	Image/picture stored in GIF format
jpg	Image/picture stored in JPEG format
htm	Web page
html	Web page
txt	Plain text
wav	Music/sound file
zip	Compressed collection of files

IR39   FTP (FILE TRANSFER PROTOCOL) SITES/SPACE

All computers/servers that allow the File Transfer Protocol are also called "FTP Sites." Using FTP allows you to both download and upload files from FTP sites on the Internet. These files can consist of software, text, and graphics.

FTPSpace is Internet-accessible disk space or what is known on the Internet as a "server" or storage space for Web pages and other files that may be shared with the Internet, e.g., AOL (ISP) provides members with space (up to 2 MG of storage space to create Web pages). This is a free perk.

FTPSpace also contains a list of Web publishing tools that you can download and use to create Web pages. Some of these tools are free and others (such as Shareware) are not.

IR40   FREEWARE/SHAREWARE

As defined in Unit 2, Shareware is copyrighted software that the programmer makes available for personal use to others.

Many Web sites offer free software. Most of the programs will be either Freeware (no charge) or Shareware (try it and then pay for it if you decide to keep using it).

IR

NOTE Reputable Web sites/programs are virus protected.

For information on Web site rating systems, see the following:
- http://www.rsac.org/
- http://www.safesurf.com/

When you copy a file/Web page from a remote computer to your computer, this is known as a download. When you copy a file/Web page from your computer to a remote computer, this is known as an upload.

NOTE Files uploaded to your FTPSpace are available to anyone on the Internet, unless they are uploaded to a "private" directory; this directory is automatically created. Other people can upload files to the directory by creating an "incoming" directory.

IR41 DOWNLOADING A PROGRAM FROM THE INTERNET

Most programs consist of multiple files and all files are needed to use the program. To avoid unloading each file separately, gather the required files together and put them in a larger file called an archive. No matter how many files the program requires, only a single file, the "Archive" file, needs to be downloaded.

These files are compressed and therefore take less room, so it is faster to download the archive than it is to download the files separately. "Compressed format" means that the file has been altered to reduce its original size.

To download and install a program from the Internet:

◆ Locate the program you want.
◆ Download the archive for the program.
◆ Unpack the archive.
◆ Install the program.

When the downloaded archive file is completed, the compressed files needs to be decompressed and restored to the normal/original size (also called "unpacking" or "unzipping").

To search an archive, use a Usenet/Netnews Search Engine. These search engines access several articles that have been posted to newsgroups around the world.

When a file is downloaded from the Net, you can use two different systems:

1. HTTP—the protocol used to transfer information between Web servers and Web client/customers.
2. Anonymous FTP—free software available on the Internet that permits reliable, worldwide distribution of software and other data.

IR42   FIREWALLS

A firewall is a combination of hardware and software that protects computer networks from unwanted intrusions. Private networks/Intranets erect firewalls to prevent access to sensitive company data except for authorized personnel, i.e., passwords.

Public Internet sites also have firewalls to prevent unscrupulous people from accessing areas that store private information, e.g., credit card numbers, customer lists, etc.

IR43   USENET/NETNEWS AND USENET/NETNEWS SEARCH ENGINES

Usenet/Netnews is a global system of thousands of different "discussion groups/newsgroups"; these "newsgroups" send in articles and topics on current events nationwide.

Usenet/Netnews Search Engines allow you to access hundreds of articles that have been posted to all the newsgroups around the world. These search engines are free; they are run by companies that sell advertising for revenue.

IR

IR44   WEB PAGES

E-business (electronic business) or B2B (business to business) have created thousands of sites where the buying and selling of products takes place. To attract potential clients or customers, entrepreneurs should create their own Web pages. The Web provides a means of exposing their business or product to a wide audience.

Web pages use a text-based code called HTML (Hypertext Markup Language), which is used to connect related text, Web pages, and graphics. Web pages can only be accessed through (hosted by) an ISP (Internet Service Provider) or a free Web hosting provider, such as Yahoo, Alta Vista, etc. Web pages are stored as files on a Web server.

IR45   CREATING WEB PAGES

◆ Create a Web page using code, e.g., use a text-based code (HTML) to connect related text, pages, and graphics; small instructions called "tags" are used to format a graphics-based Web page.

◆ Create a Web page using Web design software; most ISPs provide software for Web-page design. Many office software packages also include Web page design formats.

◆ Hire a professional to create the Web page.

NOTE   The more graphics used, the longer it takes the reader to access the Web page.

IR46 SUGGESTIONS FOR EFFECTIVE WEB PAGE DESIGN

- Create a home page that acts as an entry to the whole Web site.
- Ensure the site is easy to read, pleasant to view, and well organized.
- Use a larger font or attractive graphic (one or two preferred) to draw the attention of the reader.
- Avoid using too much information.
- Avoid linking Web pages. If necessary, ensure users can easily navigate from the home page to secondary/linked pages.
- Do not use the "blinking" feature (words that blink or flash off and on); this is distracting to the reader.
- Do not use bright or busy background pages .
- Do not use music; if you must, set it up so the reader must press a button to hear the music.
- Remember to proofread for grammar and spelling.

IR47 THE INTRANET

The Intranet is a network within an organization that uses Internet technologies such as HTTP or FTP protocols. The *Intranet* can be used to navigate between objects, documents, Web pages, and other destinations using hyperlinks.

The Company Intranet is customized software that offers organizations a number of groupware capabilities in a networked environment, e.g., annual reports, contact us, committees, clubs, departments, divisions, e-mail and phone directories, news and events, policies, search, training, technical support, and useful Web links. It is designed for sharing company information and for creating custom applications for access via Web browsers. (See page 128 for more information on Groupware.)

IR48 ADVANTAGES TO USING THE INTERNET

Although the Internet is an excellent source of information, there are advantages and disadvantages to consider when using this technology. Some advantages are found:

- in business, for marketing and access to financial information, bonds, mutual funds, and stocks
- in government, for linking agencies and sharing information, databases, etc.
- in education, for academic research, to prepare assignments, reports, and term papers
- in health care and facilities where up-to-date information is accessed quickly
- in small businesses that are run from the home (e.g., desktop publishing, etc.)

◆ in creating a reference manual for Web sites that are accessed on a regular basis, for example:

> www.canadaswonderland.ca
> www.newsworld.cbc.ca
> www.thesaurus.com
> www.nyu.edu/library/bobst/research/soc/j... (Bobst Library—Journalism and Mass Communication Resources)
> www.vacation-properties.com
> www.theweathernetwork.com
> www.stockgroupmedia.com
> www.canadianbusiness.com

◆ time saver for "instant messaging/communication."

IR49   DISADVANTAGES TO USING THE INTERNET

Some of the disadvantages of using the Internet are:

◆ delays in getting online access—the Internet is used by people all over the world, therefore sending messages or files can be time-consuming

◆ quantity/volume of information available—there is so much data that searching to find the correct information can be intimidating

◆ the environment changes daily, with new host computers being added and other sites dropped or no longer maintained

◆ validity of information—critical business/research data must be confirmed before using, as well as the copyright status of the information; make sure you access the official Web site for a person, company, or organization

◆ privacy—there is a lack of security for e-mail and file transmission; information can be intercepted, altered, or copied

◆ cost

◆ planted viruses

IR50   INTERNET TERMS

ADSL: Asynchronous Digital Subscriber Line/at a very fast speed

Browser: A type of software used to browse sites on the Net, e.g., Internet Explorer or Netscape.

Common Gateway Interface (CGI): A system used to pass data between a Web server and a program designed to process the data.

Cookie: When a user visits a Web site, a "cookie"/indicator lets the Webmaster know that the user has been surfing; "cookies" do not read hard drives; however, they do indicate when a user makes a return visit.

Cyberspace: Internet space

Cyberworld: Internet world

IR

Dial-up modem: A device that downloads data from a distant computer (e.g., at 56.6 kilobits per second or faster)

Dial-up phone number: A number users can dial to access an online bulletin board system

Domain: A string of words or letters that identify a particular Web site

Domain Name System (DNS): The DNS translates hostnames into IP (Internet Provider) addresses

*****Download**: The process of copying a file from another computer to your computer

External networks: Large, commercial networks (e.g., America Online, CompuServe, Prodigy, the Microsoft Network, and UseNet)

Extranet: Business-to-business communication using the Internet

FAQ: Frequently asked questions—answers to the most common questions asked on a specific topic

File Transfer Protocol (FTP): A communication standard that allows users to access and send files over the Internet

Flame/s: Personal criticisms/verbal attacks on other Internet users via e-mail, USENET, or mailing lists

Global domain: The last letters of a domain name that indicate the category to which a Web site belongs (e.g., .com indicates that the Web site is part of a commercial enterprise and .edu indicates that it is part of an educational domain)

Home page: The introductory page of a Web site

Hostname: The unique name given to an Internet computer

HyperText Markup Language (HTML): A special programming language for creating Web pages

HyperText Transfer Protocol (http): The communication standard established for the World Wide Web

Icon: A symbol used to represent a command

Internet e-mail address: Used to send mail electronically, it consists of the user name, the @ symbol, and the domain name of the host (mail server)

Internet Service Provider (ISP): A company that provides access to the Internet for a fee

Intranet: A network within an organization that can be connected to worldwide Web servers for the distribution of information within the company

*****Caution:** Make sure you download from a reputable site to avoid unwanted "bugs/viruses."

Intranet services: Uses the same communication technology as the Internet but access is restricted to members of a particular group or organization

Local dial-up phone number: A number customers can dial to log on to their Internet account

Modem: A communications device

Multi-tasking: Many tasks can be performed at the same time

NC: Network computer

Netiquette: How to act on the Net—remember there is a person at the computer on the other end

Platform for Internet Content Selections (PICS): A set of standards developed for creating rating systems for Internet resources

Point-of-presence: A local dial-up phone number

Query string: Use of keywords to find information

Rich text: Text written in HTML that contains regular text and elements such as boldface, italics, various typefaces, pictures, and links to Web sites

IR

Search engine: A Web tool that uses words or strings of Google words to search for information on the WWW (e.g., AltaVista, Excite, Infoseek Guide, Lycos, Magellan, Open Text Index, The Electric Library, Yahoo!)

Snail mail: Regular post office mail

Spam: Advertisements or unsolicited mail/messages sent by e-mail

Surfing the Net: Looking for Web sites for information

Tags: Files stored on a Web server contain information that will be on the page, along with special instructions called Tags. These Tags are written according to a set of specifications using HTML and indicate what components are to be used and how they should be displayed on the page.

URL (Uniform Resource Locator): A unique string of characters used to identify and navigate a specific address/Web page on the Internet, e.g., www.pearsoned.ca/pitman

Upload: To copy a file from your computer to another computer.

Visual Reality Modeling Language (VRML): A program language used to create a three-dimensional environment on the Web

Web browser: A computer program that allows users to view and interact with Web sites

WebCrawler: Lists the number of pieces of information available on a topic (e.g., television AND news AND mass communication)

Web page: A page of a Web site; Web pages are created using a special programming language called Hypertext Markup Language (HTML)

Web server/Web site: Computers where files/Web pages are stored; these pages can contain text, graphics, audio or video, and links to other pages where information is stored

IR51 COPYRIGHT

Concerns about copyright protection for original creative works transmitted via the Internet will likely produce a comprehensive revisitation of copyright law; most authors will probably not want to have their works freely pirated without their consent. If information is transmitted via the Internet, however, it should be assumed that it could become public knowledge.

NOTE Information taken from the Internet should be referenced by Web site (e.g., author, title, etc.). For example:

Morrissy, John. "Tracking New Brunswick's Economic Revolution." *The Best in the Business* Oct. 1997: 21 pars. On-line. New Brunswick Publishing Co. Available:
http://www.nbpub.nbca/bizbest/editor. htm. 10 Dec. 1997.

IR

11 JOB SEARCH SKILLS

CONTENTS

J

Applying for a job in a highly competitive market requires considerable thought and effort. The process demands a knowledge of yourself, thorough research of the job market, careful preparation, and perseverance. This unit provides ideas on how to search for the position you want, how to present yourself to best advantage in a written application, how to prepare a résumé, how to promote yourself effectively at the interview, and how to follow up afterward.

J1   JOB SEARCH PREPARATION

Be well prepared before you start your search. In today's fast-changing marketplace, the job seeker must give serious thought to career planning—to establishing a short-term objective and to setting long-term goals. If you know who you are and where you want to go, your preparation and confidence will show during the interview. The job applicant with a clear vision of the future will approach the working world with a knowledgeable and positive outlook.

With the current popularity of contract hiring (employment for only a fixed period of time), you may want to consider this style of employment as opposed to a full-time, permanent position, which may be more difficult to find.

J2 THE SEARCH

The wise job seeker carefully researches all available sources to find the most satisfying position. Explore the following avenues to help lead you to the best job for you.

J3 PERSONAL CONTACTS

Friends or relatives already employed by companies or organizations you would like to join may be able to tell you of available positions. Since many jobs are never advertised, it is a good idea to investigate companies on your own. Use the telephone to network with friends, former colleagues, relatives, and acquaintances—their recommendations can be invaluable door openers.

J4 NEWSPAPERS

Advertisers do not always word their advertisements as you might expect. Do not read the headings or titles *only*; they may be misleading. Read *all* of the advertisement. You may find you have the qualifications and that the job would interest you. Or, you may not be interested in or qualified for a job that attracted you by the heading or title only. Do not be discouraged if you do not have precisely the qualifications listed. Advertisers seeking "college plus two years' experience" may well consider someone with a college diploma, enthusiasm, and determination. Go ahead and apply. At this point, your goal is to obtain an *interview*.

J5 AGENCIES AND CAREER COUNSELLING SERVICES

Many companies use the services of employment agencies in filling their vacancies. For job seekers, the advantages of dealing with an agency are:

◆ You are not changed any fee.
◆ The agency has a "bank" of jobs, so you do not have to spend time searching.
◆ The agency conducts skills tests and sends you only to job interviews for which you are suited.

◆ The agency will offer constructive criticism about your attitude and dress.

In addition to employment agencies, a number of career counselling organizations will guide job seekers in choosing a career path—by preparing them for interviews (e.g., role-playing, watching instructional videos, working with computer programs designed to help with career selection through aptitude testing) and by directing them to the most appropriate job agencies or professional contacts. Universities and colleges offer these services, as do private firms and federal and provincial governments. Some of these organizations charge for their services, some do not. Clarify this before you commit yourself to one of them.

J6 SCHOOLS, COLLEGES, UNIVERSITIES

Refer to bulletin boards and career counsellors in student service departments at schools or placement offices at colleges or universities.

J7 DIRECT COMPANY CONTACT

Contact the human resources manager of a firm or organization that interests you. Write an inquiry letter and follow it up with a personal visit. There may be an opening now or in the near future.

Dear [obtain the name of the appropriate person]:

    The high regard in which a friend of mine (who is employed by you) holds your organization has prompted me to apply to you for a position of administrative assistant.

    With four years of business experience, preceded by a college diploma in business studies, I can offer you computer proficiency (WordPerfect for Windows, Access, Lotus 1-2-3), strong verbal and written communication skills, and accuracy and expertise in accounting. I am a good organizer, welcome new challenges and responsibilities, and enjoy being a team player in a professional environment. The enclosed résumé will provide you with the full details of my qualifications.

    I will telephone you on Tuesday, March 21. I would appreciate the opportunity to meet with you to discuss my qualifications and determine how they might suit the needs of your organization.

                        Sincerely,

Letter of inquiry (suggested wording)

J8 LOCAL CANADA EMPLOYMENT CENTRES

Canada Employment Centres maintain lists of jobs available in various fields, both locally and across Canada.

J9 PROFESSIONAL ASSOCIATIONS AND UNIONS

Make inquiries, by telephone, mail, or in person, of professional associations and unions that represent the field in which you would like to work.

J10 THE INTERNET

The Internet is becoming a very useful tool for job searching to gain access to online career centres, matching services, job centres, job banks, indexes and search engines, chat rooms, electronic networking, and e-mail on the World Wide Web.

Employment is available through the Internet, and you can fax or e-mail applications for job opportunities. You can also develop a personal Web site and establish ongoing communications with human resource personnel around the country. Keep a file of or bookmark popular Internet sites for ongoing use.

For samples of online résumés, linkup to recruitment Web sites such as:
www.monster.ca
www.careerpath.com

J11 POSTING A RÉSUMÉ ON THE NET

Posting a résumé on the Internet is an option as a job search tool. Some sites allow you to cut and paste the hard copy into the online form; others prompt you through each screen process (also known as résumé builder), e.g., monster.ca.

You can submit your résumé in English or French, it can be edited, viewed on screen, and either stored in a database where only you have access to it (inactive), or it can be "activated" at any time.

When your résumé is activated, interested employers will contact you via e-mail, and your résumé is automatically redirected from the database of the Web site where it was posted. Employers will only see an e-mail address if you respond to an inquiry.

NOTE You can also find out how often your résumé has been viewed.

Sample Résumé Format

Title:	Specific job title, i.e., administrative assistant
Objective:	Supply information on employment objective (2000-character limit/approx. two-thirds of a page)
Target locations:	Willing to relocate? If yes, select location
Work experience:	In chronological order, with dates, i.e., Oct. 2000 to Present
Work description:	Describe responsibilities/tasks for each stint of employment (2000-character limit)
Education:	List names of colleges or universities and the time-frame attended

Affiliations:	Professional associations, i.e., business organizations
Professional skills:	Specific skills, i.e., computer skills/knowledge, presentation skills, public speaking, writing, etc.
Additional information:	Additional information that may be helpful (3000-character limit/one page)
References:	Provide at least two/three references with area codes and phone numbers
Salary expected:	A figure must be selected

In some cases, the résumé can be stored with confidentially, e.g., the references and current employers are hidden.

NOTE   All required information must be provided to complete the résumé format.

Using the Internet as a job search tool has both advantages and disadvantages, as discussed below.

Advantages:

◆ You can learn about new career opportunities and job titles.

◆ You can post your résumé free of charge.

◆ Your résumé becomes part of a database where employers search for qualified candidates.

◆ You can store your résumé in a database until you choose to activate it.

◆ You can easily research prospective employers and companies.

Disadvantages:

◆ You may not be contacted.

◆ Information is freely shared; confidentiality may be an issue.

◆ You may need to check the company's reputation.

◆ You must check e-mail daily once your résumé is activated.

J

J12   THE APPLICATION

Once you hear of a job that interests you or see an appealing advertisement, you must convince someone to interview you. You do this by sending an application letter and a résumé that "sells" you.

J13   THE APPLICATION LETTER

Your letter of application must be carefully worded so that it:

◆ sells you as the right person for this job

◆ summarizes why you are applying and why you are qualified

◆ provides all of the facts asked of you

◆ is concise, specific, and to the point

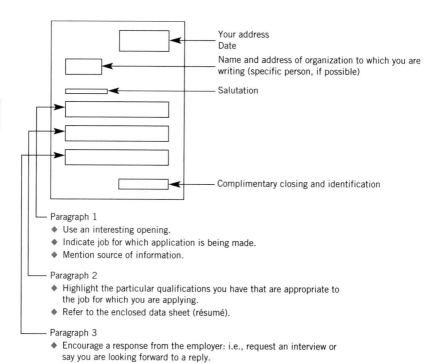

Your address
Date

Name and address of organization to which you are writing (specific person, if possible)

Salutation

Complimentary closing and identification

Paragraph 1
◆ Use an interesting opening.
◆ Indicate job for which application is being made.
◆ Mention source of information.

Paragraph 2
◆ Highlight the particular qualifications you have that are appropriate to the job for which you are applying.
◆ Refer to the enclosed data sheet (résumé).

Paragraph 3
◆ Encourage a response from the employer: i.e., request an interview or say you are looking forward to a reply.

Outline of an application letter

In preparing your letter of application (see Unit 12, K19, for format details):

◆ Use good-quality, businesslike stationery (plain white or buff-coloured, unlined).

◆ Use a computer or word-processing equipment. Although using the same letter for every application is not possible, you can save a master letter and tailor it to each application. This will permit you to create a fresh letter for each application with a minimum of effort.

◆ Include a reference to the source of your information about the job.

441 College Avenue
Brandon, MB R7A 1E8
January 20, 20--

Mr. Yves Ranier, Manager
Human Resources Department
East/West Enterprises Ltd.
3419 McDonald Avenue
Brandon, MB R7B 0B5

Dear Mr. Ranier:

I believe I have the skills and personal qualities called for in your advertisement for an administrative assistant in last night's Free Press. Please consider this letter as my application for the job.

As you will see from the enclosed résumé, I have a three-year diploma from Sheridan Park Community College. This program included training in English language skills, computer applications, accounting, human relations, and business administration. After a year of experience at Creative Solutions, my present employer, I appreciate the importance of attending to details, accuracy under pressure, and meeting deadlines. Report writing and organizing meetings are among the challenges I enjoy. I have learned to deal successfully with members of the public, to establish good relationships with co-workers, and to be a contributing team player.

It is my hope that experience as an administrative assistant will add to my qualifications and prepare me for a management position with your company.

I feel I have much to offer to East/West Enterprises Ltd. and would welcome the opportunity of discussing your needs and my capabilities in person. Please telephone me at 489-2672, or e-mail @(address) so that we can arrange an appointment.

Yours very truly,

Pietra Spenseri

Pietra Spenseri

Encl.

Application letter

◆ Ask for some action (e.g., a telephone call or written reply) leading to an interview.
◆ Keep the letter to one page if you possibly can.
◆ Carefully check any doubtful spelling or grammar.
◆ Key your name beneath the signature.
◆ Address your envelope correctly (see Unit 12, K6).
◆ Always submit an original letter of application, never a photocopy, but do keep a copy for your own records and for follow-up.
◆ Don't forget to sign the letter.

J

103 Cranberry Court
Hamilton, ON L8E 3R8
May 25, 20--

Mrs. Heather Armstrong
Human Resources Department
Cosmo Corporation
P. O. Box 2034
Hamilton, ON L8N 3T2

Dear Mrs. Armstrong

I wish to apply for the position of Administrative Assistant as advertised in (name of newspaper), on (date of issue).

As a recent graduate from (name of college/university) in the (name of program), I have acquired excellent computer skills as well as effective interpersonal relations skills and believe that I could be a valuable employee with your firm.

Enclosed is a copy of my résumé, which outlines my qualifications in various skill areas, as well as references.

I would be pleased to meet with you, at your convenience, to discuss your requirements and my suitability for the position.

Please call me at (phone number where you can be contacted during the day, as well as after working hours), or e-mail @ (address).

Yours truly,

Your Name

Encl.

Application letter

J14 THE RÉSUMÉ

The résumé (also known as the data sheet or curriculum vitae) is rarely read thoroughly by recipients. It must be short, easy to read, and organized so that it will draw attention to your most significant achievements and skills. The résumé helps the interviewer to screen applicants and derive a short list.

Ideally, of course, a new résumé should be created to precisely match each job for which you apply. If your résumé is saved on disk, you can easily make minor changes to your basic résumé. However, if saving on disk is not possible, one well-thought-out résumé can be used for most applications and your covering application letter can be designed to zero in on the specific job for which you are applying.

◆ Never drop off or send a résumé without an accompanying letter of application or letter of introduction.

NOTE   Although a résumé usually accompanies a letter of application, it can also be left as a memory jogger at companies you have contacted directly.

Getting started

Résumé writing is much easier if you begin by listing all of the information that you need to include. As step one, then, create a personal inventory (a list) of all of your skills, aptitudes, preferences, experiences, and achievements. Make your list as complete as possible. Examples of the type of information you might list are shown below. In addition, the sample résumé presented in this chapter might give you some ideas.

◆ your abilities (speaking in front of a group, language fluencies, interpersonal skills, leadership traits)

◆ your skills (keyboarding speed, accounting skill, software expertise)

◆ your priorities (being active on the job, new challenges, being given responsibility)

◆ your personal qualities (sense of humour, friendliness, punctuality)

◆ valuable work experiences (handled cash, made bank deposits, opened and closed the store, wrote company manual for XYZ software program)

Indicate part-time or full-time employment and give approximate dates (e.g., May 2001–June 2001).

◆ List volunteer work (e.g., volunteer at local food bank).

◆ Do not list political, religious, or fraternal affiliations; however, you can state that you were an election campaign volunteer.

This self-analysis will encourage you to focus on your strengths and will help you enormously in building your résumé.

Résumé presentation

A résumé is judged initially on its appearance; good presentation is essential. Follow these pointers for success:

- Use good-quality, businesslike paper.
- Use a computer if possible (eye-appealing fonts and a laser printer provide a professional look).
- Make the format neat, attractive, and easy to read. Avoid ornate typefaces.
- Highlight headings and key words.
- Ensure that your résumé is error-free.
- Restrict the résumé length to no more than two pages—employers are busy people.

NOTE The number of pages will depend on your age, employment experience, etc. Do not omit important information by trying to cut down on length. Change the format—reduce white space in setup; adjust font size (do not make too small).

- Place the résumé inside a colourful folder to add a touch of importance. A résumé with flair will be noticed and may open the door to that interview.
- Do not enclose or attach a photograph to the résumé.

Types of résumés

A *functional résumé* stresses an applicant's career achievements and responsibilities. It is often used by experienced workers and provides information under the following headings:

- personal information (name, address, telephone and/or fax number, e-mail address)
- accomplishments (e.g., brief descriptions of leadership roles played, notable organizational accomplishments, writing achievements, conference planning)
- business experience
- education
- references (optional)

A *chronological résumé* (the preferred style) is a listing of employment history in reverse chronological order (last job first). It is used by both experienced and inexperienced workers and is appropriate for beginning workers who do not have much information to include. The chronological résumé is usually presented under the following headings:

- personal information (name, address, telephone and/or fax number, e-mail address)
- career goals or objectives

- education (name of college, high school, date attended—summarize information)
- business experience—full-time and part-time
- other part-time employment/summer jobs
- interests
- references

If your education does not quite fit the job, give your work experience first. A section entitled "Additional Important Information" (as shown in the illustration of a chronological résumé in this section) works well because it helps to provide a complete picture of you.

Regardless of the type used, remember to:

- Let the résumé reflect YOU and your capabilities.
- List all of your achievements—do not be too modest.
- Be specific and positive—avoid vague statements.
- Tailor the résumé to suit the job posting and the nature of the business to which you are applying.

Key words to describe personal qualities for use in résumés:

ambitious	disciplined	loyal
analytical	discreet	reliable
conscientious	efficient	resourceful
constructive	enthusiastic	sincere
creative	hard worker	tactful
dependable	imaginative	will travel/relocate

- Relate everything in the résumé to the employer's viewpoint.
- Read your résumé carefully before mailing—it may be the key to your future!

Personal information

- State your name, address, telephone number (and fax number if you have one).
- Any other personal information you provide is voluntary. The law prohibits discrimination on the basis of gender, race, religion, marital status, age, or nationality. Such information is not relevant to any job.

Accomplishments

This section is used in a functional résumé only.

- State your language fluencies.
- Include any writings, workshops, or presentations you have done.
- List any initiatives you have taken (e.g., time-saving suggestions for tasks, cost-saving measures).
- Mention personal or sports awards or championships.

Marketable skills

List if you have experience in any of the following:

- creative writing (if you have been involved in writing for the school newspaper or local newspaper, etc.)
- planning or organization (if you have been involved in community, religious groups, or school committees)
- presentation (if you have experience using presentation skills; speaking to a group/s)
- budgeting (if you have handled a budget for an association/local group)

  Online sites will ask you to fill in boxes that are designed to provide an employer with the same information that you would provide if you were submitting a hard copy résumé. For example, the site will ask you to fill in one box with your name, another with your address, another with your last employer, and so on.

NOTE To view an online résumé builder, try linking up to one of the job search web sites we have listed in this chapter.

*Career goals can be included, omitted, or replaced with the heading: special Skills/Skill area

- leadership (if you have been a crew/section/group leader or class respresentative)
- problem solving (if you have experience in this area)
- proofreading (if you are an excellent proofreader; this is a highly marketable skill, especially in the publishing business)
- tutoring/training (if you have been a volunteer subject tutor or trainer)
- reception (if you have good telephone/reception skills)
- research (if you are proficient in researching topics and know where to find information quickly)
- meeting deadlines (if you work well under pressure)
- minute-taking or shorthand/speedwriting (if you have worked on committees)

In a chronological résumé, the above items could be listed under "Additional Important Information" or as part of the description of responsibilities in the "Business Experience" section, if appropriate.

Business experience

- List your previous jobs, starting with the most recent.
- Give approximate starting and ending dates of each job.
- Indicate your responsibilities (skills, equipment, and software used) in previous jobs—do not simply list the titles of those positions.
- Mention any promotions or increases in job responsibility. This shows the prospective employer that you developed skills on the job.

◆ Do not mention salary.

◆ If you have no work experience, demonstrate that you have developed organizational, leadership, and interpersonal skills by providing details of part-time or summer jobs, volunteer work, or co-operative education programs.

Education

◆ Do not include letters of commendation/reference.

◆ Include certificates, degrees, or diplomas earned; mention your major study areas, lengths of programs, and honours, scholarships, or special awards. Names and addresses of institutions may be shown but this is not required.

◆ Note any work-related training—evening courses, professional workshops, special training courses.

◆ Do not include elementary school information.

Interests

◆ Include this section when such information would be beneficial, such as in the case of a person new to the workforce or where such interests have some connection to the job for which the résumé is being submitted.

◆ Give data that would provide useful insights for employers (e.g., volunteer work can demonstrate valuable administrative and/or teamwork experience; work with youth groups shows leadership qualities).

◆ Include specific sports interests, hobbies, intramural activities, and involvement in social organizations. Active people are more productive employees.

NOTE Employers are impressed with people who are involved in volunteer work. If this interests you, check the Volunteer Opportunities Exchange (VOE). You can provide a profile of your skills and interests, and agencies fill out a similar form, outlining their volunteer positions. The VOE then matches skills and needs. Privacy measures ensure the confidentiality of this information.
Web site: www.volunteer.ca

References

◆ Ask permission from people you identify as references *before* you use their names.

◆ Indicate that references are available on request, but go to the interview prepared with names, positions, addresses, and telephone numbers.

◆ Give a copy of your résumé to the person(s) you use as a reference (in case they are called for information regarding data).

◆ Good references are previous or present employers, teachers, religious leaders, doctors, lawyers, businesspeople, and politicians.

◆ Do not use relatives as references.

J15 THE APPLICATION FORM

Although you have provided a comprehensive résumé, most organizations will still require you to complete an application form. You are judged on how carefully and accurately—not how quickly—you complete the form. Your attention to it tells the prospective employer whether you can follow instructions well, whether you are organized, and whether you care.

◆ Complete the form neatly and accurately. This might be the only handwritten document the interviewer has on which to judge your writing skills.

◆ Have your own copy of your résumé available to remind you of dates of previous jobs, education, etc.

◆ Be truthful but not unnecessarily modest.

◆ Do not leave any blank spaces; if the question does not apply to you, write in "N/A" (not applicable).

NOTE If you left a job under circumstances that were unpleasant (e.g., you were dismissed, for personal reasons, etc.), write in "To be discussed" (this gives you the opportunity to discuss the situation in person).

J16 THE INTERVIEW

The interview is designed to inform both the employer and the applicant. Most interviews follow a pattern and being aware of this pattern will make you a more confident interviewee.

You can expect a few minutes of introductory small talk during which the interviewer will try to make you feel comfortable. Next, the interviewer will ask you questions about your education and experience. Details of the position will then be given, and you will be invited to ask questions. Information about the company, its activities and products, will probably be mentioned. Finally, you will be asked if, after hearing about the job first-hand, you are still interested.

The following are some important points to note in successfully presenting yourself at an interview.

Before the interview

Be prepared! If you are well prepared and feel comfortable, you will appear confident. Consider some or all of the following.

Personal preparation The actual day of your interview will go smoothly if you follow these tips:

- Plan your wardrobe the night before the interview so that you look your best and are comfortable—dress "up" but dress appropriately.
- Make sure you are well rested.
- Have a positive attitude.
- Go alone. Leave family and friends at home.
- Arrive in plenty of time. Make the trip a day or two before to calculate the travelling time.
- Be polite to all staff you meet—you may have to work with them.
- Allow up to one hour for the actual interview.

Company research Try to do some or all of the following:

- Visit the organization ahead of your interview to gain background information, such as literature that details products sold, sales figures and types of sales, number of employees and branches, company history, name of the president, etc.
- Research the vendors/users of the product to learn about its quality and that of the company's service.
- Find out your interviewer's name and supervisory role.

Use this information to develop questions that will show your interest in and knowledge of the company you wish to join. Such preparation will make you stand out in a positive way.

Job research Try to obtain a job description and base your presentation on it. This might be available from:

- the interviewer (telephone and ask)
- the employment agency, if that was your job referral source

If this is not possible, create your own job description by, for example:

- asking pertinent questions of the receptionist at the organization or some other employee
- carefully analysing the job ad and building on it

Interview "kit" Go to the interview with:

- pen and pad or paper to write down pertinent information
- a file folder that includes:
  - a copy of your application letter, résumé, and any letters of recommendation
  - a copy of the "want ad" (if you are applying for a job from a newspaper ad)
  - a portfolio of job samples that show your capabilities, if possible
  - a log/record of dates, jobs applied for, and interviews (use for interview follow-up)

During the interview

The interview is your chance to convince the employer that you are the best candidate. Be prepared to talk in a confident way about yourself and your career goals.

♦ Enter confidently. Your body language will show your attitude toward the job.

♦ Let the interviewer guide the interview. Wait for, but don't expect, an offer to shake hands (then do it firmly). Don't sit down until you are invited to do so.

♦ Remember your interviewer's name.

♦ Relax, sit naturally.

♦ Avoid "yes" and "no" responses. Expand on your answers. Questions are usually designed to encourage you to talk.

♦ Listen carefully to the interviewer's questions so that you avoid evasive replies.

♦ Be sensitive to the interviewer's reactions to you; adjust your approach if necessary.

♦ Look at the interviewer. Direct eye contact signifies confidence.

♦ Smile!

♦ Keep the discussion to job-related topics. Home or social concerns have no place here.

♦ Answer questions about interests and hobbies openly.

♦ Do not chew gum.

♦ Do not smoke, even if you are invited to do so. You may need both hands at some point.

♦ Be positive and honest about your capabilities but do not be too modest. Include the fact that you learn new skills easily.

♦ Speak positively of former employers and work experiences.

♦ Use your school record, summer job, and volunteer experiences as examples of work experience.

♦ Be prepared to be tested where skills are part of the job.

♦ Do not drink alcohol if you are invited to a job interview at lunch.

The issue of salary is a sensitive one, and some employers do not discuss it during the first interview. The following should be helpful, however:

♦ Know, before going to an interview, what you are prepared to accept.

♦ Allow the prospective employer to raise the subject. If it looks as though you are going to be offered the job and salary has not been mentioned, then raise the subject yourself.

Employers today are concerned with quality and service. Applicants who demonstrate an understanding of this are more likely to succeed.

Answering and asking questions You will be asked questions, of course, and these will vary from job to job. The following are some typical ones that you would be well advised to review and be prepared to answer before you go for your interview:

◆ What are your best personal qualities?
◆ What was your greatest achievement at school? College?
◆ What is your weakest skill area? Your strongest skill area? (Be very honest; this answer could be the determining factor that gets you the job.)
◆ Were your grades in school an accurate reflection of your capabilities?
◆ What are your limitations?
◆ Why do you want to work for this company/organization?
◆ What do you know about the company/organization?
◆ Why are you interested in this job?
◆ What qualities do you think are necessary for this job?
◆ What would you like to be doing five years from now?
◆ How long would you stay with us if the job were offered to you?
◆ If you could have any position, what would it be? Why?
◆ Why do you think we should hire you?
◆ How long would it take for you to make a positive contribution?
◆ Why did you leave your previous job?
◆ What did you like least about your previous job?
◆ What is your opinion of the company where you last worked?
◆ How do you handle deadlines and working under pressure?
◆ How would you deal with a colleague who constantly interrupted you while you were involved in a job/task.
◆ Do you have references? Which one would you prefer me to contact and why?

You will also be invited to ask questions. Again, be prepared. Even if your interviewer seems to have dealt with all of the information you require, try to ask at least one relevant question when invited to do so. Questions you might consider are:

◆ What promotional and career opportunities does the company offer?
◆ Does the company provide a training program for new employees?
◆ Does the company encourage and sponsor advanced education?
◆ What are your expectations of the person chosen for this position?
◆ Will I be working as part of a small or a large team?

Not all interviews are the same, of course. You may find it informative to refer to Unit 8, H9 and H10, on the subject of how to conduct an interview, so that you are aware of what an employer is trying to find out about you.

The end of the interview Leave the interviewer with a good impression:

◆ Thank the interviewer.

◆ Ask for a date by which you can expect an answer. (If you do not hear within 10 days, write or call.)

◆ If it is clear at the conclusion of the interview that you have not been successful, be polite as you leave.

J17 INTERVIEW FOLLOW-UP

Evaluate yourself after each interview by asking yourself these questions:

◆ Was my research of the company adequate?

◆ Did I show confidence?

◆ How did I deal with the questions?

Be honest in your appraisal, work on any weaknesses, and be better prepared for the next interview.

◆ Consider sending a follow-up letter to the interviewer, expressing your thanks for the interview and indicating that you are looking forward to a reply. Use the letter to further emphasize important skills you could bring to the job and add any relevant information

J

441 College Avenue
Brandon, MB   R7A 1E8
January 28, 20--

Mr. Yves Ranier, Manager
Human Resources Department
East/West Enterprises Ltd.
3419 McDonald Avenue
Brandon, MB   R7B 0B5

Dear Mr. Ranier:

Thank you for the time you spent with me today at the interview. It was a pleasure to meet you and to find out so much about your organization. The possibility of working for such a dynamic company is most exciting.

I look forward to hearing from you very soon and, I hope, to become a part of East/West Enterprises Ltd. in the near future.

Sincerely,

Pietra Spenseri

Pietra Spenseri

Follow-up letter to interviewer

that perhaps you feel did not come across strongly during the interview.

If you are offered the job, congratulations! If you are unsuccessful, try not to be discouraged. Consider phoning the employer and asking for an evaluation of your performance at the interview. Use this feedback to better prepare yourself for future job searches.

J18 SUCCESS ON THE JOB

Constantly improving technology and the increasing availability of knowledge and data make it essential for workers who wish to progress to prepare for two or three career options and to keep abreast of the job market. Bear in mind that the key qualities of a desirable employee are genuine interest, willingness to learn, co-operation, and initiative. Demonstrate these qualities and encourage your professional growth by:

◆ finding a mentor, a role model who will guide you along your career path

◆ taking relevant courses

◆ identifying your weaknesses and planning to correct them (e.g., speaking skills, language skills, team-player qualities)

◆ subscribing to work-related magazines

◆ joining professional organizations

◆ keeping up to date with technological advances

◆ welcoming new challenges

The worker who gains new skills and is willing to change career goals to adapt to the job market will always have the greatest potential for success.

Give the job a fair chance. If you do not like your job, stay at least a year to gain the experience, and then look for another more challenging or suitable position. Keep your résumé updated on a regular basis; add new skills, courses, employment history, new references, etc.

NOTE Never leave a job unless you have another one to go to!

···· UNIT ····

12 KEYING AND FORMATTING DOCUMENTS

CONTENTS

K

T his unit will focus on the production of business commun-ications. Regardless of the equipment used, this section will answer many of your keyboarding and formatting questions. The information is presented in five major categories:

Page placement information covers paper sizes, default settings, type sizes, starting lines, and margin settings.

Formatting techniques provides the detailed information needed to help you key accurate, attractive, and effective business documents.

Style practices covers the keying of punctuation, metric expressions, and special symbols.

Editing and proofreading contains proofreading symbols.

Formats and language style covers formatting and document style practices.

K1   PAGE PLACEMENT INFORMATION

K2   PAPER SIZES

Standard (letter-size) paper dimensions

- $8^1/_2$" × 11" (21.5 cm × 28 cm)
- 6.5" wide × 66 lines deep
- available in sheets or continuous form for computer use on tractor printers. After printing, pages are detached and edges stripped off to give the appearance of cut sheets.

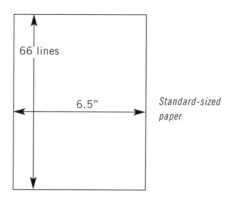

66 lines

6.5"

Standard-sized paper

Legal-size paper dimensions
* $8^1/_2$" × 14" (21.5 cm × 35.5 cm)
* 6.5" wide × 84 lines deep
* available in sheets and continuous form

NOTE Monarch and Baronial (small-size stationery) are described in this unit, K43.

K3 DEFAULT SETTINGS

All word-processing software comes with default (preset) format settings. Usually these are:

Word		*WordPerfect*
1"	top margin	1"
54	text lines	54
1"	bottom margin	1"
6"	line length	6.5"
1.25"	left margin	1"
1.25"	right margin	1"
10 pt.	point	12 pt.
single	spacing	single
5 pt.	tabs (half-inch intervals)	6 pt.

While these can be changed, they are convenient for most documents. Work with these default settings as much as possible to speed up your document production time.

K4 FONTS AND POINT SIZES

Software allows for various fonts and point sizes. All offer 10 and 12; and more. As well, printers offer various choices.

Most laser printers and software allow for typefaces and fonts to be printed in various *point sizes*. This refers to the vertical height of an upper case character, measured from the baseline to the top of the characters, e.g., if 36 point is chosen, the height from the baseline to the top of the character would be $^{1}/_{2}$ inch. This is also discussed in Unit 4, Desktop Publishing."

This is 14 point.

This is 12 point.

K5   FORMATTING TECHNIQUES

Format means the setup of a document and refers to the margins, spacing, page length, etc., that should be used. Contained in this unit are examples of most business documents. For properly formatted examples of the following business communications, consult the units indicated:

- ◆ agenda: Unit 14, "Meetings, Conferences, and Teleconferences"
- ◆ application letter (personal business style): Unit 11, "Job Search Skills"
- ◆ forms: Unit 7, "Forms and Form Design"
- ◆ itinerary: Unit 20, "Travel Arrangements"
- ◆ meeting announcements: Unit 14
- ◆ minutes: Unit 14
- ◆ press release: Unit 1, "Communications: Language Skills"

K6   ENVELOPE ADDRESSING

Canada Post has issued guidelines for a *preferred style* of addressing envelopes that is strongly recommended to ensure maximum efficiency in sorting and delivery, especially for mass mailings. However, the traditional style of envelope addressing is still acceptable, because Canada Post recognizes that some businesses have large mailing databases that were prepared this way.

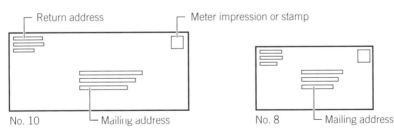

No. 10   No. 8

4 1/8 in. x 9 1/2 in. (105 mm x 241 mm)   3 5/8 in. x 6 1/2 in. (92 mm x 165 mm)

The two most frequently used business envelopes

K

General guidelines

◆ Key carefully and accurately.

◆ Single-space throughout.

◆ Include a return address in the top left-hand corner.

◆ Align the address so that each line starts at the same point.

◆ Use a maximum of six lines.

◆ Always include a postal code. Obtain this from letterheads, return addresses on envelopes, or from *Canada's Postal Code Directory*, available from Canada Post (see Unit 15).

▶ K7   Canada Post preferred style

◆ Key the entire return and mailing addresses in capitals, and single-space.

◆ Do not use punctuation of any kind, e.g., Vancouver BC V6B 4P4

◆ Attention lines, "Confidential," etc., must appear above the name and address of the company.

◆ Use the two-letter province or territory abbreviations that are provided in the Appendix.

◆ Use Canada Post abbreviations, as shown in this unit, K8.

◆ Start keying on line 15 on a No. 10 envelope, and line 13 on a No. 8 envelope, five spaces to the left of centre, so that the postal code appears within the optical character recognition (OCR) area. If necessary, start higher for each additional line needed (e.g., "Attention," "Confidential").

◆ Use standard fonts, avoiding script, italic, etc.

◆ Show suite or apartment number on the same line as the street address, after the street name.

◆ Separate the postal code from the province abbreviation by two spaces.

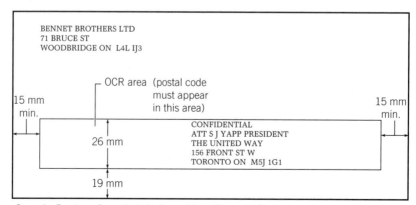

Canada Post preferred style for addressing envelopes

NOTE If envelopes or labels are generated from the inside addresses of letters, appropriate changes in the inside addresses of the letters will be needed (see this unit, K26, for an example).

▶ K8 Canada Post and traditional abbreviations

	Preferred style	Traditional style		Preferred style	Traditional style
Apartment	APT	Apt.	Heights	HTS	Hts.
Avenue	AVE	Ave.	Mountain	MTN.	Mtn.
Boulevard	BLVD	Blvd.	Parkway	PKY.	Pky.
Building	BLDG	Bldg.	Place	PL	Pl.
Centre	CTR.	Ctr.	Road	RD	Rd.
Court	CRT.	Crt.	Route	Rte.	Rte.
Crescent	CRES	Cres.	Rural Route	RR	R.R.
Drive	DR	Dr.	Street	ST	St.
Estates	EST.	Est.			

▶ K9 Places

Canadian provinces and territories

Provinces and territories	Abbreviations	
	Traditional	Preferred
Alberta	Alta.	AB
British Columbia	B.C.	BC
Labrador (part of Newfoundland)	Lab.	LB
Manitoba	Man.	MB
New Brunswick	N.B.	NB
Newfoundland	Nfld.	NF
Northwest Territories	N.W.T.	NT
Nova Scotia	N.S.	NS
Nunavut	—	NU
Ontario	Ont.	ON
Prince Edward Island	P.E.I.	PE
Quebec*	P.Q. or Que.	PQ or QC
Saskatchewan	Sask.	SK
Yukon Territory	Yuk.	YT

*QC is the official two-letter abbreviation for Quebec introduced in 1992 by Canada Post for "optical character reader" machines. However, envelopes marked with a PQ or a Que. will be delivered to their addresses in that province.

U.S. states, districts, and territories

The two-letter U.S. Postal Service abbreviations must appear on all envelope addresses.

States, districts, and territories	Abbreviations	States, districts, and territories	Abbreviations
Alabama	AL	Missouri	MO
Alaska	AK	Montana	MT
American Samoa	AS	Nebraska	NE
Arizona	AZ	Nevada	NV
Arkansas	AR	New Hampshire	NH
California	CA	New Jersey	NJ
Canal Zone	CZ	New Mexico	NM
Colorado	CO	New York	NY
Connecticut	CT	North Carolina	NC
Delaware	DE	North Dakota	ND
District of Columbia	DC	Ohio	OH
Florida	FL	Oklahoma	OK
Georgia	GA	Oregon	OR
Guam	GU	Pennsylvania	PA
Hawaii	HI	Puerto Rico	PR
Idaho	ID	Rhode Island	RI
Illinois	IL	South Carolina	SC
Indiana	IN	South Dakota	SD
Iowa	IA	Tennessee	TN
Kansas	KS	Texas	TX
Kentucky	KY	Utah	UT
Louisiana	LA	Vermont	VT
Maine	ME	Virgin Islands	VI
Maryland	MD	Virginia	VA
Massachusetts	MA	Washington	WA
Michigan	MI	West Virginia	WV
Minnesota	MN	Wisconsin	WI
Mississippi	MS	Wyoming	WY

K

▶ **K10 Envelopes with international addresses**

For international addresses, follow the preceding rules. If the traditional style of address is used, show both the place name and country in capitals. Include zip codes, postal codes, zone numbers, or postal districts before the country name. A list of U.S. state abbreviations is provided in the Appendix.

Canada Post preferred style	Traditional style
EDMOND T DRAPER 8632 ALASKA AVE N APT 107 CHICAGO IL 60652 -1187 USA	Mr. Edmond T. Draper 8632 Alaska Avenue North Apartment 107 CHICAGO, ILLINOIS 60652 -1187 U.S.A.
MISS L LARNEY ELLIOTT GALLERIES LTD 51 LUTON RD HARPENDEN HERTS AL5 2UB ENGLAND	Miss L. Larney Elliott Galleries Ltd. 51 Luton Road HARPENDEN, HERTS. AL5 2UB ENGLAND

▶ **K11   Production hints**

◆ Use your word-processing equipment to automatically produce envelopes or self-adhesive labels. These can be printed from source lists (e.g., selected clients from your database) when you produce form letters or, with some software, from inside addresses of letters. If you do this, capitalize the city or town name in the inside address as you key in the letters.

◆ Purchase continuous-form envelopes with side flaps to speed up envelope production on computers.

▶ **K12   Folding and inserting correspondence**

Enclosures should fit envelopes as closely as possible.

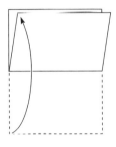

1. Place letter *face up* on desk. Fold in half.

2. Fold right third to left, making the fold slightly less than one-third of the way over.

3. Fold left third so that it extends 0.5 cm beyond the other two-thirds.

4. Insert last folded edge first.

Large envelope (No. 10)

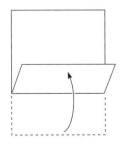

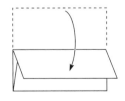

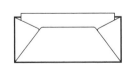

1. Place letter face up on desk. Fold slightly less han one-third up toward top.

2. Fold down top of letterhead.

3. Insert so that second fold goes in first.

K

▶ K13 Window envelopes

When you use window envelopes, be sure the enclosure fits the envelope snugly so that the address (including the postal code) cannot shift out of the window area.

Standard size specifications (with acceptable window positions) are available from Canada Post.

▶ K14 Speedy envelope sealing and stamping by hand

Sealing

◆ Use a damp sponge or other moistener.

◆ Assemble 10 envelopes one behind the other with flaps open and glued side up.

◆ Run the sponge over the first two or three envelopes. Seal them.

◆ Continue until all envelopes are sealed.

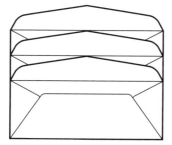

Envelopes assembled for speedy sealing by hand

NOTE   Adhesive-strip flaps are available at a higher cost than traditional-seal envelopes.

Stamping

If a franking machine is not available, do this:

◆ Assemble 10 envelopes so that the stamp area is visible.

◆ Moisten a horizontal row of 10 stamps.

◆ Quickly attach a stamp to each envelope.

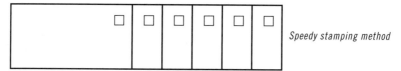

Speedy stamping method

▶ K15 Standard-sized envelopes

◆ The largest envelope for Canada Post delivery is 245 mm × 150 mm (10" × 6") and the smallest is 140 mm × 90 mm (5$\frac{1}{2}$" × 3$\frac{1}{2}$"). Courier services will handle any size.

◆ Insert the return address in the top left-hand corner.

◆ Position the mailing address so that it appears in a band 15 mm in from the sides and 19 mm up from the bottom. Key the address on the envelope itself or use a label.

NOTE Canada Post will deliver non-standard-sized mail for a higher fee.

▶ K16   Labels

Because of the time-saving feature of labels, businesses use them for regular mail, as well as for large envelopes and parcels. You may prepare them on electronic labellers, word processors, and computers, and several types are available. Be sure the address is positioned in the centre of the label and affixed to an envelope so that Canada Post rules are followed. When you use a dark envelope, light-coloured labels are particularly useful.

Electronic labellers are also available for home or office use.

K17   FINANCIAL STATEMENTS

Financial statements are reports prepared regularly for management that show the worth of the company, the operating results, the cash flow, and a host of other information used for decision making.

The two main financial statements are the balance sheet and the income statement. A properly keyed balance sheet is shown in Unit 6, "Financial Management," and the income statement is illustrated here.

For all financial statements, follow these guidelines:

◆ Financial statements usually contain a descriptive column and money columns. Leave six to eight spaces after the first (descriptive) column. Leave two spaces between the money columns.

◆ Follow the techniques of tabulation (see this unit, K70).

◆ Use an automatic "decimal tab" feature for alignment purposes if possible.

◆ Use leaders if they will make the report easier to read. Use the automatic feature of your software or leave one blank space after the first column and three before the money column if you insert them manually.

◆ If you prepare similar statements on a regular basis, save your format on disk or keep a note of your margin- and tab-setting points.

◆ Try to keep financial statements to one page and centre the document on the page.

◆ When a document must go on two pages, plan carefully so that the break occurs between major sections.

◆ If space permits, double-space the heading.

◆ Key a single underscore directly under subtotals and a double underscore directly under totals. These should start under the dollar sign.

◆ Negative figures should be shown in parentheses; e.g., (9000).

◆ Continuation lines should be indented two or three spaces.

MARTIN KOLCHETSKI
INCOME STATEMENT
For the Year Ended March 31, 20--

Income

Gross Sales	$92 206.45	
Less Returns and Allowances	969.59	
Net Sales		$91 236.86

Cost of Goods Sold

Merchandise Inventory, April 1, 20-1		$ 9 462.20	
Purchases	$54 943.15		
Less Returns and Allowances	496.96		
		54 446.19	
Cost of Goods for Sale		63 908.39	
Less Mdse. Inv., March 31, 20-2		11 220.25	
Cost of Goods Sold			52 688.14
Gross Profit			$38 548.72

Expenses

Salaries Expense	$13 731.24	
Delivery Expense	1 560.60	
General Expense	510.80	
Insurance Expense	62.00	
Supplies Expense	440.80	
Depreciation Expense	534.16	
Total Operating Expenses		16 839.60
Net Income		$21 709.12

Financial statement

K18   LEGAL DOCUMENTS

Preparing legal documents is straightforward. Simply apply the usual rules of style (see this unit, K78) and, with some modifications, the rules of report keying (see this unit, K45).

◆ If you are employed by a legal firm, follow the style guide of your office.

◆ If you do not work in a legal office and are required to complete legal documents, consult a specialized reference source.

K19 LETTERS

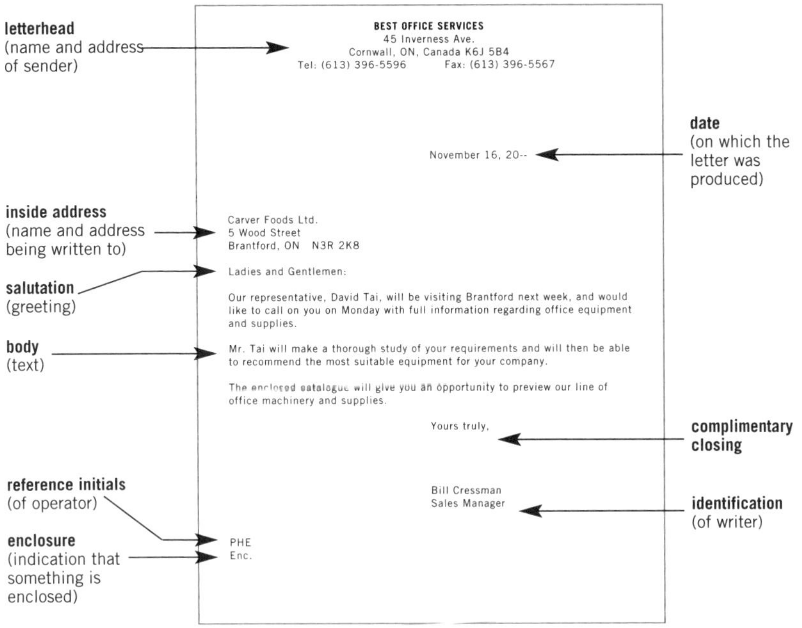
BEST OFFICE SERVICES
45 Inverness Ave.
Cornwall, ON, Canada K6J 5B4
Tel: (613) 396-5596 Fax: (613) 396-5567

November 16, 20--

Carver Foods Ltd.
5 Wood Street
Brantford, ON N3R 2K8

Ladies and Gentlemen:

Our representative, David Tai, will be visiting Brantford next week, and would like to call on you on Monday with full information regarding office equipment and supplies.

Mr. Tai will make a thorough study of your requirements and will then be able to recommend the most suitable equipment for your company.

The enclosed catalogue will give you an opportunity to preview our line of office machinery and supplies.

Yours truly,

Bill Cressman
Sales Manager

PHE
Enc.
letterhead (name and address of sender)
date (on which the letter was produced)
inside address (name and address being written to)
salutation (greeting)
body (text)
complimentary closing
reference initials (of operator)
identification (of writer)
enclosure (indication that something is enclosed)

Basic letter parts

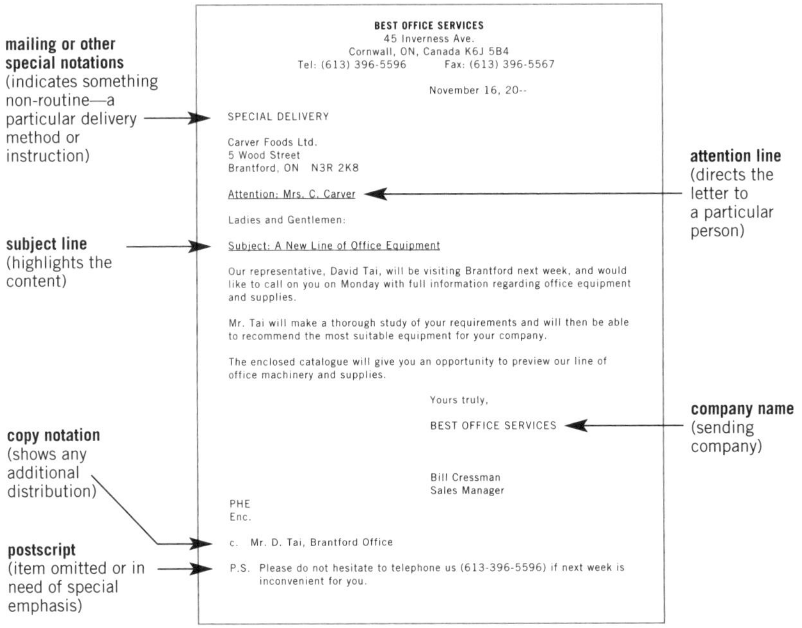
BEST OFFICE SERVICES
45 Inverness Ave.
Cornwall, ON, Canada K6J 5B4
Tel: (613) 396-5596 Fax: (613) 396-5567

November 16, 20--

SPECIAL DELIVERY

Carver Foods Ltd.
5 Wood Street
Brantford, ON N3R 2K8

Attention: Mrs. C. Carver

Ladies and Gentlemen:

Subject: A New Line of Office Equipment

Our representative, David Tai, will be visiting Brantford next week, and would like to call on you on Monday with full information regarding office equipment and supplies.

Mr. Tai will make a thorough study of your requirements and will then be able to recommend the most suitable equipment for your company.

The enclosed catalogue will give you an opportunity to preview our line of office machinery and supplies.

Yours truly,

BEST OFFICE SERVICES

Bill Cressman
Sales Manager

PHE
Enc.

c. Mr. D. Tai, Brantford Office

P.S. Please do not hesitate to telephone us (613-396-5596) if next week is inconvenient for you.
mailing or other special notations (indicates something non-routine—a particular delivery method or instruction)
attention line (directs the letter to a particular person)
subject line (highlights the content)
company name (sending company)
copy notation (shows any additional distribution)
postscript (item omitted or in need of special emphasis)

Additional letter parts

▶ **K20   Basic letter and punctuation styles**

Most business letters are formatted in one of the three basic styles and in one of the three punctuation patterns illustrated here, although closed punctuation is rarely used today.

Basic letter styles

Full block style

◆ all lines start at the left margin

Block style/Modified block style

◆ date and compli- mentary closing start at the centre

◆ all other lines start flush with the left margin

Semi-block style

◆ date and compli- mentary closing start at the centre

◆ paragraphs are indented

Basic punctuation styles

Open punctuation

◆ punctuation is *not* used after the date, inside address, salutation, complimentary closing, or identification unless these end with an abbreviation

Mixed (two-point or standard) punctuation

◆ a colon follows the salutation

◆ a comma follows the closing

◆ punctuation is *not* used after the date, inside address, company name, or identification unless these end with an abbreviation

Closed punctuation

This style is rarely used and should be avoided:

◆ a period follows the date

◆ a comma follows all lines of the inside address except the last one,* which is followed by a period

◆ a colon follows the salutation

◆ a comma follows the complimentary closing, the company name, and the individual writer's name

◆ a period follows the last word of the identification

*The postal code is *never* punctuated.

NOTE

◆ Any of the three punctuation styles shown may be used with any letter style. Full block and open punctuation are the most time-saving.

K

◆ Attention lines, subject lines, mailing notations, enclosures, reference initials, and copy notations have ending punctuation *only* if they end with an abbreviation.

◆ Time-saving tips for formatting letters appear in this unit, K88.

Basic letter and punctuation styles

August 24, 20--

Mr. Stefan Usselman
Box 24
Allan, SK SOK 0C0

Dear Mr. Usselman

Yours truly

L. Bitz

Full block style, open punctuation

August 24, 20--

Mr. Stefan Usselman
Box 24
Allan, SK SOK 0C0

Dear Mr. Usselman:

Yours truly,

L. Bitz

Block style/Modified block style, mixed punctuation

K

August 24, 20--.

Mr. Stefan Usselman,
Box 24,
Allan, SK SOK 0C0

Dear Mr. Usselman:

Yours truly,

L. Bitz, Manager.

Semi-block style, closed punctuation

206 Emerald Terrace
Saskatoon, SK S7J 4J1
August 24, 20--

Mr. Stefan Usselman
Box 24
Allan, SK SOK 0C0

Dear Stefan:

Would you be available for a brief meeting on September 17?

I am coming your way during that week and would very much like to talk to you about some new milking equipment I bought this year that is just great. Milking time is really reduced, and this leaves a few more hours each week for all those other chores that we farmers constantly face.

Give me a call or drop me a note if September 17 suits you.

Please give my best to your family. Look forward to seeing you soon.

Kindest regards,

Lyle Bitz

Personal business letter: Block style, mixed punctuation

▶ **K21   Additional letter and punctuation styles**

April 6, 20--

Mrs. Edith Tait
Nursing Co-ordinator
North York General Hospital
2005 Sheppard Avenue East
Willowdale, ON M2J 1E1

SIMPLIFIED LETTER STYLE

You might select this letter, Mrs. Tait, for use in your
office if you are looking for a way of cutting letter
production time to a minimum. Notice that letters in the
simplified style have neither a salutation nor a
complimentary closing. Note also that a subject line is
always included.

This letter is very similar to the full block style, and
should be formatted in the same way. The only major
change to make is to the subject line. This can be
located a double or triple space below the inside address
and a double or triple space above the body.

Craig Hkoury
Manager

PHE

Simplified style, open punctuation

April 6, 20--

Dear Mr. Carella:

The letter style favoured by most government
departments, civil service offices, and senior
executives for their personal correspondence is known
as the official style.

The official style is essentially a regular letter that
has the inside address as the last item. The letter may
have blocked or indented paragraphs and may be
produced in any one of the three punctuation styles.

If the letter includes a postscript, enclosure, or copy
notation, these are placed in their usual positions.

Yours sincerely,

F. Benjamin

PHE

Mr. S. Carella
247 Barrington Street
Halifax, NS B3H 2P8

Official style, mixed punctuation

April 16, 20--

Mr. G. Loric
Fleming and Sons
372 Pender Street West
Vancouver, BC V6B 1T4

Dear Mr. Fleming:

Have you been searching for a letter guaranteed to catch
the attention of your customers through its eye
appeal? Look no further! The hanging indented (or
suspended) style will do the job for you.

Paragraphs in this letter style start normally, but the
second and all succeeding lines are indented. The
indentation may be five or ten spaces, depending on
just how eye-catching you want your letter to be.

For the remaining details, simply follow the formatting
procedure for the block style letter.

Yours sincerely,

Maya Eby
Circulation Manager

PHE

*Hanging indented (suspended) style,
mixed punctuation*

April 16, 20--

MRS EDITH TAIT
NURSING COORDINATOR
NORTH YORK GENERAL HOSPITAL
2005 SHEPPARD AVE E
WILLOWDALE ON M2J 1E1

Dear Mrs. Tait

You might select this letter style because of its
simple, uncomplicated format.

Please note that the inside address is in capitals,
with no punctuation, to follow the Canada Post
guidelines.

Sincerely yours

George Lacey
Manager

*Full block letter showing Canada Post
preferred style for inside address. Use
this when envelopes and labels are
produced automatically.*

▶ **K22   Letterhead**

◆ Most organizations have preprinted letterhead.

◆ Create an elegant letterhead for your personal business letters if you have appropriate software.

 **Mobile Software Consultants**
2430 Tecumseh Rd. Windsor, ON N9E 1X8
Phone (519) 246-9870 Fax (519) 246-9873

▶ **K23   Letter placement**

Letters should be positioned on the page so that they are attractively framed by a balanced amount of white space.

◆ Word-processing software has a default (automatic) setting of a 6.5″ line, which is appropriate for most letters.

◆ Insert the date a double or triple space below the printed letterhead (or line 15). For a short letter, leave eight to ten lines between the date and inside address; for a longer letter, leave only four lines.

◆ Allow four to six lines for the signature block.

◆ Preview your letter, if possible, and adjust the spacing to achieve a balanced look before printing. This adjustment can be done by reducing or increasing the space between the date and inside address and in the signature area.

NOTE   If your organization's letterhead is not standard (e.g., demands a wide left margin) create your own default document and save it. Avoid changing margins. Leave a bottom margin of at least one inch (6 lines) for continuation pages. We provide guidelines for dealing with continuation pages in this unit at K39.

K24 Date

As mentioned, position this a double space below the letterhead or on line 15 either at the margin or the centre, depending on the letter style being used. Either of these styles is acceptable:

◆ Numeric: 20-- 07 29 (year, month, day)

◆ Standard: July 29, 20--

◆ Bring the date in from network to save keyboarding time.

K25 Mailing and special notations

◆ Show mailing notations at the left margin, midway between the date and inside address.

◆ Use these only when a special mail service, such as registered mail, is used.

K

♦ Use this position also for special notations such as "Confidential," "Personal," etc.

♦ In the rare situation where you might have both a mailing and a special notation, position them one above the other.

♦ Use capitals or initial caps and underscore, or boldface and no underscore.

PERSONAL   – or –   Personal   – or –   **Personal**

K26 Inside address

Canada Post preferred style

Canada Post has a preferred style for envelopes. When you use the inside address of your letter to generate envelopes or labels, you will need to use this style in your letters (see this unit, K6). If you key envelopes as a separate step, follow the traditional style for keying inside addresses.

Canada Post Preferred Envelope Style	*Traditional Style*
MS LAURA LARNEY	Ms. Laura Larney
ELLIOTT GALLERIES LTD	Elliott Galleries Ltd.
1257 SALT SPRING RD	1257 Salt Spring Road
VANCOUVER BC V1R 6R7	Vancouver, BC V1R 6R7

Traditional style

♦ Use at least three lines for the address.

♦ Keep line lengths approximately equal.

♦ Avoid abbreviations as much as possible. For acceptable street abbreviations, see this unit, K8; for provincial and state abbreviations, see K9.

♦ Indent any continuation lines by two spaces.

♦ Include a social title—Mr., Mrs., Miss, Ms., Messrs. (plural male), Mesdames or Mmes (plural female). In cases where gender is unknown (e.g., Chris Fisher), omit social title.

♦ Professional titles and special titles such as Professor, Reverend, etc., are not usually abbreviated, but Doctor (Dr.) may be.

♦ Do not show titles *and* degrees—use one or the other, but not both (B. Turcotte, Ph.D. or Dr. B. Turcotte).

♦ Check the proper form of address if you are writing to a prominent person in public life, politics, the clergy, or the military (see Unit 1, "Communications: Language Skills").

♦ A person's position in an organization may be shown in these ways (note the use of the comma):

Mr. F. Sharman, President   Mrs. Jane Tobias
Buttonville Golf Club   Director of Services
                                   Collingwood Consultants Ltd.

Mr. F. Ciampaglia
President, BIB Inc.

- Key names of organizations so that they match those on letterheads for spelling, capitalization, and abbreviations.
- When street names are numbers, use words for one to ten and use numbers for over ten:

  160 Seventh Street   32 South 13th Street   43 – 13 Street

- Separate the town from the province with a comma.
- Do not capitalize city or town names.
- Provinces may be shown in full or in the abbreviated form (see the Appendix).
- Show the postal code as the *last* item, immediately after the province and separated from it by two spaces, or on its own line.
- For addresses in the United States, include the zip code after the name of the state and "U.S.A." as the last line.
- Place routing codes for overseas addresses *before* the country name:

  Mme D. Dupont
  5, rue des College
  F-61760 Barr
  France

NOTE   French addresses take a comma after the street number.

- See this unit, K6, for more illustrations.

K27 Attention line

- Locate the attention line two lines below the inside address, centred, or starting from the left margin (preferred). All of the following are acceptable styles:

  Attention Mr. J. Dunn   ATTENTION MR. J. DUNN
  Attention: Mrs. J. Crisp   ATTENTION: *Miss M. Elliott*
  Attention: Mr. J. Dunn   Attention of the Traffic Dept.

- If you use a computer and want to produce your envelopes or labels from the inside address of your letter or you are using window envelopes, incorporate the attention line into the inside address:

  Attention Mr. John James
  Aoko Golf Wearhouse
  137 Bishop Crescent
  MARKHAM, ON L3P 4N5

K28 Salutation

- Position the salutation two lines below the address (or attention line if there is one and it is shown below the address).
- Capitalize the first word and all nouns:

  Dear Mr. Waugh   Ladies and Gentlemen
  Dear Chris Fisher (gender unknown)   Dear Ms. Patel
  Dear G. O'Keefe (first name and gender unknown)

◆ See Unit 1, "Communications: Language Skills," for help in selecting the appropriate salutation.

K29 Subject line

◆ The subject line is placed two lines below the salutation, centred, or starting from the left margin (much preferred). The following are all acceptable styles:

SUBJECT: ANNUAL SALES CONVENTION   Annual Sales Convention
Subject: Annual Sales Convention   Re: Annual Sales Convention

K30 Body (message part of the letter)

◆ Begin the body two lines below the salutation or subject line.

◆ Single-space; double-space between paragraphs. In the case of an extremely short letter, the entire body may be double-spaced.

◆ Paragraph indents will be determined by the letter style used.

K31 Complimentary closing

◆ Place the complimentary closing a double space below the body, starting at either the left margin or the centre, depending on the letter style used.

◆ Capitalize the first word only:

Yours truly   Very sincerely yours

◆ See Unit 1, "Communications: Language Skills," for help in selecting the appropriate complimentary closing.

K32 Company name in closing

◆ If the company name is used in the closing, key the company name in capitals a double space below the complimentary closing:

Yours truly

GRANATO GRAIN CO.

◆ When the company name is long, it may be centred under the complimentary closing. In this case, be consistent and centre the identification line(s) also:

Yours truly

GRANATO CANADIAN GRAIN COMPANY

(4–6 lines)

Rosalie Granato

K33 Identification line (author's name and position)

◆ Locate the identification line anywhere from four to seven lines below the closing or company name.

◆ Use it as a balancing line. For example, if you have only a small amount of space left at the lower edge of the page, leave four lines, but stretch this to seven lines if there is surplus space to be used.

◆ Show the name of the author and/or the position held:

Yours truly

↓ 2

PARANI, WONG & COMPANY

↓ 4–6

Jason D. Wong
Sales Director

Yours sincerely

↓ 4–6

Vikki Cranfield, Ph.D.
Chair, History Department

◆ A man does not usually indicate his courtesy title in the closing; a woman has choices:

Grant Parker, President   Ms. M. Chantrell
Mary Chantrell   Miss M. Chantrell, Principal
M. Chantrell   Mrs. M. Chantrell

◆ When the courtesy title is not shown, you may include it with the handwritten signature, but it rarely is:

Yours sincerely

Mary Chantrell

Miss M. Chantrell

Yours sincerely

Miss M. Chantrell

Mary Chantrell

◆ Use one or two lines, but do not let the identification extend beyond the margins.

◆ If you are authorized to sign a letter in the author/signer's absence, use one of these forms:

Barb Davison
per
Charmaine Reynolds

Charmaine Reynolds
for
Barb Davison

(The author is Barb Davison; the signer is Charmaine Reynolds.)

K34 Reference initials

◆ Insert reference initials at the left margin. Use the same line as the identification line or two lines below it.

◆ If the author's name is keyed in the identification, it is not necessary to show his or her initials. If both author's and operator's initials are

K

used, show the author's initials first, and the operator's initials second. Choose from these styles:

PHE:LF   – *or* –   PHE:lf

LF   – *or* –   lf   (only operator's initials shown)

K35 Enclosure/attachment notation

◆ Use this notation when something is to be included with the letter.

◆ Show the notation one or two spaces below the reference initials. Choose from any of these styles:

Enc:	Enclosure	Enc. Cheque $453.95	
Encl.	Enc. (2)	Enc. 3	Encls.
Attach.	Attachment	Attach. (Report)	Attachments

NOTE Attachment indicates that the material is held together by a paper clip or is stapled.

K36 Copy notation

◆ Use this notation when one or more people are receiving copies of the letter.

◆ Insert the notation one or two spaces below the enclosure notation (or whatever comes last in the letter), at the left margin. The following are acceptable styles:

c Mrs. M. Daniel	Copy to	Mr. F. Rocca
cc Mr. D. Ling	Copies to	Mr. W. Roswell
		Ms. F. Fiore

Fax Mrs. G. Rollins   **or**   fc(fax copy)   Mrs. G. Rollins

◆ When the distribution of the copies is not to be shown on the original, a blind copy notation should be used on the copies only:

bc Mr. D. Roswell

◆ Some organizations prefer the use of *pc* (photocopy) in place of *c* or *cc*:

pc Mr. D. Ling

K37 Postscript

◆ Use the postscript (P.S.) to add emphasis or to include something omitted from the body.

◆ Position it a double space below the last item, and set up in either style shown:

P.S.   Thank you so much for your lunch invitation. I'm sorry I can't make it this time.

P.S.   Thank you so much for your lunch invitation. I'm sorry I can't make it this time.

▶ K38   Filing Notation/path and filename

This is a coded notation that indicates where the document is stored or saved on disk. Most software packages have an automatic filename insert feature.

◆ Use a small font size (8- or 9-point) for the filing notation.

◆ Key the filing notation on the left as a footer or a double space below the reference initials, the enclosure notation, or the copy notation, whichever is last.

PHE:oi

A:\unit12.wpd

NOTE   *oi* means operator's initials

▶ K39   Multi-page letters

◆ When letters take up more than one page, insert a heading on successive pages showing the addressee, the page number, and the date.

◆ Use the same quality stationery as used for page 1, but use a plain sheet (unless your firm has printed continuation-page stationery).

◆ Position the heading on line 7. Continue the body of the letter a triple or double space under the heading.

line 7→ Cooper Lumber Co.   2   20-- 08 12

↓ 2 or 3

cheque will be received from you within the next few days. If this cheque is not received, the matter will be...

line 7→ Newfoundland Lumber Supply Company
Page 2
20-- 08 12

↓ 2 or 3

cheque will be received from you within the...

◆ Use the addressee's name as it appears on the first line of the inside address on page 1.

◆ Do *not* have fewer than two lines of a paragraph at the foot of one page or at the top of the continuation page.

◆ Do not isolate the signature block. Have at least two lines of the body on the page with it.

◆ Use your header feature and your widow/orphan protect feature for very long letters.

▶ **K40 Displayed information**

Numbered sentences or items in a list

♦ Leave a line of space above and below each numbered item.

♦ Single-space each numbered item and double-space between them.

♦ Either line up the numbers with the existing margin or indent five spaces from the left margin.

♦ Computer users should use the automatic indent feature.

Numbered sentences

Quoted or inset information

♦ Leave a line of space above and below any information that has been quoted or that must be set off from the rest of the body.

♦ Indent five spaces from the left and right margins.

♦ Single-space the quoted or inset text.

19th April 2001

The Toronto Star
One Yonge Street
Toronto, ON   M5E 1E5

Gentlemen:

Please insert the following advertisement in the classified
advertising section of your paper in category 710, General
Help Wanted.

Automotive parts manufacturing firm requires
person to perform packaging and warehouse
duties in the Toronto distribution centre. We
offer a full benefits program, 5-day week, and
good starting salary. Phone (416) 232-3198.

Please make the advertisement a small one and arrange
for it to appear on Thursday and Friday, July 10 and 11.

Yours truly,

M. Walesa
Human Resources Manager

cb

Quoted or inset information

Tabulated information

- Follow the rules for keying tables (see this unit, K70).
- Leave a line of space above and below the table.
- If the table has a short line length (i.e., is narrower than the line length of your letter, set up the tabulation normally.
- If the table is a long one (i.e., is longer than the line length of your letter), first calculate for the tabulation and then set your margins for the rest of the letter. Set your margins five spaces to the right and to the left of the tabulation line length. This will guarantee that your table fits within the line length of the letter.

Dear Mrs. McMaster:

Please send us a quotation on each of the following
items:

5 cm steel casing	SC4	5 sections
1.5 cm Logan pump	LP1	4 sections
3 cm twist steel cable	TS7	400 m

Please show f.o.b. to Prince George, British
Columbia.

Special effects

When a particularly eye-catching letter or insert is needed and you have electronic equipment:

◆ Use different fonts and type sizes.

◆ Highlight sections in boldface.

◆ Justify inset or quoted blocks

◆ Use your line-draw feature.

▶ K41 Form letters

Form letters contain basic information that will be sent to a number of people, yet each letter must appear to be individually produced. Use the mail/merge feature of your software to achieve this.

◆ Create and save the master letter.

◆ Create and save the source list of variables (names, addresses, dates, amounts).

◆ Use the merge option to produce the finished letters.

Current Date

FIELD(Title) FIELD(Initial) FIELD(Last Name)
FIELD(Address)
FIELD(City, FIELD(Province) FIELD(Postal Code)

Dear FIELD(Title) FIELD(Last Name)

Thank you for applying for a charge account with us. Enclosed is your credit card as approval of your application. We are pleased to inform you that your credit limit has been set at FIELD(Amount of Credit) and that your account balance will be calculated on the FIELD(Date of Account Balance) day of each month.

We appreciate the opportunity to be of service to you and welcome you as a Lockwood charge account holder.

Yours very sincerely,

D. Kappelhoff
Credit Manager

Enc.
oi

Master of form letter showing merge codes

FIELDNAMES(Title;Initial;Last Name;Address;City;Province;Postal Code;Amount of Credit;Date of Account Balance)ENDRECORD
Mr.ENDFIELD
G.ENDFIELD
GrevenitisENDFIELD
556 Wynford PlaceENDFIELD
ActonENDFIELD
ONENDFIELD
L7J 2L5ENDFIELD
$2000ENDFIELD
19thENDFIELD
ENDRECORD

Mr.ENDFIELD
P.ENDFIELD
DeragonENDFIELD
95 Kingsgate CourtENDFIELD
DundasENDFIELD
ONENDFIELD
L9H 3Z6ENDFIELD
$1500ENDFIELD
19thENDFIELD
ENDRECORD

Mr.ENDFIELD
B.ENDFIELD
HennickENDFIELD
15 Wildewood AvenueENDFIELD
HamiltonENDFIELD
ONENDFIELD
L8T 1X4ENDFIELD
$2200ENDFIELD
19thENDFIELD
ENDRECORD

Variables source list with merge codes

Form letters contain basic information that will be sent to a number of people, yet each letter must appear to be individually produced. Use the mail/merge feature of your software to achieve this.

◆ Create and save the master letter.

◆ Create and save the source list of variables (names, addresses, dates, amounts).

◆ Use the merge option to produce the finished letters.

NOTE   Usually you can automatically produce envelopes or labels from your variables source list. Check your software instruction manual.

Mr. G. Grevenitis
556 Wynford Place
Acton, ON L7J 2L5

Dear Mr. Grevenitis:

Thank you for applying for a charge account with us. Enclosed is your credit card as approval of your application. We are pleased to inform you that your credit limit has been set at $2000 and that your account balance will be calculated on the 19th day of each month.

We appreciate the opportunity to be of service to you and welcome you as a Lockwood charge account holder.

Yours very sincerely,

D. Kappelhoff
Credit Manager

Enc.
oi

Form letter ready for mailing

▶ **K42   Merged letters**

You can use electronic equipment to produce form letters by saving on disk paragraphs that are frequently used. These prepared paragraphs can be assembled and merged as needed. An example of such paragraphs is shown on the following page.

1. Thank you for your interest in establishing a charge account with Fleming Fashions.

2. Your application for a charge account has been approved and an account number has been established for you. Your credit card showing your assigned number is enclosed.

3. We regret to inform you that your application for a charge account cannot be accepted. You are encouraged to apply again in the future when your credit status improves.

4. Your application for a charge account is on hold because we need some further information from you. The enclosed card and envelope are for your reply. When your application is complete, you will hear from us again.

5. As always, we look forward to satisfying your needs for clothing with style. Won't you stop in soon to use your new credit card?

6. As always, we look forward to satisfying your needs for clothing with style.

Merged paragraphs

Dear Mrs. Zarengo:

Thank you for your interest in establishing a charge account with Fleming Fashions.

Your application for a charge account has been approved and an account number has been established for you. Your credit card showing your assigned number is enclosed.

As always, we look forward to satisfying your needs for clothing with style. Won't you stop in soon to use your new credit card?

Sincerely yours,

Finally assembled letter text (using paragraphs 1, 2, and 5)

▶ K43 Letters on small stationery

◆ The names given to stationery that is smaller than standard are Monarch and Baronial.

◆ Senior business executives may use them to add distinction to their letters or when it is necessary to catch a reader's attention.

◆ Set margins of one inch (2.5 cm) from each side and follow the standard formatting rules for letters.

K

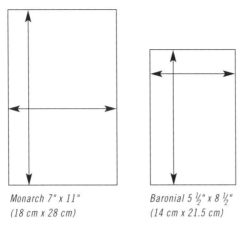

Monarch 7" x 11"
(18 cm x 28 cm)

Baronial 5 ½" x 8 ½"
(14 cm x 21.5 cm)

K44 MEMORANDUMS

Use interoffice memorandums (memos) when written communication between company employees is necessary.

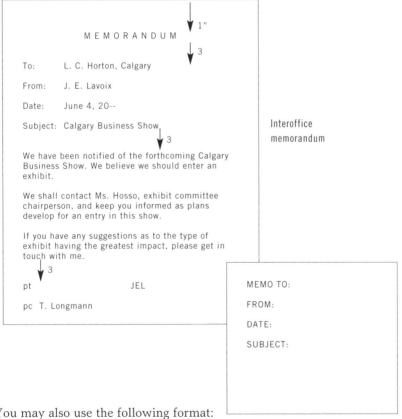

MEMORANDUM

↓ 1"

↓ 3

To: L. C. Horton, Calgary

From: J. E. Lavoix

Date: June 4, 20--

Subject: Calgary Business Show

↓ 3

We have been notified of the forthcoming Calgary Business Show. We believe we should enter an exhibit.

We shall contact Ms. Hosso, exhibit committee chairperson, and keep you informed as plans develop for an entry in this show.

If you have any suggestions as to the type of exhibit having the greatest impact, please get in touch with me.

↓ 3

pt   JEL

pc T. Longmann

Interoffice
memorandum

MEMO TO:

FROM:

DATE:

SUBJECT:

K

You may also use the following format:

Omit MEMORANDUM in top line

◆ Inside address, salutation, and complimentary closing are not used.

◆ Use the default setting of a 6.5" line.

- Use block style (i.e., do not indent paragraphs).
- Do not repeat the author's name in the signature area if it is given at the top. Reference initials may, however, be shown at the centre or left side, a double or triple space below the body.
- Titles are not needed in the "To" and "From" sections but may, as a matter of courtesy, be used in the "To" section only.
- Format details for enclosure and copy notations, postscripts, and multiple pages are the same as for letters (see this unit, K35–K40).
- If preprinted stationery is not used, "Memo To" or "To," "From," "Date," and "Subject" may be located one under the other as illustrated. With printed stationery, insert the relevant information to suit the stationery.

NOTE The copy (copies) notation may also be keyed at the top of the memo.

Example:

Memorandum

To: Erika Darling

Copies to: L. Bognar, T. Longman

From: Steven Campbell

Date: March 4, 2001

Subject: Environmental Issues

M E M O R A N D U M

TO: L. C. Horton, Calgary

FROM: J. K. Drury

DATE: June 4, 20--

SUBJECT: Calgary Business Show

We have been notified of the forthcoming Calgary Business Show. We believe we should enter an exhibit.

Once we have contacted Ms. Hanna Hosso, the exhibit committee chairperson, we will let you know how plans develop for an entry in this show.

If you have any suggestions as to the type of exhibit having the greatest impact, please get in touch with me.

pt   JKD

pc   T. Longmann

Interoffice memorandum on preprinted stationery

K45 REPORTS, ESSAYS, MANUSCRIPTS

Reports may be formal or informal. When they are informal, the memo format described in the previous section is generally acceptable. If a formal report is required, the following will be helpful:

◆ Reports, essays, and manuscripts are enough alike that the instructions here apply to reports used in business, to formal academic essays, and to material being prepared for publication.

◆ Reports, essays, and manuscripts usually consist of a title page, contents page, body, and bibliography. Some may also contain a preface, appendices, a glossary, and an index.

◆ Use the many automatic functions of your word-processing equipment as you produce reports. These features are discussed here because some parts of reports can be generated automatically.

◆ Use good-quality, plain white, letter-size paper, unpunched.

◆ Always save a copy on disk or make a photocopy of the document.

▶ K46 Title page

The title page (also known as the cover page) shows the name of the company, organization, or institution; document title (topic); name of author; name of person and/or company to whom submitted; and the submission date.

◆ Format the page so that it is attractive and easy to follow.

THE MARITIME PAPER COMPANY

Head Office

THE BUSINESS REPORT—ITS FINISHED APPEARANCE

Submitted to
Mr. E. J. Reynolds, President

by
Robert L. Craig
Office Manager

20-- 07 15

Centred title page

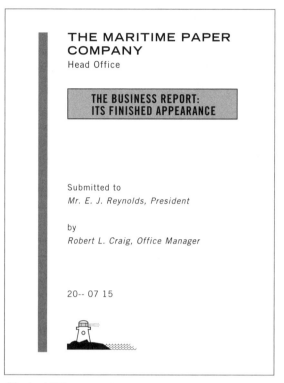

Blocked title page

- ◆ Use your software to good advantage (lines, bold, italics, different fonts) but don't overdo it—a simple, conservative style is best.
- ◆ Leave at least six blank lines at the top and bottom.
- ◆ The paper used can be heavier than that used for the body.

▶ K47 Preface

The preface (also known as the introduction, abstract, foreword, synopsis, summary, or digest) outlines the purpose of the work, its scope and limitations, the methods of research employed, the major ideas, the name of the person who authorized it, and any special observations or acknowledgments.

- ◆ Key the preface as a separate page.
- ◆ When a contents page is used, the preface will precede it. When there is no contents page, the preface will go between the title page and the body.
- ◆ Use the same margins, placement, and spacing as for page 1 of the body but leave the page unnumbered.

PREFACE

The results of research into the importance of the visual effect of reports indicates that their appearance is indeed a significant factor in their impact.

It is hoped that this report will have the effect of making report writers in the company aware of the need to devote sufficient time and energy to illustrations, reproduction means, and binding methods.

4

Acknowledgments

2

In presenting this report, we wish to acknowledge the assistance and co-operation received from the print shop staff and the desktop publishing personnel.

▶ K48   Contents page

The contents page lists each major section (and sometimes subsections) of the document, as well as page numbers. It is needed only in longer reports (10 or more pages) and should be prepared *after* the rest of the report has been finished so that accurate page numbers can be included.

The contents page can be produced automatically with some software. Check your manual and use this feature if you can. If not:

◆ Use the same margin settings as in the body.

◆ If the contents list is a short one, centre the material vertically on the page. No page number is needed.

◆ If the contents list is a long one and likely to take up more than one page, insert the heading 2″ from the top of page and finish 1″ from the bottom edge line. Start the continuation page 1″ from the top of page. Use roman numerals to number these contents pages and place them at the bottom of page.

◆ The contents page should follow the heading pattern and/or numbering system used in the report, essay, or manuscript itself.

K

TABLE OF CONTENTS

K

NOTE An informal report usually does not include a glossary or an index.

▶ **K49 Body of the report**

K50 Placement guide

Starting line	Page 1	$1\frac{1}{2}$" or 2"
(top margin)	Page 2, etc.	1"*
	(If the document is presented in chapters or separate units, start these 2" from top of pages.)	
Line length	6"/6.5"	
(side margins)	1" left/right margins	
Last line	1"	
(Bottom margin)		

*Default settings with all word-processing software

NOTE Increase the left margin by $1/2$" for a bound report containing paper printed on one side only. Increase *both* margins by $1/2$" if paper is printed on both sides. The printer menu of some software provides a binding feature. If you use this, you will not have to change margins from the default settings.

2"

THE BUSINESS REPORT: ITS FINISHED APPEARANCE
↓ 2"

An effective business report requires research, organization, and writing skill. The final layout and appearance must also be carefully considered if the report is to achieve its desired effect.
↓ 2

ILLUSTRATIONS
↓ 2

Pictures, graphs, or illustrations will help you get an idea across quickly or emphasize a particular point. Remember that:
↓ 2

• Graphs and charts have more impact than tables.

• Each graph, chart, or picture should make only one point.

• Keep the graph or picture as close to the related text as possible.
↓ 2

HEADINGS
↓ 2

"Headings and subheadings pinpoint and summarize ideas for easy absorption by the reader."[1] If you want your message to be acted upon, make it as easy to read and understand as possible.

---

[1] Farmiloe, Dorothy, Creative Communication for Business Students, Holt, Rinehart & Winston, Toronto, 1991, p. 186.

K

NOTE Use double-spacing throughout report for productivity (e.g., before side headings, subheadings, and paragraph headings).

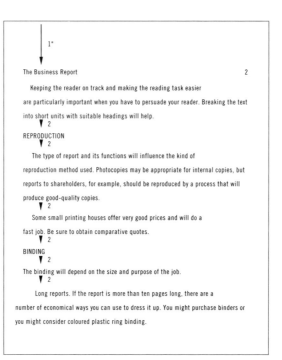

The Business Report   2

Keeping the reader on track and making the reading task easier
are particularly important when you have to persuade your reader. Breaking the text
into short units with suitable headings will help.
▼ 2
REPRODUCTION
▼ 2
The type of report and its functions will influence the kind of
reproduction method used. Photocopies may be appropriate for internal copies, but
reports to shareholders, for example, should be reproduced by a process that will
produce good-quality copies.
▼ 2
Some small printing houses offer very good prices and will do a
fast job. Be sure to obtain comparative quotes.
▼ 2
BINDING
▼ 2
The binding will depend on the size and purpose of the job.
▼ 2
Long reports. If the report is more than ten pages long, there are a
number of economical ways you can use to dress it up. You might purchase binders or
you might consider coloured plastic ring binding.

K51 Starting lines

K

For page 1 of the body and major units or chapters, key the heading 2"
from the top. For continuation pages, key the number 1" from the top.

K52 Spacing and indents

◆ Use double spacing and a half-inch paragraph indent. For business
reports, economic and/or environmental-concern considerations
might call for single or $1^1/_2$ spacing. The first rough draft should,
however, be double-spaced.

◆ Use single spacing for displayed information (e.g., long quotations,
numbered lists, tables).

K53 Headings

◆ Use headings and subheadings to organize the material, to show
relationships, and to indicate the relative importance of the separate
sections of the report.

◆ Decide what your heading pattern will be and stick to it.

◆ Use of a full header is an option on page two and succeeding pages of
a report and can be keyed in Initial Caps or ALL CAPS: e.g., THE
BUSINESS REPORT Page 2.

◆ Suggested styles that will permit five levels of subheads as above are:
  • capitals, centred (if the heading is long, use two lines and centre
    both)
  • capitals, side

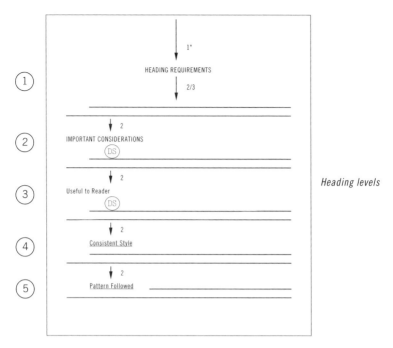

Heading levels

- initial capitals, side, underscored or boldfaced
- initial capitals, side, indented five, underscored or boldfaced
- initial capitals, side, underscored or boldfaced, and run in (indented five)

◆ To speed up your keying, if you are working from a draft, decide on heading categories *before* you start keying and then code each heading in the job (e.g., number them from one to five). Follow your code sheet as you proceed.

NOTE Use styles feature of word-processing software for headings and body text.

◆ Because mixing double- and triple-spacing on a computer can be both a nuisance and time-consuming, use double-spacing throughout the report. Always tab for new paragraphs when using double-spacing.

K54 Numbering systems

If information will be presented in sections and subsections, use a consistent pattern of numbers, letters, and indents so that the reader can easily identify the relative importance of the material. The following system works well.

    I. A major topic.
       A. A section of the major topic.
          1. The next subsection.
             a. Part of 1, above.
                (1) A subsection of a.
                (2) A second subsection of a.

b. Another part of 1, above.

2. A second subsection.

B. Another section of the major topic.

II. The next major topic.

A. A section of this major topic.

NOTE The five-space tabs preset on your software are useful here.

K55 Ending the pages

Each page should have a bottom margin of 1". *Exception*: You can adjust the bottom margin by $1/_2$" to accommodate one lone line.

Your computer will page automatically but you must follow these rules and make adjustments if necessary:

◆ Keep at least two lines of a paragraph at the foot of one page and always show at least two lines at the top of the next page so that you avoid widows and orphans.

Orphan The first line of a paragraph appearing by itself on the last line of a page

Widow The last line of a paragraph appearing by itself as the first line of a page

Some software has automatic widow/orphan protection.

◆ With three-line paragraphs, fit all three at the foot of one page or carry all three over to the top of the next. Use *block protect* to accomplish this, if possible.

◆ Do *not* key a heading on one page and the body on the next so that the heading is isolated. (Block protect can help here.)

◆ Do *not* break tables unless they are very long and have natural breaking points in them. Block protect will automatically keep them intact for you.

K56 Numbering the pages

Introduction (table of contents, preface)

◆ Leave these unnumbered unless many pages are involved.

◆ Use roman numerals or letters of the alphabet if several pages are involved with each section, and place these at the foot, centred. Count the title page as *i* (1), but do not show the number.

Body

◆ Word-processing software can automatically insert *headers* and *footers* (page titles and page numbers). At your choice, the information will remain the same; the page number will increase automatically.

◆ Leave the first page unnumbered. If you use automatic page numbering, you can suppress page 1.

◆ Number the second and succeeding pages either 1″ from the top line or 1″ from the bottom edge of the page, at the centre or on the right-hand side.

◆ Discontinue the headers on the endnotes or notes pages, but keep the page numbers on these pages.

Ending (appendixes, bibliography, index)

◆ Number these as part of the report or as separate sections.

◆ Use roman numerals, arabic numerals in parentheses, or letters of the alphabet if several pages are involved within each section, and place these at the foot.

◆ Use a numbering system that has not already been used in the introductory pages.

K57 Displayed information

Numbered lists

◆ Start these indented $^1/_2$″ on each side or align them with the margins. Aligning with the margin and using the automatic indent is the faster method.

NOTE Use auto-numbering feature of word-processing software.

◆ Single-space each numbered item but double-space between them.

1. Enumerations occur frequently in reports and deserve special treatment.

2. Display these by means of spacing and indents.

Tabulated material

If the material has already been keyed in a spreadsheet or other document, import it into the new document if possible so that rekeying is avoided. If keying is needed:

◆ Follow the rules given for tables (see this unit, K70).

◆ Do *not* let tables extend beyond the margins of the body text.

◆ Use single spacing.

◆ Consider using a different font. This could be used to highlight material or so that the table takes less space.

◆ Leave a blank line above and below the table.

◆ Insert a footnote for a table directly below it, rather than at the foot of the page.

K

K58 Graphics

Graphics—pie charts, line graphs, bar graphs—can be used effectively in reports to replace text and present complex information in a simple format.

◆ If you are using integrated software, prepare graphics separately and then incorporated them into the text. Graphics from spreadsheets done on non-integrated software can be imported into most word-processing software.

◆ If a list of illustrations is required, insert this as a separate sheet after the body of the report and before the bibliography.

K59 Special effects

Your software can help to make your report more effective. Change print sizes and fonts for variety. Justify the right margin to add a professional look. Use lines and shading effectively. Keep your pages simple and uncluttered. Don't overdo it, though. These text enhancers lose their value if they are overused.

White space is a very important tool to use with page design. White space is empty space—margins, spacing between lines, etc. Use this space to set off the design of the page and to give the page a look of balance, clarity, simplicity, and organization. Again, don't overdo it (see this unit, K89).

K

K60 Quoted material

Short quotations

Quotations of three lines or fewer should appear in the body of the report within quotation marks. End each with a raised numeral indicating a footnote or endnote reference. If your software cannot produce raised numbers (superscript), show the numerals in brackets [1] or parentheses (1).

Quoting complete sentences

Use quotation marks, begin the quotation with a capital, and end it with a period:

> Writers should be aware that "Quotations of just a few lines are double-spaced and placed within quotation marks."[2]

Quoting parts of sentences

Use the ellipsis (...) to indicate that not all of the sentence from which the quotation is taken has been used:

> Writers should be aware that quotations and paraphrases "...of just a few lines are double-spaced."[1]

> Writers should be aware that quotations "...of just a few lines..."[1] are double-spaced and may be introduced and ended by the ellipsis.

NOTE   Use *four* periods if the closing ellipsis comes at the end of the sentence.

Long quotations

For quotation, longer than three lines:

◆ Leave a line of space above and below them.

◆ Single-space the quoted material.

◆ Indent five spaces on each side of the margins.

◆ Do *not* use quotation marks.

◆ Indent the first line an additional five spaces if you are quoting from the beginning of a paragraph:

> Dorothy Farmiloe says on this subject:
>
> > An appendix is the place to put supplementary material not essential to the report but which may aid the reader's understanding of it in some way.[2]

◆ If the quotation opens part way through a sentence, use an ellipsis to begin the quotation.

◆ If the quotation closes with an incomplete sentence, use the ellipsis *plus* a period at the end.

K61 Footnotes, endnotes, and textnotes

◆ Footnotes appear on the page on which the referenced material appears.

◆ Endnotes provide the same information as footnotes but are keyed on one separate sheet headed "Notes" or "Endnotes" at the end of the section, chapter, or report.

◆ Textnotes provide a third choice for showing references. Here, the writer records the information source in parentheses at the appropriate point in the document. Textnotes are not numbered. Usually a short version is used and full information is provided in a bibliography.

> Bartering involved the exchange of goods or services for other goods or services; no money changed hands. (Bedford et al., *The Canadian Office*, p. 2)

Textnote example

For academic situations, follow the style stipulated by the institution. For other situations, endnotes and textnotes are increasingly used because they are so easy to produce.

Footnotes, endnotes, and textnotes are also used to:

◆ provide additional useful information on a particular topic to that noted in the body of the report:

6. For more detailed information on Canada's population, consult the statistical data published regularly by Statistics Canada.

♦ identify the source of information quoted exactly or paraphrased:

11. H. Ramsey Fowler et al., <u>The Little, Brown Handbook</u>, 2nd Canadian ed. (Don Mills, ON: Addison-Wesley, 1998), p 117.

K62 Numbering notes

Textnotes are not numbered. Sophisticated software offers automatic footnoting or endnoting and is very easy to use. If this feature is not available, do the following:

♦ Use arabic numerals and number each quotation or reference consecutively. Use asterisks when only a few references are needed.

♦ In the body, insert the reference numbers a half line above the regular keying line at the *end* of the quotation or reference, outside any punctuation, and without space before it. If your software does not offer superscript, number as in example 2 on the page that follows.

1. ...spacing is as you would expect."[2]
2. ...spacing is as you would expect."[2]

In the footnote or endnote itself, the numeral may or may not be raised (see below). When you use the automatic footnoting feature of your word-processing equipment, this decision will be made by the software used.

K63 Keying footnotes

Footnotes must be inserted on the page on which the reference appears. Software with automatic footnoting does most of the work for you. You simply key in the appropriate reference information when you key in the quotation, and the software positions the reference correctly.

♦ Single-space footnote references and leave a single space between them.

♦ If the text is short on the last page, still insert footnotes at the *foot* of the page.

♦ Follow the style of either example shown below. They will suit most applications. However, academic institutions may have specific requirements and these must, of course, be followed.

♦ Follow the order and punctuation shown in this unit, K65, which vary with the type of publication being cited.

1. Jonathon Whelan, E-Mail @Work: Get Moving with Digital Communications, (Toronto: Pearson Education Canada, 2000), p. 204 (Toronto: Pearson Education Canada, 2000, p. 204.

NOTE Italicize or underline names of books, magazines, newspapers, and periodicals.

K64 Keying endnotes

Sophisticated software keys endnotes automatically. When this feature is not available, follow these guidelines:

◆ Use a separate sheet.

◆ Start 2″ from top margin.

◆ Use the Heading "Notes"/"Endnotes" and centre it.

◆ Single-space each reference and double-space after each one.

◆ If continuation pages are required, start 1″ from top margin and use a page numbering system that has not already been used (e.g., lower-case roman numerals).

◆ Place the finished page(s) after the body of the document and in front of the bibliography.

NOTES/Endnotes

↓ 2 or 3

1. Aspasia Kaplaneris, "Earthbound...for Now," *Between Worlds: A Reader, Rhetoric, and Handbook*, 1st Canadian ed., ed. Susan Bachmann, Melinda Barth, and Karen Golets Pancer (Don Mills, ON: Addison-Wesley, 1998), p. 139.

2. Chris Howard, "Performance Appraisals: Appraise This!" *Canadian Business*, 29 May 1998, p. 24.

K65 Keying textnotes

◆ If a work is short and no bibliography is to be provided, include a full reference the first time it is used and a short one thereafter:

Jonathon Whelan, E-Mail @Work: Get Moving with Digital Communications, (Toronto: Pearson Education Canada, 2000), p. 204

◆ If a bibliography is provided, short references are appropriate throughout the document:

Whelan et al., *E-mail @Work*, p. 204

K66 Constructing references

Provided here are standard, acceptable methods. Some academic institutions and publishers have set rules in this regard and their preferences should be followed. Simplicity is the keynote in the style suggested here.

Anthologies and collections

In references to a selection from the collected works of one author, state the author and the work, the title (underscored or in italic), the name(s) of the editor(s), the place of publication, the publisher, the year of publication, and the page number:

K

1. W.B. Yeats, "The Lake Isle of Innisfree," <u>W.B. Yeats Selected Poems</u> (New York: Gramercy Books, 1992), p. 57.

1. W.B. Yeats, "The Lake Isle of Innisfree," *W.B. Yeats Selected Poems* (New York: Gramercy Books, 1992), p. 57.

If a reference is made to a work in an anthology, follow this pattern:

1. Alice Walker, "Even as I Hold You," *Poetry: A Longman Pocket Anthology*, 2nd ed., ed. R.S. Gwynn (New York: Addison-Wesley Educational Publishers Inc., 1998), p. 313.

Books

Full footnote　The standard footnote includes the footnote number, the author(s) and/or editor(s), the book title, the place of publication, the publisher, the year of publication, and the page number(s):

5. H. Ramsey Fowler, et al., <u>The Little, Brown Handbook</u>, 2nd Canadian ed. (Don Mills, ON: Addison-Wesley, 1998), p. 117.

◆ For two authors, list their names in the order used on the title page of the book:

6. T. Palmer and V. D'Amico, <u>Accounting for Canadian Colleges</u>, 2nd ed. (Toronto: Addison Wesley, 2001), p. 206.

◆ For more than two authors, state the first author and then add *et al.* (and others):

7. Burnett et al., <u>Introduction to Integrated Marketing Communications</u> (Toronto, ON: Prentice Hall Inc., 2001), p. 25.

Non-print sources

For CD-ROMs, recordings, tapes, interviews, speeches, videos, and performances, provide sufficient information for the reader to identify and locate the source if necessary:

17. Personal interview with Mr. Alan Nelson, Manager, Mentor Guaranty Ltd., Red Deer, Alberta, December 21, 20--.

18. Ramsden, Peter G. "Iroquois," in *The 1997 Canadian World Encyclopedia* (CD-ROM), Toronto: McClelland and Stewart, 1997.

The Internet

When referencing information from the Internet, give the Web site name, location, etc.:

www.bloomberg.com./markets/currency/currcalc.cgi/currcalc.html

• to calculate the worth of the Canadian dollar in other currencies
www.chrc.ca

• Canadian Human Rights Commission
www.canadapost.ca

• to gain access to Canadian postal codes

www.stockgroupmedia.com

• resource for investors; allows investors to do basic research on public companies traded on most North American stock exchanges

Magazines and newspapers

State the author's name, the article title (in quotation marks), the magazine or newspaper name (italicized or underscored), the month and year of publication, and the page numbers if possible:

11. Brian Bergman, "Software on Demand," *Maclean's*, 25 May 1998, p. 48.

12. Lisa Wright, "Selling Yourself the Write Way: How to Sharpen Your Résumé," <u>Toronto Star</u>, June 3, 1998, E1.

Others

For referencing sources other than printed material, you might divide them into sections, for example, Section A, Interviews; Section B, Radio/television programs; Section C, Movies; Section D, Musical performances or compositions; and Section E, Videotapes, etc.:

Section A—Interviews

Interview with Gordon Burwood, Corporate Travel Agent, Dennis Heming Travel, Hamilton, ON. January 29, 1998.

Interview with Dennis Heming, DHT Travel, Owner, Hamilton, ON. February 16, 1998.

Section B—Television programs

The Money Market, prod. John Sourdough, CBC Special, February 13, 1998.

Investing for the Future, prod. Carmen Bisson, NBC Special, June, 1998.

Section C—Movies

Titanic, dir. James Cameron, Leonardo DiCaprio and Kate Winslet, Paramount and 20th Century Fox, 1998.

Section D—Musical performances

George Frideric Handel, *Messiah*, ed. Watkins Shaw, Novello Handel Edition (Sevenoaks, Eng.: Novello, n. d.).

NOTE n. d. means no date

Section E—Videotapes

Serenade, chor. George Balanchine. Perf. San Francisco Ballet. Dir. Hilary Bean. 1981. Videocassette. PBS Video, 1987.

Shortened and recurring references

After a work has been cited in full once or is to be shown in the bibliography, shortened references may be used following any of these styles:

◆ the *short form* (author, title, page number)

- et al. (*et alii* meaning "and other people"): this refers to three or more authors; list only the first author's name followed by et al.
- ibid. (short form of *ibidem*, meaning in the same place): this refers the reader back to the immediately preceding footnote
- op. cit. (*opere citato*, in the work cited): this refers the reader back to a previously cited work but a different page number
- loc. cit. (*loco citato*, in the place cited): this refers the reader back to the previously cited work, same page number

> 11. Palmer and D'Amico, <u>Accounting for Canadian Colleges</u>, p. 283.
>
> 12. Ibid., p. 304.
>
> 13. Sharman, <u>The Business Bible</u>, p. 147.
>
> 14. Reid, op. cit., p. 326.
>
> 15. Sharman, loc. cit.

NOTE Of these methods, the short form is preferred in business reports and academic papers. The other references are rarely used now.

▶ K67   Bibliography and References

The bibliography is an alphabetical list of all of the source material consulted by the author in the preparation of the report. Usually shown in each entry are the author(s) and/or editor(s), title, place of publication, publisher, and date of publication.

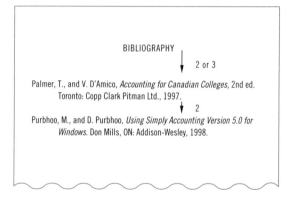

> BIBLIOGRAPHY
>
> ↓ 2 or 3
>
> Palmer, T., and V. D'Amico, *Accounting for Canadian Colleges*, 2nd ed. Toronto: Copp Clark Pitman Ltd., 1997.
>
> ↓ 2
>
> Purbhoo, M., and D. Purbhoo, *Using Simply Accounting Version 5.0 for Windows*. Don Mills, ON: Addison-Wesley, 1998.

If you have used the footnoting feature on your software, you can automatically generate a bibliography with no need to rekey. If you must create one yourself:

- Key the bibliography on a separate page (or pages).
- Use the same margins as for the body. Start the first page 2" from the top edge of the paper and succeeding pages 1" from the top.
- Number pages as part of the report, or use roman numerals but leave the first page unnumbered.

◆ Centre and capitalize the main heading.

◆ Start the first line at the margin and indent the second and succeeding continuation lines five or ten spaces.

◆ Single-space each reference and leave a single space between them.

◆ Do not number bibliographic references.

◆ Follow the punctuation shown in the illustration.

◆ Note that the first author is listed by family name first.

◆ When the work either does not have an author or editor or the person's name is not known, position the work in alphabetical order by the first word in the title, ignoring *A, An,* or *The.*

TYPICAL BIBLIOGRAPHY ENTRIES

One author	Rock, Michael E. *Ethics: To live by, to work by.* Toronto: Holt, Rinehart, 1992.
Two authors	Cox, Michael, and Michael Rock. *The Seven Pillars of Visionary Leadership.* Toronto: Dryden, 1997.
Three or more authors	Bedford, Jennie M. et al. *The Canadian Office: Systems and Procedures.* Toronto. Copp Clark Pitman Ltd., 1995.
Second book by same author(s)	——. *The Canadian Office: Systems and Procedures, Instructor's Manual.* Toronto: Copp Clark Pitman Ltd., 1995.
Editor(s) as authors	Hattersley, M., and McJanet L. (eds.). *Management Communication: Principles and Practice.* Boston: McGraw-Hill, 1997.
Magazine article	Howard, Chris, "Performance Appraisals: Appraise This!" *Canadian Business*, 29 May 1998, p. 24.
Newspaper	Wright, Lisa, "Selling Yourself the Write Way: How to Sharpen Your Résumé." *Toronto Star*, June 3, 1998, E1.
Institution as author and publisher	Certified General Accountant's Association of Canada. *International Financial Management*, ed. Jim Storrey. Vancouver: Certified General Accountant's Association of Canada, 1997.
Government publication	Canada. *Career Handbook.* Ottawa: Human Resources Development Canada, 1996.
Non-print sources	Cockburn, Bruce. *The Charity of Night.* Toronto: True North, 1997.

NOTE   You can also use the term References (same as Bibliography) to indicate sources of information used in the report. If the report is short, you can place the References a double-space below the body of the report. If there are several references, use the traditional format and place on a separate page.

▶ K68 Glossary

The glossary is a list of difficult or special technical terms used in a report, thesis, or book. It is usually included in formal or lengthy reports.

▶ K69 Index

An index is an alphabetical listing of all topics and their page numbers. It is often provided with very lengthy reports and academic papers.

Indexes will vary considerably with the nature of the material. However, use the same margins and starting and finishing lines as the rest of the document. Plan your work so that the information is easy to follow.

Some software permits the automatic generation of an index if the required references are indicated as the document is keyed.

K70 TABLES (TABULATION)

To tabulate means to set up information in columns so that it is easy to read and attractive in format.

SCOTT NEHLAWI ENTERPRISES
Sales by Area: May 20--

Area	Dealer	Amount
N. Ontario	Maria Kim	$92 468
Manitoba	Raj Kumar	90 650
Quebec	Daniel Keith	87 943

Spreadsheet software does *all* of the work for you. Word-processing software offers features such as tables and decimal tabs that simplify the keying of tabulations. However, you must position margins and tab stops.

Before you get into time-consuming calculations, take advantage of the many shortcuts your software offers you, such as:

◆ Use the pre-set (default) tabs and take an educated guess at how the tabulation will look on the page. You can easily insert or delete space or move blocks later.

◆ Use the auto table feature.

◆ Use the *column* feature if this is available.

◆ Save on disk the format for tabulations you do frequently (e.g., in monthly reports) and use it again.

When precise placement of a tabulation is needed, the following will be helpful.

▶ K71   Centring tabular columns horizontally

Planning the job

The first step in tabulation is to find the longest (key) item:

✓ N. Ontario ⑩	Maria Kiu	✓	$92 468 ⑦
Manitoba	Raj Kumar		90 650
Quebec	✓ Daniel Keith ⑫		87 943

1. Locate the longest item in each column (key item). Sometimes the key item is the column heading.

2. Decide on the number of spaces to leave between columns. Six is standard for most work but anywhere from two to twelve is acceptable; three is standard for financial work, but two is acceptable.

3. Draw a plan showing columns and spaces and note on it the character count of each item and the amount of space to be left between columns:

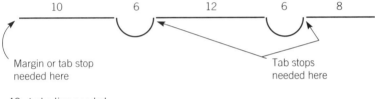

42-stroke line needed
(10 + 6 + 12 + 6 + 8 = 42)

Most software provides a *ruler bar*, with preset (default) margin and tab stops.

With most software, you key your new tab and margin positions directly on the ruler bar or through a dialogue box.

Setting your ruler

1. Clear the default tab stops.

2. Set margins or tabs for the line length needed for the table (i.e., add all of the numbers on your plan and set that line length).

3. Set tabs for the start of the second and all succeeding columns. Space or cursor forward from the left margin for the number of characters in the key item in the column plus the spaces in between and then set the tab.

Column headings

Blocked headings Simply start the headings at the left margin and at all tab stops:

SALES	RETURNS
$1 205 512	$127

Centred headings Centre these headings over the columns.

A. Short heads (headings shorter than columns)

SALES

$102 375.12

◆ Use your automatic centring feature for centring column heads. When precise help is needed, the following will be useful:
1. Follow instructions 1 through 3 for setting the machine.
2 Key in the main table heading (title) and triple- or double-space after it.
3. Count the number of characters in the column heading. Subtract this number from the character count of the key item in the first column and divide the result by two (drop any fractions). Space forward the resulting number from the left margin stop and key in the column heading.
4. Depress the tab key. Repeat the procedure given in step 3 for the other column headings.
5. Double-space and key the remainder of the tabulation.

B. Long heads (headings longer than columns)

SALES BUDGET

$17 000

K

Long column heads will be the key item (longest line) for your column count. Your tab stop will, in fact, be set for the column head.
1. Key in the main table heading and double- or triple-space.
2. Insert the column headings at the tab set points.
3. Centre the column *under* the head as follows:
   a) Find the longest item in the *column* and count the characters.
   b) Subtract this character count from the heading count.
   c) Divide the result by 2 (ignore any fractions).
   d) Reset the margin at the number found.
   e) Depress the tab key. Repeat steps *a*, *b*, and *c*.
   f) Clear the tab.
   g) Space forward by the number found and reset the tab.
   h) Key in the rest of the table.

NOTE   Align single-line headings with the *lower* line of two-line heads and either centre or block them.

Sales
Department   Total

17 172   14 854

◆ Make sure headings are not isolated from columns.
◆ Repeat the column heads at the top of the continuation page and use the word "continued" to help the reader if the tabulation is a complex

one. If you use "Copy to clipboard" and "Copy from" commands on your software, no rekeying will be needed.

▶ K72   Table feature

Use the table feature on software if possible.

◆ Format your tabulation as already described.

◆ Key in the horizontal rules as you proceed.

◆ Begin and end the horizontal rules at the left and right margin stops, respectively.

◆ Note carefully the returns needed to obtain the effect of a line of space above and below column headings, the body, and totals.

JANUARY TOTALS

	N. Ontario	Manitoba	Quebec
(return twice) ———————————————————			
	N. Ontario	Manitoba	Quebec
(return once) ———————————————————			
	72 468	100 650	67 943
	9 005	20 725	6 319
	37 291	5 432	18 250
	118 764	126 807	92 512

Computer

▶ K73   Boxed tables

If possible, use table draw feature of your software. If not:

◆ Key the horizontal rules as you proceed and leave the vertical rules until you have finished the tabulation.

◆ Follow the points noted for ruled tables.

◆ To insert the vertical rules, remove the paper, reinsert it sideways, and use the underscore, placing the rules in the *centre* of the available space. Begin and end the vertical rules *at* (not beyond) the bottom and top horizontal rules.

◆ The outside edges of the table may be ruled/closed or left open.

JANUARY TOTALS

N. Ontario	Manitoba	Quebec
72 468	100 650	67 943
9 005	20 725	6 319
37 291	5 432	18 250
118 764	126 807	92 512

K

▶ K74   Tables with braced headings

Braced headings are ones that are centred over a number of column headings. Set margins and tabs for column headings and key in the main heading. Your word-processing equipment will centre the braced heading automatically if you block the area over which it is to be centred or invoke the merge cells command when using auto tables.

To insert the braced heading manually:

1. Find the width over which the braced heading is to be centred (i.e., add the character count in the key items of the columns involved plus the spaces between).
2. Count the characters and spaces in the braced heading.
3. Subtract the two results from each other and divide by two.
4. From the tab set for the first of the columns over which the braced heading is to be centred, space forward the number found in step 3 and insert the braced heading. Repeat this procedure for each braced heading.
5. Complete the tabulation.

REPORT FOR WEEK ENDING FEBRUARY 28, 20--

Western Provinces				Eastern Provinces		
B.C.	Alta.	Sask.	Man.	Ont.	Que.	Maritimes

▶ K75   Positioning tables in documents

If your tabulation is to be keyed on one page, it should be centred on the page by using the page-centring feature on your software.

◆ Try to keep tables to one page.

◆ If the table is part of a document, it should be designed to fit within the margins of the rest of the document. Ideally, a five-space indent should appear on each side.

◆ Avoid breaking a table. Note the following possibilities for dealing with this situation:
   • Carry all of the tabulation to the next page and leave extra space on one page.
   • Position the tabulation in an appropriate spot where it will fit and not disrupt the flow of the reading. Provide a reference for the reader as to the location (e.g., "See Tab 3, p. 4").
   • Change spacing from double to single or to $1^1/_2$ if possible.
   • Print the table in a smaller font.

◆ If you must break the table, find a place where a natural break occurs (e.g., between sections) and repeat the column heads on the continuation page.

NOTE   Use the auto heading repeat and row break features available in the auto table feature of your word-processing software.

▶ K76   Keying tabulations

In addition to the formatting guidelines given here, note the following points.

Abbreviations

To save space in tables, abbreviations are permitted. However, use these sparingly and consult Unit 1, C96, for help with standard ones.

Numbers

Whole numbers Align these from the right (units, tens, hundreds, etc.):

```
127
 32
159
```

Separate digits into groups of three by means of spaces, not commas.

```
1 205              12 141
           – but –
1 630               1 630
```

NOTE   The metric system in Canada uses spaces rather than commas to separate digits into groups of three for numbers greater than 9999. The major accounting associations consulted do not have a set policy on comma usage. Most accounting firms use the comma, as do law firms (the comma is the natural connector for keeping numbers together).

Decimals Align these by the decimal point, using a consistent style. Use your decimal tab feature as a great time-saver here, bearing in mind that tabs must be set for the decimal point, not the start of the column.

```
9.00          9.         0.93            s.93
       – but –             – not –
15.51         15.51      2.91            2.91
```

Dollar signs Position these to accommodate the longest line but insert at the beginning of columns and in subtotals and totals only:

```
$   37
 1021
$1058
```

Percentage signs Place these after the figure. Use after the first entry and on totals or subtotals only.

```
50%
```

Times Align the hours and minutes at the colon:

```
9:15 a.m.
10:36 p.m.
```

K

Totals Follow the spacing shown below unless space is at a premium:

```
127
 32

159
```

References

Source references used with tabulations are normally positioned *under* the table rather than in a footnote or endnote.

JANUARY TOTALS*

N. Ontario	Manitoba	Quebec
72 468	100 650	67 943
9 005	20 725	6 319
37 291	5 432	18 250
118 764	126 807	92 512

*Statistics Canada, May 20--

Spacing

Double- or triple-space under the main head. Where a two-line (or more) heading is involved, centre each of the lines and single-space between them:

SALES REPORT FOR WEEK ENDING FEBRUARY 28, 20--

✓ TS or DS
✓

Monday	Tuesday	Friday	Total
✓	✓ DS	✓	✓
317	298	312	927

◆ Position any subheadings a double space below the main heading:

JANUARY TOTALS
✓
Prepared by T. Navratilova
✓ TS or DS
✓

N. Ontario	Manitoba	Quebec
✓	✓	✓
73 468	100 650	67 943

◆ Double-space under the column heads.

◆ Single- or double-spacing is acceptable in the body of tabulations. Use whichever will produce a table that is attractive and easy to read.

◆ For continuation (run-on) lines, single-space and indent two or three spaces.

▶ **K77 Using software to best advantage**

As well as noting the suggestions made in this unit, K70, take advantage of your software to produce attractive and easy-to-read tabulations. Where possible:

◆ Use table feature.

◆ Use small type for headings and thus avoid the need to abbreviate.

◆ Use italic and boldface as a change from underscoring.

◆ Use $1^1/_2$-spacing if double is too space-consuming or if single makes reading difficult.

◆ Use a sans serif face if the document it is contained within has a serif face.

◆ Remember that automatic leaders are available on most software packages.

K78 STYLE PRACTICES

This section outlines the correct style to use when keying metric expressions and the correct spacing to use after punctuation marks and special characters. For information on the current style practices for the following, consult the sections indicated:

◆ abbreviations: Unit 1, "Communications: Language Skills," C96

◆ capitalization: Unit 1, C108

◆ numbers: Unit 1, C124

◆ roman numerals: Appendix

◆ word division: Unit 1, C137

K79 METRIC EXPRESSIONS

The style to be used in keying common metric terms, units of measure, and their symbols is as follows.

▶ **K80 Symbols**

◆ Use only the symbols specified in the SI metric system (see Appendix).

◆ Use symbols rather than terms with numbers:

30 m   – *not* –   30 metres   – *but* –   thirty metres

◆ Use lower-case, except when the symbol is derived from the name of an individual:

mm for millimetre   Exception: Use capital *L* for litre:
N for Newton   3 mL   2 L
C for Celsius

◆ Leave a space between quantity and symbols:

   2.75 m

   The degree sign occupies the space in temperature expressions:

   32°C

◆ Do not start a sentence with a symbol:

   Distance is expressed in metres.

   – *not* –

   m is used to express distance.

◆ Do not pluralize metric symbols—the singular and plural forms are the same:

   1 kg   75 kg

◆ Symbols are not abbreviations. Use a period only if the symbol occurs at the end of a sentence:

   He bought 0.75 kg of cherries.
   He bought 0.75 kg.

◆ Show square and cubic symbols by means of exponents (numerals keyed a half-line higher). Use superscript on your word-processing equipment or a half-line on a typewriter.

   $16 \, m^2$ $32 \, cm^3$

◆ Use the solidus (/) to represent *per:*

   He drove at 60 km/h.

▶ **K81   Numbers**

◆ Express fractions as decimals:

   2.75 kg   – *not* – $2^3/_4$ kg

◆ Use a zero in front of the decimal point when no whole number is shown:

   0.75 kg

◆ Use hard spaces/non-breaking spaces to group figures into blocks of three for numbers over 9999. This applies to grouping on both sides of the decimal point. The space may be omitted in four-digit numbers unless these numbers are listed in a column with other numbers of five digits or more.

   17[ ]243.57 m   1467[ ]m

▶ **K82   Numeric times and dates**

Numeric times and dates are not metric expressions but are related because they are methods of measurement.

◆ Key numeric dates in this sequence: year, month, day; year (four digits), space, month (two digits), space, day (two digits):

20-- 04 12 (meaning April 12, 20--)

◆ Bring date in from the network for productivity purposes.

◆ When times are based on the 12-hour clock, use four digits and separate hours and minutes with a colon:

12:00 P.M.   11:42 A.M.

◆ When times are based on the 24-hour clock, no punctuation is used between the hours and the minutes:

0430   1622

K83   SPACING RULES

▶ K84   Spacing rules for symbols

Symbol	Spacing	Example
Addition	one on each side	$3 + 2 = 5$
Ampersand (&)	one before and one after*	Smith & Wesson
At (@) (each costing)	one on each side	$2 @ \$15 = \$30$
Cent sign	one after	He paid 75¢ for it.
Decimal	no space	1.05
Degree symbol	no space	30°C
Division	one on each side	$6 \div 2 = 3$
Dollar sign	one before	She paid $15.
Equality	one on each side	$6 \times 2 = 12$
Feet	no space before, one after	He was 6' tall.
Inches	no space before, one after	He was 6' 2" tall.
Multiplication	one on each side	6×2
Number (#)	one before, none after	17 Avenue Rd., #3
Oblique/solidus	no space	3 3/5; and/or; 31 km/h
Percentage (%)	none before, one after	5% plus 10%
Subtraction	one on each side	$6 - 2 = 4$

*But not in all-cap abbreviations: R&D

▶ K85   Spacing rules for punctuation marks

Punctuation mark	Spacing	Example
Apostrophe		
as possessive	no space	The manager's office
as omission sign	no space	Aren't you coming?
Colon		
as punctuation	two after with non-proportional type, one with proportional	He bought: disks, He bought: disks,

(continued...)

Punctuation mark	Spacing	Example
as time	none before or after	10:30 p.m.
as ratio	none before or after	3:6 is 1:2
Comma	one after	a desk, a chair, a phone
Dash*	two hyphens without spaces	He can--he said.
Exclamation mark	two after, one with proportional type	Good grief! What Good grief! What
Hyphen	no space	editor-in-chief
Parentheses	one before the opening, one after the closing	Can you (as a friend) do this?
Period		
◆ at sentence end	two spaces, one after proportional type	Go home. It's time. Go home. It's time.
◆ after abbreviations with:		
◆ one abbreviation in caps	one space	Mr. J. Hwong
◆ two abbreviations or more in caps	no space	S.C.I.B.
◆ any abbreviations in lower case	no space	f.o.b.
Question mark	two after, one with proportional type	Can you? Will you? Can you? Will you?
Quotation marks	one before opening quotation and one or two after completing quotation (if a punctuation mark ends the closing quotation, use the spacing required by that punctuation mark)	"Is the letter ready?" Mr. Winters asked.
Semicolon	one after	She went east; he went west.

*Em dash (—) A long dash or two dashes used to indicate a sudden break in thought; originally, the length of an em dash was the portion of a line occupied by the letter *m*; now it refers to the square of any size of type

Em space A square of a given point size; a 12-point em space would be a square of 12×12 points

En dash (–) half the length of an em dash but longer than a hyphen; used mainly to indicate continuing or inclusive numbers (e.g., 1997–1999, pages 56–59).

En space half the width of an em space; most commonly it is the width of the character 0 (zero). To insert the *em dash* or *en dash*, use the special character function on your software.

NOTE See this unit, K79, for spacing in metric expressions.

K86 EDITING AND PROOFREADING

Editing and proofreading are often thought to mean the same thing. In fact, they don't.

Editing means checking and revising content and style, asking questions such as: Is it accurate? Is it clear? Does it say what I want? Have I made the best selection of words? Does it develop logically? If you are editing someone else's work and have questions about the content, check with the originator.

Proofreading means checking against the original to ensure there are no errors or omissions; checking for the mechanics of language such as grammar, punctuation, and spelling; and checking that the format details are correct.

The better job you do of on-screen proofing and editing, the more productive, efficient, and cost-effective you will be. This is an area where care is needed because on-screen proofing is more difficult than proofing from hard copy.

◆ Use the spell-check feature of your software program to find obvious errors. Do not rely solely on the spell-check feature as there may be many errors that it cannot check. Spell check does not recognize homonyms (words that sound alike but are spelled differently). It does not know what words or sections have been omitted and cannot indicate inaccuracies in figures, for example. Fortunately for keyboarders, some software packages offer a feature that will automatically correct common spelling errors as you key, such as transposed characters—*adn* will be corrected to *and*, *recieve* corrected to *receive*, etc.

◆ Use the thesaurus if you keep running into the same word. It will quickly provide you with choices so that the writing is varied.

◆ Grammar- and style-checker features of your software program are also useful in this area. However, use them with discretion. You do not have to accept every suggestion for improvement that they make.

◆ Redlining is a useful feature for group proofing and editing. Changes made are not final.

◆ Check that you have been consistent in your word treatments (e.g., did you use "e-mail" or "E-mail" throughout that report?). Global search and replace can be valuable here.

◆ Move the cursor from line to line as you read.

◆ Ask someone else to proofread the screen as you read aloud from the original.

◆ For complex tasks—tabulations, for example—isolate them by putting them into a second document and check them there.

The editing of documents that word-processing software permits can cause its own problems:

◆ Be sure that if a paragraph is replaced, the old one has been deleted.

K

◆ Be sure that if text has been moved, it is in the right place.

◆ Be sure that text that is moved does not appear twice.

◆ Be sure that new, added, or imported material is consistent in format with the rest.

Frequently recurring errors to watch for include:

◆ errors in headings

◆ repeats of words at the beginnings and ends of lines

◆ keying *you* for *your, now* for *not*

◆ transposing numbers, such as phone numbers, money amounts, street addresses, e.g., *1081* for *1801*, etc.

◆ errors in titles, e.g., *Ms.* instead of *Mrs.*

◆ errors in spacing

◆ format inconsistencies, e.g, indenting paragraphs

When lists of items are keyed, count them to make sure nothing has been missed.

Proofread the hard copy as well when you have printed it out.

K87 PROOFREADING MARKS

These symbols are generally used in correcting communications produced as rough drafts. The list includes those needed for desktop publishing applications as well as those used in routine document production. (See pages 387–88.)

K

K88 FORMATS AND LANGUAGE STYLE

Despite the incredible changes information processing has brought about in business offices, few have occurred in the formats and language style used in written communications. Speed is crucial for cost effectiveness, of course, and the best formatting and style practices are the simplest. Consider these productivity hints for your office:

◆ For letters, use the full block or simplified style and open punctuation.

◆ Eliminate periods after initials.

◆ Because mixing double- and triple-spacing in some software can be a problem, double-spacing after main headings, before side headings, and under page numbers in headings is quite acceptable.

◆ With proportional spacing, use only one space after periods, question marks, exclamation marks, and colons.

Meaning	Symbol	Edited	Correction
Align horizontally	=	By Lakshmi	By Lakshmi
Align vertically	||	Bluffers Park Guildwood	Bluffers Park Guildwood
Change hyphen to dash	– –	ready-made to	ready—made to
Change punctuation to a period	⊙	Stay there⊙	Stay there.
Change word	—	manufacture We produce	We manufacture
Close up	⌣	per cent	percent
Delete and close up	⌒	per/cent	percent
Delete letter	ℯ	better writings	better writing
Delete underscore	ℓ⌒ℓ	very long day	very long day
Delete word	⌒ℓ	offer you quality	offer quality
Double space	ds⌈	ds ⌈That should be ⌊the way to work.	That should be the way to work.
Drop below the line	∧	∧ H2O	H_2O
Indent 1 em space	⊡	⊡Tea's ready!	Tea's ready!
Insert 1 en dash	$\frac{1}{N}$	1997 $\frac{1}{N}$1998	1997–1998
Insert 1 em dash	$\frac{1}{M}$	the desk$\frac{1}{M}$not used	the desk—not used
Insert a hyphen	⹀∧	ready⹀made	ready-made
Insert letter or word	∧	i it prize and was	prize and it was
Insert punctuation mark(s)	⟨⟩ ∧ ∧ ♢ ⟩⟩	⟨⟩Home James∧ don't spare the horses⟩⟩	"Home, James; don't spare the horses."
Insert space	# ∧ ⟨	# withit forthe ∧	with it for the
Leave in, do not omit (stet)	_ _ _ _	This service will	This service will
Make all capitals	≡	Benjamin	BENJAMIN
Make boldface	⌇	at this point	at **this** point

(continued...)

Meaning	Symbol	Edited	Correction
Make capital letter small (lc)	/	at this ¢ompany	at this company
Make italic	—	P.O.H.	*P.O.H.*
Make a small letter capital (uc)	≡	when she arrives	When she arrives
Move as shown	♂	is available (to you)	is available
Move number of spaces in direction shown	5⌐	5⌐By the time	By the time
	⌐5	⌐5By the time	By the time
New paragraph	¶	¶During the last	During the last
Raise above this line	∨	according to Jones∨	according to Jones[1]
Single space	SS	⌐payroll preparation various employees	payroll preparation various employees
Spell out, do not abbreviate	◯	Bring(4)books. Third(Ave.)	Bring four books. Third Avenue
Transpose letters or words	∿	recieve receipts/cheques and	receive receipts and cheques
Others Bottom margin	*bm*		Break the page here.
Top margin	*tm*		Natural page break.
Hard page break	*Hpg*		
Soft page break	*Spg*		
Wrong font	*wf*	*wf* Be bold.	Be bold.

K89 MAKING DOCUMENTS ATTRACTIVE

Today's software permits better-looking documents, close to what is achieved with desktop publishing (DTP). Some offer a variety of fonts and some basic drawing and charting tools. You can create multiple newspaper-style columns. You can also include bulleted lists and graphics from the package or from supplementary clip-art packages.

Use some creativity and make your work visually stunning but also businesslike. Business documents do not have to look dull. Some suggestions are:

♦ Use an appropriate graphic on the cover page of a report.

Special effects ideas

- ◆ Use the line-draw feature to draw boxes around information that should be emphasized.
- ◆ Use the vast array of fonts available to add some sparkle. Use the fonts with knowledge, however. A serif font, such as Times Roman, is good for most applications because the serifs (small "feet" attached to the letters) make the work easier to read. Sans serif (without serifs) like Geneva and Helvetica are harder to read but are excellent for headings.
- ◆ Change the spacing if you wish. Most software will allow, for example, spacing that is a little wider than single-spacing but not as great as double or a little more than double, and so on. This can add interesting variety to an otherwise dull-looking document.
- ◆ Some software provides character sets to enhance document appearance (dashes, bullets, fractions, multinational symbols, box drawing, icons, and math and science symbols). Use these to good effect.

K90 DOCUMENT STYLE MANUALS

A major advantage of word processing—particularly in a centralized setup—is the opportunity to achieve consistency of document formats and styles throughout the organization. A style manual is a major contributor to achieving this consistency.

The style manual can take many forms. It might be a simple binder containing samples of properly formatted and keyed documents. In its most sophisticated form, it might be a professionally produced document containing examples of communications, inputting procedures, records management procedures, and language and style instructions. Ideally, the pages that make up the manual will be saved on disk and updated and reissued as needed. On a networked system, a hard copy is not really necessary provided a proper back-up system is in place. Users can simply access relevant parts from a shared database as required. Make sure updated information is made available to all support staff who will benefit from the information.

K91 PRODUCTIVITY TIPS

Whether you prepare transcripts from your own notes, a recorded tape, a handwritten or keyed draft, or an in-person dictation, you should aim for productivity in the workplace. Prepare in advance by using the following guidelines:

◆ Gather any special supplies and reference sources (e.g., articles, books, magazines, or file folders) with pertinent information that may be needed.

◆ Look up information *before* you begin keying the documents (e.g., proper spelling of names, addresses, etc.).

◆ Keep a reference section in your files or on disk (for speedy access).

◆ Keep the information updated for future use.

◆ Set aside time for large keying jobs in order that you can make progress and save time.

◆ Proofread your work carefully; have someone else look it over before sending to print if there is going to be a mass mailing or printing of the material (saves time and money).

Keying from written notes

◆ Check for urgent items and deal with them first (prioritize your work).

◆ Read each item through before you begin keying and check on special instructions to make sure you understand what must be done.

◆ Keep special notes or instructions in a steno notepad (i.e., shorthand or short-form notes) and draw a diagonal line through each item as you complete it. If you use a steno notepad, place a rubber band around the last page you transcribed so that you are ready for the next dictation session.

Keying from recorded tapes

See Unit 21, WP22, for in-depth information on machine/micro-transcription.

13 MATH AND CALCULATOR SKILLS

CONTENTS

M

The computer makes the calculating task easy and has taken the drudgery out of many office-related calculating jobs. However, basic numeracy skills are essential for every office worker because some computer applications (e.g., spreadsheets) need mathematical expertise. Also, knowing how to use an electronic calculator is mandatory for small, everyday tasks. With this in mind, this unit focuses on three issues:

◆ how to use a calculator
◆ how to convert numbers into decimal equivalents for processing
◆ how to solve typical business-related mathematical problems

M1 USING A CALCULATOR

M2 CALCULATOR TYPES

Calculators are available in two main types: the hand-held pocket calculator with a visual display, and the desktop calculator with either a visual display (readout) or paper tape (printout), or both. You can also use computers as calculators, but use a desktop or hand-held calculator most day-to-day calculations.

All calculators perform the basic functions of add, subtract, multiply, and divide. Some offer such additional features as percentage keys, memory keys, and constants. Some have fixed point and some have floating decimals.

Some calculators operate like small computers and are programmed with preset formulas that are useful for mathematical and/or scientific applications. Others can be programmed to use formulas chosen by the user. It is impossible to provide detailed instructions on how to use all calculators. The major features will be dealt with here, but you should carefully study the instruction manual for your particular calculator so that you become familiar with all of its features.

Many computer software packages include calculating functions so that routine calculations can be handled on-screen as part of the word-processing procedure. Spreadsheets can also be incorporated into documents so that you do not have to redo calculations already completed.

M3 BASIC OPERATIONS

The method a calculator uses to process numbers is known as the *logic* of the machine. There are two major kinds: algebraic logic and arithmetic logic. It is important to know the difference between them because it affects the order in which you depress some operations keys — ⊞ , ⊟.

Algebraic logic

7 ⊞ 3 ⊟ 2 ⊟ 8   10 ⊞ 2 ⊟ 12

7 ⊠ 3 ⊟ 21   10 ⊟ 2 ⊟ 8

10 ⊡ 2 ⊟ 5

Arithmetic logic

7 ⊞ 3 ⊞ 2 ⊟ readout 8 (or ⋇ 8)

7 ⊠ 3 ⊟ 21   10 ⊞ 2 read 12

10 ⊟ 2 ⊟ 5   10 ⊞ 2 ⊟ read 8

Note that multiplication and division operations are identical, but the order of operations for add and subtract is different.

Most pocket calculators use algebraic logic; most desktop versions use arithmetic. Experiment with your calculator or refer to the instruction manual to ascertain which type you have. The examples used in this unit were calculated on a desktop, arithmetic-logic calculator.

M4   THE DECIMAL INDICATOR

Calculators have either fixed point or floating decimals. Fixed point allows you to preset your needs; with floating, the machine inserts the decimal automatically in the correct position in the display. Fixed point can be useful in dealing with, for example, money calculations, where only two decimal places are needed.

M5   PRINTOUT VS. READOUT

The hard copy available from calculators with paper tapes rather than only visual displays can be useful in several ways:

◆ in entry checking (i.e., proofreading)
◆ by providing a permanent record for filing
◆ by permitting printed subtotals where needed

M6   PERCENTAGE KEY

Percentages can be worked out on even the most simple calculator, but a single percentage key saves time and effort. What the key does, in fact, is divide a number by 100. See this unit, M16, for more information.

M7   MEMORY

The memory feature permits the operator to store one or more calculations while working on another. Typical calculator memory keys are:

| M+ | add to memory | CM | clear memory |
| M− | subtract from memory | RM | recall from memory |

Again, consult your manual for precise operating instructions.

M8   CONSTANT KEY

Some calculators have a built-in constant key for storing a number required for repeated multiplication and division calculations. For example, if you wanted to calculate 1.5% of each employee's salary for bonus purposes, enter 1.5 in the constant and then key in each salary amount and the ☒ key to obtain the answer for each employee.

M9   CLEAR KEY

All calculators have a clear key.

☐ C *Clear* permits you to begin a new calculation by deleting everything connected with previous calculations. The effect is the same as that of switching the machine off.

☐ CE *Clear entry* permits you to correct a mistake in the number you are entering without clearing the whole of the calculation from the machine. On some machines ☐ C and ☐ CE are combined into one key ☐ C/CE. Press once for clear entry and twice for full clearance.

It is a good idea to touch the clear key before starting any new calculation, to ensure that nothing has been retained from an earlier one.

M10   TOUCH FINGERING

Become an efficient calculator operator by using touch fingering, as shown in the illustration. The right index finger strikes the 1, 4, and 7 keys; the middle finger the 2, 5, and 8 keys; and the fourth finger the 3, 6, and 9 keys. The thumb strikes the zero and the right little finger strikes the + − ÷ × = and total keys.

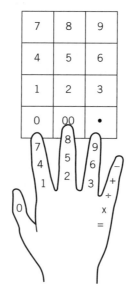

M

M11 Decimals, Fractions, Percentages

This section is concerned with part quantities—decimals, fractions, and percentages—and the different ways of expressing them and calculating with them.

M12 DECIMALS

Calculators and computers can work only with whole numbers and decimals. For example, a calculator cannot multiply by $12\frac{1}{4}$. You must change $12\frac{1}{4}$ to its decimal equivalent.

The decimal equivalent of $\frac{1}{4}$ is 0.25 (see the table of equivalents in this unit, M18, or convert according to the instructions provided in M15). The problem then becomes simply a matter of keying in the numbers and operations keys and reading the result. To multiply $12\frac{1}{4}$ by 4, key in as follows:

12.25 $\boxed{\times}$ 4 $\boxed{=}$ 49

NOTE In written work, always precede a decimal value of less than one with a zero: 0.25, not .25.

▶ M13   Decimal places

For most business situations, working to two decimal places is sufficient (i.e., two figures after the decimal place). If your calculator does not allow you to set specific decimal places, round off as follows. Take 5 and over up one; leave 4 and below at the second decimal number.

427.6**75** to two decimal places = 427.6**8**
427.6**73** to two decimal places = 427.6**7**

Where a greater number of decimal places is required, follow the same basic rule:

427.6763 to three decimal places is 427.676
427.676678 to five decimal places is 427.67668

M14   FRACTIONS

Fractions are parts of whole numbers and can be expressed as decimal fractions (0.25) or common fractions ($\frac{1}{4}$). Common fractions must be converted into their decimal equivalents before a calculator or computer can accept them for processing.

M

▶ **M15 Converting fractions into decimals**

To convert fractions into their decimal equivalents
Divide the numerator by the denominator:

$\dfrac{3}{5}$ (numerator)
(denominator)

3 ⊟÷ 5 ⊟= 0.6

The decimal equivalent of $^3/_5$ is 0.6.

To change whole numbers and fractions into decimals
Change the fraction to its decimal equivalent by dividing the numerator by the denominator, and then write the result after the whole number:

$^5/_8$ as a decimal is 5 ⊟÷ 8 ⊟= 0.625

The decimal equivalent of $6^5/_8$ is therefore 6.625.

> For overtime, employees earn $1^1/_2$ times their normal pay rate. An employee's hourly pay is $12.10. If the employee worked one hour overtime, what was the overtime pay? The calculation is:
>
> $1^1/_2 \times 12.10$
>
> Convert $1^1/_2$ to decimal $= 1.5$
>
> Key in 1.5 ⊠× 12.10 ⊟= readout 18.15 (to two decimal places)
>
> The employee's overtime pay was $18.15.

M16 PERCENTAGES

A percentage of a number is a one-hundredth part of that number. For example, 5 percent of a number is 5 one-hundredths of that number and can be expressed as:

$^5/_{100}$ or 0.05 or 5%

Percentage key
Use your calculator ⊠% key for routine percentage calculations, as follows:

Calculate 35% of 15:

15 ⊠× 35 ⊠%

Display shows 5.25 (i.e., 35% of 15 = 5.25).

When no ⊠% key is available, multiply the two figures and divide by 100 (which is the same as moving the decimal two places to the left):

Calculate 35% of 15:

$$\frac{35}{750} \times 15 = \frac{525}{100} = 5.25 \quad -or- \quad 0.35 \;\boxed{\times}\; 15 \;\boxed{=}\; 5.25$$

To change a fraction to a percentage

Divide the numerator by the denominator and multiply the result (quotient) by 100 (which is the same as moving the decimal two places to the right).

(numerator)

$$\frac{4}{5} \times 100$$

(denominator)

$$= 0.80 \times 100 = 80\%$$

$4/5$ expressed as a percentage is 80%.

To change a percentage to a decimal

Divide the percentage figure by 100; that is, move the decimal point two places to the left, and remove the % sign.

1/2% expressed as a decimal is 0.005.
35% expressed as a decimal is 0.35.
189% expressed as a decimal is 1.89.

To change a decimal to a percentage

Multiply the decimal by 100; that is, move the decimal point two places to the right, and add the percentage sign:

1.34 expressed as a percentage is $1.34 \times 100 = 134\%$.
0.75 expressed as a percentage is $0.75 \times 100 = 75\%$.
0.025 expressed as a percentage is $0.025 \times 100 = 2.5\%$.

To find what percentage one number is of another

Divide the base number into the other number (the amount) and multiply by 100 (the base number will usually follow "of"):

What percentage of 25 is 5?

(amount)

$$\frac{5}{25} \times 100 = 20$$

(base number)

5 is 20% of 25.

M

Of $750 worth of total footwear sales, $150 was in socks. What percentage of total sales was in socks (or, more simply, what percentage is 150 of 750)?

┌──── (sock sales) (amount)
▼
$\frac{150}{750}$ × 100
▲
└──── (total sales) (base number)

[=] readout 20

Socks made up 20% of the total sales.

To find the full number of which a percentage is known

Divide the known number by the known percentage and multiply by 100.

If 10 is 20% of the total number, what is the total?

┌──── (known number)
▼
$\frac{10}{20}$ × 100 = 50
▲
└──── (known percentage)

10 is 20% of 50 (the total).

▶ M17   Percentage increases and decreases

Routine percentage increases and decreases can be done on the calculator by simply depressing the [+] or [−] key after the [%] key, as illustrated in these two examples:

What will be the new selling price if the price of an item costing $15 is increased by 35%?

Key in 15 [×] 35 [%] [+] [=]

Display shows 20.25 (i.e., the new selling price is $20.25).

What will be the selling price if the price of an item costing $15 is decreased by 35%?

Key in 15 [×] 35 [%] [−] [=]

Display shows 9.75 (i.e., the new price will be $9.75).

To plan budgets and projections, organizations need to analyze figures and make comparisons. If you assist in these tasks and do not use a spreadsheet, it is useful to know how to calculate percentage increases and decreases and to understand the process involved. The following examples will assist you.

To find the percentage increase of one number over another
Subtract the base number from the increased number to find the *amount* of the increase. Divide the *base number* into the amount of the increase and multiply by 100.

If 25 increases to 30, what is the percentage increase?
30 (increased number) − 25 (base number) = 5 (amount of increase)

$\dfrac{5}{25} \times 100 = 20$

┌──── (amount of increase)
└──── (base number)

The rate of increase of 30 over 25 is 20%.

If sales rose from $4000 (base number) to $5000 (increased number), what was the percentage increase?

5000 $-$ 4000 $=$ 1000

1000 $\div$ 4000 $\times$ 100 $=$ 25

Sales increased by 25%.

To find the amount of increase when the base number and percentage increase are known
Add the rate of increase to 100, divide this total by 100, and multiply by the base number.

If 60 is increased by 15%, what will be the new amount?
15 (rate of increase) + 100

$\dfrac{115}{100} \times 60$ (base number)

= 69

60 increased by 15% is 69.

If sales of $4000 must be increased by 25%, to what amount must sales increase?

$\dfrac{25 + 100}{100} = 1.25$

$1.25 \times 4000 = 5000$

Sales must increase to $5000.

To find the amount of decrease when the base number and percentage decrease are known

Subtract the rate of decrease from 100, divide the result by 100, and multiply by the base figure.

If 60 is decreased by 15%, what will be the new amount?

$$\underset{\displaystyle \overline{100}}{\dfrac{85}{}} \times 60 \text{ (base figure)} \quad \text{(100 – decrease of 15))}$$

$$= 51$$

60 decreased by 15% is 51.

If sales of $4000 decreased by 25%, to what amount did sales decrease?

$$\dfrac{25 - 100}{100} = 0.75$$

$$0.75 \times 4000 = 3000$$

Sales of $4000 decreased by 25% equal $3000.

M18 COMMON EQUIVALENTS

Percent (%)	Decimal fraction	Common fraction	Percent (%)	Decimal fraction	Common fraction
1	0.01	$\frac{1}{100}$	$37\frac{1}{2}$	0.375	$\frac{3}{8}$
5	0.05	$\frac{1}{20}$	40	0.40	$\frac{2}{5}$
$6\frac{1}{4}$	0.0625	$\frac{1}{16}$	50	0.50	$\frac{1}{2}$
$8\frac{1}{3}$	0.083	$\frac{1}{12}$	60	0.60	$\frac{3}{5}$
10	0.10	$\frac{1}{10}$	$62\frac{1}{2}$	0.625	$\frac{5}{8}$
$12\frac{1}{2}$	0.125	$\frac{1}{8}$	$66\frac{2}{3}$	0.666	$\frac{2}{3}$
$16\frac{2}{3}$	0.1666	$\frac{1}{6}$	70	0.70	$\frac{7}{10}$
20	0.20	$\frac{1}{5}$	75	0.75	$\frac{3}{4}$
25	0.25	$\frac{1}{4}$	80	0.80	$\frac{4}{5}$
30	0.30	$\frac{3}{10}$	$87\frac{1}{2}$	0.875	$\frac{7}{8}$
$33\frac{1}{3}$	0.333	$\frac{1}{3}$	90	0.90	$\frac{9}{10}$
			100	1.00	

Table of common equivalents

Certain percentages and their decimal and fractional equivalents are used so frequently that knowing them can save a great deal of unnecessary calculation time.

M19 TYPICAL BUSINESS MATH APPLICATIONS

In addition to the typical business mathematics examples that follow, see also Unit 6, "Financial Management," for account reconciliations, financial statements, payroll, and petty cash.

To help develop accuracy in your calculations, it is a good idea to estimate as well as verify answers and, when a printout is available, to proofread carefully.

Estimating answers

Although calculators make mathematical calculations easy, try always to "guesstimate" an answer first.

Multiply 596.86 by 21.63

Round the figures up or down to the nearest whole numbers that are easy to work with: 600 × 20

The "guesstimate" answer can be quickly calculated mentally as 12 000

The actual answer when 596.86 is multiplied by 21.63 is 12 910.08

Note how the "guesstimate" answer helps to ensure the correct placement of the decimal point in the actual answer—a frequent problem where large numbers are involved.

Verifying answers

The skilled calculator user will routinely check answers and carefully proofread printouts. The following are two suggestions for verifying answers.

Once you have completed a calculation such as:

What is 20% of 120?

(Enter 120 ×️ 20 %️ readout 24),

double-check by doing the calculation again or working the problem backwards:

Enter 24 ×️ 100 =️ readout 2400.

Divide by 20 = readout 120.

Verify a column of figures by working once from top to bottom and then from bottom to top.

M20 BILLING (INVOICING)

Billing is the process of completing an invoice—a record of a customer's purchases. This will show the unit cost, extensions, and some or all of discounts, taxes, and shipping charges. Note the sequence in which calculations must be made as indicated by the following example.

20	packages computer paper @ 19.95/pkg.	399.00
4	boxes 3.5" disks @ 7.00/box	28.00
		427.00
	Less 15% trade discount	64.05
		362.95*
	Plus 7% GST	25.41
		388.36
	Plus 8% PST	29.04
		417.40
	Plus shipping charge	5.00
	TOTAL	422.40

NOTE   See "Sales Taxes" (this unit, M27). In some provinces, PST (provincial sales tax) is calculated on the basic invoice amount*; in others it is calculated on the invoice amount plus the GST (goods and services tax).

M21   COMMISSIONS

Commission is a percentage of the total amount of sales made by a sales representative that is payable to that representative. To calculate commissions payable, multiply amount of sales by rate of commission:

If the commission rate is $1\frac{1}{4}$%, what commission is payable on sales of $1784.50?

Convert $1\frac{1}{4}$% to a decimal: 1.25%

Key in 1784.50 $\boxed{\times}$ 1.25 $\boxed{\%}$ readout 22.31

Alternatively, key in as $\frac{125}{100}$ $\boxed{\times}$ 1784.50

Commission payable is $22.31.

If a real estate agent sells a house for $195 000 and the total commission is 6% (3% of which is payable to the agent and 3% to the real estate broker), what will the agent earn?

Key in 195 000 $\boxed{\times}$ 6 $\boxed{\%}$ readout 11 700.00

Since one-half is payable to the broker and one-half to the agent, divide the total by 2. The agent therefore earns $5850 on the sale ($11 700 $\boxed{\div}$ 2).

This can also be keyed in as:

$\frac{6}{100}$ × 195 000   (6 $\boxed{\times}$ 195 000 $\boxed{\div}$ 100)

M22 COMPARISONS

Businesses frequently compare costs, percentages, etc., to make forecasts or prepare budgets. An example of such a calculation follows:

Sales in year 1 were $270 963, with expenses of $7852. In year 2, sales were $279 061 and expenses were $6981. Compare the relationship of expenses to sales in each year.

Year 1: $\dfrac{7852}{270\ 963} \times 100$

Key in 785 200 $\boxed{\div}$ 270 963 readout 2.8978

Expenses are 2.9% of sales.

Year 2: $\dfrac{6981}{279\ 061} \times 100$

Key in 698 100 $\boxed{\div}$ 279 061 readout 2.5016

Expenses are 2.5% of sales.

Financial statements provide useful opportunities for comparing operating results. See Unit 6 for examples of comparative balance sheets and income statements.

M23 DISCOUNTS

A discount is a percentage deduction off a selling price and may be offered as an inducement to buy for a number of reasons. Discounts are granted by wholesalers to retailers as short-term promotional gimmicks or for prompt payment of invoices, for example.

Trade and special discounts

To calculate the discount, change the percentage rate of the discount to its decimal equivalent (as described in this unit, M16) and multiply by the total price:

A special summer discount of 5% is allowed on sales of tropical plants:

Total price (gross amount) for 5 plants at $6.20 each	=	$31.00
Discount of 5% is 0.05 (decimal equivalent of 5%) × 31	=	1.55
Amount payable (net amount) is total − discount	=	$29.45

NOTE Discounts of this type are deducted *before* sales taxes are calculated.

Cash discounts

Cash discounts are frequently offered to encourage prompt payment of a bill. For example, if the payment terms quoted are 2/10, N/30, this means that a 2% discount can be deducted if the invoice is paid within 10 days of the invoice date. If the discount is not claimed, full payment must be made within 30 days.

What discount can be claimed on an invoice for $140 with terms of 2/10, N/30?

Convert 2% to its decimal equivalent = 0.02

Multiply by $140 (140 × 0.02) = $2.80

Subtract the discount amount of $2.80 from the invoice amount of $140. The amount payable is ($140 − $2.80) $137.20.

Chain discounts

When a series of discounts is granted (e.g., for quantity buying, as a special promotion, to particular industries or types of buyers), this is known as a chain discount.

The first discount is taken off the list price. The second discount is taken off the remainder, and so on. Successive discounts cannot be added together.

$1000		• list (basic) price
− 200	• 20% trade discount	• decimal equivalent of 20% (0.20) × 1000
800		
− 80	• 10% large-quantity discount	• decimal equivalent of 10% (0.10) × 800
720		
− 36	• 5% special summer promotional discount	• decimal equivalent of 5% (0.05) × 720
$ 684		• amount payable

Total discount allowed is:
List (basic) price ($1000) − amount payable before taxes ($684) = $316.

M24   FOREIGN CURRENCY EXCHANGE

The foreign currency exchange rate is the rate at which one country's currency can be exchanged for that of another's at a financial institution. Newspapers frequently publish lists of exchange rates, but the exchange rate quoted by institutions may vary from these because of the constant fluctuations caused by economic and political factors. Most currencies are now expressed as decimals and conversions are simple.

Change $25 U.S. to Canadian dollars where:

$1.00 U.S.   = $ 1.5537 Canadian (November 16, 2000 quote)
25 × $1.5537   = $38.84 Canadian

Therefore, $25 U.S. equals $38.84 Canadian

To change Canadian currency to U.S. currency at the same rate (i. e., $1.5537 Canadian = $1.00 U.S.), the calculation is:

$$\frac{1}{\$1.5537} = \$0.6436$$

Therefore, $1.00 Canadian = $0.6436 U.S.

Change $25 Canadian to U.S. dollars where:

$1.00 Canadian	=	$0.6436 U.S.
25 × $0.6436	=	$16.09 U.S.

In other words, it will cost you $25 Canadian to buy $16.09 worth of U.S. currency.

M25   INTEREST

Interest may be earned or paid—earned on bank accounts, term deposits, or promissory notes; or paid on bank loans or mortgages. Essentially there are two types of interest: simple and compound.

Simple   Where interest is calculated only on the original principal, the simple interest formula is $I = Prt$ (I = interest, P = principal, r = annual rate, and t = time in years), but may also be expressed as:

$$P = \frac{1}{rt} \quad \text{or} \quad T = \frac{1}{Pr} \quad \text{or} \quad r = \frac{1}{Pt}$$

NOTE   Where the time involved is less than one year, express it as a fraction of a year. For example, express 60 days as $^{60}/_{365}$; 6 months as $^{6}/_{12}$. If time is 1 year, show as 1.

M

What is the principal amount (P) when interest (I) is $18, rate ($r$) is 9%, and time ($t$) is 2 years?

$$P = \frac{1}{rt}$$

$$P = \frac{18}{0.09 \times 2} \quad \text{(0.09 is the decimal equivalent of 9%)}$$

$$P = \$100$$

Compound   Where interest is calculated periodically and added to the principal so that for succeeding periods interest is calculated on the original principal plus the accumulated interest, the formula is:

$$A = P(1 + i)^n$$

A = amount that the principal (P) will accumulate to at i rate of interest per interest period for n interest periods.

Interest tables that do the compound interest calculations for you are available in book form, as supplements to mathematics texts, and through financial institutions.

Two other interest-related formulas that may be useful are *effective interest rate* and *amortization*.

Effective interest rate

$$r = \frac{2Nc}{A(n+1)}$$

r = annual interest rate
N = number of payments in one year
c = cost of borrowing
A = amount borrowed
n = number of payments to pay loan in full

Assume that a person wants to buy a used car offered at $6000 with a $400 down payment. The arrangement offered is 36 equal payments of $170 with a cost of borrowing of $520, or 5.9%. The effective interest rate calculation will be:

$$r = \frac{2 \cdot 12 \cdot 520}{5600 \times \cdot 37}$$ *The basic cost minus the down payment

$$r = \frac{12\,480}{20\,7200}$$

$$r = .0602$$

Expressed as a percentage, the true interest rate is 6.02% (i.e., the decimal point was moved two places to the right).

NOTE When you work with algebraic expressions on a calculator, be careful about the sequence used to carry out the operations.

Amortization formula (mortgage payments)

◆ Repayment of a mortgage is a long-term process that may take 25 or 30 years. The time it takes to completely repay a mortgage, which is established when the mortgage is first negotiated, is called the *amortization period*.

◆ Most mortgages are arranged for six months to five years. This is known as the *mortgage term*.

◆ The formula for calculating the amount to be paid against a mortgage is:

$$p = \frac{P\,i\,1+i^{\,n}}{A\,1+i^{\,n} - 1}$$

p = amount to be paid per payment period
P = principal
i = interest rate per time period
n = total number of payment periods

◆ Books and software are available that provide the calculated information in table form. (Mortgage lenders, real estate agents, and libraries can also help.) These sources show amounts of interest payable under each option and consequences of paying the loan off faster, and should be consulted if this type of information is needed.

Calculating mortgage payments

The table below provides a rapid calculation of mortgage payments. Multiply the principal amount of the mortgage (in thousands) by the monthly payment factor shown in the appropriate amortization period opposite the current interest rate in the following table.

For example, for a principal mortgage amount of $95 000 amortized over 25 years at an interest rate of 8.00%, the monthly payment would be $95 \times 7.63 = \$724.85$.

Interest Rate %	Monthly Payment Factors		
	15 Yrs.	20 Yrs.	25 Yrs.
6.00	8.40	7.13	6.40
6.25	8.54	7.27	6.55
6.50	8.67	7.41	6.70
6.75	8.80	7.55	6.86
7.00	8.94	7.70	7.01
7.25	9.07	7.84	7.16
7.50	9.21	7.99	7.32
7.75	9.34	8.13	7.47
8.00	9.48	8.28	7.63
8.25	9.62	8.43	7.79
8.50	9.76	8.59	7.95
8.75	9.90	8.74	8.12
9.00	10.05	8.89	8.28
9.25	10.19	9.05	8.44
9.50	10.33	9.20	8.61
9.75	10.48	9.36	8.78
10.00	10.63	9.52	8.95

M26 PRICING GOODS FOR SALE

Pricing means to establish the price at which goods can be sold, taking into consideration discounts or other allowances to be given, transportation costs, pricing legislation, demand, the type of business, competition, and the profit margin (i.e., percentage return on sales or investment).

Markup and margin

Most retail and wholesale prices are established by using markups. A markup is a percentage added to the cost price of the goods to cover operating expenses and to provide a reasonable net profit.

If the owner of a business seeks a net profit of, for example, 12% of sales and the operating expenses of the business are expected to be 27% of sales, the selling price must produce a gross profit (margin) of 39%. The cost price of each article should, therefore, be 61% of its selling price.

sales (100%) – cost price (61%) = gross profit (margin) (39%)

gross profit (39%) – expenses (27%) = net profit (12%)

If cost price = $56, then 61% of the selling price is $56

The selling price = $56 \times \dfrac{100}{61} = \$91.80$

Therefore, markup = $91.80 – $56.00 = $35.80

NOTE Margin and markup are the same in amount but different in percentage because margin is related to selling price and markup is related to cost price.

If the selling price is known to be $91.80, then the margin is $35.80, or 39% of the selling price; if the cost price is known to be $56, then the markup is $35.80, or 64%.

Markdown
A markdown is often called a discount. It means a reduction in the regular price and is usually offered by the seller to attract customers and increase sales.

Break-even point
For a business to be worthwhile, income must exceed expenses. The point at which income and expense intersect is known as the break-even point (BEP). (Above the BEP, profit; below the BEP, loss!) The break-even point is calculated to determine the minimum output or sales necessary for income to cover costs. Break-even point analysis is particularly useful for comparing pricing alternatives:

$$BEP = \frac{\text{total fixed costs (costs that cannot be changed)}}{\text{suggested selling price per unit – variable costs (costs that can be changed) per unit}}$$

Total fixed costs for publishing a book are $90 000, variable costs per unit amount to $5.50, and the suggested selling price is $10.50:

$$BEP = \frac{90\,000}{10.5 - 5.50} = \frac{90\,000}{5} = 18\,000 \text{ units}$$

Therefore, 18 000 copies of the book must be sold before a profit is achieved. To improve this position, the selling price might be raised or some way of cutting variable costs (e.g., using less expensive paper) might be sought.

M27 SALES TAXES
Federal and provincial taxes are charged on most sales. Calculate sales tax as a percentage of the total value of the purchase, and add.

The federal goods and services tax is 7% of the invoice amount. This 7% is charged on most goods and services, unlike provincial sales taxes, which tend to apply to merchandise transactions only. Provincial sales tax rates and the way in which provincial sales tax is charged vary from province to province. In some provinces, the provincial sales tax is charged on the base invoice amount. In others, the provincial sales tax is charged on the invoice price plus the GST. Examples of the two methods follow.

◆ Tax calculation showing taxes based on invoice price (PST charged on base invoice price):

Invoice amount	$250.00
Plus 7% GST	17.50
	267.50
Plus 8% PST	20.00
Amount payable	$287.50

◆ Tax calculation showing tax charged on invoice amount plus tax (PST charged on invoice price plus GST):

Invoice amount	$250.00
Plus 7% GST	17.50
	267.50
Plus 8% PST	21.40
Amount payable	$288.90

Check your provincial rules to ascertain the method to use in your province. More information on GST is available from Canada Customs and Revenue Agency (CCRA) in Ottawa or CCRA Excise GST offices in major centres throughout the country, which can be contacted toll-free in Canada. Procedures for accounting for GST are explained in Unit 6, "Financial Management."

NOTE Merchandise that is purchased to manufacture items for retail sale (e.g., paper for making greeting cards) is taxed only when it is in its final form. A sales tax licence number on an invoice is used to indicate that the material is exempt from sales tax because this is not the final (end) sale of the paper.

Notes on tax calculations

◆ Calculate taxes payable before adding shipping charges.
◆ Deduct all discounts before calculating taxes.
◆ Use the memory or constant feature of your calculator when many similar tax calculations must be made.

M

M28 STATISTICAL DATA

Frequently, business information is presented in the form of averages and ratios to indicate comparisons and trends.

▶ M29 Averages

Mean

An average or mean is a single number that represents a central tendency in a group of numbers. Averages (means) may be simple or weighted.

Simple average Find a simple average by dividing the sum of a series of numbers by the total number of members of the series:

T-shirts sold for $10.95 in the spring sale, for $12.00 at the regular price, and for $11.50 in the fall sale. The simple average selling price was:

$$\frac{\$10.95 + \$12.00 + \$11.50}{3} = \frac{\$34.45}{3} = \$11.48$$

Weighted average The *simple* average is based on only one unit of each number being added and then divided by the sum of the units. A *weighted* average is calculated when there is more than one unit in each item. A weighted average is calculated when a more accurate figure than that provided by a simple average is needed. To find a weighted average, multiply each quantity by its unit value, add the products, and then divide by the sum of the quantities:

120 T-shirts were sold at $10.95 in the spring sale, 230 at the regular price of $12, and 90 at $11.50 in the fall sale. The average (weighted) selling price was:

$$\frac{(\$10.95 \times 120) + (\$12.00 \times 230) + (\$11.50 \cdot 90)}{120 + 230 + 90} =$$

$$\frac{\$1314 + \$2760 + \$1035}{440} =$$

$$\frac{\$5109}{440} = \$11.61$$

Compare this weighted average with $11.48, the simple average calculated above.

Mode

Mode is the figure occurring most frequently in a list of numbers:

6, 7, 9, 6, 7, 8, 7, 8

The mode in this example is 7 since it occurs three times.

This type of statistical information is most interesting to a shoe retailer, for example, who wishes to know the most common selling shoe size.

Median

The median (middle value) in a series of numbers arranged in numerical order is the quantity that appears at the mid-point of the list. One-half of the quantities have a higher value and one-half have a lower value.

Find the median figure by arranging the series of numbers in order of size or value and then selecting the middle one.

Seven students earned these marks: 24, 76, 10, 73, 74, 70, 66.

Arrange in order: 10, 24, 66, 70, 73, 74, 76.

The median mark is 70. There are three numbers higher than 70 and three lower. When the number of items is even, the median is the simple average of the two middle numbers.

▶ M3U Ratio

The ratio of two numbers is the comparison of the size or value of one number with the size or value of another number.

There are 5 management staff and 20 support staff in the office. The ratio of management staff to support staff is 5:20 or 1:4 (reduced to its simplest form).

▶ M31 Proportion

The term *proportion* is used to indicate that two ratios are equal: 1:4 is proportional to 2:8. When two ratios are equal, their cross products are also equal:

$$\frac{1}{4} \times \frac{2}{8}$$

If three terms in a proportion are known, the fourth is easily found:

y:16 is proportional to 3:12

$$\frac{y}{16} \times \frac{3}{12} \qquad \begin{aligned} 12y &= 48 \\ y &= \frac{48}{12} \\ y &= 4 \end{aligned}$$

4:16 is proportional to 3:12.

A firm has a policy of taking co-op students in proportion to its full-time staff. If the established ratio is 5 co-op students to every 100 full-time employees, what number of co-op students will there be if the present full-time staff numbers 360?

$$\frac{5}{100} \times \frac{y}{360}$$

$$100y = 1800$$
$$y = 18$$

Therefore, there will be 18 co-op students for a staff of 360 because 5:100 is proportional to 18:360.

M32 SPREADSHEETS

Most businesses make considerable use of computer spreadsheet software to increase productivity and to provide a great deal of useful financial and numerical data. While extensive mathematical skill is not needed to operate a spreadsheet program, an understanding of the basics of formula creation and the use of mathematical symbols is needed. The information in Unit 2, "Computers: Hardware and Software," CO26, will provide the necessary understanding.

If you have access to computer spreadsheet software, use it as much as possible for applications in which repeat calculations are required. Such programs are fast and accurate and will recalculate everything instantly if there is a need for any change. Unit 2 also provides information on possible spreadsheet uses.

M

UNIT

14 MEETINGS, CONFERENCES, AND TELECONFERENCES

CONTENTS

MC

Meetings, conferences, and teleconferences are a regular and important part of business activities. *Meeting* usually refers to a small gathering of people; *conference* or *convention* is applied to a much larger one; and teleconference refers to electronic communication when a face-to-face meeting is not necessary or possible.

Meetings may be quite informal sessions, designed to permit participants to exchange ideas and information in a relaxed atmosphere. For example, staff meetings are held regularly to discuss and solve problems, project team meetings may be held at various stages during a project, and committee meetings are called when one particular objective is the focus. Formal meetings, on the other hand, are conducted strictly according to the organization's constitution and bylaws (the official meeting rules of conduct). For example, annual general meetings (AGMs) are the official gatherings of shareholders and are conducted under strict parliamentary procedure (see this unit, MC6).

Conferences are frequently held over several days in hotels, convention centres, or resorts and may include both business and social activities.

Teleconferences are invaluable when it is impossible or unnecessary to physically bring together all participants.

Although meetings and conferences vary in purpose, size, length, and degree of formality, the planning, announcing, conducting, and recording procedures are very similar. Advance plans must be well laid, the sessions must be conducted efficiently, and points raised and decisions made must be recorded accurately. This unit will help you to successfully organize any type of meeting or conference.

MC1 PLANNING A MEETING

Before taking any action, clarify these points:

- purpose of the meeting
- type of accommodation needed, and whether breakout rooms (additional seminar rooms) will be required
- number of participants
- desired location
- most suitable time
- budget allocation
- specialized equipment needed
- whether a meeting/convention planning agency or consultant should be used

MC

Whether the meeting is to be held on the company's premises, in a hotel, or in other accommodation, book and confirm the space and services well in advance. List what needs to be done before the date set and do each job early enough to guard against problems. Make calendar entries to remind you when each arrangement is to be checked and confirmed. (For help with conferences and conventions see this unit, MC16; for help with teleconferences, see MC25.)

- Once the meeting date(s) have been set, reserve the meeting room and double-check the booking later. Ensure that the room will accommodate the number of attendees expected.
- Notify all potential attendees of the confirmed meeting date(s) and location.
- Plan, order, and confirm refreshments and/or meals, glasses and water.
- Invite speaker(s) or special guest(s) well in advance.
- Make and confirm hotel bookings for out-of-town participants.
- Be sure that any required sound equipment is ordered.
- Ensure that blackout curtains are available if needed.
- Check that lecterns, podiums, tables, etc., are available.

◆ Arrange for pencils, pads, copies of agendas, committee reports, and other required materials.

◆ Plan the seating so that everyone can see and participate equally well.

Room layout Depending on the type of meeting and the size of the group, choose from the following standard set-ups:

◆ Boardroom style: Formal setting, small groups.

◆ Classroom style: Long, narrow room, good for speaker focus and note-taking.

◆ Round-table style: Informal, small groups and discussion groups.

◆ Theatre style: Lecture presentation from a stage, large audiences.

◆ U-shaped set-up: Medium-sized group, interaction desired.

Meetings involving meals Take special care when food is to be served at or during a meeting:

◆ Reserve a table in a reputable restaurant. Provide a contact name, telephone and fax numbers, the number in the party, the time of arrival, and the method of bill payment.

◆ For an elaborate mealtime meeting, you may be asked to arrange a cocktail hour, select the menu, make a seating plan, and organize after-dinner entertainment. Hotels and restaurants frequently employ specialists who assist with such details.

MC2   ANNOUNCING A MEETING

Meetings may be announced verbally (and then confirmed), in writing, or via communicating computers and electronic calendars. To identify a convenient date for all (or most) participants:

◆ Offer three possible dates and notify all attendees of the one chosen by most.

◆ When you use electronic calendars, check the participants' schedules, "book" the meeting date, time, etc., and ask them to confirm their attendance by e-mail.

NOTE   If you plan regularly scheduled meetings, create and save a "Notice of Meeting" form (see examples on the next page) on your computer or word processor and simply fill in the blanks for each meeting.

When you invite participants to a meeting, note the following:

◆ Include the time, date, location, purpose, and if possible, the length of the meeting.

◆ Send out the notice far enough in advance so that people can fit the meeting into their plans but not so early that it can be forgotten.

◆ For formal meetings, send out the announcement in writing far enough in advance to allow the necessary length of time specified in the constitution or by-laws.

MC

ELLIOTT GALLERIES
82 Charlotte Drive
Victoria, BC V9B 4N6

Telephone No. (205) 987-2424
Fax No. (205) 987-2447

To: Members of the Board   20-- 11 20

NOTICE OF MEETING

A meeting of the Board of Directors will be held at
10:00 a.m. on Wednesday, December 12, 20--, in the
Confederation Room of the High Ridge Hotel at 24
Marine Drive, Victoria. The agenda is attached.

S. Dominelli
Executive Secretary
Elliott Galleries

Formal notice of meeting

INTEROFFICE MEMO

To: Sales Representatives
From: D. Sanderson, Sales Manager
Subject: Quarterly Sales Meeting
Date: February 26, 20--

Please be sure to attend the sales meeting for the
second quarter of this year on March 20, 20--, at 10:30
a.m. in the conference room. The items to be covered
are:

Sales to date by area
(I will provide this data and comment on
performance to date)

Public relations and promotion suggestions
(each of you will be expected to contribute your
thoughts in this area—10 minutes or so)

Quotas for the second quarter
(Mary, our budget officer, will provide details)

Discussion
(this will provide an opportunity to share mutual
concerns)

I have arranged lunch at the Board of Trade for all of us
at 1:00 p.m. If we haven't covered all items on the
agenda by then, we can continue the meeting over
lunch.

PHE   D.S.

Informal notice of meeting

◆ With a formal meeting, send out the notice of the upcoming meeting with a copy of the agenda and the minutes of the previous meeting.

MC3   THE AGENDA

The agenda is the *plan* for the meeting. It lists the purpose, place, date, and time of the meeting, as well as the items of business to be discussed and the order in which they are to be dealt with. No fixed format needs to be followed in preparing agendas. An interoffice memo indicating the discussion topics serves well for small, informal meetings. A detailed agenda indicating discussion topics and length of discussion times may be useful for larger gatherings with much to cover. Send the agenda out in advance of the meeting so that participants can be properly prepared. Otherwise, a copy should be put at each attendee's place at the meeting or handed out prior to the meeting.

NOTE   For regular meetings conducted under an identical format, consider creating and saving a template, filling in the blanks each time.

NOTE   Send out important motions and items requiring special consideration, such as reports, with the agenda at least four days prior to the meeting.

MC

Elliott Galleries
Board of Directors Meeting
20-- 12 12
High Ridge Hotel

Agenda

1. Call to order

2. Reading and approval of minutes

3. Reports from officers

4. Matters arising from the minutes

5. New business

6. Next meeting

7. Adjournment

Procedure

1. Chairperson starts the meeting, conveys apologies sent by absent members.
   • Secretary takes attendance.
   • Secretary announces whether a quorum (minimum number of members) is present for voting purposes.

2. Secretary reads minutes of last meeting. Chairperson asks for corrections. Group votes on changes, if any; if not, minutes are approved as read.

3. Reports from officers are read; copies are given to attending members.

4. Unfinished business from the last meeting is taken up.

5. New items are discussed. For example, nominations of new officers and elections could take place.

6. Date of next meeting is decided.

7. Chairperson closes the meeting.

Agenda and procedure for formal meeting

```
          ELLIOTT GALLERIES
          Quarterly Sales Meeting
          Conference Room
          20-- 03 20
          10:30 a.m.


              A G E N D A

  10:30  Welcome and introductions

  10:40  Reports:

         Sales update by area: D. Sanderson

         Public relations and promotion suggestions: sales
         representatives by area

         Quotas for second quarter: M. Misener

  12:00  Discussion

  12:30  Lunch (at the Board of Trade)
```

Informal meeting agenda

MC4 LAST-MINUTE PREPARATIONS

◆ Conduct a last-minute check of all details.

◆ Try out any special equipment (e.g., VCR, tape recorder, projector, or computer) to see that it works properly. Check that overhead pens, etc., are available if needed.

◆ Check the room temperature and furniture arrangement so that a comfortable working atmosphere exists. (See "Room Layout," MC1.)

◆ Have available where appropriate:
  • name tags if participants do not know one another
  • a list of names and affiliations of those attending
  • extra agendas
  • extra copies of the minutes of the last meeting
  • the minute book or file
  • copies of the constitution and by-laws
  • any previously submitted motions
  • copies of reports to be presented

MC5 CONDUCTING A MEETING

Meetings are conducted by a chairperson. With informal meetings, the chairperson's role is simply to maintain order, ensure that the meeting follows the agenda, and facilitate the proper communication of ideas and dissemination of information.

In some formal meetings, parliamentary procedure (formal rules of order) may be used, and it is the chairperson's task to see that these rules are followed. Although the rules of order might seem cumbersome, they do give everyone an equal right to be heard, to have all points of view considered, and to vote. In particular, the chairperson:

◆ ensures there is a quorum present. A quorum—the minimum number of members that must be present—is required before a formal meeting can proceed. Unless a quorum is present, the business conducted at the meeting cannot be considered legal or binding. The size of the quorum is established in the constitution of the organization

◆ calls the meeting to order (i.e., makes sure that it starts on time)

◆ maintains order

◆ explains and decides all questions of procedure

◆ announces and clarifies all business under consideration

◆ states motions (formal proposals) and resolutions (expressions of opinion) on which a vote is to be taken

◆ suggests a time limit for discussion on any particular topic or motion

◆ when necessary, keeps track of those wishing to speak to a motion and calls on them in order

◆ formally calls an end to the discussion before voting is to begin

◆ conducts voting

◆ announces voting results

MC6 PARLIAMENTARY PROCEDURE

▶ MC7 Presenting a motion

Parliamentary procedure requires that certain formal rules of order be followed when initiating discussion on a topic. When a proposal is made at a formal meeting, it is referred to as a *motion* and must have the support of another person, who is referred to as the *seconder*. Chairpersons do not require seconders for motions they propose.

The participant making the motion should rise and be recognized by the chairperson. After the motion has been made and seconded, the mover speaks on behalf of it. Next follows a debate during which supporters and opponents of the motion speak. The mover makes the final comment and the chairperson then puts the motion to the vote.

A typical motion begins, "I move that..."
A typical motion support begins, "I second the motion..."
Discussion and, perhaps, amendment of the motion follow.

NOTE Although motions to amend a motion may be made, only one main motion at a time can be handled. Motions to amend must be discussed and voted on so that the main motion is properly amended before it is finally discussed and a vote taken. For example:

Main motion
I move that the staff receive a bonus this year.
Seconded by J. Persaud.

MC

Amendment

I move to amend the motion that the staff receive a bonus this year only if the company earns a profit in excess of 10 percent.
Seconded by S. Boquist.
Discussion
Vote carried.

Amended main motion

I move that the staff receive a bonus this year, provided that the company earns a profit in excess of 10 percent.

The chairperson finally conducts the voting (by ballot or show of hands) on the motion as amended and announces the result of the vote. If more than half of the voters are in favour, the motion is adopted (carried). If there is a tie or less than half are in favour, the motion is defeated. If a motion is not voted on, the procedure for disposing of it is to *lay it on the table*, or, as this is more commonly expressed, to *table it*. A tabled motion can be revived, debated, and voted on at a subsequent meeting.

▶ MC8   Point of order

If a meeting member feels that a debating rule has been broken, that member can interrupt the person speaking and address the chairperson directly, without waiting for recognition, by saying, "Mr. (or Madam) Chairperson, I rise to a point of order." An example of a broken debating rule that might initiate a point of order would be the introduction of a topic totally unrelated to the motion under discussion.

Points of order must be made immediately after the alleged violation. They are not debatable, and the member who was interrupted must yield until the matter is clarified.

NOTE   Only a brief outline of parliamentary debating procedure has been included here. Full details appear in *Robert's Rules of Order*, available in paperback or hardbound editions. Anyone who is required to conduct or take notes at an important formal meeting should become familiar with Robert's Rules.

MC9 PROXIES

The constitution and by-laws of most organizations permit a person who cannot attend important meetings to be represented by proxy. A proxy can be either:

◆ another person who can attend the meeting with authority to vote and make decisions on behalf of the absent person

◆ a ballot (voting card) that has been sent out before the meeting and has been completed and returned by the absent person

MC

MC10 RECORDING A MEETING

MC11 MEETING MINUTES

Minutes are a permanent document designed to record, first, that a meeting was held and, second, the decisions made at the meeting. In addition, some minutes record proposals made and rejected as well as a summary of the discussion. Minutes must provide sufficient information for those not present to have a clear picture of what took place. Most companies keep a minute book in which copies of minutes are filed.

Minutes are legal documents, so it is important that they be accurate. Properly prepared minutes:

◆ clearly state the name, purpose, time, date, and place of the meeting

◆ record who was present (and sometimes who was absent)

◆ are accurate, concise, impersonal, and unbiased

◆ provide a summary of the results, not a complete description of the proceedings

◆ contain exact statements of motions, movers, and seconders

◆ state the terms of any resolutions adopted

◆ indicate the method of voting used and the outcome of the voting

◆ note appointments made

◆ make mention of the adjournment, including the time at which the meeting ended

◆ give notice of when the next meeting will be held

◆ contain the secretary's and chairperson's signatures

MC

MC12 TAKING NOTES FOR THE MINUTES

◆ Sit close enough to the chairperson so that you can get his or her attention if you miss a detail. Make sure you are comfortable.

◆ Study the agenda in advance and read over any specified papers prior to the meeting so that you are familiar with names and terms.

◆ Go over the minutes of the previous meeting to familiarize yourself with previous discussion topics.

◆ Prepare in advance a list of people who should attend so that only a check mark is needed to designate their absence or attendance.

◆ Make a seating plan and assign a number to each person present. Identify each person by some feature that will help you to recall names.

◆ Set up your note pad so that you have room for names and discussion topics. Organize your notes so that all discussion on any one subject is kept together. Note the name of each person introducing a topic. (You might consider preparing a template, an outline that you can use at every meeting, on which information can be quickly inserted.)

♦ Take more notes than necessary; they can be edited later.

♦ For formal meetings, a preprinted note-making sheet would be useful. It is especially helpful for motions because they must be recorded verbatim (word for word). Record whether a motion was adopted, defeated, referred to a committee, or tabled. Record also the names of those involved.

♦ Note anything that demands action after the meeting.

♦ Do not hesitate to interrupt discreetly to ask for restatement of a motion, clarification of a point, or identification of a speaker; or perhaps arrange a signal with the chairperson, who will then stop the meeting and have the point clarified.

♦ Be prepared to read back a motion at the chairperson's request before the vote is called.

NOTE If possible, take a laptop or notebook computer into the meeting. This will simplify final preparation of the minutes.

MC13 TAPE-RECORDING THE MINUTES

It is often helpful to use tape-recording as a backup reference to your own written meeting notes. Before using a tape recorder, remember these disadvantages:

♦ Some people may object to being taped.

♦ It may be technically difficult to set up so that the voices of all members are audible.

♦ Playing back and transcribing may be time-consuming.

♦ Speakers' voices may be difficult to identify.

If you do use a tape recorder:

♦ Change tapes during pauses in meetings or use two recorders and start recording on the second tape as the previous one is ending.

♦ Number and identify each tape.

MC14 PRODUCTION AND APPROVAL OF THE MINUTES

♦ Prepare a rough draft while the information is still fresh in your mind (preferably on a computer or word processor and saved so that if changes are needed you can avoid complete rekeying).

♦ Follow the sequence of topics used in the agenda.

♦ Refer to previous minutes and use the same style and format.

♦ Make motions and resolutions stand out in some way (e.g., use capitals).

- Language must be concise and impersonal. Do not use contractions (Unit 1, C38), interjections (C35), or direct quotations (C44).

- Be objective—do not include personal opinions.

- Record whether a motion was adopted, defeated, referred to a committee, or tabled.

- Reports, depending on their importance, can be:
  - summarized and the summary attached to the minutes
  - attached in their entirety
  - referred to in the body of the minutes

- Submit the final draft to the chairperson of the meeting for approval— within 24 hours is advisable. When possible, use communicating computers to permit shared editing of the draft.

- Produce enough copies for participants, others on the distribution list, and for the file (or official minute book), as well as extras for the next meeting.

- Members must approve minutes at the next meeting. If changes or additions are necessary, they can be written into the next minutes in the case of small or informal meetings. Where formal meetings are concerned, the minutes represent a legal document, and changes and/or additions are inked into the original and initialled by the chairperson. Once the minutes have been officially approved, no further changes are allowed.

> NOTE   An example of minutes from a formal meeting appears opposite.

MC

MC15 MEETING FOLLOW-UP

- Distribute the minutes soon after the meeting.

- Deal with any requests that may have arisen at the meeting (e.g., for additional information, for example).

- Send reminders, if necessary, about action to be taken. (Send copies of the committee's conclusions to those responsible for their implementation.)

- If feasible, circulate minutes of the previous meeting with the notice and agenda of the next meeting, so that participants can check items in advance for accuracy, and absentees can be kept informed.

- Send out appropriate thank-you notes.

- Note required items for the next meeting on your calendar.

- Note the date of the next meeting on your own and any other calendar for which you may be responsible.

```
                          Elliott Galleries
                       Board of Directors Meeting
                             20-- 12 12
                           High Ridge Hotel

                           M I N U T E S
```

Attendance	Present: J. Elliott, N. McCune, J. Ackroyd, S. Dominelli, R. Wilson, D. Darrigo, V. Vanlaarhove, W. Chan, G. Kotzell. Regrets: J. Revell, M. Toren, P. Lutz
Call to Order	Jayne Elliott, the President, chaired the meeting and called it to order at 10:00 a.m. by wishing all directors the compliments of the season and a successful new year.
Approval of Minutes	The minutes of the August 10 meeting were read. Norman McCune moved that the minutes be approved and David Darrigo seconded the motion.
Matters Arising	Since there were no matters arising from the previous minutes, the Chairperson proceeded with the business at hand.
In-House Desktop Publishing	Joachim Ackroyd informed the meeting that after extensive research by his department it seemed advisable, in view of present economic times, for the organization to invest in an in-house desktop publishing program. The cost- and time-saving benefits would be apparent in the first year, he felt. Copies of the report were distributed and the recommendation was discussed.
Motion	BE IT RESOLVED that the purchase of an in-house desktop publishing system be approved, and that Mr. Ackroyd provide quarterly reports on the operation of the program. Moved by J. Vanlaarhove, seconded by R. Wilson. The motion was carried unanimously.
Announcement	The next Board of Directors meeting will be held on 20-- 03 07.
Adjournment	The Chairperson adjourned the meeting at 12:40 p.m.

```
                                   Chairperson _____

              Date _____        Secretary  _____
```

Minutes of formal meeting

MC16 CONFERENCES AND CONVENTIONS

Conferences and conventions are large (sometimes massive) meetings of people with a common bond—such as members of a nationwide organization, association, or profession—gathering to exchange information and ideas, to make decisions, and to socialize. Many are annual events. Because conferences and conventions often involve a stay of several days in one centre and may include people from many locations, a considerable amount of highly detailed planning is required well in advance of the event.

MC17 PROGRAM

- ◆ Obtain speakers and/or panellists and confirm their attendance in writing early (even as much as a year in advance, in some cases).
- ◆ Contact potential sponsors early and obtain commitment.
- ◆ Invite and confirm possible exhibitors.
- ◆ Where workshops, seminars, or study sessions are included, allow time for study and reflection.
- ◆ Provide time for relaxation, exercise, or simply for enjoying the hotel or resort facilities.
- ◆ Include activities for family members accompanying delegates, if appropriate.

MC18 PUBLICITY

Promotion of the event may be handled in several ways, such as by:

- ◆ announcements placed in magazines and journals
- ◆ a mailing to each member that includes a description of the program, details of date, times, and location, and a registration form

Whichever method is used, early promotion is desirable.

MC19 CONFERENCE OR CONVENTION SITE

MC

In establishing the conference or convention site, the planner will be required to compare costs and facilities offered by the various possible locations. The information needed to obtain cost comparisons includes: the number of delegates, the type of meeting, dates, arrival and departure times, accommodation required, number of hospitality suites required, preregistration and registration procedures anticipated.

Be aware that sites capable of accommodating very large conventions are limited and may have to be booked as much as five years in advance.

The following are key points for comparison of various possible sites: cost per delegate, convenience of location, type of accommodation offered, number and size of meeting rooms, banquet facilities, services offered, and recreation facilities available.

Most major hotels, resorts, and convention centres employ specialists in conference planning. These people will assist with such tasks as registration of delegates, name tags, meeting room layouts, arrangement of facilities required by speakers, and organization of social activities. They should be relied on; they are experts.

Once you have chosen the venue, confirm the booking in writing and insist on written confirmation. It is a good idea to send along a checklist of your requirements so that there is no doubt as to what has been agreed.

MC20   PREPARATION OF MATERIALS

Arrangements must be made for:

◆ printing of announcements and programs, and for such other items as name cards, tickets for special events, and flyers describing local events and other activities

◆ preparation of information packages for each delegate, containing details of sessions and locations, local attractions, hotel services, meal tickets, etc.

NOTE   Use your computer to good effect. Your word-processing merge feature will minimize repetitious tasks in your preparation of notices, letters, and programs; a database will be invaluable in record-keeping and follow-up; and an electronic spreadsheet will simplify budgeting and financial management.

MC21   EQUIPMENT NEEDS

◆ Prepare a list for all audio-visual aids, flipcharts, bulletin boards, computers, and sound and other equipment that may be required for each of the separate meetings or sessions.

MC22   PREREGISTRATION AND REGISTRATION

◆ Make arrangements with the conference or convention location staff for dealing with those who register early or at the start of the event.

◆ Set up a registration desk where delegate materials, such as information packages and name tags, can be distributed.

MC23   REPORT OF THE PROCEEDINGS

◆ When the conference or convention is over, a report of the proceedings is frequently required. Some organizations keep a summary only; others prefer to keep a verbatim report, which may include copies of papers presented by speakers.

◆ Some organizations distribute the report of the proceedings free; others charge a fee.

MC24   CONFERENCE OR CONVENTION WRAP-UP

◆ Send thank-you letters to speakers and others.

◆ Follow up on and then file comments and ideas suggested by participants and organizers for the next conference.

MC

MC25 TELECONFERENCES

Teleconferencing is a viable alternative to traditional face-to-face meetings. It allows people to communicate across distances without leaving their offices. Through the medium of telecommunications, teleconferencing offers the benefits of voice-to-voice communication or voice-and-visual communication. Although expensive, teleconferencing can save an organization money and time if used properly. Plan conferences well in advance so that relevant materials can be distributed and studied by the scheduled participants.

In its simplest form, a teleconference can take place among three people, each at his/her own telephone. In more complex forms, it can take place among several individuals on their own telephones in various locations, communicating with one person or a group of people at company headquarters. It can also be an audio and visual communication among several people in one centre and their colleagues in one remote location, or among groups in various locations, hearing and seeing each other as if they were in one room.

The three categories of teleconference service are audio conferencing, audio-plus conferencing, and video conferencing.

MC26 AUDIO CONFERENCING

Audio conferencing is a simple telephone hookup among several people in different locations. Speakerphones or audio terminals permit discussion by all participants.

The chairperson can direct-dial to connect all members, or each participant can call in to a prespecified number, or the telephone company operator can arrange to set up the conference.

MC27 AUDIO-PLUS CONFERENCING

Audio-plus conferencing is useful in situations where people need to share documents or graphics. Speakerphones or audio terminals transmit speech exchanges and a terminal screen and/or console allows document transmission via facsimile, electronic messaging, or an electronic blackboard (the blackboard can be seen by the other participants). In planning such conferences, note the following:

◆ Arrange the seating plan so that all participants can see the graphics monitor or screen and each other.

◆ Check the lighting to ensure comfortable viewing.

◆ Provide light pens or other equipment for members to use.

◆ If microphones (small clip-on models are effective) are necessary, position the sound speakers carefully.

The telephone company operator is required to set up an audio-plus conference.

MC

MC28 VIDEO CONFERENCING

Video conferencing via a screen, console, and audio equipment is available where face-to face communication is essential but a physical meeting is not feasible. The features of audio conferencing are also included in this service. A video conference can be held in two ways:

◆ *Point-to-point:* Participants in two locations are involved in an exchange and discussion.

◆ *Point-to-multipoint:* Participants in one location can address people in several locations, but no discussion can take place.

The high costs associated with video conferencing limit its use to large organizations. High-end video cameras must be set up at the participating locations. The cameras are wired to a large black box called a codec. Just as modem means modulation/demodulation, codec stands for compression/decompression. The codec compresses the video signal into manageable chunks of data and transmits the data stream along to an integrated services data network (ISDN) modem set up next to the codec.

ISDN is a technology used to carry large volumes of data over telephone wires at very high speeds. The modems can transmit the data to the telephone lines and on to the receiving location where a modem and codec decompress the signal, relaying the data to a screen projector and then onto a screen for viewing.

Some large organizations and hotels provide video conferencing facilities for other businesses. It is more common, however, to use the facilities of telephone companies that handle the planning, setup, etc. When planning a video conference in this way, make reservations at least six weeks in advance.

MC29 PREPARATION FOR A TELECONFERENCE

Since teleconferences are charged for on the basis of time, participants must arrive early and be thoroughly prepared. Participants must know well in advance that a teleconference rather than a regular meeting is being arranged in order to avoid costly delays.

MC30 COMPUTER CONFERENCING

Computer conferencing enables people to conduct meetings via linked computers. Participants can communicate simultaneously or call up stored messages at their convenience.

MC

MC31 Terms

Ad hoc committee: A committee created to deal with a specific issue

Agenda: A list of items to be handled at a meeting

Amendment: A change to a motion that has been presented

Motion: A proposal requiring a proposer and a seconder

Parliamentary procedure: Rules governing the proper conduct of formal meetings

Point of order: A question about the validity of meeting procedures

Proxy: A person delegated to vote for an absent meeting member or a voting ballot sent in prior to the meeting

Quorum: The minimum number of members that must be present before a meeting can take place

Resolution: A formal decision approved at a meeting

Tabled: Postponement of a motion or discussion until a later date

MC

15 POSTAL AND SHIPPING SERVICES

CONTENTS

P

PART 1

POSTAL SERVICES

Technology has made possible the instant exchange of many types of information among businesses. However, the traditional method of delivering documents still has a major role to play. It offers the best service for some circumstances, and it offers the most economical services for some types of businesses. Knowledge of the wide range of postal services available and how to use them most efficiently is, therefore, important to all office workers.

Part 1 of this unit outlines suggestions for dealing with incoming and outgoing mail, a presentation of the key services offered by Canada Post, and a discussion of some alternative delivery methods. Part 2 provides information about shipping procedures and documentation requirements.

NOTE Electronic mail is discussed in Unit 5.

P1 MAIL-HANDLING TECHNIQUES

Processing mail efficiently is important in the successful operation of any business, regardless of size. Knowledge of mail-handling equipment and procedures is a useful asset, therefore.

P2 INCOMING MAIL

In a small firm, one person is expected to open and process all incoming mail. In a large organization, a mail department with specialized procedures and trained staff is responsible for dealing with it.

If you are designated to handle incoming mail, you may be required to do some or all of the following:

- **Sort** the incoming mail into categories:
  - priority (letters, invoices, interoffice memos, or any items requiring prompt attention)
  - newspapers and periodicals
  - advertising materials
- **Open and date-stamp** all but *personal and confidential* correspondence. Use letter-opening equipment if it is available.
- **Read and annotate** the mail. If this is part of your duties, after reading each document, highlight or underline the important passages and make marginal notes to help the recipient formulate a reply. You can also use stick-on notes. Scan the tables of contents of magazines and journals and identify any articles that might be of interest to colleagues or your supervisor.

♦ **Distribute** the mail to the appropriate people by placing it on their desks or in their mail slots or in-trays. Use a routing slip (see Unit 3, E5) for periodicals or non-urgent material.

Business etiquette calls for prompt responses to mail. This is also important if you are expected to reply to incoming mail in someone's absence.

Once incoming mail has been responded to, it should be marked for follow-up (see Unit 16, RM38), filed, or disposed of.

P3   OUTGOING MAIL

Efficient mail procedures speed up the communications process. The following tips, based on established postal standards, will help to ensure prompt delivery of your mail by the Canada Post Corporation.

♦ **Address mail carefully**. Refer to Unit 12, K6, for guidance in correctly keying addresses for domestic and international mail. Include postal codes for countries that use these.

Because of automated mail-sorting equipment, machine-printed or keyed mail can be sorted faster than handwritten mail. Mail that has no postal code may take longer to reach its destination. If a postal code is unknown, look it up in *Canada's Postal Code Directory*. This directory can be obtained at a reasonable cost at some post offices and postal outlets in Canada or can be ordered from:

NATIONAL PHILATELIC CENTRE
CANADA POST CORPORATION,
STATION 1
75 NINIAN STREET
ANTIGONISH, NS B2G 2R8

P

NEW BRUNSWICK/NOUVEAU BRUNSWICK

	Street Number from	to	Postal CODE		Street Number from	to	Postal CODE
	No de la maison de	á	CODE Postal		No de la maison de	á	CODE Postal
LEGION DR				Even/Pair	98	104	E3A 1V4
Odd/Impair	101	105	E3A 2K9		200	228	E3A 1V6
	107	–	E3A 2L1	**MACKENZIE RD**			
Even/Pair	100	122	E3A 2K8	Odd/Impair	15	–	E3B 6B5
LEICESTER ST					55	65	E3B 6B6
Odd/Impair	7	23	E3B 4N3	Even/Pair	30	–	E3B 6B7
	63	75	E3B 4N5	**MACLAREN AVE**			
Even/Pair	4	–	E3B 4N2	Odd/Impair	537	603	E3A 3K9
	22	70	E3B 4N4		623	639	E3A 3L1
LESLIE ST					713	767	E3A 3L4
Even/Pair	52	–	E3B 5B2		771	777	E3A 3L6
LEVERMAN ST					781	807	E3A 3L8
Odd/Impair	9	–	E3A 4H7	Even/Pair	528	–	E3A 3K7
LILAC CRES					542	614	E3A 3K8
Odd/Impair	3	27	E3A 2G7		626	668	E3A 3L2
	29	65	E3A 2G8		672	686	E3A 3L3
Even/Pair	2	24	E3A 2G6		732	758	E3A 3L5

Canada's Postal Code Directory page

If you need a postal code immediately and do not have a directory, you can find a postal code information number in the telephone book under the Canada Post Corporation listing.

Within the section for each province, towns and cities are arranged alphabetically, with rural route and lock box number lists appearing at the end of each. To find the postal code in the directory, locate the town or city, the street (arranged in alphabetical order), and then the street number.

`NOTE`   Standard-sized, meter-stamped mail without a postal code is more expensive than coded mail. Uncoded business mail may be returned to sender for the application of additional postage. The extra amount is collected by Canada Post when the organization replenishes its postage.

◆ **Use a return address.** In case of non-delivery, a return address enables Canada Post to return the item. Non-delivery of mail is usually caused by an incorrect address. Mail that cannot be delivered and has no return address is kept by Canada Post for a reasonable time, then opened and the contents sold at an annual public auction.

◆ **Use the correct Canada Post service and affix sufficient postage.** If there is a deficiency in the amount of postage paid, the item is returned to the sender.

◆ **Use standard-sized envelopes.** Envelopes that are larger or smaller than the limits set by Canada Post must be sorted manually. As a result, they require more postage.

`NOTE`   If you are mailing a disk, enclose a covering letter that identifies the contents of the disk and mark the disk clearly. Encase the disk in cardboard or heavy plastic wrap and use a padded envelope or box for mailing.

◆ **Wrap parcels carefully.** Packages must be carefully wrapped to avoid damage, breakage, leakage of contents, or injury to postal handlers. See this unit, P10, for information on prohibited articles.

◆ **Mail early.** Avoid the end-of-day rush at the post office by mailing early, and sort your mail into in-town and out-of-town batches if street letter boxes in your area are dedicated in this fashion. Mailing departments of large corporations generally have their own deadlines (usually mid-afternoon).

P4   MAIL-HANDLING EQUIPMENT

Your company's size will determine the sophistication of the equipment used to process mail. The following are examples of some of the mail-handling equipment available.

Folders

If you must mail large quantities of documents often, machines that fold letters, reports, etc., for mailing are helpful. Some models can also perforate, score, or slit documents as well as fold them. Other models can fold and insert documents as well as seal envelopes.

Mail openers

These automatic machines are designed to open large volumes of mail quickly.

Postage scales

These weigh scales are used to ensure that correct postage is affixed. Items must be placed one at a time on the scale, so these scales are useful only for companies that have small volumes of mail.

Mail-handling systems

Several types of systems are available that provide combinations of mail-handling processes. There are three basic types: manual, automatic, and electronic (computerized).

◆ *Manual systems* accept hand-fed mail and seal and stamp it.
◆ *Automatic systems* accept mail from a stack and automatically seal it, postmark it, meter-stamp it, count the pieces of mail, and restack it.

 You can rent or buy manual and automatic meter/mail-handling machines from postage meter manufacturing companies. They are available in two types. One type must be taken to the post office, where a bulk amount of postage credit is purchased and entered into it. When that amount has been used up, a further amount can be purchased. The other type, which is attached to a special base, can be replenished by simply telephoning the post office.
◆ *Electronic mail-handling systems* (which are used by many companies with high volumes of mail) comprise several pieces of linked equipment. These machines can:
 • handle single sheets or continuous business forms (e.g., invoices) that are automatically fed through a burster to be separated
 • feed documents into a folder and inserter, where they are folded, combined with any required inserts (e.g., return envelopes), and stuffed into mailing envelopes
 • move the envelopes on a conveyor belt through a postage meter to be automatically sealed, weighed, categorized, and stamped

Electronic mailing systems can also provide reports such as:

◆ breakdown of costs by department or other desired category
◆ daily total cost of mail
◆ daily cost of mail by postal-service category
◆ batch totals
◆ cost of postage per batch

Electronic mail-handling systems can be custom-designed to take documents of varying dimensions through the stages of inserting, sealing, addressing, weighing, and stamping. These expensive systems are useful for mass mailings.

NOTE Computer software is available to assist in parcel handling. A weigh scale is connected to a microcomputer; after placing a parcel on the scale, the operator keys in such information as parcel identification number, destination, and the number of the invoice enclosed. The computer calculates the postage rate and can print out address labels if desired. An automatic report of daily parcel shipment activities can also be provided.

P5   CANADA POST SERVICE

The amount of postage payable depends on the type of service used, the mass of the item, the destination, and any additional services required. Because postal rates change from time to time, it is wise to keep current postal information in your office. The *Canada Postal Guide* can be purchased from the Canada Post Corporation at the National Philatelic Centre address provided in this unit, P3. Canada Post rate-information leaflets are available free at any post office.

P6   CANADA POST SERVICE WITHIN CANADA

For Canada Post service to the United States and overseas, see this unit, P31 and P39, respectively.

▶ P7   Lettermail

Mail in this category consists of letters, business documents, greeting cards, and postcards that weigh up to 500 g. Items in envelopes larger or smaller than the limits specified by Canada Post are more costly to mail. In Canada, all lettermail is sent by air or the fastest possible land route.

▶ P8   Publications

A service is available only to companies that ship large quantities of printed matter (e.g., magazines). Contact a Canada Post commercial sales representative for information regarding this service.

▶ P9   Unaddressed mail

Items addressed simply to "Householder" or "Occupant" or bearing no address at all can be sent by this service. It is the most economical postal service for distributing catalogues, samples, promotional leaflets, etc. The company sending out the mailing specifies to the post office the district to be covered and the letter carrier then distributes one mailing piece to every householder or occupant in that district. The charge is a fee per item, plus a sum per kilogram.

Exception: Those who have indicated "NO ADMAIL HERE" on their mailbox or receptacle. A similar service is available for addressed admail.

▶ P10 Parcel mail

For parcels weighing up to a maximum of 30 kg, four services are available:

- ◆ **Regular post:** Most economical service. Deliveries are available for confirmation and signature for an additional fee.
- ◆ **Expedited parcels:** A fast ground service is available to commercial customers only. Local is service next day, regional service is one to three days, and national destinations can take up to seven days.
- ◆ **Xpresspost:** A service that offers the advantages of speed and economy, with local delivery the next business day, delivery between major centres within two days, and regional one to two days delivery; this service includes delivery confirmation.

Package size	Cost
◆ up to 1 m in length, width, or depth	◆ basic rate is chargeed
◆ any dimension exceeding 1 m	◆ surcharge is levied
◆ over 3 m length and girth or any dimension over 2 m	◆ not accepted by Canada Post

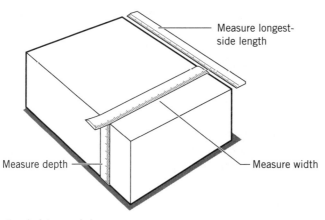

How to calculate parcel size

- ◆ **Priority Courier:** The fastest and most costly Canada Post parcel delivery service. It provides next-day delivery of envelopes and packages (maximum 30 kg) to certain designated areas in Canada, computer tracking of items, signature on delivery option, and indemnity up to a specific level.

Prohibited articles include animals, perishables, plants, liquor, drug samples, and explosives. For more detailed information, consult the *Canada Postal Guide.*

▶ **P11   Special Canada Post services**

P12 Aerogrammes (air letters)

An aerogramme is a self-contained, pre-stamped letter/envelope for airmail correspondence.

P13 Business reply cards and envelopes (prepaid—Canada only)

These are used by companies to encourage inquiries in response to advertisements, completion of consumer survey questionnaires, etc. The initiating organization is charged a fee per card or envelope plus the postage on each one returned.

P14 COD (Canada only)

This service is available to organizations that mail items requiring payment on delivery. The amount to be collected (maximum of $1000, when the amount is to be collected in cash, and a maximum of $25 000 if the amount is in the form of a cheque payable to the sender) is paid to the letter carrier on delivery, and a receipt is given as proof of payment. Items in excess of $500 must be picked up at the post office unless they are payable by cheque. The sender pays a small fee for the service and receives payment for the goods mailed by means of a money order. If the goods are lost or damaged, the post office will reimburse the sender for their declared value.

P15 Change of address cards (Canada and the United States)

A kit containing change of address cards can be purchased from the post office. The cards, which the sender completes and mails to correspondents, require letter or airmail postage.

NOTE For an additional charge, the post office will, for four months, hold mail for you or redirect it.

P16 Volume electronic mail

This service is available for large volumes (5000 letters or more each year). Canada Post receives text and a mailing list is provided in an electronic format. The material is electronically transmitted to regional production centres and converted to hard copy for delivery.

P17 Electronic statement of mailing

Canada Post's electronic statement of mailing is an order-entry software tool available free to commercial customers that use any of the following Canada Post services:

- Addressed Admail
- Catalogue Mail
- International/USA Incentive Letter-post
- Lettermail
- Publications Mail
- Unaddressed Admail

This software allows customers to complete their billing statements and make calculations automatically ensuring accurate rates, and eliminates the need to develop their own software for data entry.

Approved commercial customers can download the software from the Canada Post Web site: www.canadapost.com/CPC2/common/pages/questions.html

P18 Postal code products

For customers wishing to prepare their own mailings, postal code data are available for use in a company's database, for a fee, on CD-ROM, 6250 BPI or 1600 BPI Magnetic tapes, and IBM 3480 cartridge. While the initial fee is quite costly ($800 to $2000, depending on requirements), customers receive monthly updates.

P19 Coverage for loss or damage

Compensation to a maximum of $5000 in Canada, and $1000 in the United States or designated countries, is provided for damage, loss, or rifling of mail. The coverage fee (plus regular postage) is based on the value of the article. Check the *Canada Postal Guide* for a list of acceptable/insurable items.

P20 Lock boxes

These are the equivalent of postal office boxes (see this unit, P23) located at retail outlets for customer convenience.

P21 Members of Parliament mailing privileges (franked mail)

Mail to or from the prime minister, Governor General, senators, and parliamentary members of the federal government, either in Ottawa or in their constituencies, may be sent free of charge, except during election periods.

P22 Money orders

Postal money orders permit the safe sending of money almost anywhere in the world. They can be purchased at post offices for a small fee and can be cashed at the recipient's post office at no cost. Because they are numbered and the sale recorded, money orders can be replaced if lost.

NOTE You can purchase money orders at banks and some other financial institutions.

P23 Post office boxes (lock boxes and bags)

Lock boxes and bags are rented by businesses and individuals not wishing to use a full address and by those who want to pick up their mail at the post office or when letter carrier service is not available. The renter pays an annual fee, is allocated a box or bag number, and is given a key. He or she has sole access to the contents. Lock boxes are available in five sizes.

P24 Postage-paid-in-cash permit system

Businesses sending large volumes of addressed, identical-weight packages may take advantage of this special discount service. Consult the post office or the *Canada Postal Guide*, Part 1.

P25 Priority Courier

This service exists to provide next-day delivery of envelopes or packages (maximum 30 kg) to certain designated areas in Canada. A contract arrangement is possible when packages are sent frequently from one address to another (e.g., head office to branch office). Pickup and delivery service is available. Individual customers can also use this service by taking the item to a post office and purchasing a proper Priority Courier envelope. Consult the Canada Post sales department for details of designated areas and contract terms.

P26 Scheduled pickup for a fee

Account customers may use the scheduled pickup service. The weekly fee is dependent on the total volume of mail shipped for the week.

P27 On-demand pickup

Available to account customers for a fee.

P28 Registered mail

This proof-of-mailing service is useful when an important document or small item is to be mailed. The item to be registered must be taken to the post office. On payment of lettermail postage to Canadian destinations or small packet postage to the U.S., plus a registration fee, the sender is given a numbered receipt. When the item is delivered, the addressee or authorized representative must sign for it. If a registered item does not arrive at its destination, the registration number facilitates tracing the package.

P

P29   Acknowledgment-of-receipt card

For a small fee, the sender of a registered item can request an acknowledgment-of-receipt card. On receipt of the item, the recipient signs the card, which Canada Post then returns to the sender as proof of delivery.

NOTE   Canada Post provides many other services, such as the sale of traveller's cheques and the latest Canadian stamp releases, or to make a suggestion for a new stamp design.   Refer to the *Canada Postal Guide/CD* for complete information on these and other services.

P30   CANADA POST SERVICE TO THE UNITED STATES

▶ P31   Letter mail

Letter mail travels by air to the United States and costs a little more than mail to be delivered in Canada. It includes materials up to 500 g and is required to comply with Canada Post standards. The rate and weight structure is quite specific:

◆ Cheapest rate: Standard-sized letters and cards up to 50 g

◆ More expensive rate: Over-sized (within Canada Post limits) items up to 500 g

◆ Most expensive: Larger than over-sized letter mail up to 500 g

P32 Direct bags (printed materials—United States and international only)

Businesses that send up to 30 kg of material to a single address may use this economical surface mail service e.g., printing firms sending books to libraries.

▶ P33   Printed materials (surface mail only)

This is an economical service for mailing printed materials up to a maximum of 1 kg.

▶ P34   Small parcels

Packets up to 1 kg in weight can be sent by surface or by air, with the latter being more expensive. Printed materials are sent by surface only. Small packets may be registered but not insured.

▶ P35   Airmail parcels

For urgent mail packages between 1 kg and 30 kg, airmail service is available. Size restrictions are a maximum of 1 m for length or width, and a maximum dimension of 2 m for length, plus girth.

▶ P36   Surface parcels

Mail from 1 kg to 30 kg with the same size restrictions as airmail packages but of a less urgent nature may be sent for a much lower price by this service.

▶ P37   Special Canada Post services to the United States

The following special services are available for mail delivery to the United States (see previous sections of this unit): direct bags, coverage foe loss or damage, money orders, registered mail, Express Post USA, and Purolator delivery.

▶ P38   Customs declaration

Customs regulations demand that the contents, their value, and the name and address of sender be declared on every package leaving Canada. Forms are available at the post office.

P

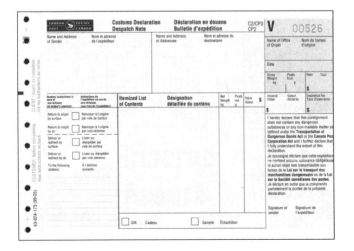

P39 CANADA POST SERVICE TO INTERNATIONAL DESTINATIONS

P40 Special delivery (International)

This service is used when high-speed delivery is required. The sender must take the item to the post office. The amount paid is a fee plus applicable postage to certain countries.

► P41   Aerogrammes (air letters)

You can buy a self-contained, pre-stamped letter/envelope form from the post office for the same price as an airmail stamp. Writing space is limited and no enclosures are permitted.

► P42   Letter mail and postcards

Letters of a business or personal nature and postcards to a maximum of 500 g travel by air only.

► P43   Letter packages

Business or personal letter mail between 500 g and 2 kg in weight travels by this costly air service.

► P44   Printed matter

You may send packages of printed matter up to 2 kg in weight by airmail or by surface route (ship and land), which is slower but less costly. Direct bags go by surface mail only and are for the use of publishers and other mailers sending a quantity (up to 30 kg) of mail to one address.

► P45   Small packets

Packages in this category weigh up to 2 kg and may be sent by airmail or by surface mail, depending on the urgency. Airmail is costlier than surface. Small packets may be registered but not insured.

► P46   Parcels

You may send parcels weighing more than 2 kg and less than 20 kg to most countries, and less than 30 kg to more than 80 countries by air or surface mail. See *Canada Postal Guide* for country guidelines.

► P47   Special Canada Post services to overseas destinations

The following special services are available for mail to many countries (see previous sections in this unit for descriptions): direct bags, insurance, international reply coupons, money orders, registered mail, special delivery, and Purolator. Consult the *Canada Postal Guide* or your post office or postal outlet for a list of those countries to which these services apply.

▶ P48   Customs declaration

Customs regulations demand that the contents, their value, and the name and address of sender be declared on every package leaving Canada (see illustration, this unit, P38). The forms are available at the post office or postal outlets.

▶ P49   DUTY-FREE AND TAX-EXEMPT IMPORTATIONS BY MAIL

The Canada Customs and Revenue Agency (CCRA) can examine any items that come into Canada by mail. Duty can be charged as well as any goods and services tax (GST), or harmonized sales tax (HST), on a mail item you receive. This is determined by the item's value in Canadian dollars, and whether it is a gift.

If someone mails you an item that is worth $20 Canadian or less, then you are not charged duty, GST, or HST on the item. If the item is worth more than $20 Canadian, however, then you must pay duty and the taxes on the full value of the item.

NOTE   Alcoholic beverages, books, magazines, periodicals, tobacco, and goods ordered through a Canadian post office box, or intermediary *do not* qualify for the $20 exemption.

TIP   To obtain delivery status information on *Priority Courier, Expresspost, Purolator International* and *Delivery Confirmation/Registered* items: Call Customer Service: 1-888-550-6333.

NOTE   Canada Post provides many other services, such as the sale of traveller's cheques, and are constantly adding to the list. Refer to the *Canada Postal Guide*/CD-ROM or your local post office for complete information on these and other services.

Web site: www.canadapost.ca

P50 ALTERNATIVES TO CANADA POST SERVICES

P51   AIRLINES

Several airline companies offer fast, economical air delivery of letters and packages to destinations in North America and overseas. Refer to the Yellow Pages under "Airlines" or "Courier Service" or contact an airline company (see also Part 2 of this unit).

P52   BUS PARCEL EXPRESS (BPX)

A bus will transport letters or packages of a personal or business nature from one destination to another in Canada and the United States.

◆ The sender can take the package to the bus terminal and have it picked up at the arrival terminal.

◆ Door-to-door pickup and delivery service is available for an additional fee.

◆ Same-day delivery is possible, depending on the locations of sender and addressee.

◆ Maximum weight allowance is 35 kg (77 lb.).

P53 COURIERS

A number of courier organizations offer delivery services within cities, between provinces and states, and around the world. Charges are based on package weight (limit: 35 kg/package), destination, and the time period requested for delivery. Services normally operate on a five-day-week basis, although some urban areas offer seven-day-week services. A signature is usually required on delivery.

▶ P54 Standard services

◆ same-day delivery (depending on destination, more expensive than next-day service)

◆ pickup and delivery

◆ specialized letter service for overseas next-day delivery

▶ P55 Additional possible services

◆ drop boxes similar to mailboxes, with specific pickup times

◆ shipments up to 2.25 tonnes (5000 lb.)

◆ acceptance of some dangerous commodities (provided the package and bill of lading clearly identify the contents)

◆ electronic tracking

◆ weekend service for an additional fee

◆ radio-dispatched vehicles for rapid pickup

◆ linked services with the receiving country's postal system

Check the Yellow Pages under "Courier Service" or "Delivery Service."

▶ P56 Using courier services wisely

If possible:

◆ Use computer-aided shipping, if offered. This saves paperwork, links you with courier agents, and permits tracking of parcels.

◆ Take advantage of volume discounts—use one courier rather than several and set up an account.

◆ Use deferred delivery—overnight or next-day service is cheaper than same-day delivery.

- Consolidate shipments—send all packages to one city in one bag once a day.
- Use courier drop boxes when possible to save pickup charges.
- Compare rates when insurance is needed and use the cheaper—your own insurer's rate or the courier's.
- Negotiate prices for non-routine arrangements and inquire also about package deals.
- Be a smart consumer—comparison-shop for the courier that offers the services that best meet your needs at the lowest cost.

P57   TAXIS

If a courier is unavailable for same-day delivery, consider using a taxi for an urgent local delivery.

 **2**

SHIPPING SERVICES

Vast quantities of raw materials and manufactured products are shipped daily across Canada. This unit provides basic information about the types of shipping services that are available.

P58 "SHIPPING SERVICES" CHART

The "Shipping Services" chart on the following pages provides some general information on the services available when shipping commercial goods in Canada by various modes of transportation. Before choosing a particular type of transportation, however, consider the factors outlined below.

Charges for transportation services are based on:

- the nature of goods being carried
- their destination
- their mass or volume, whichever is greater

and can be paid in one of the following ways:

- prepaid by the shipper (consignor) in cash
- charged to the shipper's account
- COD, paid by the recipient (consignee)

P59 CHOOSING A TRANSPORTATION MODE

Whether you choose air, rail, or truck, consider these factors:

◆ Air:
- is fastest but usually most expensive
- may have mass or volume restrictions
- may have restrictions on certain goods

◆ Rail and truck:
- are best for heavy or high-volume goods
- can be interchanged (e.g., piggypack), but transfer from one mode to another costs more

If you are shipping hazardous goods, contact Transport Canada for full instructions regarding packaging, marking, and documentation. The transportation of these materials is the combined responsibility of consignor and carrier.

SHIPPING SERVICES

Transportation mode	Pickup and delivery	Restrictions	Special services	Points to note
AIR				
Same Day	• available at extra cost	• see P59	• guaranteed airport-to-airport delivery	• 24-hour service • same-day delivery
Overnight	• available at extra cost	• see P59	• airport-to-airport delivery	• next day delivery possible if goods received by a particular time
Air Freight	• available at extra cost	• see P59	• door-to-door delivery during standard 5-day business week • container service • animal transport • refrigeration facilities	• 24- to 72-hour delivery • certain documents might be required in addition to a awaybill; check with the carrier

NOTE For small packages with a maximum mass of 1 kg, Airvelops (tear-resistant, waterproof envelopes) are available at airline cargo centres.

RAIL FREIGHT	• included for piggyback door to door	• full boxcars only (91 tonnes)	• heated and refrigerated units available • container capability • piggyback capability	• best suited to large, out-of-town shipments • pool-car service for partial loads (rail company) • charges based on perishability, mass/volume, distance, need for special services • faster service available for extra charge

P

Transportation mode	Pickup and delivery	Restrictions	Special services	Points to note
TRUCK	• usually included	• see P60	• heated and refrigerated units available • container capability	• delivery possible to places not served by trains or airplanes • charges based on mass/volume, distance, type of goods • full truckload rate is cheaper than partial load • usually instant computer access to locate shipment
BOAT (Steamship)	• usually not included	• containers only, except for consumer goods	• tank containers • refrigerated and heated units available • open-top containers	• best suited to heavy, bulky goods, machinery, where speed is not a priority • personal effects must be prepaid
BUS	• available at extra cost	• maximum 35 kg maximum girth + length: 360 cm		• packages usually must be prepaid
COURIER	• included in service charge	• maximum mass varies from courier to courier	• acknowledgment of delivery for additional charge • reduced rates for prepaid envelopes • guaranteed delivery times	• prepaid shipments a good alternative to postal services • overnight door-to-door service in most of Canada • instant tracking of parcels • drop boxes often conveniently located in commercial areas

Because costs and types of services vary, and because all carriers do not offer all services, you should comparison-shop to find the most suitable and economical carrier for your shipment.

P60 FREIGHT FORWARDERS

These agents offer a useful service for companies that ship merchandise requiring less than a full load. The freight forwarder leases a full load and uses the space to ship several small (part) loads from various consignors. In spite of the fee charged, the advantages to the shipper are:

- *cost-saving* because of the full-load rate
- *time-saving* because the agent is familiar with carriers, routes, and rates; can monitor the shipment during transit; and serves as intermediary between shipper and carrier.

P61 SHIPPER'S RESPONSIBILITIES

The shipper usually pays the freight charges. If a shipment is being sent COD, however, the shipper should obtain a written or electronic commitment from the consignee that payment will be made to the carrier on delivery of the goods.

A company shipping goods should check the maximum liability for merchandise lost or damaged by the carrier and perhaps consider additional insurance coverage.

P62 DOCUMENTATION

Prepare a *bill of lading* (often called a *waybill*) for each shipment. Blank forms are provided by the carrier but must be completed by the shipper. When the carrier picks up the shipment, the driver signs the bill of lading, acknowledging the carrier's contract to deliver the goods to the given destination. The bill of lading, which is a contract, also:

- acts as the shipper's receipt from the carrier, acknowledging that the shipment is in good condition and that the number of packages in the shipment is correct
- provides the carrier with all relevant information on the destination of the goods
- can sometimes be used as a supporting document for loss, damage, or shortage claims by the shipper

A bill of lading must therefore be carefully prepared and its accuracy confirmed before a shipment is loaded.

The carrier supplies multiple-copy bills of lading. The consignor and the consignee each receive at least one copy and the carrier keeps the rest.

P63 PRO BILL

A *pro bill* form, which contains details pertinent to the carrier only, must also accompany a shipment. If a pro bill is not available, a *pro sticker* is completed from information taken from the shaded areas of the bill of lading.

P64 EDI

Currently, in many cases, shippers transmit all of the necessary information by electronic data exchange (EDI: see Unit 9). For example, some parts of shipping processes are completed by the use of bar code labels on packages that can be read by hand-held scanners carried by transportation company drivers. In some cases, however, paper documents are still required for the actual shipping process because of the need for the signatures of the carrier and the consignee (in special cases, proof of identification is also required).

P65 INTERNATIONAL SHIPPING

The importing and exporting of goods involves preparation of many Customs documents and adherence to a strict set of procedures. Companies that conduct international trade usually either have Customs experts on staff or use the services of Customs brokers or consultants. If you are ever required to handle any aspect of importation or exportation and do not have an in-house expert, consult a Customs representative at Canada Customs and Revenue Agency or a Customs broker or consultant.

P

16 RECORDS MANAGEMENT

CONTENTS

RM

R ecords management involves the safe and orderly storage of records, using a system that ensures fast and easy retrieval of required information. An organization's information might be stored in the form of paper documents or might be stored using magnetic, electronic, or optical media. Today's office worker, therefore, must be familiar with the techniques for successfully managing records of a great many types and complexities. This unit will provide the information you need to meet the challenge, regardless of whether the system is manual or electronic. You will be guided through the management and control of storing documents, magnetic media, microfilm, and optical disks; you will be introduced to various types of storage equipment; you will find out about computer-based systems; and you will learn the terms used in the records management process.

RM

RM1 THE ALPHABET IN RECORDS MANAGEMENT

Because the alphabet is the basis of many records management systems, one uniform set of rules for placing file captions (names, places, subjects) in alphabetic order must be followed by everyone who uses the records in the system. The rules that follow are based on those developed by the Association of Records Managers and Administrators International (ARMA) for standardizing alphabetic filing. These rules also take into account the needs of electronic systems and should be adopted so that there is consistency between both manual and electronic sorting methods.

RM2 INDEXING

Before file captions (names, places, subjects) can be arranged in alphabetic order, they must be indexed. *Indexing* means determining the most important part of a caption and then putting that word or set of words first, if necessary. The indexed version of the caption should be placed on the file folder, record card, or record container.

If you index for an electronic sorting system (for database records, for example), you must take special care because, while the software can sort with amazing speed, it cannot make indexing decisions.

Normal order	Indexed order
Laura L. Fleming	Fleming, Laura L.
The Sharp Electronics Company	Sharp Electronics Company, The

NOTE Commas are used to indicate that parts of a caption have been rearranged.

If a database is used for automatically preparing envelopes or labels, depending on the software, you may need to use several fields: one for producing alphabetic lists and one for mailing purposes, as the following illustrates:

Field 1:	Mailing label name:	Miss Elaine Cheng
Field 2:	Family name:	Cheng
Field 3:	Given name:	Elaine

Field 1 will be used for labels and envelopes; fields 2 and 3 will be used for alphabetic lists.

The easiest way to handle the indexing process if you have doubts is to set up the information in unit order as illustrated below:

Unit 1	Unit 2	Unit 3	Unit 4
Jack	Bird	Plumbing	Co.
Fleming	Laura	L.	
Sharp	Electronics	Company	The

RM3 ALPHABETIC SEQUENCING

Consider each part of the caption as a separate unit, working from left to right until a comparison point is reached. For correct filing order, always follow the rule *Nothing comes before something.*

Unit 1	Unit 2	Unit 3
Bird	J.	
Bird	Jack	
Bird	Shop	The
Birde	J.	John

◆ Use all units, including articles, prepositions, and conjunctions. If words such as *the*, *a*, *an* come first, treat them as the last unit.

RM4   NAMES OF INDIVIDUALS

◆ Consider family names first, given names or initials second, middle names or initials third.

◆ A family name standing alone precedes a family name with initials.

◆ A family name with initials precedes a family name with a full given name:

> Johnson
> Johnson, N.
> Johnson, Nadia

NOTE   The name of a married woman may be alphabetically sequenced as given and cross-referenced to her husband's name, depending on how the woman prefers to be known:

> Jones, Sara (Mrs.)
> Cross-reference: Jones, Robert (Mrs.) <u>see</u>
> Jones, Sara (Mrs.)
>
> Jones, Sarah (Mrs.)
> cross-reference: Jones, Allan (Mrs.) <u>see</u>
> Jones, Sarah (Mrs.)

Non-English names

When it is difficult to distinguish the family name from the first name, index the name as it appears. Cross-reference when there is doubt:

As written	**Unit 1**	**Unit 2**	**Unit 3**
* Leung Hung Pok	Leung	Hung	Pok
Daniel To	To	Daniel	
* <u>See</u> Pok, Leung Hung			

RM5   NAMES OF COMPANIES

Company names are usually filed as written:

> Ford Motor Company, The
> Pourquoi Pas Restaurants Ltd.
> Sara Lee Kitchens
> Spruce Springs Antiques

NOTE   In cases in which a company is named after a person and is generally referred to by the family name, cross-referencing might be considered to avoid confusion. For example, "Terence Singh Electronics Ltd." might be referred to generally as "Singh's." In this case, it would be filed as written to follow ARMA rules and could be cross-referenced under "Singh, Terence, Electronics" to avoid possible confusion.

RM6 TITLES AND DEGREES

Disregard these for alphabetic sequencing purposes (unless required to distinguish between identical names) but key on to the caption after the name:

Normal order	Caption order
Mrs. Jane Alexander, B.A.	Alexander, Jane (B.A.) (Mrs.)
Dr. Alan H. Draper	Draper, Alan H. (Dr.)
Captain James Morgan	Morgan, James (Captain)

If a title is part of a person's given name or a business name, file it as written:

Normal order	Caption order
Lord Simcoe Hotel	Lord Simcoe Hotel
Sir Nicholas Restaurant	Sir Nicholas Restaurant
Sister Gabriella	Sister Gabriella

Social or courtesy titles are used for indexing only when two or more names are identical:

Pearson	Phil	Miss
Pearson	Phil	Mr.
Pearson	Phil	Mrs.
Pearson	Phil	Ms.

RM7 INITIALS AND ACRONYMS

When initials or acronyms form all or part of the name of an organization, treat them as one filing unit. Also treat TV and radio call letters as one unit:

	Unit 1	Unit 2
CAC Realty	CAC	Realty
CFMT Television	CFMT	Television

When the meaning of the initials or acronym is known, cross-reference to avoid confusion (e.g., IBM Canada Ltd.; cross-reference: Use for International Business Machines Canada Ltd.). This allows you to file under the common abbreviation while acknowledging the full title. See RM37 for information on cross-referencing.

RM8 ABBREVIATIONS

Treat as they are written and indexed alphabetically. Note that Saint, St., or Ste. when used as a title is considered a separate unit. When Saint, St., or Ste. is a prefix to a personal name, it is considered part of the name.

As written	First unit	Second unit
Saint Patrick's Church	Saint	Patrick's
St. John's Bookstore	St.	John's
Jacques Ste. Marie	Ste. Marie	Jacques

RM

James Brown	Brown	James
Jane Brown	Brown	Jane
Jas. Brown	Brown	Jas.

RM9 PREFIXES

In names that contain a prefix, such as D', Da, De, De la, Des, Di, El, Fitz, L', La, Las, Mac, Mc, O', St., Ste., Ten, Van, and Von, the prefix is considered to be part of the name (i.e., prefix plus name equals one word). In other words, ignore spacing, punctuation, and capitalization in alphabetic sequencing in such names:

P. D'Ambrosia	D'Ambrosia, P. (considered as if spelled <u>Dambrosia</u>)
O. De Kleine	De Kleine, O. (considered as if spelled <u>Dekleine</u>)
P. St. Clair	St. Clair, P. (considered as if spelled <u>StClair</u>)
D. von der Heidt	von der Heidt, D. (considered as if spelled <u>vonderheidt</u>)

El Matador (considered as if spelled <u>Elmatador</u>)
La Scala Dining Room (considered as if spelled <u>Lascala</u>)
Le Chien Élégant (considered as if spelled <u>Lechien</u>)

RM10 PUNCTUATION

Ignore all punctuation in alphabetic sequencing, no matter where it occurs, but key it into the caption:

LeLarge Inc.
Lela's Hairstyling
Lelas, T.
L'Élégant Beauty Salon
L'Élégant Ltd.

RM11 HYPHENATED NAMES

Treat hyphenated names as one filing unit; disregard the hyphen while establishing filing order but key it into the caption:

	Unit 1	Unit 2	Unit 3
Canadian-American Pen Co.	Canadian-American	Pen	Co.
James William Curtis	Curtis	James	William
Ellen Curtis-Brown	Curtis-Brown	Ellen	
Winston Curtis-Jones	Curtis-Jones	Winston	
Nu-Style Beauty Salon	Nu-Style	Beauty	Salon

RM12 SYMBOLS

Treat these as though they are spelled out, and each is considered to be a separate unit:

	Unit 1	Unit 2	Unit 3	Unit 4
Chui & Kwak Ltd. (*treat as*)	Chui	and	Kwak	Ltd.
Easy $ Car Rental (*treat as*)	Easy	Dollar	Car	Rental

RM

RM13 GEOGRAPHIC NAMES

Treat these as though each word is a separate unit (i.e., they are filed as written). However, treat geographic names starting with non-English articles or prefixes as one unit:

	Unit 1	Unit 2	Unit 3
Lake Huron Fisheries	Lake	Huron	Fisheries
Las Olas Importers	Las Olas	Importers	
Mount Vernon Antiques	Mount	Vernon	Antiques

RM14 COMPASS POINTS IN NAMES

When names include compass points, consider the compass points as they are written (i.e., each word will be a separate unit):

Unit 1	Unit 2	Unit 3
North	Atlantic	Fisheries
North	West	Airlines
North-West	Sportswear	
Northwestern	Auto	Service

RM15 NUMBERS

Several rules apply in relation to captions that include numbers:

1. Place captions beginning with *arabic numerals* in numeric order and list these before all alphabetic files.

   747 Travel Agency before Able 2 Taxi Service

2. Place captions starting with *roman numerals* after those starting with arabic numerals.

   747 Travel Agency before III Star Club

3. File names beginning with *spelled-out numbers* in appropriate alphabetical sequence.

   Four Seas Fashions after Able 2 Taxi Service

4. When numbers come *within a name*, consider these as spelled out.

   Able 2 Taxi Service = Able Two Taxi Service

   747 Travel Agency
   III Star Club
   Able 2 Taxi Service
   Able II Taxi Service
   Four Seas Fashions

RM16 ASSOCIATIONS, SOCIETIES, ORGANIZATIONS, BANKS, RELIGIOUS INSTITUTIONS, COLLEGES, SCHOOLS, UNIVERSITIES

These remain unchanged for filing purposes:

Normal order	Indexed order
Bank of Montreal	Bank of Montreal
Church of the Redeemer	Church of the Redeemer
L'Amoreaux Collegiate	L'Amoreaux Collegiate
R.H. King Academy	R.H. King Academy
Stephen Leacock College	Stephen Leacock College
University of Manitoba	University of Manitoba

Cross-reference, if necessary, to avoid confusion (e.g., Montreal, Bank of).

RM17 BOARDS, COMMITTEES, ESTATES, TRUSTEES

Rearrange names of boards, etc., to bring the most important word to the front:

Normal order	Indexed order
Board of Governors	Governors, Board of
Estate of D. Chung	Chung, D., Estate of

Cross-reference to the normal order of the words, if necessary, to avoid confusion.

RM18 GOVERNMENTS AND THEIR DIVISIONS

File these under the name of the particular level of government (federal, provincial, municipal), with further subdivisions where necessary:

Normal order	Indexed order
Government of Canada	Canada, Government of
Ministry of Agriculture	Agriculture, Ministry of
Saskatchewan Ministry of Health	Saskatchewan, Province of, Health, Ministry of
Windsor Board of Education	Windsor, Education, Board of

Foreign government names

File these in the order of the country, department, bureau, or other subdivisions:

Normal order	Indexed order
Ministry of Trade, Korea	Korea, Trade, Ministry of

RM19 IDENTICAL NAMES

If two or more names are identical, distinguish among them by proceeding through the following steps until a point of comparison is found:

RM

1. personal/professional, courtesy title
2. geographic location
3. address

Barbara Brogly, B.A.	Brogly, Barbara (B.A.)
Dr. Barbara Brogly	Brogly, Barbara (Dr.)
Ms. Barbara Brogly	Brogly, Barbara (Ms.)
Prof. Barbara Brogly	Brogly, Barbara (Prof.)

If no titles of any type are given for identical personal names or if identical company names occur, file alphabetically by location (i.e., the province/state/country is compared first; then town/city; then street name; then street number, numerically):

Brogly, Barbara, Nova Scotia
Brogly, Barbara, Saskatchewan

General Goods Co., Main Street, Edmonton, Alberta
General Goods Co., 73 Fifth Street, Charlottetown, Prince Edward Island
General Goods Co., 49 Third Avenue, Charlottetown, Prince Edward Island
General Goods Co., 150 Third Avenue, Charlottetown, Prince Edward Island

RM20   TELEPHONE DIRECTORY ALPHABETIC SEQUENCING

Telephone directories do not follow all ARMA rules. If you are looking for information in a telephone directory, note the following possible variations in alphabetic sequencing:

◆ Company names that include individuals' first and last names may be listed under the family name.
◆ Some abbreviations are treated as though spelled out. (e.g., Assoc., Insce.). Ampersands (&) are disregarded.
◆ Numbers are treated as though spelled out (e.g., "7-Eleven Stores" after "Sevcenko, E.").
◆ Hyphenated names are sometimes treated as separate units and sometimes as one (e.g., "Servo-Clean" after "Servite Inc.").
◆ Government organizations are listed within the government body (i.e., federal, provincial, and municipal) and appear separately in the Blue Pages.

RM

RM21 Basic Document Records Organization and Supplies

Despite the increased use of such records management technology as magnetic disks, optical disks, and EDI (electronic data interchange), vast quantities of document records are still kept by both large and small organizations.

RM22   PARTS OF A TYPICAL ALPHABETIC DOCUMENT FILE

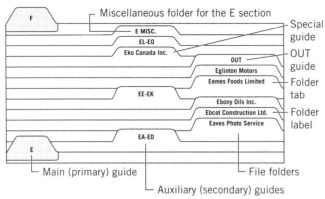

Parts of a typical document file

▶ RM23   Guides

Use *main* (primary) and *auxiliary* (secondary) guides (folder-sized cardboard with metal or plastic tabs) to separate file folders into divisions and subdivisions to facilitate filing and retrieval. Use *special* guides when files for particular subjects or correspondents are frequently referred to and must be speedily located.

▶ RM24   Folders (legal- or letter-size)

Individual Prepared for each person, organization, or subject; placed in alphabetic order behind the relevant guide.

Miscellaneous Prepared for documents concerning a new correspondent or subject; placed at the back of the proper subdivision until at least five documents have accumulated. An individual folder is then prepared and moved to the appropriate position.

▶ RM25   Suspension folders

So that file folders do not slide around in file drawers, place them inside suspension folders that hang from a special framework inserted in the file drawer.

Folder tabs

Folders are available in a variety of *cuts* that leave a tab visible in the file drawer or on the file shelf.

RM

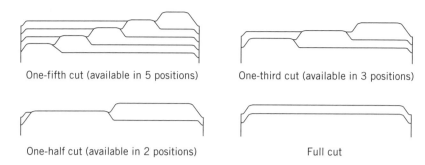

One-fifth cut (available in 5 positions)   One-third cut (available in 3 positions)

One-half cut (available in 2 positions)   Full cut

Folder tabs with top cuts

You can use same cut for all folders in a system, or cuts may varied to stagger folders so that one folder tab is not obscured behind another. Cuts may be top tab or side tab. Use side tab folders for lateral filing cabinets and shelf filing systems. See this unit, RM47 and RM48.

Folder labels

Folder captions are usually keyed on labels available in roll or sheet form and in various colours. Key captions neatly in a consistent style and position the labels carefully so that the captions can be easily seen. You can use colour to indicate particular years, particular departments, etc. Plastic tabs are provided with suspension folders to readily identify the file folders they house.

RM26 RECORDS MANAGEMENT SYSTEMS

Records may be arranged alphabetically, by geographic location, by subject, by number, or by a combination of letters and numbers.

Below is a description of how these systems accommodate document records. The principles of alphabetic, numeric, geographic, subject, and chronological records management can also be applied to electronic, optical, and micrographic media.

RM

RM27   ALPHABETIC FILING

◆ Names and subjects are filed in simple alphabetic order (see this unit, RM3).

◆ Main guides indicate each letter of the alphabet.

◆ Auxiliary guides break down each letter of the alphabet into sections. Folders are arranged alphabetically by name behind these guides. The user merely looks for the first two or three letters on the auxiliary guide and then looks behind for the desired folder.

◆ This system is simple, easy to operate, but difficult to expand.

◆ Alphabetic filing is used in small organizations where specialized breakdown by subject or location is not needed.

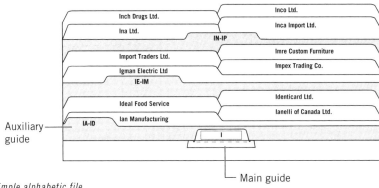

Auxiliary guide

Main guide

Simple alphabetic file

RM28 GEOGRAPHIC FILING

◆ Files are grouped by geographic location from the largest geographic division to the smallest (e.g., from province to town).

◆ The largest divisions (provinces) appear on the main guides, and the cities or towns on the auxiliary guides. File folders for correspondents in each city or town are placed alphabetically behind these guides.

◆ This system is useful for firms or departments whose main interest is territorial data (e.g., sales records); however, it should be noted that the successful operation of a geographic system demands sound geographic knowledge.

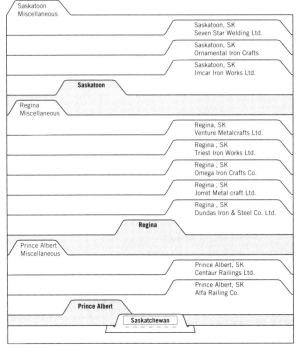

Typical geographic file

RM29 SUBJECT FILING

◆ Subject filing means organizing records by topic (i.e., the content of the material) and then arranging the files alphabetically by those topics.

◆ The main guide indicates the main topic breakdown in the filing system. Auxiliary guides indicate any necessary subdivisions of the topic. Folders are arranged alphabetically by topic behind the appropriate guide.

◆ Establishing subject classifications demands care and considerable knowledge of the organization's activities.

◆ To facilitate retrieval, an alphabetic master list or card index is needed that shows all of the main subject divisions, auxiliary divisions, and individual folder categories.

◆ Many cross-references are likely to be required.

◆ This filing system is used when subject matter is more important than correspondents' names.

▶ RM30 Use of letters and numbers in subject filing

Subject files may also be identified by letters and numbers used in combination or sometimes by numbers alone. Such systems are particularly useful in large, centralized document filing systems because they can overcome the restrictions generally imposed by simple alphabetic subject systems. These variations offer flexibility, diminish misfiling possibilities, and ease expansion difficulties.

Alpha-numeric

A combination of letters and numbers is used. Main topics are given letters and related subtopics are assigned numbers:

A	ADMINISTRATION
A1	**Human Resources**
A1-1	Company Policies
A1-1-1	Absenteeism
A1-2	Employee Records
A2	**Physical Plant**
A2-1	Electrical Wiring
A2-1-1	Alarm System
A2-2	Fixtures
B	CUSTOMER SERVICE

Decimal

This system is based on the concept that all materials can be grouped into 10 or fewer main categories. Each of the 10 major subjects may be subdivided into 10 more parts and so on indefinitely:

100	ADMINISTRATION
110	**Human Resources**
111	Company Policies
111.1	Absenteeism
112	Employee Records
120	**Physical Plant**
121	Electrical Wiring
121.1	Alarm System
122	Fixtures
200	CUSTOMER SERVICE

Duplex-numeric

A combination of numbers is used. Each primary topic is given a consecutive number, and secondary and tertiary (third subdivision) topics are subdivided down from that number:

1	ADMINISTRATION
1–1	**Human Resources**
1–1–1	Company Policies
1–1–1–1	Absenteeism
1–1–2	Employee Records
1–2	**Physical Plant**
1–2–1	Electrical Wiring
1–2–1–1	Alarm System
1–2–2	Fixtures
2	CUSTOMER SERVICE

Subject-numeric

Subject groups are assigned alphabetic codes (usually of three letters) and secondary and other categories are represented by numerals:

ADM.00	ADMINISTRATION
ADM.01	**Human Resources**
ADM.01–0	Company Policies
ADM.01–0–1	Absenteeism
ADM.01–1	Employee Records
ADM.02	**Physical Plant**
ADM.02–0	Electrical Wiring
ADM.02–0–1	Alarm System
ADM.02–1	Fixtures
CST.00	CUSTOMER SERVICE

RM31   NUMERIC FILING

Numeric filing offers accuracy, confidentiality, and unrestricted possibilities for expansion.

Sequential numeric system

In sequential numeric systems, one number is used to cover all of the records of a client, case, or account:

♦ As new folders are required, new numbers are added in sequence.

♦ Main guides are used to indicate round numbers.

♦ Auxiliary guides are used to break down the round numbers into smaller categories.

♦ When a file is opened, a number is allocated and an alphabetic record (computerized list or index card) is made up.

♦ The number to be used for a new file is determined by consulting the *access register*, a record of file numbers already allocated. The next unused number is allocated to the new file.

♦ The system *must* have a complementary alphabetic system that shows the client's name, address, assigned number, and any other pertinent information. If the file number is unknown, consult the alphabetic system and the file number is easily located.

Costa Tailoring Sevice   **Acct. No. 107**

Cliffside Repair Sevice   **Acct. No. 103**
34 Rupert Road
Kenora, ON P9N 3B5
          Telephone No. 529-1024
President: S. Boquist

Alphabetic record system that complements the numeric filing system

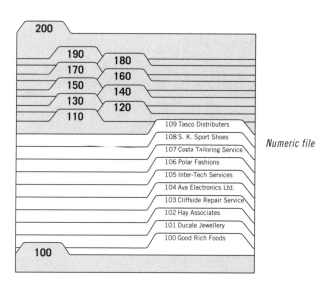

Numeric file

RM

NOTE Some companies use both a name and a number on the file folder, but where confidentiality is required, only a number is used.

Terminal digit filing

- In this type of numeric filing system, you read numbers from right to left in equal groups of numbers (i.e., the first two numbers at the right are *primary*, the next two are *secondary*, and the rest are *tertiary*). For example, file Number 091832 is read as 32 18 09.

- To file or retrieve, you first look under section 32 of the file, then under section 18, and finally under section 09. In such a system, 32 could be the cabinet number, 18 the drawer number, and 09 the client number within the folder. Spaces, hyphens, and periods can be used to separate numbers.

- Users of this system include insurance companies and hospitals.

- The main reason for using this system is to avoid the concentration of new files in one file drawer or shelf.

- The system speeds retrieval.

RM32 MANAGEMENT AND CONTROL OF RECORDS

A well-planned records management system has the following features:

- clear objectives
- a person or people in charge with knowledge of the needs of the entire organization
- a procedures manual
- an up-to-date list of files and storage locations
- a standard classification system that is understood and used by all employees
- a control program
- a records retention schedule
- a planned transfer program for movement of files from active to inactive

NOTE Analysis of needs and prior planning are essential to discover the true potential for automation of records management and to identify the most appropriate technology. Such an analysis can also uncover wasteful procedures and show existing inadequacies.

RM

RM33 THE RECORDS CYCLE

The management of records by an organization is most easily viewed as having four stages. This is generally referred to as the records cycle.

Creation A record is prepared by an organization or received by it.

Maintenance and use The record is stored efficiently and accurately so that it can be retrieved quickly.

Transfer The record is moved from active to inactive storage (known as archives), which may be on- or off-site.

Destruction The record is finally removed from the system.

RM34 MANAGING DOCUMENT RECORDS

In some organizations, records are kept in a *centralized* storage area under the direction of a records manager; in other departments, records are retained in individual departments (i.e., they are *decentralized*). Regardless of the size or sophistication of the system, a consistent and careful routine is necessary for efficient records management.

You must routinely check all documents to ensure proper *releasing* for filing; then they should be *coded* and, if necessary, marked for *cross-reference* and *follow-up*. In addition, efficient *charge-out* and transfer procedures must be used.

RM35 RELEASING

◆ No document should be filed until somebody has released it (i.e., indicated that all necessary action has been taken).

◆ Initials, a rubber stamp, or a copy of a reply attached to the original document are generally used as filing releases.

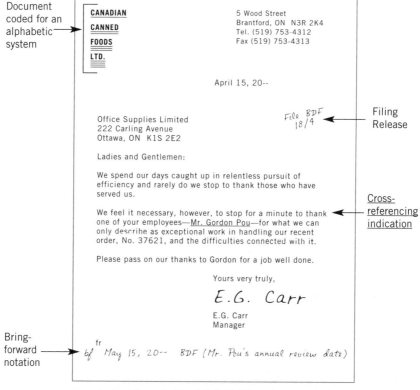

Example of a letter coded for alphabetic filing, showing typical release, cross-reference, and bring-forward (follow-up) notations

RM36   CODING

Coding means identifying on the record where it is to be filed.

◆ Underscore or circle the word(s) under which the document is to be filed, or write the appropriate caption on the document.

◆ The filing units may be indicated quite simply by the use of one or more underscores:

Unit 1	**Unit 2**	**Unit 3**	**Unit 4**
Canadian	Canned	Foods	Ltd.

◆ In the case of a numeric system, the appropriate number is underscored, circled, or written on the document.

NOTE   Coding makes refiling easier if documents taken from the system must be replaced.

RM37   CROSS-REFERENCING

Cross-referencing means indicating in one or more places where a record is located. File records under the most important classification and cross-reference them under the other(s).

```
                    CROSS-REFERENCE

NAME OR                                    Folder No. _____
SUBJECT    Dixon Pencil Co. Ltd.

Address    531 Davis Drive
           Newmarket, ON   L3Y 2P1


REFER TO
Folder No.  Eberhard Faber (Canada) Ltd.      _____
            531 Davis Drive
            Newmarket, ON   L3Y 2P1
            (Division of Dixon Pencil Co.)
            Date of letter or paper:  November 8  20 __
            Remarks:  Inquiry about automated
                      storage systems


SEE ALSO
Folder No. _____     _____
           _____
           _____
           _____
           _____

    File this cross-reference under the name or subject written at
    the top of this page.
```

Cross-reference sheet

RM

Use cross-references when a document refers to more than one subject or when a file might be looked for under more than one heading. For example:

◆ when names contain several important words:

Vancouver Board of Education

◆ for names that sound alike but have different spellings:

Noel/Nowell

◆ for companies referred to by initials when the meaning of the initials is known:

CBC/Canadian Broadcasting Corporation

Three cross-referencing devices are:

Cross-referencing sheets Specially designed letter-size sheets that can be filed inside the cross-referenced folder as though they were correspondence. These direct the searcher to the correct folder.

Cross-referencing folders Tabbed half-folders placed in the file drawer or shelf in the cross-referenced position as though they were actual folders. These half-folders are labelled to indicate the position of the actual correspondence folder.

Cross-referencing computerized lists or small index cards Used in a large system in which many cross-references occur. Keep lists in folders or binders; keep cards in a separate drawer.

> Dixon Pencil Co. Ltd.
>
> See: Eberhard Faber (Canada) Ltd.

Cross-reference shown on the tab of a half-folder

```
DIXON PENCIL CO. LTD.
531 Davis Drive
Newmarket, ON  L3Y 2P1

See:  Eberhard Faber (Canada) Ltd.
      531 Davis Drive
      Newmarket, ON  L3Y 2P1

Note: Eberhard Faber is a division of Dixon
      Pencil Co.
```

Cross-reference card

RM38 FOLLOW-UP OR REMINDER (TICKLER) SYSTEMS

A good follow-up system ensures that documents that will require attention in the future are brought forward at the proper time. Any document that has a "bring forward" notation on it should have the request recorded in one of the following devices before you place the document in the files.

Desk calendar

On the appropriate day, note the reminder request and the location of the material.

Follow-up or chronological file

◆ Label 31 folders (one for each day of the month) and 12 folders (one for each month).

◆ Place the folders in a file drawer.

◆ File a follow-up request for the current month in the appropriate *day* folder. If the follow-up is for a future month, place it in the appropriate *month* folder.

◆ Deal with material in each day's folder on the appropriate day then move the empty folder to the back of the *day* folders.

◆ At the beginning of each month, move the previous month's empty folder to the back and transfer papers from the current month's folders into the daily folders.

◆ Do not use dates of weekends or holidays for bringing forward documents unless business is usually conducted on those days.

◆ For a very large system, set up daily folders for a *year*.

NOTE The material in the folder may be the original, a copy, or simply a note to serve as the follow-up reminder.

Tickler file

This system is identical to the follow-up file except that it is in card form and is housed in a small index card container. You can make reminder notes on separate cards and insert them behind the appropriate day or month guides.

Electronic reminder systems

The follow-up reminder is keyed onto an electronic calendar and is seen on the appropriate day. See Unit 2, "Computers: Hardware and Software," for information on electronic calendar software.

RM

RM39 CHARGE-OUT PROCEDURES (BORROWING STORED MATERIALS)

Every records management system should have an efficient charge-out procedure for establishing the whereabouts of a record or a file while it is out on loan.

◆ Keep careful record of all documents and files out on loan in case they are needed by someone else. Simple ways of achieving this are by means of a completed requisition form; small index cards that show the name of the borrower, date of borrowing, description of the record or title of the file; or a computer record that can be easily updated.

♦ While the record is out on loan, use an OUT guide or an OUT folder to replace it. OUT guides are satisfactory for single documents. OUT folders are best for replacing complete folders because new records can be safely stored in them while the folders are out on loan.

♦ Ensure strict follow-up of overdue material to make sure that borrowed material is returned. Use a bring-forward tickler system, a desk diary, or electronic calendar for this purpose.

♦ If the record is given by the borrower to another person (rerouted), the borrower should inform the records department and you should change the OUT guide and follow-up record to show the new borrower's name.

♦ Two ways of guarding against the non-return of material are:
  • demanding written requests, or (but more costly)
  • copying what has been lent

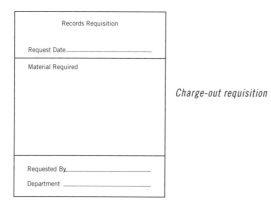

Charge-out requisition

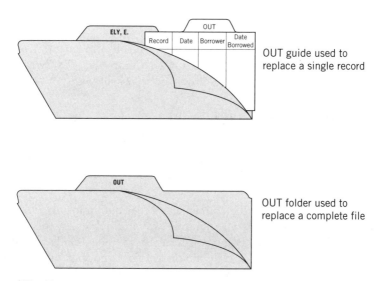

OUT guide used to
replace a single record

OUT folder used to
replace a complete file

OUT guides

Machine-readable labels (barcoding)

This system for charging out files requires a dedicated microprocessor. Labels on file folders contain bar codes that can be read by a photoelectric wand.

◆ When a file is requested, it is removed from shelf storage and the operator passes the wand over the bar code.

◆ The file is then taken out of inventory and the information stored in the wand is entered into the records centre database.

◆ This action records the location of the file in the computer, and thus overdue items are automatically indicated.

◆ Records for archival storage can be easily identified in this system.

RM40 DOCUMENT FILING TIPS

◆ For faster filing, sort papers into large groupings that follow the arrangement used in the cabinets or shelves (e.g., A–G, H–L, M–S, T–Z). Sorters are available in desktop models or large portable-tub types.

◆ Place documents in file folders with the left edge against the crease in the folder.

◆ Arrange documents in chronological order, with the most recent date on the top.

◆ Keep a "Miscellaneous" folder at the back of each alphabetic or numeric division to hold documents that are not designated to a specific file. When five documents have accumulated for a client or subject, make up an individual folder.

◆ A folder should hold a maximum of 100 sheets. Do not exceed the space provided by the creases. Use an expansion folder for heavy correspondence.

◆ Suspension folders in cabinets keep materials neater and make files easier to handle.

◆ Boxed suspension folders are useful when a folder and other bulky records must be kept together.

◆ Do not crowd file drawers or shelves. Allow 10 cm (4") of unused space.

◆ Use coloured labels. Colour speeds retrieval and prevents misfiles because the interruption that a misfile makes in the bands of colour is quickly identified.

◆ Colour can also be used effectively to indicate time periods and therefore can make the job of transferring old files easier.

◆ File every day if possible.

◆ Develop a filing manual outlining all of the procedures you use so that someone else can take over if necessary.

RM

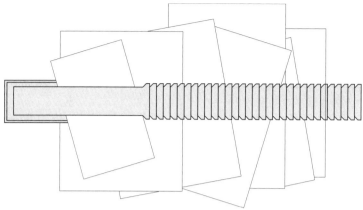

Desktop sorter

RM41 ELECTRONIC RECORDS

Electronic records are those kept in digital form on tape or on disk. The system may be centralized, decentralized, or a combination of both. In a centralized system, information is saved centrally in word processing, database, or spreadsheet files. Network users can retrieve information onto their own screens from remote locations. Files may be open to all users or may require the use of a password or code for access. If a system is decentralized, users have stand-alone computers and their own disks.

The terms used in electronic record-keeping tend to be similar to those used in non-electronic systems. Depending on the software used, reference will be made to directories, files, folders, cabinets, etc.

RM42 MANAGING ELECTRONIC RECORDS

The management of centralized electronic records systems tends to be a specialized field under the control of trained records management experts. For managing a smaller, decentralized system, the following information will be useful.

RM

Storage
◆ A systematic approach similar to that described for documents is needed (see this unit, RM46).
◆ Records produced can include disks, cassettes, cartridges, and printouts. These may be stored in standard file cabinets, but specialized equipment is available that provides for safety and ease of access, including:
  • three-ring binders with heavy-gauge vinyl pockets
  • boxes, racks, and rotary stands
  • shelves
  • binders that fit on suspension racks

◆ Disks and tapes are vulnerable to climatic conditions and should be maintained at constant acceptable temperature and humidity levels.

◆ For the sake of safety, do not store disks or store tapes and hard copies (printouts) together.

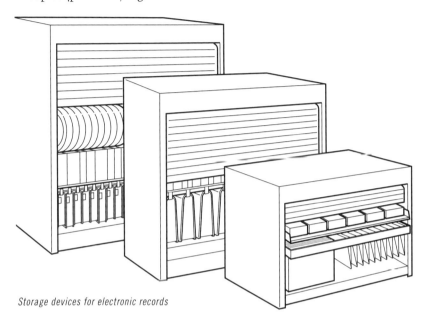

Storage devices for electronic records

Record identification

The value of an expensive electronic facility is seriously diminished if the operator is unable to locate records quickly. Identify clearly disks, cassettes, CD-ROMs, etc., through a standard alphabetic, alphanumeric, or subject system that is understandable by others. This applies both to the storage device and to the records stored in it.

◆ Decide on what disk and under what directory folder the file should be located and follow a consistent procedure for naming files. Clear identification is essential.

◆ Label each disk with a general classification and date.

◆ Print a directory, which can be folded and placed in the disk jacket or kept separately.

◆ If one disk is full, use the same general classification and add "1," "2," etc., to successive disks.

Coding

◆ On the record, key a descriptive file name and the initials of the author (e.g., Saleslet3.DM). See Unit 21, "Word Processing," WP14, for ideas. If a hard copy of the record is also filed, the file name recorded on the document permits fast and easy retrieval of the disk.

RM

Control

- ◆ Make backup copies of important storage disks and all software and store them with care.
- ◆ Control borrowing (charge-out) carefully.
- ◆ Create a procedures manual that contains a complete description of your storage system and procedures to assist users if you are absent.
- ◆ If confidentiality is required for records stored on disk or tape, use passwords or codes so that the directory or index is meaningless in the wrong hands.
- ◆ Regularly purge your system of old files.

RM43 RECORDS RETENTION

Periodically clean out and purge records and purging of disks to dispose of outdated or unnecessary material. Routine correspondence may be destroyed but legal considerations control the retention of some materials. Seek the advice of legal counsel or an auditor as to which records must legally be retained by each type of business.

The paper pollution problem can be eased by a careful assessment of which records might be kept on film, tape, or disk, and which—because of legal requirements—must be retained in the original form.

A records retention schedule (a timetable for the life of a record) is essential. The schedule should show the types of records and the time periods for which they should be kept; it should contain instructions for their eventual disposal or destruction (e.g., transfer from active to inactive storage, microfilmed, stored on disk, or authorized destruction). The records retention schedule is usually drawn up by management, the records manager, and the company's legal counsel and, perhaps, auditor.

RM44 TRANSFER METHODS

Inactive files, containing records that are old and not in use but that should be kept for some reason, should be removed (transferred) from the active files and stored elsewhere so that there is no unnecessary crowding of the active files. The transfer method to be used will be determined by the nature of the business and will be either perpetual or periodic.

Perpetual transfer When a particular piece of work (e.g., a legal case) is finished, the file is transferred into storage.

Periodic transfer After a certain period (e.g., on a particular date each year), all of the files are transferred.

RM45   DESTRUCTION

A few records can be disposed of by simply placing them in the garbage or arranging for recycling. However, most require special treatment because of the need for confidentiality. Shred records of this type.

Shredders   Organizations usually purchase their own equipment for paper disposal.

RM46 RECORDS STORAGE EQUIPMENT

RM47   FILE CABINETS

Lateral file cabinets have the length of the file against the wall and offer a considerable saving in time and space requirements over the once-popular vertical file cabinets.

- ◆ Lateral cabinets have up to five pull-out drawers or shelves and are available in letter and legal size.
- ◆ The drawers may be fitted with a cradle over which hanging (suspension) folders may be hooked, either to serve as file folders or to house other, smaller folders.

RM48   SHELVES

- ◆ Shelves, which may be open or closed, are advantageous where large quantities of files are maintained. Shelves save space and offer a plentiful storage area. Most systems use boxes or suspension units that attach to the shelves to house materials.
- ◆ Shelves offer great flexibility and can, for example, be adapted to house computer printouts and magnetic tape reels.
- ◆ If floor space is limited, shelves can provide maximum filing capacity.

RM

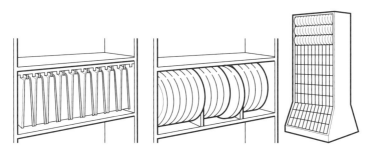

Shelves adapted to house suspended file units and tape reels

RM49 MOBILE CARRIAGE SYSTEMS

Also known as laterally rolling modular filing systems, these space-saving systems may have movable rows or stationary back rows and laterally rolling middle and front rows. Depending on the make, the rows may be moved manually, mechanically, electrically, or electronically. This system allows easy access to any file in any row. Built-in safety features ensure that staff members cannot be caught between moving shelves.

◆ Some systems offer microprocessor electronic controls that permit keyboard commands and computer control.

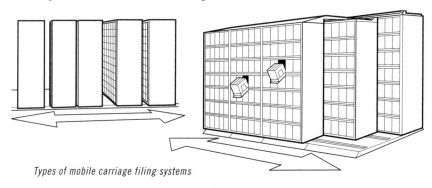

Types of mobile carriage filing systems

RM50 ROTARY (CIRCULAR) FILES

These are available in several versions, including an electronically driven one. They *bring* files to the operator.

RM51 SPECIAL FILING EQUIPMENT

Special equipment—plan files, card record systems, binding cases, magnetic disks and tape containers, and optical disk "juke box" storage devices, etc.—is available from office supply companies. Alternatively, manufacturers will build special equipment and provide expert consultation services if necessary.

RM52 AUTOMATED FILING EQUIPMENT

Automated storage means that the location and replacement of a particular record (file, tape, reel, card, cheque, etc.) is handled by push-button command.

◆ The system is controlled by an operator who sits at a simple keyboard.

◆ The operator keys in the record identification and gives the *Start* command.

◆ A mechanism then moves to the appropriate location, couples itself to the requested file container, and transports the container to the workstation.

◆ After the file has been dealt with, the operator gives a *Re-Store* command and the mechanism automatically returns the file container to its proper position.

◆ The system can be interfaced with a computer.

RM53 IMAGE TECHNOLOGY

This is today's term for records management systems based on *micrographics* or *optical disks* (usually referred to as *image processing*). Micrographics systems are *analog*; image processing systems are *digital*.

RM54 MICROGRAPHICS

Micrographics involves microminiature recording on film and permits records storage in two or three percent of the space needed for storage of original documents. Equipment needed is:

◆ a *camera* to film (record) documents

◆ a *processor* for processing and duplicating exposed film (or the exposed film can be sent to a specialist for processing)

◆ a *microfilm/microfiche* reader to magnify the microfilm back to readable size (microfilm can be enlarged to its original size without loss of detail)

◆ a *printer* to produce hard copies (printouts) of the microfilmed documents of the same size as the original documents.

NOTE The reader and printer are frequently one combined unit rather than two separate units.

▶ RM55 Types of microfilm

Microfilm comes in three sizes for various applications:

◆ 16-mm rolls or flat film

◆ 35-mm rolls or flat film

◆ 105-mm solely for microfiche

◆ microfiche jackets (16- and 35-mm film)

◆ aperture cards (35-mm frame by frame)

   16-mm film is used for letter-, legal-, and cheque-sized documents, newspapers, or any business-type documentation up to 28-cm × 43-cm (11″ × 17″) sized paper.

   35-mm film is used primarily for architectural drawings, maps, and specifications (i.e., documentation larger than 28 cm × 43 cm), or records that would be hard to read if they were too small.

   105-mm film is used for microfiche and COM (see this unit, RM59).

RM

▶ RM56 Microforms

A microform is the medium that holds the microimages in place for storage or for reading the individual record images or microrecords. The choice of microform will depend on the nature and the amount of the material to be stored and might be any of the following.

Reels (or cartridges)

◆ Reels are rolls of uncut film that are used when all of the microfilmed documents are related to each other (e.g., when libraries store old newspapers).

◆ Reels and cartridges offer the advantage of low cost and high density (i.e., they can hold up to 6000 images) but they are difficult to search and update.

Film jackets

◆ These are transparent cards with sleeves into which strips of film are inserted.

◆ These covers are used for storing strips (up to 75 per jacket) of microfilm.

◆ The jackets are particularly suited to *active* systems when frequent consultation and update are involved.

Aperture cards

◆ These are computer input cards that house a microfilm frame.

◆ This storage medium combines the microfilm with electronic data processing because the input card can be coded with related data.

Microfiche

◆ This is the term for 100-mm × 150-mm (4" × 6") flat sheets that contain rows of microfilm frames.

◆ Each microfiche can hold from 30 to 420 microimages.

◆ This method is suited to situations in which, for example, film versions of entire reports arc to be kept.

◆ Microfiche is easier to update than other film storage devices.

Ultrafiche

◆ This microform contains microrecords with a very high reduction ratio (more than 90 times) and therefore permits storage capacity of 4000 or more images.

◆ Because of the density of images, there is usually an index of that particular fiche in the lower right-hand corner.

▶ RM57 Microfilm storage systems

Equipment designed specifically for housing the various types of microfilm storage devices (binders, cabinets, small tubs) is available

RM

from office equipment suppliers. An indexing system for locating microfilmed material could be a card index, a punched card index, or any record identification method used in numeric, alphabetic, or alphanumeric systems (see this unit, RM26).

▶ RM58   Micrographics and the computer

Micrographics can play an important role in information processing. Data generated by a computer can be converted directly into microimages (computer output microfilm: COM) and also retrieved by a computer (computer-assisted retrieval: CAR).

NOTE   Computer output to laser disk (COLD) is becoming popular in mainframe data centres as a replacement for COM.

RM59 Computer output microfilm (COM)

In a COM system, computer output is transferred directly onto microfilm instead of onto paper. An operator can access a specific document within seconds for viewing on a monitor and for hard-copy printing if needed.

The system is advantageous because it is space-saving and permits very rapid retrieval. The high cost of COM makes it best suited to large, sophisticated records management situations. For smaller companies, the Yellow Pages list service companies that specialize in COM.

RM60 Computer-assisted retrieval (CAR)

In CAR, the capability of the computer is linked to the searching of microform files. Microrecords are located within seconds and the microform can be read on a separate viewer or, in an integrated (networked) office, on the screen of the terminal from which the request was initiated. The microrecord is marked with a machine-readable code that assists automatic retrieval.

RM61 Computer input microfilm (CIM)

RM

CIM is the reverse of COM—microfilm is used as input to the computer. The microfilm is scanned and converted into machine-readable format on magnetic tape. This tape can then be used by the computer to read and manipulate information processed and stored earlier on the microfilm.

RM62   IMAGE PROCESSING

Image processing is a digital technology that is being used increasingly in records management. Documents are scanned or read in and the computer stores them on optical disks. The strength of the system lies in its ability to capture, store, process, and retrieve documents for information, printing, and distribution, regardless of format or content.

Image processing is heavily used in insurance claims processing, banking, health care, business, the professions, and government.

▶ RM63 Optical disk storage

◆ A scanner captures data and a laser records it onto high-density 5.25" or 3.5" optical disks. Storage of text, graphics, photographs, and sound is possible.

◆ Optical disk technology offers quick access, sophisticated indexing capabilities, and extensive cross-reference possibilities.

◆ Made from aluminum, sturdy, and long-lasting, optical media are particularly attractive because they are impervious to damage by magnetic or electrical spikes or surges.

◆ Data can be accessed by several users at the same time.

NOTE For full details of the kinds of optical disks available, see Unit 2, "Computers: Hardware and Software," CO36.

RM64 DOCUMENT-BASED MANAGEMENT SYSTEMS (DBMS)

DBMS are the core of image processing systems and applications. They allow for complete integration of a company's document records and can be used for storage of active or inactive files.

◆ The system uses optical disks as the storage medium.

◆ Imaging guarantees absolute accuracy, as opposed to keying. Document files are scanned in; files stored on disk or tape are read in.

◆ Users do not have to wait. Information on disk can be accessed quickly and easily and in many ways because of cross-referencing.

◆ Files are always accounted for because they are not removed from the system.

◆ Information can be customized to each company's preferences.

◆ In some systems, a change in one record can be registered automatically in other relevant documents.

◆ Correspondence and responses can be matched in files.

◆ Responses to queries can be handled immediately because there is less dependence on other people to provide information.

In an accounts receivable application, for example, a complete customer file can be maintained electronically. An electronic invoice is generated from the mainframe computer, a signed bill of lading indicating proof of delivery is scanned in, and a "notes" function is available to allow details such as telephone calls to be recorded. The system can be fax-enabled for instant transmission of information.

RM65 OTHER ELECTRONIC RECORDS SYSTEMS

RM66 COMPUTER OUTPUT TO LASER DISK (COLD)

Computer output to laser (optical) disk is becoming widely used in mainframe data centres to replace COM, computer-generated printouts, and magnetic tape storage.

RM67 DATABASES

Some records may simply be facts—names, telephone numbers, addresses, inventory stock items, policy numbers, information on customer buying habits, client credit ratings, etc. Records of this type are frequently kept in an electronic database, a computerized system that permits highly organized storage of such data. The information is cross-referenced in several ways so that it can be searched for under many categories. (See Unit 2, "Computers: Hardware and Software," CO17.)

RM68 ELECTRONIC DATA INTERCHANGE

Electronic data interchange (EDI; Unit 9, "Information Processing and Integrated Office Automation," IP4 and IP5) will bring an end to most paper records in many organizations and an increased focus on electronic records.

RM69 LEGAL ADMISSIBILITY OF MICROGRAPHIC AND ELECTRONIC RECORDS

In Canada, microfilm is accepted as being legal if the following guidelines are followed:

◆ *MICROFILM AND ELECTRONIC RECORDS AS DOCUMENTARY EVIDENCE* (CAN/CGSB-72.11.93)

◆ *Canada Evidence Act* (Publication #YXC35)

◆ *Ontario Evidence Act* (Publication #110559)

Where records are kept on tape or disk, a lawyer should be consulted before the decision is made to eliminate the hard copy versions.

RM

17 REPROGRAPHICS

CONTENTS

R

Reprographics—the term used to describe any type of copying or duplicating process—is an important part of the office worker's world. Those using reprographic systems are responsible for choosing the best and cheapest one for each task and knowing how to use that system wisely.

In this unit, you will be introduced to the equipment and processes available to you, shown how to use the equipment or process to best advantage, made aware of copyright restrictions, and helped in choosing the most appropriate equipment for your office, should this be required of you.

R1   REPROGRAPHIC IMAGING TECHNOLOGIES

There are two basic technologies in image processing: analog and digital. An understanding of both provides a guide to their applications.

Analog

Analog is the technology of the most common photocopying process now used. In this process, light is reflected through mirrors and lenses to a drum, creating a latent image. The drum is applied to paper, where it leaves a pattern created by static electricity. Toner, a black powder, sticks to the statically charged places and a copy is created. Originals are scanned by the equipment each time a copy is made.

Digital

Digital reprographics uses the binary technology of the computer. The original is scanned once, a digital film master is made, and printing is done from the master. If necessary, the user can manipulate and edit the digital signals before the film master is made.

R2   MAKING THE RIGHT CHOICE

You have three options for handling your copying and duplicating requirements. The choices are:

◆ **Do the work yourself**. This is convenient and fast but may not offer the range of services provided by more specialized services.

◆ **Use a centralized, in-house** (within the company) **service** if one exists. This can provide a more professional-looking product but may not offer the speed required.

◆ **Send the work out**. You will usually get both speed and quality from commercial houses but this is economical only if you need a large number of copies.

When choosing reprographic service, consider the number of copies needed, the quality of reproduction required, the intended use of the finished product, speed, and cost.

R

R3 PHOTOCOPYING

R4 TYPES OF PHOTOCOPYING EQUIPMENT

Photocopying equipment tends to fall into three major categories:

1. Low-volume (convenience): For a requirement of less than 20 000 copies each month. Speed: Up to 50 copies a minute.
2. Mid-volume: For from 20 000 to 50 000 copies each month. Speed: From 20 to 50 copies a minute.
3. High-volume: For from 50 000 to 100 000 copies each month. Speed: 50 to 120 copies a minute.

R5 CONVENIENCE PHOTOCOPIERS

Usually several convenience photocopiers are used in larger organizations, located in places where the greatest need arises. They may be situated within one department or shared among several. They are:

- small, relatively inexpensive, desktop or console (floor) models
- simple to operate and require no special training
- able to use plain paper—they do not need specially treated stationery
- useful for volumes of less then 20 000 copies a month
- available in speeds ranging from 3 to 50 copies a minute, with the low-speed type being suited only to very low-volume, light usage

For light business or home use, small, portable personal copiers are available. These versatile little machines even permit colour copying if needed.

R6 PHOTOCOPIER FEATURES

The trend in photocopying is to high productivity. New machines provide unattended copying, as they offer automatic handling of originals and sorting and finishing of copies. These machines feature paper trays and hoppers that can carry hundreds of sheets and can automatically switch from one tray to another so that there is no risk of running out of paper. Technology is facilitating even greater efficiencies. For example, job settings can be stored in memory or on small plastic insertable cards and maintenance problems can be resolved automatically over telephone lines.

The basic photocopier comes with an automatic counting device, exposure control, and the ability to handle letter- and legal-sized paper. In addition, copiers may have all or some of the following features:

- automatic document feeding: You stack the documents in a tray and the machine feeds one copy at a time automatically

- semi-automatic document feed: You feed the originals one by one into the input tray and the machine takes and positions them for copying
- continuous-form feeder: It feeds unburst computer paper, making copies of each page on separate sheets
- photomode: Some machines do this automatically. They sense and set the proper exposure. Provides clean, clear copies of black-and-white or colour photographs, screened artwork, and half-tones
- collating, sorting, stacking, stapling, and hole-punching
- stitching, thermal binding, and hole-punching
- reversing or recirculating automatic document feeder: Copier turns a two-sided document over to copy both sides (single documents or stacks)
- automatic handling of stacks of mixed-size originals: Some machines can "read" document size and select the proper paper size
- original-size to copy-size keys: Can copy from any common paper size to another automatically
- environment protection:
  - photoconductor drums can be recycled by some manufacturers
  - toner cartridges can be recycled
  - some machines use approved recycled paper
  - some manufacturers use packaging materials that are ozone-friendly
- edge-to-edge copying
- margin shift: Adjusts right or left margin up to 16 mm ($\frac{5}{8}$") for hole-punching
- edge-erase: Eliminates black edges and shadows when copying from books or second-generation originals
- reducing and enlarging of originals to various sizes: Possible percentages of reduction and enlargement vary with the make of machine (e.g., 127%, 98%, 76%, etc.), which can have either a preset, push-button, or zoom mechanism. Some zoom mechanisms go from 50% to 200% in 1% increments. On some machines, a zoom preview guide allows you to ensure the right size the first time
- toner saving: This allows for ordinary images for extra file copies, for example, when less toner is required. The regular amount of toner would be required for special presentation copies, however
- five-way paper supply: Can accommodate, for example, letter-size plain paper, letterheads, statements, ledger paper, labels, transparencies
- cover sheet insertion
- remote diagnostics: Equipment comes with modems that will automatically contact the nearest equipment service depot over a fax line when jams or other problems occur. Internal diagnostics systems keep track of the service and maintenance history of the machine

R

- self-diagnostics to indicate causes of machine malfunction (e.g., paper jam/toner requirement)
- adding highlight colour to black copies: Colour is added through an optional electronic edit pad. User designates the area of the original to be highlighted
- reproducing in full colour or in one or more of the four primary colours in quick-change modules
- large-copy format: Some copiers can handle large blueprints; film; and opaque, translucent, or plain paper, without shadows or background variations. Can handle originals up to 6 mm ($^1/_4$") thick
- multi-function memory: Preset instructions related to specific types of copying jobs can be put into the equipment's memory for future recall on frequently run jobs
- interruption and job recovery: The machine remembers the point at which a job was interrupted and continues on from there
- return to position: The control for number of copies is automatically set back to 1 a few seconds after the user has finished
- 35-mm or large-slide format copying
- dual-page book copying: Produces letter-sized copies of each page without repositioning the original
- image editing: Provides cut-and-paste capability. You can delete elements of an original from the copy or combine elements from two or more originals to create a new original. The terms used in this process are *trimming* (for erasing borders), *masking* (for erasing parts), and *image overlay* (for combining). Push-button colour may also be used with the editing feature to permit highlighting or used as a second colour with black.

R7   PRODUCING QUALITY COPIES

The image should be sharp, the background should be white, and the copy should be spot- and streak-free.

- If copy quality is unsatisfactory, check your toner and developer levels, ensure that the glass plate is clean, and then request a service call if the problem has not been eliminated.
- Use pen instead of pencil for sharp reproduction.
- Carefully made corrections will not show—use cover-up liquids and tapes.
- Use cut-and-paste techniques to create documents that are as good as originals if your photocopier does not have image editing capability.
- Keep your original properly positioned if you do not have the automatic feed feature. It is wasteful to run off a large number of copies and then discover that the top heading is missing, for example, or that the type is going uphill!

- Make any needed exposure adjustments when you are working with a coloured original.
- If you are working with punched paper, be sure the holes will come out on the correct side before you start the print run.
- Take care when loading feeder trays that the paper is right side up.
- Fan paper to reduce paper jams.

R8   USING YOUR COPIER ECONOMICALLY

Avoid such costly and wasteful practices as:

- producing copies for distribution to staff members when circulation of the original document would do
- using a photocopier when a cheaper process would serve
- making more copies than you actually need

NOTE   If you accidentally make too many copies, use the blank sides for notepads or printing drafts on your laser printer.

To make the best use of your copier:

- Save your copying until you have several items: avoid frequent walks to and from the machine.
- Use the right size of paper for the job.
- Make the exact number of copies needed.
- Use two-sided copying (duplexing) as much as possible.
- Make use of the collating feature if one is available.
- Label a separate bin in which employees can place spoiled or unneeded copies (with the exception of confidential materials, which should be properly disposed of). Use these copies for other office uses, such as notepads.

R9   MONITORING COPIER USE

Some organizations control copier use. This serves several purposes: costs may have to be billed to customers, usage by departments may need to be monitored, or copier abuse (such as overcopying and personal copying) may need to be prevented. Copy management systems may take the form of:

- a log showing date, number of copies, department, and name of person making the copies
- a full-time operator who works only from a requisition form approved by a supervisor
- a key, cartridge, or plastic card provided by the machine vendor that may be issued to only a few people. Some of these devices have counters built into them.
- the allocation of codes as passwords for individuals and/or departments

R

NOTE   Using office copiers for personal use is a form of theft from the workplace.

R10   KEY OPERATORS

Key operators are specially appointed people in an organization who are responsible for maintaining the copying equipment. The name(s) of the key operator(s) should be clearly indicated on the equipment.

If you are the key operator, be sure you:

♦ familiarize yourself with the equipment by requesting a vendor demonstration

♦ understand how to read the self-diagnostic indicators

♦ know how to use the hotline service if one exists, and to follow instructions given

♦ know how to clear routine jams

♦ know when and how to add toner/developer

R11   MID- AND HIGH-VOLUME COPYING

Mid- and high-volume machines are used for mid-volume (20 000 to 50 000 copies a month) and high-volume (50 000 to 100 000 copies a month) tasks and are capable of speeds up to 120 copies a minute. They are usually centrally located and are generally the responsibility of a few key operators specially trained in their use. These expensive machines are:

♦ able to offer cheaper unit costs on long runs that cannot be achieved with convenience copiers

♦ useful to organizations with many reports and other in-house copying requirements

♦ equipped to provide easier control over use than are convenience copiers

♦ available in models capable of duplexing, collating, and stapling, and of adding tabs, dividers, and covers

R

R12 CENTRALIZED COPYING SERVICES

A centralized in-house copying service can reduce costs, control equipment use, and permit direct charging of costs against users or jobs. A full-time, trained staff is on hand and high-powered, sophisticated equipment is available. Some centres—also known as graphic arts centres or print shops—are large and sophisticated enough that they can often provide a full range of services, including artwork and binding.

The creation of desktop publishing masters (see Unit 4, "Desktop Publishing") as originals for copying or duplicating has led to an increase in in-house printing and the use of large copier-duplicators. Some print shops also offer phototypesetting among their services (see next section).

R13 PHOTOTYPESETTING

For in-house phototypesetting (or photocomposition), text is entered directly into a special phototypesetting unit (much like a word processor) or through word-processing equipment or an OCR (Optical Character Reader) unit linked to it. The result is professional typesetting, offering proportional spacing, justified text, and a variety of fonts and spacing. Where in-house phototypesetting is not available, some specialized commercial printers can convert text stored on disk into phototypesetting.

R14 USING A CENTRALIZED SERVICE

Complete a copy centre request form indicating your specific requirements. Careful completion is essential as this is used to prioritize requests and will be rigidly followed by the operator.

```
          COPY CENTRE WORK REQUISITION

   Name _____      Date  _____
   Department_____      Required Date  _____
   Telephone_____      Required Time  _____
   Charge to Account No._____

   ┌──────────────────────────────────────────────┐
   │  Copy Centre Use:  Job No. _____    │
   │                    Cost _____      │
   │  Time Received:_____   Time completed:_____│
   └──────────────────────────────────────────────┘

   No. of Originals _____    No. of copies each _____
   Job Description_____

   Delivery Method:  To be picked up  ❑
                     To be delivered  ❑

   ┌──────────────────────────────────────┬──────────┐
   │  Instructions:                        │ Cost:    │
   │  ❑ print one-sided    ❑ two-sided     │          │
   │  ❑ 3-hole punched paper  ❑ unpunched paper │     │
   │  ❑ coloured paper     colour:         │          │
   │  ❑ other size paper    size:          │          │
   │  ❑ collate                            │          │
   │  ❑ staple                             │          │
   │  ❑ bind     type:                     │          │
   │  ❑ special instructions               │          │
   └──────────────────────────────────────┴──────────┘

   Copies to: Copy Centre, Billing Dept., Requester
```

Copy centre request form

R15 SPECIALIZED COPIERS

R16 INTELLIGENT COPIERS

The intelligent copier is a sophisticated, computer-based piece of equipment. It combines the technology of the microprocessor, laser printer, and photocopier and has certain features of both printers and copiers. It can accept text, graphics, and instructions from computers, word processors, or magnetic media, and it can be programmed to form paragraphs, locate information from memory, image edit, and copy at high speed directly from the digitized information it receives. It can then distribute information to other compatible equipment in the network. The intelligent copier offers many of the features of convenience copiers and can be operated as a convenience copier when required.

As business moves closer to integrating office practices, the current trend is to increased digital applications, because these allow for the creation, manufacture, management, and delivery of a document in one process. Current digital copiers comprise scanners and printers that will network with faxes, printers, and computers. Future models will combine into one unit a copier, fax, scanner, telephone, printer, and computer.

R17 DIGITAL CAMERAS

A digital camera is similar to a 35-mm camera in that it takes and stores pictures on a memory card. When you take a picture on a digital camera, you first press the shutter release button, then the automatic focus is applied and the CCD (charged-couple device) charges up and prepares for the picture to be taken. When the shutter button is fully depressed, the shutter opens, allowing light to enter the camera and strike the CCD. The light is measured electronically on the CCD, and then it is sent to the internal memory (the buffer) of the camera. When the image information reaches the buffer, it is compressed (if selected) into JPEG format. The completed image is then transferred to the memory card of the camera. Some cameras have an internal buffer large enough to hold many pictures, and can take multiple pictures in a row; this is called "burst shooting."

Digital photography options allow you to store, delete, or print images in record mode before they are stored on memory cards.

The memory card is an electronic storage device that stores each picture until it is uploaded to the computer; you can use these stored images for internal pages, presentations, printed publications, and other applications.

Digital cameras offer high-quality image enhancement technology and are instantly ready to print out. Send the images through e-mail, or view them on television using a video cable.

R18 DIGITAL DUPLICATORS

Digital duplicators scan originals once, making a digital film master of the image and then printing directly from the master. (Regular photocopiers scan originals once for every image made.) Cost per copy decreases as more copies are printed.

R19 OFFSET DUPLICATING

Offset duplicating is a lithographic process that can produce thousands of high-quality copies that closely resemble commercial printing. Specially trained operators must run the duplicating machine, but preparation of the offset master requires only keyboarding skills. Because of the special skill needed to operate the equipment, most office workers will not become directly involved with offset duplicating but should be aware of the existence of the process and its capabilities. Offset duplicators are usually a feature of the centralized printing service described earlier. Two new trends in offset duplicating are:

◆ a direct link between desktop publishing systems and offset presses that automates the production of printing plates and eliminates the necessity to make film

◆ automation and mechanical improvement of the presses to speed production, making presses easier to use and enhancing quality, particularly when using colour

R20 COMPUTER PRINTERS

Information on computer printers can be found in Unit 2, "Computers: Hardware and Software," and in Unit 4, "Desktop Publishing."

NOTE See Unit 2, CO12, for information on scanners.

R21 COMMERCIAL COPYING SERVICES

When a copying job is too big or is needed more quickly than your in-house facility can accommodate, consider a commercial copying or printing service. Consult the Yellow Pages of your telephone book for local companies and compare their services based on rate, quality, and speed. Be sure to provide full details of the job, and request quotations.

R22 COPYRIGHT PROBLEMS

The illegal use of copyright materials is an issue of serious concern to authors and publishers, who justifiably view such use as theft of their property. The *Copyright Act* provides severe penalties for the unauthorized copying and use of copyright printed and published materials and software. Anyone copying and/or using photocopied material should be aware that written permission is usually required before copyright materials may be reproduced and distributed. Among materials that may not be copied are bank notes, birth certificates, books, periodicals, and computer software.

> **NOTE** Copyright symbol ©
> Example: Cover images copyright © 1999 PhotoDisc, Inc.

R23 Finishing Equipment

Among the array of finishing equipment that allows documents to be presented attractively are the following. Consult the catalogues of office equipment suppliers and stationers for more details.

- collators
- specialized staplers (power, long, heavy-duty)
- binding machines
- folding, inserting, sealing, addressing, and meter-stamping equipment
- headliners (typesetting devices that produce print in various sizes and fonts)

Additional information on finishing is provided in Unit 4, "Desktop Publishing."

R24 Choosing Reprographic Equipment

If you are involved in selecting copying equipment for your office, bear the following in mind. For the greatest efficiency at the lowest cost, choose the right equipment for the job. Several basic considerations should be kept in mind:

- Cost: Which is best—buying, leasing, or renting?
- Speed: How important is speed? Is the extra cost involved in obtaining faster copying justified for your needs?
- Space: How large a space do you have available in an area that is accessible yet removed enough that noise is not a problem?
- Monthly needs: How much copying do you need? The system should be the right size: not so powerful that its capability is wasted; not so small that overuse poses a problem of frequent breakdown.
- Quality of copy produced: Will the copy quality meet all of the firm's requirements?
- Type of material to be copied: Is the system capable of handling all of your needs for both in-house and outside use?

◆ Needs for the future: Will the system fit in with future expansion possibilities? Are you moving toward desktop publishing, for example?

Comparative details

Considerable care must go into the selection of the office copier because many types and makes are available. Compare copiers on at least the following basic points:

◆ trade-in value of present machine
◆ warranty details
◆ lease to purchase option
◆ cost of service contract
◆ noise level
◆ speed
◆ service response time
◆ ease of restocking the machine with paper, developer, and toner
◆ movability
◆ special wiring or power supply needed
◆ "instant on" or warm-up period
◆ control devices available so that the machine use can be measured and/or restricted
◆ additional features available (see this unit, R6)

R

UNIT

18 SOCIAL AND INTERPERSONAL SKILLS

CONTENTS

S

S1   SOCIAL SKILLS

The social skills demanded of people in their business lives are essentially no different from those that apply in their private lives. Tact and courtesy in dealing with other people are the keys to successful relationships. Whether business is conducted at home or abroad, employees are required to possess social skills that will reflect well on their organizations. Knowing how to behave correctly in any situation leads to the comfort of all concerned and can play a significant part in job promotion. Social skills are so important in today's business world that agencies exist for the sole purpose of training personnel in the art of good manners.

Some companies (such as law firms, advertising agencies, government departments) schedule professional development days to update employees on social etiquette/protocol. Training courses/seminars may also be provided for employees who must interact with out-of-country personnel, such as training on social protocol during government functions.

S2   COMMUNICATIONS

For guidance on situations requiring written communications, see Unit 1, C138; for guidance on oral communications, see Unit 1, C166.

In responding to written and other communications, bear these two guidelines in mind:

◆ Answer letters within 48 hours.

◆ Deal with telephone calls, e-mail, and fax messages promptly.

S3   DINING OUT

Eating out is often part of the working day. If you are called on to represent your employer at a club, restaurant, or social event, do not let inexperience deter you from enjoying the occasion.

◆ For business meetings, choose a quiet restaurant and make a reservation. Use a restaurant that you know offers good food and service and has the right atmosphere.

◆ If *you* are inviting people, let them choose the time. Ask if they have preferences as to type of food (vegetarian, seafood, a national favourite).

◆ Arrive before your guests and wait at your table, but do not order anything.

◆ Sit opposite your guests for best eye contact.

Order a light meal at a business meeting, especially during the working day.

▶ S4   Dress

If you are doubtful as to what to wear, check with your host or ask a more experienced colleague or another member of the party.

▶ S5   Dining etiquette

Small talk is an invaluable tool for breaking the ice at a business meal. Good topics to open the conversation include vacations; sports; a new house or apartment; the latest play, movie, or bestseller. Avoid discussing politics and other controversial issues. Once your guests are at ease, you can address business matters.

S

◆ Be careful about alcohol consumption. Don't feel pressured to drink if you don't wish to do so.

◆ If you are a guest, wait for your host to begin eating before starting yourself.

◆ If toasts are part of the occasion:
  • go well prepared if you are to make the toast
  • remain seated and don't drink to the toast if *you* are being toasted

Smoking

Smoking is unacceptable while anyone is eating. It is a good idea to ask permission before you smoke, even after the meal has ended. If you are in the no-smoking section of a restaurant, you may not, of course, smoke at all.

▶ S6 Table etiquette

Some basic guidelines in table manners follow.

Cocktails Garnishes (except citrus fruit) may be eaten.

Soup If soup is served in a cup with two handles, use both to pick up the cup. If soup is served in a bowl on a serving plate, spoon the soup away from you, and leave the spoon in the bowl when you have finished. Don't slurp or blow on soup. If it's too hot, wait for it to cool a little.

Wine If you are not experienced in wine selection, choose a known favourite or ask your table server or wine server for advice. The wine waiter, after uncorking the wine, pours some into the glass of the person who placed the order. After approval of the wine, the server will fill all of the glasses. If you are the person who placed the order and you are not satisfied with the temperature or the taste of the wine, say so.

Table setting

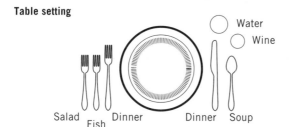

Water

Wine

Salad Fish Dinner Dinner Soup

If you are faced with many pieces of silverware, work from the outside in.

Used cutlery

Knife and fork in finished position

NOTE House wine should *never* be tasted for approval.

S

Bread Break (do not cut) the bread or roll; butter enough for only one or two mouthfuls at a time. Take butter from the serving dish and put it on the side of your side plate. Never take it straight from the dish onto your bread.

Vegetables If they are served in individual dishes, you may eat them from the dish or transfer them from the dish onto your dinner plate.

Bones These belong on the plate at all times.

Seafood It is acceptable to use your fingers when peeling shrimp or cracking lobster or crab shells. If you need to add lemon, use a fork to hold the lemon wedge and your other hand to squeeze the lemon.

Fresh fruit Use a knife to cut and a knife and fork to eat fresh fruit such as oranges, apples, pears, plums. With oranges, cut the outer skin in quarters and peel it off. Then cut the fruit itself into quarters and then into smaller sections for eating. With apples, etc., cut the fruit into quarters, remove the core, and then cut into bite-sized pieces.

Napkin Place your napkin on your lap. Do not tuck it into your neck. Use it to dab at, rather than wipe across, your mouth. Place the napkin on your chair if you have to leave your guests temporarily. Only at the end of the meal is it correct to place the napkin (unfolded) on the table.

General

◆ Keep elbows off the table at all times.

◆ Avoid speaking with your mouth full.

◆ Avoid heavy dinner conversation topics, such as politics and religion.

◆ Do not monopolize the conversation; allow each person time to speak.

◆ Avoid telling tasteless jokes.

◆ Turn off your cell phone unless you are expecting an emergency call.

▶ S7   The bill

It is customary for the person who issues the invitation to pay for the meal. If you are the host and anticipate a dispute about payment of the bill, arrange with the server before the end of the meal for you to take care of it. Payment by credit card usually assists in resolving this kind of situation. Check the bill carefully as errors can occur.

When in a group, it is acceptable to request separate bills; do this before ordering.

▶ S8   Tipping

The customary tip for good service is 15 percent of the cost of the meal, not including tax. If you are dissatisfied with the meal or the service, the amount of the tip (if any at all) is your choice. If a group dinner has been arranged, it would be wise to check about tipping. On these occasions, service is often included in the total charge per person.

NOTE   Tipping may vary from country to country.

S9 INTRODUCTIONS

Business presents constant opportunities for meeting new clients, employees, or supervisors. When someone is introduced to you, good etiquette demands that you stand as you greet the person. When you are called on to introduce a prospective employee, a friend or relative, or any one person to another, follow these general guidelines:

1. *Introduce the person holding the less important position to the person holding the more important one.* For example, the president of a company (Mr. Lin) is to be introduced to a new accounts receivable clerk: "Mr. Lin, I'd like you to meet Sandy Ross, who joined us on Monday." In reply to Mr. Lin's greeting, the new clerk would say, "How do you do?"

2. *Introduce the younger person to the older one.* For example, a person is about to introduce his or her mother to a colleague: "Mother, may I introduce Miss Gauthier (Ann)?" "Ann, this is my mother, Mrs. Duncan."

3. *Introduce the man to the woman.* For example, when two people of equally important positions are introduced: "Mrs. Hussain, may I introduce Mr. Weir?" However, if the male president of a company is meeting a female employee for the first time, the woman would be introduced to the man, "Mr. Stanley, I'd like you to meet our new staff member, Keetah Pimi."

4. *Introduce the new employee to the supervisor:* "Mrs. Oliver, I'd like you to meet our new receptionist, Ms. Natarajan."

5. *If spouses have different names, make this clear.*

NOTE   If you develop the habit of saying first the name of the older person or the name of the person holding the more important position, the rest follows automatically.

On being introduced

◆ If you did not hear the introduction clearly, ask to have it repeated.

◆ If you forget a name, admit it.

◆ Introduce yourself, using your first and last names.

◆ Stand when someone senior is being introduced.

Handshakes

◆ Take the initiative and extend your hand.

◆ Shake firmly, allowing genuine enthusiasm to show but don't make it a bone crusher.

◆ Confident, friendly eye contact at the same time as the handshake complements the process.

◆ If the handshake is rejected, don't be alarmed. It may be that health problems, such as arthritis, are the cause, or there may be a cultural reason involved.

S10   INVITATIONS

For such special occasions as weddings and formal dinners, formal invitations are often used. The invitation may be engraved, partially engraved, or handwritten. Keyed formal invitations are not considered good etiquette. Formal invitations should follow this format:

> *Mr. and Mrs. Terence Jones*
> *request the pleasure of*
> *Mr. and Mrs. James Meilleur's*
> *company at a dinner*
> *in honour of*
> *The Right Honourable Ramon Hnatyshyn*
> *on Friday, the seventh of September*
> *at half past eight o'clock*
> *Safari Room, Deerfield Lodge*
> *Charlottetown*
>
> *R.S.V.P.*   *Formal*

Printed or engraved invitation

Invitations should be sent out three to five weeks ahead of the event (except for extremely prestigious dinners, which require at least eight weeks' notice).

Invitations should be answered within one week.

NOTE   Responding to an invitation even though an R.S.V.P. is not requested is a thoughtful gesture.

▶ S11   Acceptance

The acceptance should contain virtually the same words as the invitation. It should be handwritten in the third person, as the following illustration shows, on fine-quality, double-folded stationery.

> *Mr. and Mrs. James Meilleur*
> *accept with pleasure*
> *the kind invitation*
> *of*
> *Mr. and Mrs. Jones*
> *to attend a dinner*
> *on Friday, the seventh of September*
> *at half past eight o'clock.*

Formal acceptance

S

▶ **S12 Regrets**

To decline an invitation, write a regrets note on good-quality paper. The wording follows the same pattern as the acceptance.

> *Mr. and Mrs James Meilleur*
> *regret that they will*
> *be unable to accept*
> *the very kind invitation*
> *of*
> *Mr. and Mrs. Jones*
> *to attend a dinner*
> *on Friday, the seventh of September*
> *as they have already accepted*
> *an invitation for that evening.*

Formal regret

S13 GENDER EQUITY

The rules of etiquette might change over time, but good manners based on courtesy are always in fashion. The following reflect current business practices:

◆ When leaving an elevator, equality prevails. A speedy exit is what counts, so either male or female may exit first.

◆ As far as opening doors is concerned, whoever is in the lead should open the door and hold it for others. Visitors should be allowed to go through the door first. Whoever opens the door should be thanked for the gesture.

◆ For greetings in public, a handshake is acceptable, but kissing is not.

◆ Men should not stand up to acknowledge the arrival of women at business meetings, except under the circumstances outlined in the "Introductions" sections of this unit, S9.

◆ All staff should rise:
   if a visitor comes to the office or to a meeting
   for a higher-ranking executive who is an infrequent visitor

◆ Men should not feel obliged to pay the meal bills for women, unless playing the role of host.

◆ Men are not required to help female co-workers with their chairs or with putting on their coats unless asked.

◆ No one should make comments about a person's physical appearance, nor should sexist jokes be told.

◆ Either a male or a female may hail a cab.

◆ Avoid office romances.

S

S14 SMOKING

Be careful. Most public and government buildings do not permit smoking.

A visitor to a firm should check the rules of the organization before smoking in any part of the building and should put out smoking materials before entering a reception room or being received by his or her host.

Even if the rules permit smoking in some areas, a visitor should ask permission to smoke.

S15 INTERPERSONAL SKILLS

In very simple terms, interpersonal skills are those needed to assist us to get along with people. Human interaction is an integral part of any job because no job exists where contact with others does not occur. We are all team players.

The successful employee demonstrates many characteristics—all of the technical skills needed to complete the job and the interpersonal skills such as thoughtfulness, insight, sensitivity, and concern for others—that permit him or her to be a successful and accepted part of the office team.

◆ Master the art of listening, to improve accuracy and save time (see this unit, S27).

◆ Be co-operative. If something is not your responsibility, don't say, "That's not my job." You might suggest, "Joe looks after that. Would you like me to get him to do it for you?"

◆ Offer assistance if you are not too busy and a co-worker is obviously under pressure.

◆ Look like a professional. Dress for success! First impressions are very important in the business world. A negative image reflects poor self-confidence and self-worth. Make a statement about yourself with colours, fabrics, clothes, hair, and personal hygiene. Keep your wardrobe neat, clean, in good repair, and varied.

Fingernails should be clean, kept fairly short, and have a well-cared-for look. If you use polish, wear a subtle shade. Keep your hair well brushed and clean (if coloured, maintain roots on a regular basis)—no overstyled hairstyles. Avoid flashy, dangling, and noisy jewellery.

◆ Be careful about language. Profanities are never acceptable.

◆ Watch your body language. Your energy level tells a lot about you. Vitality is noticed, but don't overdo it. Check your posture and project a comfortable but confident image. Hunched shoulders or crossed arms and legs suggest a defensive attitude.

◆ Keep an open mind and show yourself to be receptive to new ideas and procedures.

S

S16 COMMUNICATING

The most important ingredient for success in developing interpersonal skills is the ability to communicate well. Communicating well means sharing a message or idea in such a way that there is a high level of understanding between the sender and the receiver of the message. Communication breakdowns can lead to misunderstanding, frustration, and even costly errors. Breakdowns in communications are often avoidable and usually occur because of:

◆ *poor language skills* (inappropriate and poorly chosen words)

◆ *poor listening skills* (not concentrating fully on what has been said)

◆ *emotional involvement* (judging the speaker or writer rather than the words)

All of the above barriers can be overcome with the right effort.

◆ Choose words with care and develop a vocabulary extensive enough to assist you to use words with precision.

◆ Learn to listen well (see Unit 3, E11). As a listener, try to empathize with the feelings and ideas that a person is communicating. If the message is not clear, ask for clarification. As a speaker, be aware that you may be misinterpreted and seek confirmation that you have been understood.

◆ Be as objective as possible. Avoid letting personal biases and prejudices get in the way.

How to have an effective discussion

A discussion is not a conversation. A conversation can involve a variety of subjects, whereas a discussion should be focussed on a specific topic or list of topics. A conversation generally has no specific purpose, but a discussion is aimed at a definite objective—it may be to solve a problem, to decide on a course of action, or to reconcile conflicting opinions. The people involved in a discussion are joined in a kind of partnership by working towards a conclusion acceptable to all sides. The success of some of our most important relationships, whether personal or business, will depend on the success of discussing things.

The motto of an effective discussion should be "We can work it out":

◆ What is the objective? The aim is to reach an understanding with the involved parties.

◆ Be prepared. A discussion should embrace all points of view and all the facts should be disclosed; if important opinions or facts are left unspoken out of politeness or tact, the resolution of the question may never come to completion.

◆ Allow equal time for each speaker. People who view a discussion as a battle to be won often try to win it by attrition—they will make the same point over and over again in attempts to wear down the opponents.

◆ Keep the discussion from getting personal. Sarcasm or sharp criticism aimed at an individual can prompt retaliation, but incompatibility need not be an obstacle for a successful discussion. Take a break if the discussion is getting heated and personal.

◆ A little comic relief is welcome in serious discussions, but there is a fine line between a jest and a jeer.

◆ A discussion should not be taken as an occasion to show off one's wit or superior knowledge; the participants involved should not feel intimidated. For example, although W.S. Gilbert and Sir Arthur Sullivan loathed each other, they formed one of the most fruitful partnerships in the history of the musical theatre.

◆ Try not to confuse assumptions with facts. A fact is something that is capable of verification by demonstration. Never pretend to know something you actually don't know. Facts should not be assumed, nor should they be twisted to fit one's opinions. No matter how objective we like to think we are, our convictions are bound to be subject to a degree of distortion arising out of various backgrounds and interests.

◆ Talk *to* the people involved not *at* them. Whenever we talk *at* people, we turn what should have been dialogue into diatribe.

◆ A discussion is a matter of alternately speaking and listening. One important qualification for being a good discusser is to be a good listener.

◆ Improve your listening skills by asking questions whenever you are unclear about the meaning of a statement.

◆ Summarize your understanding of a statement to verify that you have heard it accurately.

◆ Be on guard against the tendency to hear what you want to hear; people are subject to a form of wishful thinking, changing the meaning of what is being said.

◆ Replace the general language to specific language in order to refine the terms for all to understand.

S17 E-MAIL/VOICE-MAIL PLANNING

The process of using e-mail and voice mail is so easy that sometimes people are guilty of using them without planning properly. This can leave people and their messages open to all kinds of misinterpretation.

◆ Think through your message before you respond.

◆ Bear in mind that e-mail may not be private. Many unfortunate rumours have been started this way.

◆ Use your e-mail facility as a business communications tool only.

Follow the basic rules of writing when you use this medium: keep your messages short and businesslike but not so brief that they can be construed as being abrupt and hostile. (See Unit 5, EM14, for more information on this.)

S18   INTERPERSONAL SKILLS ON THE JOB

At work, relationships exist with co-workers, with employers, and with customers and visitors, and the successful office worker will know how to relate successfully to all three groups. The employee demonstrating good interpersonal skills usually follows these guidelines:

◆ *leaves personal troubles at home*

◆ *learns to accept the lifestyles and values of others* (beliefs, eating habits, housing, education, leisure activities, dress style), respecting the rights of others to choose how to live and behave

◆ *avoids making judgments* without having all of the information

◆ *maintains a good appearance*
  • pays attention to health care and personal hygiene
  • knows that office workers represent their organizations to the outside world and have a responsibility to maintain good grooming and appropriate dress standards

◆ *displays a good and co-operative attitude*
  • demonstrates a willingness to work hard and carry his/her own weight
  • avoids getting involved in gossip
  • avoids being part of the problem; becomes part of the solution
  • gives an honest day's work and saves time and money where possible
  • shows adaptability by, for example, being willing to help out in "rush" situations
  • is anxious to learn and move ahead on the job
  • is courteous, respectful, and considerate of others and is generally cheerful and approachable
  • shows respect for more senior personnel; is sensitive to the level of company language informality and addresses senior staff formally until invited to use first names
  • respects co-workers' time by avoiding interrupting them
  • is an excellent listener
  • is tactful and sensitive in dealing with others
  • displays self-discipline, competence, loyalty, trustworthiness, honesty, and responsibility
  • does not impose on others by abusing sick leave, taking long breaks, or coming in late and leaving early

◆ *observes rules*
  • knows and follows both the written and unwritten rules of the organization

◆ *respects the work and personal space of colleagues*

◆ *develops tolerance*
  • is aware that some mannerisms can be irritating (loud laughter, bragging, complaining, gossiping, vulgar language), and recognizes the things that cannot be controlled or changed and learns to live with them
◆ *attempts to separate the behaviour from the person*
  • knows that although a person may have done something that was offensive, that person has not become totally offensive
◆ *gets ahead while maintaining good relations with co-workers*
  In seeking advancement, the person displaying good interpersonal skills is aware of the pitfalls to avoid:
  • does not become a winner by making others look like losers
  • knows that getting along with co-workers must always be a priority
  • accepts praise gracefully and resists bragging about it
  • shares credit where it is due
  • flatters only with sincerity
  • acknowledges thoughtfulness

S19   ETHICS

Ethics is concerned with morality—the right and wrong of a situation—and is different from legality. Photocopying copyright printed materials (such as sheet music) for resale is illegal, while photocopying a personal document would be unethical. Employees use unethical business practices when they do any of the following: they are frequently unpunctual or take prolonged breaks; they use office equipment and supplies for personal matters; or play computer games or surf the Net on company time; they are disloyal to the organization in any way.

Not all office-related ethical or moral issues are clear-cut; some may require serious thought. For example, in the following situations, what will you do if you:

◆ are asked to cover for the "boss" when you know he or she is in the office
◆ observe other employees violating company rules

If you cannot establish satisfactory solutions to such problems and your personal ethics are frequently in conflict with those of your organization, you may need to seek a new position.

S20   CONFLICT RESOLUTION

Occasionally, a misunderstanding or error in communication can lead to hurt feelings, embarrassment, or loss of temper. See this unit, S16, for ways to resolve conflict through discussion. A recommended process of resolving conflicts is outlined in Unit 8, "Human Resources Management," H33.

S21 GENDER ROLE STEREOTYPING AND DISCRIMINATION

Sexual harassment is against the law. Most companies also have anti-harassment and fair-treatment policies and programs that stress the value of a diverse work force. If your company does not have a stated policy, be very careful on the following issues:

◆ Know that females prefer to be addressed as "women" rather than as "ladies" or "girls."

◆ Avoid comments or behaviour that may be considered sexist, racist, or harassing. Think about how you might feel if such comments were directed toward you.

◆ Avoid jokes that may be construed as sexist or racist.

◆ Use gender-inclusive language (see Unit 1, C14).

◆ Be aware that ageism is a form of discrimination and must be avoided.

S22 FRONT-LINE RECEPTION, PUBLIC RELATIONS AND CLIENT/CUSTOMER SERVICE EXCELLENCE

All organizations are concerned about the image they present to outsiders and must provide clear guidelines for employees to follow. Be aware of and follow your organization's wishes in dealing with visitors. Some employers, for example, want to see *all* visitors; others, only after an interview has been arranged and the visitor has been announced.

Whatever approach is taken by your employer, be aware that goodwill, an invaluable business asset, is created by customer satisfaction. Goodwill is the friendly, honest, warm feeling that can be conveyed by employees and is as important as the good reputation of the product or service sold. The good reputation of a company can be fostered by employees who:

◆ demonstrate a genuinely helpful attitude

◆ offer a pleasant, friendly smile and cheerful greeting

◆ remember and recognize customers

◆ show courtesy, understanding, and respect

◆ demonstrate competence

S23 GREETING VISITORS

◆ Always dress professionally.

◆ Never chew gum when greeting clients/visitors.

◆ Never ignore a person who comes into the reception area for an appointment or requesting assistance.

◆ Deal with everyone with equal kindness, patience, and concern.

- If you are handling a phone call, ask the caller to hold momentarily in order for you to acknowledge the client/visitor.
- Give the visitor your complete attention; smile and make eye contact.
- Listen patiently and carefully to people who may have difficulty expressing themselves because of unfamiliarity with the language.
- Write down pertinent information, such as the visitor's name (ask for the spelling of the name if it is a long or difficult one to remember, name of company, etc.).
- Make visitors feel at ease and comfortable. Introduce yourself. Hang up coats and offer refreshments and reading materials (if appropriate) if the visitor must wait.
- Arrange to have daily newspaper(s) available in the reception area.
- Ensure that the caller sees the person who can best help him or her.
- Make visitors feel important. Address them by name when speaking to them or advising them that Mr. or Mrs. *(whomever they have come to see)* will see them now.
- Make introductions properly and confidently (see this unit, S9).
- It is not necessary to carry on a conversation with a client, but if he or she initiates a conversation, keep it light and be courteous and polite; the conversation should be on a very impersonal note.
- Never discuss personal or company business with a client, and do not get involved in conversations about company business with other co-workers when a client/visitor is present.
- Do not eat in the reception area or at your desk if you are greeting/receiving clients.
- Maintain a professional work area (e.g., a tidy desk with no food or drink on it).
- Never judge a visitor by appearance. Appearances can deceive!

Handling complaints

- Deal with complaints yourself if possible. If not, find the right person to do so. Customers must never just be passed on to someone else and have to repeat their story one or more times.
- Offer sincere apologies and be genuinely interested in solving the problem.
- Know your company policies, procedures, and products well so that you can provide accurate information in response to questions.

S24 DEALING WITH DIFFICULT VISITORS

- Some visitors will be hard to handle and will require special treatment.
- Be tactful but firm. Ask visitors wishing not to announce themselves or state their business to write this information down so that it can be given in confidence to the appropriate person.

- ◆ Where the employer is unwilling to see visitors who have not made appointments, explain the company policy and tactfully suggest that the visitor might like to write in to arrange an appointment.
- ◆ Be cautious with people who try to obtain information about the company or particular employees. If their inquiries seem to be legitimate and do not involve a breach of company confidentiality, respond to them politely.
- ◆ Try to be a good listener and avoid arguing with the caller. Frequently, the anger will be exhausted if the person is given an opportunity to get the matter off his/her chest. The customer may not always be right, but the customer's viewpoint must always be considered.
- ◆ Don't take problems personally. The irate customer is not really mad at *you*. Maintain your poise and stay calm.

See Unit 19, TT7, for hints on dealing with difficult telephone callers.

S25 HINTS ON REMEMBERING NAMES

- ◆ Write down the name if possible.
- ◆ Make a determined effort to remember a name by listening carefully and paying attention as it is said and by asking for spelling or pronunciation, if needed.
- ◆ Say the name out loud.
- ◆ Watch for names on business cards, name tags, office doors, documents, etc.
- ◆ Use the name in greetings and partings.
- ◆ Maintain a card file or database record.

S26 SCHEDULING APPOINTMENTS

- ◆ Write down the name, company, and phone number of the client/visitor.
- ◆ Check that the information is correct; always spell the name and repeat the phone number for the client to ensure that all information is correct.
- ◆ Check your employer's appointment calendar at the end of each day in order to be better prepared for daily activities, i.e., write down names, company names, phone numbers, etc. (in case of a delay or for rescheduling in case of an emergency).
- ◆ Make sure your calendar is up to date with your employer's and with other office workers' for whom you are scheduling appointments.
- ◆ If you are using office scheduling software, make sure you key in information correctly, and keep the appointments and scheduler up to date.

◆ Make sure another employee is trained for backup and is aware of your scheduling procedures (in case of illness or vacation, leave of absence, etc.).

S27   LISTENING SKILLS

Studies show that the average person spends about 80 percent of his or her waking hours engaged in communication. This communication time is divided among four skills: listening, speaking, reading, and writing.

The average adult listens at no better than a 25 percent efficiency level. For example, after listening to a 10-minute oral presentation, the average person understands and remembers less than half of what was said. If a speaker talks for more than 10 minutes, as often happens in the classroom and in seminars, conferences, and business meetings, efficiency in listening might well be less than 25 percent.

Employees who do not listen effectively can cost organizations billions of dollars. Poor listening skills can account for letters, contracts, and reports that must be rekeyed and shipments that must be reshipped; they can lead to co-worker misunderstandings and the loss of valuable clients/customers.

Techniques of a good listener

Improve your attitude—you must realize the **importance** of good listening skills and develop them to become a better listener.

◆ Good listeners pay **attention** to whomever is speaking. They concentrate on what is being said, avoid distractions, and do not let the mind wander.

◆ Good listeners are **interested** in what is being said; poor listeners usually decide after hearing a few words from the speaker that they do not really like the topic and then lose interest, missing out on valuable information.

◆ Good listeners are **motivated** and want to gain knowledge; the more they know about the topic, the more they can contribute.

◆ Good listeners maintain eye contact with the speaker and try to listen and **learn** as much as they can about the subject.

◆ Good listeners do not interrupt or change the subject until the speaker indicates that he/she is **finished speaking** on the topic.

◆ Good listeners take notes and then ask questions in order to clarify information; they **listen attentively** rather than mentally rehearsing what they are going to say next (they think before they speak).

Good listening skills can assist with problem solving, making you a valued employee: "The chronic kicker, even the most violent critic, will frequently soften and be subdued in the presence of a patient, sympathetic listener—a listener who will be silent while the irate faultfinder dilates like a king cobra and spews the poison out of his system" (Dale Carnegie).

Remember: Knowledge is power, and knowledge workers are an asset in the work force.

S28 BUSINESS ETIQUETTE ABROAD

As Canadian business becomes increasingly global, Canadians must become more aware of how business is conducted in other lands. Consulates and trade offices exist to help with advice on customs and practices in particular countries. In general, the following should prove useful.

Doing business   In some countries, it is not standard practice to get right down to business. Take time for the social niceties first, as custom dictates.

Business cards   Handle business cards (and present your own) with respect. Never write on business cards. If you do much business in a particular country, have your cards printed bilingually, one language on each side.

Decision making   In some cultures, this can take longer than in North America because team decisions are typical.

Punctuality   Most nations favour punctuality, but its importance can vary. Research the attitude toward punctuality in any country you might visit.

Holidays (and holy days)   Know what they are and avoid scheduling business on those days.

Name usage and greetings   Ask the correct method of addressing your business counterpart. In China, for instance, the surname precedes the first name. Although handshakes are the most common form of business greeting, this is not always so. Some research will help.

Body language   Hand or facial gestures, touching, even handshakes, have varying connotations. Do your homework *before* you leave home.

Eye contact   Eye contact does not denote politeness or interest everywhere. This should be investigated.

Status   North American informality is not the norm worldwide, so business travellers should be prepared for some of the following:

◆ Hierarchical lines of communication must be strictly observed, especially in correspondence.

◆ Educational and position titles are commonly used in addressing businesspeople abroad. Use these until invited to be less formal.

◆ Know that formal and informal language levels exist for addressing individuals in some cultures.

Language usage: Oral   Communicate clearly. Avoid jargon, slang, colloquialisms, humour, proverbs, or clichés that might confuse your business counterpart. Speak at a rate that is not too fast but is also not slow and patronizing, and do not hesitate to repeat to clarify your point.

Language usage: Written Keep your correspondence simple and try to deal with one issue at a time. Be conscious of the time needed for translation and decision making.

Clothing and shoes Dress to suit your surroundings in the visited country. Be aware of shoe removal and specific dress customs.

Tipping Check the level of tipping that is customary. Overtipping is unacceptable everywhere. In some situations, little gifts could be useful alternatives.

Gift giving and receiving In many countries, gift giving is standard procedure, for varying reasons. Let the customs of the country guide you. You may be wise to carry uniquely Canadian items to give to your client(s) when this is appropriate.

Thank-you notes Don't delay thank-you notes until you're home—take personalized notepaper with you on your trip.

Being a good host When on foreign soil, visitors—especially from status- and group-oriented cultures—require careful attention. Make them comfortable and provide all of the support they need to do their job here. Their dietary and religious habits should be respected and their style of entertainment researched to avoid possible embarrassment.

S

UNIT

19 TELEPHONE TECHNIQUES AND SERVICES

CONTENTS

TT

Today's sophisticated telephone technology interconnects telephone lines, fibre optics, digital systems, microwaves, and satellites to transmit voice, text, data, and images across the world. The never-ending additions to the telephone service, as well as portable telephones and telephones in cars, planes, and trains, have reinforced the telephone as a key player in the business world. This unit provides details on the telephone, its many features, and the services available.

TT1 TELEPHONE TECHNIQUES

TT2 ANSWERING CALLS

Often the voice at the other end of the business telephone line is the introduction to a company. Sometimes it is the only impression a caller gets. A warm and enthusiastic greeting encourages client and vendor alike. Businesspeople can be good ambassadors for their organizations if they are knowledgeable about company operations, and if they employ good telephone techniques.

NOTE Usually a caller can detect the mood of the person answering the phone. A bored or disinterested voice shows indifference. A tired voice reflects a tired employee. A harried voice indicates confusion at the other end.

Be alert: Bosses have been known to call their companies to check on how employees are answering phone calls. *Never* use the company phone for personal calls unless it is an emergency. Companies can check phone bills for abuse of company phone lines. All calls can be traced back to the extension or user.

TT3 IDENTIFYING YOURSELF

Answer promptly—before the third ring—and identify yourself and your affiliation. Listen actively: concentrate on the caller's voice and remember to be helpful and tactful. Welcome callers courteously and professionally with "Good morning," "Good afternoon," etc., followed by the appropriate identification:

For a firm "Elliott Galleries. How can I help you?"

Your own telephone "Gilles Beaupré (or Mr. Beaupré). Can I help you?"

Department telephone "Credit Department. Rajan Sharma speaking."

Another's telephone "Mr. Lieberman's office. Rajan Sharma speaking. Can I help you?"

Make your callers comfortable by bearing these points in mind:

Voice, language, and tone
◆ Give all callers an attentive ear.
◆ Enunciate clearly:
  • Speak distinctly; do not smoke, chew, or conduct other conversations at the same time.

◆ Be natural; keep your voice volume moderate.

◆ Train your emotions, voice, and vocabulary to be positive, even on a "down" day. For example, say, "Let me see if [name of person] can help," rather than "We can't help you." Or, "[Name of person] will be available at 10 tomorrow morning. May I have her call you?" rather than "Sorry, [name of person] has gone for the day."

◆ Stay away from the slang, "OK" and "no problem"; use "certainly," "very well," "all right," instead.

NOTE Do *not* have a radio on when you are answering a phone—the background noise is amplified on the receiving end and is not appreciated by callers.

◆ Did you know you are amplifying your voice when you cover the mouth section of the receiver or if you hold the phone to your chest?

◆ Did you know that most callers can tell when a person is not telling the truth?

TT4 TRANSFERRING CALLS

◆ Transfer only when it is essential and only if the caller agrees.

◆ Complete the transfer within 20 seconds.

◆ If you do not know who should handle the call, note the caller's name and number and have the appropriate person call back.

◆ If you *do* know who should handle the call, make sure that person is available and give a brief explanation of the call before you transfer it.

◆ If you must leave your desk, arrange for your telephone to be answered (e.g., use call forwarding; see this unit, TT37).

TT5 MONITORING CALLS

◆ Avoid keeping callers on the line. Offer a choice such as, "That line is busy. Will you hold or shall [name of person] call you back?" Offer to call back if you need to obtain information for the caller. If you must leave the line, first ask the caller's permission and then provide progress reports every half-minute.

TT6 TAKING MESSAGES

◆ Keep a note or message pad and pen near the telephone.

◆ Take messages correctly: check doubtful spellings with the caller; note information accurately and repeat it if you are in doubt.

◆ Always note the number (including area code) to save time later.

◆ Make sure the company directory is current. Keep names, job titles, job transfers, changes in phone numbers or extensions, and new employee additions up-to-date. It is embarrassing if you cannot locate a person when a client calls.

TT

◆ Do not say, "I have never heard of that person." Ask the caller/client to hold and make inquiries to verify the employee's name and extension number. For additional information, see Unit 18, S23, "Greeting Visitors."

◆ Print the name of person who received the phone message; this is important in case of a follow-up inquiry.

MESSAGE FOR

M S. _Jean Won_

WHILE YOU WERE OUT

M r. _Liboc_

OF _Central Library_

PHONE NO. _236-9102_

TELEPHONED	√	RETURNED YOUR CALL	
CALLED TO SEE YOU		PLEASE CALL	
WANTS TO SEE YOU		WILL CALL AGAIN	

MESSAGE: _The books you wanted are in._

DATE _July 6_ TIME _2:30_

RECEIVED BY _B H_

Telephone message form

TT7   DEALING WITH DIFFICULT CALLERS

If an angry or aggressive person attacks your company or you in a tirade, calm the caller by saying:

◆ "I understand your irritation..." *or*

◆ "I apologize for the inconvenience..."

and always be loyal to colleagues and company.

When an irate caller says, "Why do you want to know who's calling?" you could reply "This will enable [name of person] to give you better service when he or she answers."

◆ Deal with complaints and aggressive calls by listening, offering a sympathetic voice, and suggesting a reasonable solution.

TT

TT8 BEING TACTFUL AND DISCREET

◆ Deal with wrong numbers efficiently and courteously.

◆ Don't tell callers that people being called are on holiday, at lunch or on a break, or sick. Give a return date or time and suggest that you transfer the call to someone else who could handle the inquiry.

◆ Encourage callers to come to the point quickly by politely questioning them as to their needs.

◆ Maintain and display a calm demeanour, especially when flooded with, or transferring, calls.

◆ Handle persistent callers by addressing them by name and cheerfully discouraging them.

◆ If you are required to screen calls:
  • say the person called is unavailable, or "[Name of person] is working on a report right now. May I tell her you called?"

TT9 MAKING CALLS

Use a cheerful and businesslike greeting, followed by an appropriate identification:

For a firm "Laura Larney of Elliott Galleries here."

Your own telephone "It's Yuying Hou calling."

Your department "This is Winston Kennedy of the sales department."

◆ Keep an up-to-date directory of frequently called numbers (including area codes). Do this on your computer so that you can take advantage of automatic dialling if this feature is available to you, or program frequently called numbers into your telephone.

◆ Plan ahead: check the number, have questions ready, make notes if necessary, and/or have files available.

◆ Identify yourself and your affiliation.

◆ Use the most appropriate service and dial direct if possible.

◆ Consider time zones when making long-distance calls (see Appendix).

◆ Take advantage of any special rates or discounts (see the front section of your telephone directory).

◆ If you contact a wrong long-distance number, call the operator (0) to have the charge cancelled.

◆ Anticipate that you may be answered by a recording and have a brief message thought out (see this unit, TT11).

TT10 RETURNING CALLS

◆ Do this within six hours if possible, for the sake of courtesy, even if only to acknowledge the call.

◆ When asking someone to return a long-distance call, suggest "collect" if company policy permits.

TT

TT11   LEAVING MESSAGES

As a result of office automation, a caller is frequently connected to a recorded message instead of a person. Be prepared for this and have your message clearly thought out and complete before even making the call. Keep the message short—as little as 30 seconds might be allowed after the "beep."

◆ Give your name, affiliation, number, and the date and time.
◆ State the reason for your call.
◆ Ask for a return call or say you will call back.

If the recorded message offers several alternatives, be patient, keep a pen handy, and listen carefully in order to obtain the information you want without delay and frustration.

Creating your own recorded message

Start with a warm, professional greeting (without gimmicks) identifying yourself and your company and asking the caller to leave a name, number, message, time, and date. Assure the caller of a quick response. Write out and practise the message before recording it.

> This is Heidi Schwartz of Cape Breton Fashions. Please leave your name, number, and a short message after the beep and I'll call you as soon as I can.

TT12   TELEPHONE SERVICES

A wide variety of types of calls and special services is available to telephone customers. Information about such calls and services, as well as information pertaining to calls in specific areas, is provided in the introductory pages of the telephone directory. Consult these pages before making a long-distance call.

Because telephone service is now open to competition, some organizations and individuals subscribe to companies offering alternative long-distance services to those provided by the telephone company in each province.

To use such services, the caller enters a system access number or a password on a touch-tone telephone before dialling the rest of the number as usual. Long-distance calls are then billed separately.

TT13   AREA CODE OVERLAYS

Local call dialling using 10-digit dialling was introduced in January 2001, e.g., local calls in the 416 and 905 areas now must include their area code as part of their phone number. This means 647 for Toronto's 416 area, and 289 for the surrounding 905 communities, i.e., (416) 647-549-6789 or (905) 289-576-1223.

TT

* Reprogram any modems/Internet diallers, fax machines, home security systems, options such as call forwarding, speed diallers and lists, and wireless phones.

For more information, access www.bell.ca/areacodes.

TT14   LONG-DISTANCE CALLS (NORTH AMERICA)

Direct dialling (from one number to another) is the most economical way of phoning long distance. Whenever an operator is used, the cost of telephoning increases.

NOTE   Packages as well as discount plans are available for long-distance callers. Check with your phone service provider for special rates.

Long-distance inquiries   For long-distance inquiries, dial 1 + area code + 555-1212 and give the operator the name and address of the person you are calling.

Time zones   Check the phone directory for the time zone map showing area codes, or see the appendix at the end of this book, for example:

Time difference/TD

Pacific time	8:00 a.m.
Mountain time	9:00 a.m.
Central time	10:00 a.m.
Eastern time	11:00 a.m.
Atlantic time	12:00 noon
Newfoundland time	12:30 p.m.

▶ TT15   Dial direct

Station-to-station   A direct call with operator intervention only for particulars of billing. The charge begins when the called telephone is picked up. To call within your own area or outside it, dial 1 (access code) + area code + the number.

From St. John's to Corner Brook, Newfoundland (same area code [709]):
Dial 1 + 709 + 721-8014

From Toronto to Deerfield Beach, Florida (different area code):
Dial 1 + 305 + 421-4353

Collect   The person receiving the call agrees to accept the charge.

Dial 0 + area code + number. When the operator responds, say "collect" and give your name.

Bill to a third number   A call made from one number but billed to another.

Dial 0 + area code + number. When the operator responds, say "bill to" and give the area code and number to which the call should be charged. If the call is made from a public telephone, the operator will confirm acceptance with someone at the third number before connecting the caller.

Calling card (credit card) Available from the telephone company, and very convenient for anyone who travels frequently and makes many calls. The person or company named on the card is billed monthly.

NOTE Calling cards can no longer be used for calls outside North America. Major credit cards can, however, be used from appropriately equipped telephones.

> Dial 0 + area code + number. When the operator responds, say "credit card" and give the telephone credit card number.

▶ TT16   Operator assisted

Person to person This service is useful when contact is required with a specific person or department. The charge begins when the specified contact is made. Person-to-person calls are more expensive than station-to-station calls.

> Dial 0 + area code + number. When the operator responds, give the name of the person you wish to reach. Collect, bill to third number, and calling card services may be requested with person-to-person calls.

TT17   OVERSEAS CALLS

The most economical overseas telephone call is made by dialling direct.

Overseas inquiries To obtain the telephone number of an overseas party, dial 0 and ask the operator for the number.

There is an access charge on all international/overseas directory assistance requests. There is no charge if the foreign directory service cannot be reached. Customers may request up to two listings per call if supplied by the same foreign directory operator at the same time.

▶ TT18   Dial direct (see telephone directory for listing of countries)

Station to station Cheapest type of overseas call.

> Dial 011 + country code (2 or 3 digits) + routing code (1 to 5 digits) + local number (2 to 9 digits). The country code and routing code are obtainable from the telephone directory.

Collect, calling card, bill to third number, and person to person May be requested at an additional charge.

> Dial 01 + country code + routing code + local number. When the operator answers, identify the kind of call you want and give the information shown in "Dial Direct" (see this unit, TT15).

TT

▶ **TT19   Operator assisted**

Where direct dialling is not possible, dial 0 and the overseas operator will make the call for you.

TT20   SPECIAL TYPES OF CALLS

▶ **TT21   Conference**

This type of call is made when several people at different locations (domestic and/or international) all wish to confer at the same time. Plan the call in advance. Dial 0 and ask for the conference operator (see also "Teleconferences," Unit 14).

▶ **TT22   Marine**

Used for communicating with ships equipped for radio-telephone service. Dial 0 and ask for the marine operator.

▶ **TT23   Mobile**

Used to contact cars and trucks that have *manual* mobile telephone service. Dial 0 and ask for the mobile operator.

To call Access 450 customers (those with direct-dial mobile equipment), dial the 7-digit mobile number (preceded by the area code, if necessary).

Mobile telephones are different from cellular telephones, which enable users to contact *any* telephone number by simply dialling (this unit, TT34).

NOTE   In some countries, cellular telephone are called mobiles.

▶ **TT24   900 and 976 Services**

Lines are available to sponsors of information programs. The content of these services is the responsibility of the companies that provide the information. The person who dials up the program is charged for the call.

▶ **TT25   WATS (Wide-Area Transmission Service)/Toll Free**

Inwats (INcoming WATS—Code 800/Toll Free)   This system is used by businesses and service companies to encourage customers to call long distance free of charge within a certain radius. Dial 1 + 800 + special Inwats number. For example, this service is used by hotels to accept reservations from out-of-town clients.

Outwats (OUTgoing WATS)   This service is available to companies that make many wide-area calls. The charge is lower than for regular long-distance calls because customers usually pay on a flat-rate basis.

TT

There are six WATS zones across Canada. The subscriber pays according to the zone coverage desired. In addition, a choice of rate structures based on hours of usage is possible.

NOTE Contac and Zenith Services were discontinued in February 1999 and have been replaced with the Advantage Optimum Plan.

TT26 TELEPHONE DIRECTORIES

The telephone company directory is in two parts: alphabetic (White Pages) and classified (Yellow Pages).

▶ TT27 Alphabetic directory (White Pages)

Names, addresses, and telephone numbers of individuals and organizations are listed alphabetically by name. Names of subscribers are automatically listed free of charge, but a monthly charge is levied against subscribers wanting unlisted numbers.

The introductory pages list worldwide area codes, the types and rates of calls, telephone services available, and other useful facts. For ease of reference, government department listings are placed together and printed on blue paper (Blue Pages).

▶ TT28 Classified directory (Yellow Pages)

Organizations wishing to be listed alphabetically by service or product and to advertise their services or products subscribe to the Yellow Pages. A charge is made for each listing and each advertisement.

This directory also contains the "Talking Yellow Pages" for obtaining current information on, for example, business news, community events, investments, and weather forecasts. All calls are free.

NOTE In large metropolitan centres, the White and Yellow Pages may come in separate directories; in smaller communities, one telephone directory may be issued consisting of White and Yellow Pages.

▶ TT29 Personal directory

Frequently used telephone numbers can be organized for quick reference in a personal directory. This may be a list, a card index file, an indexed container, or an electronic (computerized) directory. The list should be organized alphabetically and should show the area code, the number, and the extension, if appropriate.

If you are on a network or have a modem, your electronic directory can function as an auto-dialler also.

TT

TT30 BUSINESS TELEPHONE SYSTEMS AND EQUIPMENT

Telephone lines are leased from telephone companies; telephone systems and equipment can be purchased, leased, or rented from and installed by telephone companies and numerous other suppliers.

TT31 CENTRALIZED ANSWERING

The type of central answering service an organization has will be determined by the number of trunk (in/out) lines, extension lines, and services it requires. All calls coming into an organization are dealt with through some type of switching equipment.

PBX (private branch exchange)

The *manual* PBX requires an operator to complete the connections for all incoming, outgoing, and interoffice calls. The switching system is usually located on the company premises.

The *electronic* PBX requires a switchboard operator—normally located on the company premises—to handle only incoming calls. Outgoing and interoffice calls are dealt with by employees directly.

A screen and keyboard can be added to this equipment that enables the operator to monitor constantly all extensions and thus deal with incoming calls more quickly and efficiently.

The *automatic* PBX not only switches all calls but can also keep a record of communications patterns and expenses. You can also program it for special functions such as transmitting data, providing an electronic directory, and acting as a message centre for telephone mail.

Centrex

This is a large switchboard in one location—usually not on the company premises—that has its own exchange number. Every telephone number in the system has the same first three digits, with the last four digits changing from telephone to telephone. Thus, each employee has an individual telephone number and can make and receive direct as well as interoffice calls. Extremely large corporations and governments use Centrex.

TT32 KEY TELEPHONE SYSTEMS

These are equipped with a number of buttons or keys that can be used in various ways. For example, a simple key telephone system comes with incoming (trunk) line buttons, an intercom button, and a hold button. Large versions of these desktop systems can accommodate up to 150 ports or lines with number of trunk and local lines decided by the user. They can provide central answering services for a company or within a department. The operator handles only incoming calls.

How a basic key telephone system works

◆ A call is signalled when a bell or buzzer rings and a button light flashes on and off.

◆ When the lighted button is depressed and the receiver lifted, the light stays on but the flashing stops.

◆ The *hold* button is depressed if a caller is asked to wait.

◆ The *intercom* button is depressed when connection to an inside-company extension must be made.

Modularity (the addition of segments) permits the expansion of services on single- or multiple-line keyed telephone sets by simply adding on the required equipment. For example, to speed up the handling of incoming calls, a monitor with a "busy lamp field" can be connected to the "switchboard" to indicate to the attendant which individuals are actually using their telephones.

Cordless telephones

The advantage of these devices is that you can use them several hundred metres away from their base attachment.

TT33   COMPUTER-BASED TELEPHONE SYSTEMS

Computerized telephone systems are available for any size of installation. These can provide all of the services of PBX or Centrex, plus integrated voice and data communications, as well as many features listed in "Additional Features" (see this unit, TT37).

For example, voice mail can be integrated into these telephone systems. The caller, on being connected, says a number and is automatically transferred to the correct "mailbox" and offered a list of options. The caller then selects an option and receives a response or some desired information.

TT34   CELLULAR TELEPHONE SYSTEMS

These portable units permit users to make and receive telephone calls while they are in transit or off the company premises, at any distance. Pocket-sized models can be purchased and many special features, such as call forwarding and fax connection, are available (see this unit, TT37). As with any telephone, the caller simply dials the desired number (local or long distance) to make a connection.

Calling areas are referred to as *cells*. The greater the distance the called cell is from the caller, the more expensive the call will be.

TT35   CELL PHONE ETIQUETTE

◆ Do not talk on a cell phone while driving; pull over for safety reasons.

◆ Avoid talking on your cell phone in restaurants or public places (since this can be annoying for other patrons).

TT

- Turn off your cell phone when attending a religious group, funeral or wedding ceremonies, the theatre, classroom lectures, or examinations/testing areas.
- Do not use your cell phone in restricted hospital areas/wards (for patients' safety).
- Avoid using your cell phone for personal use while in the workplace, i.e., incoming/outgoing calls. This is misuse of company time.

Above all, use your cell phone discreetly.

TT36 VIDEOPHONE

This equipment comprises a telephone linked to a TV screen through a computer installed with a circuit board with a digital data unit and software, and a miniature video camera. It enables two or more people in different locations to converse, to see each other as though in person, and to exchange text and graphics on the screen at the same time. Check with computer manufacturers and large retailers for detailed information.

TT37 ADDITIONAL FEATURES

Because a wide array of features are available on telephone systems, check with telephone suppliers for your specific requirements. Centralized equipment usually incorporates standard as well as optional features, both of which are included in the sample list that follows.

Audio conferencing and audio-plus conferencing See Unit 14, "Meetings, Conferences, and Teleconferences," for details.

Automated billing service Calls can be collect, billed to a phone card, or billed to a third number.

Automated call attendant system A one-line telephone rings and a recorded voice welcomes callers and guides them to the required extension. Callers are then automatically switched to another telephone number or to a fax machine.

Automatic Dialling-Announcing Devices (ADADS) This feature can store or produce telephone numbers to be called and deliver either a pre-recorded or synthesized voice message.

Automatic hold of central office (CO) Incoming calls can automatically be placed on hold.

Automatic ring again When a busy station or outside line is free, the telephone rings again.

Call answer Messages are taken for you when your phone is busy or unanswered. Use any touch-tone phone to record a personal greeting or to access messages. Callers have three minutes to leave a message.

Pager notification With this option and *Call answer*, your pager can be notified each time a message is left in your *Call answer* mailbox.

TT

◆ *Extension call answer:* This service allows personal answering for up to four people. Subscribers can send, reply, or forward messages to each other.

Call answer plus   This service allows the caller 45 seconds to record a greeting, stores up to 50 messages of up to five minutes each, and gives the subscriber unlimited use of *message monitor.* There is an additional monthly fee for this service.

Call blocking   This feature stops or "blocks" the subscriber's name and telephone number from being viewed by the person being called.

◆ *Occasional blocking:* Before dialling a number, press *67 on a touch-tone phone or dial 1167 on a rotary dial phone. A message will be displayed or transmitted to the caller: "PRIVATE NAME/PRIVATE NUMBER." There is no charge for this service.

◆ *Permanent blocking:* This is a service that permanently blocks both the name and number on the line. This option is available only to shelters for victims of domestic violence, crisis lines, public law enforcement agencies, social service agencies, and victims and potential victims of violence. For further information, contact the customer service at the phone service provider.

Call display   This consists of *number display* and *name option* services. *Number display* service and a telephone with a display screen allow you to see the number of the caller. *Name option* allows you to see the name of the caller.

Private Name Display   This feature replaces your name with the message "PRIVATE NAME." If you are calling someone who has *Call display* with the name display option, he or she will see "PRIVATE NAME" and your telephone number.

Call editor   This phone service connected to a personal computer can block unwanted calls or fax messages, record incoming calls, or forward calls automatically.

Call forwarding (call transfer)   Calls are automatically forwarded from one extension or telephone number to another as instructed, without attendant help.

Call return
◆ If the number called is busy, this feature monitors that line for 30 minutes and automatically dials it when it is free.
◆ The last call placed can be redialled with a simple code number.
◆ The last call received can be returned with a code number.

Call screen   Unwanted calls from up to 12 numbers can be diverted with a message saying calls are not being taken.

Call switching   If an extension is to be left unattended, incoming calls may be switched to another extension for answering.

TT

Call trace The last caller's number can be traced and recorded by the telephone company, if desired.

Call transaction processing Callers can select services or information by calling a telephone linked to a computer-based system.

Call waiting A person on a call gets a light *beep* tone periodically to warn of another call waiting. The waiting call can be taken without disconnecting the original caller. A long-short-short ring indicates that the call is long distance.

Calling line identification The answering telephone automatically identifies the calling number (which is linked to a computer) that instantly alerts the computer to bring up the calling person's data. Thus, all pertinent information is immediately available to the person taking the call.

Camp on If a number called is busy, the caller can wait without hanging up and be automatically connected when the line is free.

Community voice mail This is an option that allows groups to create a distribution list of members and to send messages by touching a button.

Conference calling A third person—on some equipment, up to three additional people—can be brought in on a conversation.

Control features These features are available for companies that wish to monitor costs or to control telephone use.

◆ *Toll restrictions:* Telephones in the system can be programmed to restrict users from making outside calls, from making long-distance calls, from calling the operator or directory assistance, from calling to specific area codes, from contacting numbers in an area code, or from using certain telephone lines (e.g., WATS).

◆ *Call-detail recording:* This control feature, which requires a computer interface, enables an organization to record calls by individuals, by departments, by clients called, etc., for accounting purposes. The data is stored and can be printed on command.

Dial access to central dictating systems The caller can dial and dictate into the telephone. For more details, see Unit 21, "Word Processing," WP20.

Display line A digital readout (LCD: liquid crystal display) can give day, date, time, name and/or number of caller, name or number of company dialled, length of call, and number of messages waiting.

Do not disturb This facility enables the user to block out all but emergency calls.

Facsimile and modem compatible A modem connection permits data and document transmission.

NOTE To stop unwanted fax calls on your phone line: dial *69 to identify the phone number of the business or fax machine that is sending the fax, or report the problem to repair service.

Group listening A speaker in the handset is switched on to enable those present to hear both sides of a telephone conversation.

Hands-free features

◆ *Hands-free dialling:* The telephone receiver can be left in place until dialling is complete.

◆ *Hands-free—listen on hold:* If you are placed on hold, you may hang up and a built-in speaker will monitor the line for you. When you are reconnected, you can pick up the handset.

◆ *Hands-free speakerphone:* This permits the user to move about the room and even hold conferences with several people present.

Ident-a-call This service provides the convenience of a maximum of two extra phone numbers on one line. Each phone number has a distinguishable ring that allows you to identify the number being called.

Intercom link A single button permits multi-link connection among several offices or departments at one time.

*Last call return (*69)* A voice message gives the telephone number of the last person who called.

Last number redial This feature automatically redials the last number the caller tried to reach.

Message waiting A light tells the user that a message awaits.

Microphone mute This button permits one-way listening—the user can hear intercom announcements but cannot be tuned into.

Multiple-line conference Additional people can be brought in on a two-way conversation.

Music-on-hold Callers hear music or a recorded message while they wait.

Name that Number If you have a phone number but no name, call 1-416-555-1313 (no charge) to identify the caller. You will be charged a fee for each name found.

Obscene or harrassing calls Hang up when you receive an obscene call. If calls persist or are threatening, use the *call trace* feature or *last call return (*69)*. The *call trace* should only be used in serious situations where legal action is taken. Contact the phone service provider and the local police. The phone company will only release a traced number with legal authorization. *Call trace* service is only available to residence and individual line business customers in areas where it is technically possible to offer it.

Paging access This provides dial access to one or more personal paging systems or to a loudspeaker paging system.

Prime-line executive service One telephone line can reach you anywhere you travel—for telephone, fax, or pager.

TT

Priority signal This alerts the user to urgent calls or messages, despite the "Do Not Disturb" connection.

Ring reader The telephone recognizes the ring of the incoming call and automatically sends the call to an extension, fax, or answering machine.

Saved number redial This allows you to store a number while you make or receive other calls and then redial the stored number automatically.

Speed calling This service allows the subscriber to dial up to eight numbers from any phone in the home, by using a one-digit code.

Star message system This allows a caller to press the star on the telephone key pad and record a message if the number called is busy or not answered. The number is then dialled every 20 min, for up to four hours, until the message is delivered. A toll-free number can be called to ascertain that the message was delivered.

Teleconferencing See Unit 14, "Meetings, Conferences, and Teleconferences," and Unit 5, "Electronic Mail."

Teleguard This service can block unauthorized outgoing calls to numbers such as 900 numbers, long distance, and others.

Three-way calling A third party can be contacted while you have the caller on hold, or a three-way conversation can be conducted.

Tie-trunks These provide direct system-to-system links to multiple location businesses—a one-digit number will connect the user to the long-distance location; then just the local number is dialled.

Video conferencing See Unit 14, "Meetings, Conferences, and Teleconferences."

Wide-area paging When your cellular number is dialled, the system searches you out (even in another city) and connects the caller.

The telephone system is constantly adding new developments to its range of services. A call to your telephone company or supplier will inform you about specific systems or equipment to suit your company's needs.

NOTE For more information, refer to the front pages of the Telephone Directory or call your local Business Office.

Web site: www.customer.concerns@bell.ca

TT38 VOICE-MAIL SYSTEMS (MESSAGE SERVICES)

The Net

This service of Stentor Canadian Network Management (the group of telephone companies in Canada) permits voice-messaging by linking a company's telephone and data terminal to The Net system.

The caller uses a touch-tone telephone to enter the message, which is stored on computer, and the recipient hears the saved message on a similar telephone by touch of a button.

Pre-recorded messages and lists of questions (with time allotted for answers) are examples of how voice-mail systems can be used in taking orders and collecting information. (See Unit 5, "Electronic Mail," for more information.)

TT39 PAGERS

A pager is allocated a number. When this is dialled, the type of pager determines how the call is handled.

◆ The receiving pager displays the calling number, which the recipient contacts.

◆ An operator receives the call, sends the message (which appears as a readout) to the recipient, who then contacts the caller.

◆ An operator receives the call and leaves a voice message on the recipient's pager. The message can be tuned in and may or may not require a response.

TT40 TELEPHONE-ANSWERING SERVICES

Organizations exist that will answer telephone calls on a subscriber's behalf, for a fee. Such services are available on a 24-hour basis if needed. The telephone can be answered in the name of an individual, the name of a company, or any other identification requested. Some organizations simply take messages; others offer paging services. Consult the Yellow Pages of your telephone directory for a list of the answering-service organizations in your area.

> **NOTE**   Web site: www.bell.ca
> E-mail: forum@bell.ca
> Fax: 1-800-554-5148 (no charge)

TT41 INTERNET/PHONE LINE

A dedicated phone line (cable) is recommended for frequent Internet users, otherwise callers will receive a busy signal if you are online. You could miss important incoming calls.

TT42 VOICE TECHNOLOGY

Cable companies are currently developing plans to offer telephone service over the Internet (known as *IP telephony*).

IP telephony is a phone call in which a person's voice is broken down into packets of data that are then sent to their destination over the Internet. The shift to *IP Telephony*, with the prospect of free long-distance calling, is predicted to occur over the next five years.

* Reference: Peter Verberg, Alberta bureau chief of *Canadian Business.*

UNIT

20 TRAVEL ARRANGEMENTS

CONTENTS

TA

P lanning a trip for business or pleasure involves making travel reservations, booking accommodation and rental cars, arranging for the necessary travel documentation, buying foreign currency, and organizing a host of other details. Large corporations may have their own travel departments with direct computer access to carriers, hotels, etc., but more often office workers will use the services of a travel agent or do the work themselves.

Corporate travel includes business people travelling from one city, province, or state to other countries around the globe. These travellers are usually attending business meetings, seminars, conferences, or international conventions.

TA1 USING A TRAVEL AGENT

Travel agents are paid by transportation companies (carriers) and hotels; there is no charge to the user. These travel counsellors can reduce the travel arrangement workload because they have instant access to all travel-related data. Travel agencies can offer excellent advice on accommodation, package tours, travel documents, car rentals, overseas travel, etc. In addition, they can be helpful about exchange rates, suitable clothing, climatic conditions, Customs arrangements, special events, and places of interest. However, an incompetent or unscrupulous agent can be a costly one, so before you employ an agency, check its reputation with the Better Business Bureau or the local chamber of commerce.

NOTE   For those who prefer not to use the services of a travel agent, the *Official Airline Guide*, a detailed listing of flights and services, may prove useful. The Official Airline Guide is also available for a fee in online electronic database form for those with computers that have access capability. Also, direct booking with carriers is available on the Internet for no fee.

E-mail reference for travel in Canada: **www.travelcanada.ca/tct**

TA2 AIR TRAVEL

You can make reservations by telephone or in person at the airport, at an airline ticket office, at a travel agency, or via the Internet. Tickets are prepared when payment has been made or credit has been established. Some companies maintain monthly accounts with travel agencies or airlines; other organizations provide key employees with credit cards for charging their travel bookings. You can also pay via bank, airline, hotel, and oil company credit cards.

The reservation information needed includes:

◆ name(s) of traveller(s)

◆ date(s) and preferred times of travel

◆ departure and arrival airports

TA

- class of service
- method of payment
- frequent-flier number
- contact telephone number(s) of the traveller(s)

Frequent-flyer plans/Air miles

Some organizations award bonus air miles to people who fly frequently on a particular airline or who use certain credit cards, hotels, and car rental agencies. These plans allow you to accumulate air miles through business or personal travel, car rentals, and credit card purchases.

- Be prepared to be flexible when you apply to use your "free" air miles.
- Do your own research regarding these plans—travel agents are too busy.
- Know all of the details of the frequent-flyer plans you choose.
- Check your company's policy on frequent-flyer points for personal use.
- Remember to provide individual air mile plan numbers at the time of booking hotels, air travel, car rentals, and vacation packages (where applicable).

Client statements are usually mailed out monthly or after the completion of air travel, vacations, etc. Check each statement to make sure that the earned air miles have been properly credited to the client's account. Also check expiry dates for use of accumulated points.

TA3   FARES

First class   This most expensive fare provides passengers with special check-in privileges: a VIP airport lounge, spacious, more comfortable seating, and greater personalized service than other classes receive.

Business or executive class   Passengers in this category are entitled to a special check-in counter, first choice of meals and literature, and a more comfortable seat than economy-class travellers.

Economy class   This service is the cheapest of those available in the regular-fare category.

▶ TA4   Discounted fares

Discounted fares are individual round-trip fares that sell for less than two one-way tickets. Airlines provide a limited number of seats in economy-class cabins for these special bargain fares, which are offered on some flights.

APEX (Advance Purchase EXcursion)

APEX purchasers must travel during specific time limits, they must make bookings well in advance of the journey and pay shortly after booking, and they must adhere to prearranged departure and return dates. A charge is made for cancellation or any change in the reservation.

TA

Super APEX

This extra-special discount fare is lower than regular APEX and usually requires a deposit within one week of booking. The same limitations apply to Super APEX as to APEX fares. Check with the airline or your travel agent.

Seat saver

This extra-special discounted fare applies to specific domestic destinations.

Group fare

Group-fare purchasers travel economy class as members of groups on scheduled flights and usually must purchase a land arrangement such as a hotel or rental car.

Family plan

The head of the family pays full fare; other members of the family receive discounts.

TA5 TYPES OF FLIGHTS

Scheduled flight The regular flight established by an airline that departs regardless of the number of seats sold.

Nonstop flight No stops are made until the aircraft reaches its destination.

Direct flight A stop or stops along the way will be made, but there will be no need to change aircraft.

Connecting flight Passengers must get off one aircraft along the route and board another. Some airlines routinely route all traffic through their hubs (home bases). This usually means a change of aircraft though not necessarily of airline.

Charter flight An aircraft booked exclusively for group travel. This is among the cheaper forms of air travel but passengers should anticipate full planes, a penalty for cancelling, inflexibility in changing dates, and a possible weight restriction on baggage.

NOTE

- ◆ Complimentary meals are included on all flights, and complimentary bar service is provided for first- and executive-class passengers.
- ◆ Passengers can make calls from aircraft by using telephone company credit cards.

TA6 CONFIRMATION AND CANCELLATION

It is important to confirm and/or cancel flights within the time period established by the airline. If your travel plans change, call the airline and cancel your reservations. Failure to do so may result in penalties.

TA

Remember, of course, that with certain fares, cancellations result in losing of the total cost.

TA7 BAGGAGE

Although international carriers sometimes base their free baggage allowance on mass, the usual practice is as follows: Each adult is permitted two articles to be checked (maximum dimensions of the first piece are 1.6 m (5.25') in length, height, and width; of the second piece, 1.35 m (4.25') in length, height, and width); and cabin luggage (maximum dimensions 1.2 m [4'] in length, height, and width if it will fit under the seat). No single piece of luggage may exceed 31.8 kg (70 lbs.). Airlines provide packaging for unusual or fragile items as well as special handling for these articles. Luggage allowance for charter passengers varies with the carrier. Check with the airline if in doubt.

Airline liability for lost or damaged baggage is limited in accordance with its current tariffs. Verify these at any ticket office. The airline accepts no liability for loss or damage to fragile or perishable items, money, jewellery, or negotiable securities.

TA8 CHECK-IN CONSIDERATIONS

Airline passengers should make sure they allow adequate time before actual departure to:

- ◆ check in (at least two hours before an international flight)
- ◆ deal with current stringent security regulations
- ◆ contend with special or excess baggage arrangements
- ◆ pay airport improvement fees
- ◆ handle last-minute details such as duty-free purchases and perhaps foreign currency exchange

Travellers should have on hand at least $20 Canadian cash (or equivalent, if leaving from a foreign airport) per person in case the airport charges a departure fee and does not accept credit cards.

NOTE Because adverse weather conditions or other problems can cause delays, it is wise to confirm that your flight is on time before leaving for the airport.

TA9 GETTING TO AND FROM THE AIRPORT

TA

Taxis and limousines are the usual means of transportation to and from airports. Airport buses operate from major hotels and local transit stations on a regular schedule; many hotels transport their clients by minibus. Helicopter services may also be available. Compare costs and time involved. Consult the Yellow Pages.

TA10   CHARTERED PLANES

If all commercial flights are fully booked, consider arranging a specially chartered flight. Check with airports in the vicinity or private airline companies.

TA11   TRAIN TRAVEL

You can make train reservations and purchase tickets (with or without reservations) through a travel agent. VIA Rail will accept first-class reservations by telephone, but travellers must book coach class in person. Reservations are required for most types of train accommodation. Credit cards are accepted. Reservation information needed includes:

◆ destination

◆ departure and return dates and times

◆ type of accommodation required

For more information, contact 1www.viarail.ca

NOTE   Via Rail provides an eSchedule downloading to hand-held computers using the Palm operating system, including Series III, V, and VII, and other products, i.e., Handspring Visors. The program requires about 27 KB of memory and a further 155 KB for data, or approximately 200 KB in total.

www.viarail.ca

TA12   FARES

Although regular fares are available year-round, a wide range of discounted fares is also available. Special excursion fares with discounts of 25 to 40 percent are available for journeys of one day, two to five days, and one to ten days on short runs. Special fare reductions are offered for groups, children up to 11 years of age, students, and passengers over 60. A Canrail Pass provides unlimited travel in Canada for a specified period of time. Consult your VIA Rail office or a travel agent, and book early.

TA13   CLASSES OF ACCOMMODATION

Coach   Reclining seat with footrest; snack and beverage included in cost of fare; bar service available at seat.

First class   Reclining seat with footrest; fare includes a hot meal and complimentary glass of wine.

Upper or lower berth   The upper berth is folded down from the side of the car to become a bed. During the day, with the upper berth in its folded position, passengers use the lower berth as seating accommodation.

TA

Roomette* Private compartment with washroom facilities. It sleeps one person.

Bedroom* Private compartment with washroom facilities. It sleeps two people. Chairs are provided during the day.

Ensuite* Two bedrooms separated by a collapsible wall. It sleeps up to four people.

Drawing Room* Three adjoining bedrooms.

*Passengers in these types of accommodation have priority for dining car service.

A snack bar with lounge facilities (often attached to the bar car) is available for all passengers and operates on trains between most major centres. The Transcontinental (the cross-Canada train) is equipped with a dome car, lounges, a bar, a café, and a dining car with a chef for full meal service.

TA14 CANCELLATIONS

Train ticket cancellations must be made quickly. Refunds are made on regular fares, but cancellation of excursion or high-season fares normally involves a penalty. Consult your booking agent.

TA15 BAGGAGE

Up to 70 kg (155 lbs.) per passenger is carried free in the baggage car (two suitcases is the maximum suggested for luggage in the passenger car). Arrangements can be made to transport animals in the baggage car only. Feeding, etc., is the responsibility of the owner.

TA16 AUTO TRANSPORT

Some companies will arrange to send your car by rail for you. These operate in all major centres. Consult the local telephone directory.

TA17 BUS TRAVEL

Buses provide economical, efficient, and reasonably comfortable travel. Most buses are air-conditioned and many have washrooms. The disadvantages of bus travel are that you cannot make reservations in advance, schedules are at the mercy of the weather, sleeping accommodation is not provided, and food is not served. This type of travel is most suitable for short trips and for travelling to centres not served by air or rail lines.

Occasionally, excursion fares are available for travel within Canada as well as the United States for limited times. For passengers travelling the entire country, special cross-Canada tickets may be purchased.

Passengers are permitted to carry free of charge up to three pieces of luggage, totalling 70 kg (155 lbs.) maximum.

TA

TA18 SEA TRAVEL

Although ships now tend to be used mainly for holiday cruises, passenger-carrying liners occasionally sail from the North American east coast to Europe and from the west coast for stops in the Pacific. Travel agents and shipping lines can provide information and make arrangements.

TA19 RENTAL CARS

Travellers wanting to rent cars can do so at airports, bus and train stations, hotels; through travel agents or airlines; or directly from the car rental companies. Advance reservations are essential and comparison shopping is recommended. Some companies quote unlimited distance rates and others a flat fee plus a charge per kilometre. Obtain written information on what is included in the daily or weekly rental fee, then ask about additional charges (e.g., daily road tax; gas; state, county, or provincial tax).

Carefully check all details of the insurance coverage offered by the rental company and be certain to purchase enough insurance to provide adequate but not excessive protection. Find out the amount of your liability (deductible amount) in the event of an accident or theft, and find out the amount to be paid if you drop off the car at another location.

TA20 HOTEL/MOTEL ACCOMMODATION

There are many ways of reserving hotel or motel accommodation:
- Large hotel chains provide toll-free telephone numbers for travellers across the continent. They might also have computer, fax, or telephone tieline hookups with their branches.
- Independent hotels are accessible by telephone, computer, fax, or letter.
- A travel agent could arrange reservations.
- An airline company might arrange discounted accommodation at designated hotels if you travel with that airline.

In requesting accommodation, state the type and size of room required, if non-smoking accommodation is required, the length of occupancy, and the arrival and departure dates. Rates are based on double occupancy of the room per night; a small additional charge is made for accommodating more people.

Hotels consisting of suites only might be considered for team and/or lengthy out-of-town visits. Be sure to take advantage of any special guest rates, convention group rates, or corporate discounts available to members of the Canadian Professional Sales Association or other registered associations and to others who give hotels regular business. Room rates do not include meals and taxes, although a continental breakfast is sometimes provided. In some hotels, parking may appear as

TA

a daily charge on your room bill, and there may be a charge for every local call that you make.

Check availability of fax, modem, and other communications equipment.

For women travellers, in-room amenities sometimes include make-up mirrors, hair dryers, and special clothes hangers. As well, for the security of women clients, many hotels have installed more secure room door-locking systems, brighter lighting in halls and other public areas, surveillance cameras, and easily identifiable alarm systems in underground garages for assistance in emergencies.

NOTE Private bathrooms are a standard feature in North American hotels but not necessarily in hotels in other parts of the world.

Guaranteed bookings

Hotels do not generally hold a reservation beyond 6 p.m. unless a guaranteed booking is requested. A guaranteed booking means that the room is held indefinitely and a bill will be sent even if the room is not used. Cancellation before 6 p.m. is permissible without penalty, however. Use a credit card to guarantee a booking.

NOTE *The Official Hotel and Resort Guide*, an annual publication that provides information on North American hotels, motels, resorts, and meeting facilities, or the Internet, may be useful reference sources if you have to make many bookings.

TA21   HOTEL AND RESTAURANT TERMS

If you are considering a package travel plan, the following definitions may be helpful:

- single: room occupied by one person
- double: room with one large bed or two twin or double beds for two persons
- twin: room with two beds for two persons
- suite: a living or sitting room connected to one or more bedrooms
- European Plan (EP): no meals included
- American Plan (AP): room and meals
- Modified American Plan (MAP): room, breakfast, and dinner
- Continental Plan: room and breakfast
- table d'hôte: fixed charge for the meal
- prix fixe: fixed charge for the meal
- à la carte: each dish on the menu is charged separately

TA22   THE ITINERARY

An itinerary is a detailed list of travel arrangements, accommodation, appointments to be kept, and essential reminders. If you are making arrangements through a travel agent, the agent will provide a travel itinerary as part of the service.

In drawing up a workable itinerary, allow sufficient time for checking in at airports, ensure that the traveller knows that arrival and departure times are local times, remind the traveller to reconfirm return international flights, and allow sufficient travel recovery time before meetings are scheduled.

TA23 TRAVELLERS' ELECTRONIC BUSINESS KIT

Electronic communications equipment may be part of your luggage. To make sure that your kit is complete, compile a list that shows each piece of equipment, its serial number, and ancillary items required, as shown below.

Equipment	Serial No.	Ancillary item
cellular phone	ES-37201	batteries (2)
portable fax	91-3247019	paper, spare ink cartridge, cables
dictation equipment	17-0933	batteries (3), tapes (2)
laptop or "notebook" computer	VZ-78517	batteries (4), disks (2), modem

Use the list to check off each item before and after the trip, and remember to register the equipment with Customs before you leave Canada. Check with the nearest Canada Customs office to find out how this is done.

TA24 SUPPORT STAFF RESPONSIBILITIES

If as a member of the support staff you are responsible for keeping the office running smoothly during the absence of another staff member, these points may help:

◆ In the absence of the senior executive:
  • deal with telephone calls and incoming mail by:
    – forwarding or referring them for action
    – answering them yourself
  • keep a record of your actions (a daily log is efficient)
  • open a file for all of the messages, correspondence, and data. Prioritize the documents for action

◆ On the executive's return:
  • allow a day or so for catching up (do not schedule demanding meetings)
  • present the action file
  • follow up on tasks activated by the trip
  • assist with thank-you letters
  • update computer files; distribute new information
  • help prepare the expense report

TA

	ITINERARY, RESERVATIONS, and APPOINTMENTS for James Viegas April 15–18, 20—	
Date	**Appointments/Departure Information**	**Locations/Reservations**
Sunday, April 15		
2:00 p.m. (14:00)	Air Transit pickup 423 Oak Crescent	To Pearson International Airport, Terminal 1
5:00 p.m. (17:00)	Leave Toronto Air Canada Flight 129	To Montreal Dorval Airport
6:30 p.m. (18:30)	Arrive in Montreal	Cab to Four Seasons Hotel Reservation #V36054 Confirmation #312 (attach.) Late Check-in
Monday, April 16		
9:00 a.m.–11:30 a.m.	Meeting with Managers of Communications Division Contact: Laura Elliott Ph. 514-671-4887	Four Seasons Hotel Conference Rm. West 3A
12 noon–1:30p.m. (13:30)	Luncheon Meeting with John Wilson, CEO	Mr. Wilson will meet you in hotel lobby at 12 noon
2:00 p.m.–4:30 p.m. (14:00–16:30)	Meet with Eileen Jacques of Laurier Products	1791 Sherbrooke West Ph. 514-673-4550
7:00 p.m. (19:00)	Leave Montreal Air Canada Flight 222	To Quebec City
8:30 p.m. (20:30)	Arrive in Quebec City	Cab to Laurentian Hotel Reservation #5608 Confirmation #756 (attach.)
Tuesday, April 17		
8:30 a.m.–10:30 a.m.	Breakfast meeting with Mme. Danielle Coté of Office Systems Inc.	Laurentian Hotel Willows Dining Room
12 noon–1:30 p.m. (13:30)	Meeting and Lunch with William Dubois and Support Staff of Caspar Electronics	Caspar Electronics 198 Rue St. Laurent Ph. 514-396-7122
4:00 p.m.	Leave for Airport	Note: Take laptop computer to this meeting
5:30 p.m. (17:30)	Air Canada Flight 172	Cab to Airport
7:00 p.m. (19:00)	Arrive in Ottawa Uplands Airport	To Ottawa Cab to Radisson Hotel Sparks Street Reservation #4450 Confirmation #2119 (attach.)
Wednesday, April 18		House of Commons
9:00 a.m. – Noon	Meeting with Minister of Finance, Mr. Paul Martin	Langevin Bldg. Proposals in briefcase (two extra copies enclosed)
4:00 p.m. (16:00)	Leave Ottawa for Toronto Air Canada Flight #176	Cab from Hotel to Airport
5:00 p.m. (17:00)	Arrive at Pearson International Airport	Terminal 1
	Ground Transportation	To home

Itinerary prepared by: Gladys Jones, Ext. 450   *Sample Business Itinerary*

TA25 TRAVEL FUNDS

To avoid the need to carry large sums of cash, take funds in one of these forms:

◆ *Credit cards:* Credit cards such as Visa and American Express are acceptable for most purchases in and outside of Canada.

◆ *Traveller's cheques:* (See Unit 6, FM58.) These are easily replaced if lost or stolen and are widely accepted. They are available in varying denominations. It is usually a good idea to obtain traveller's cheques in the currency of the country to be visited.

◆ *Letters of credit:* (See Unit 6, FM48.) These permit the holder to obtain amounts of cash up to a set limit in any branch of the bank that issued the letters.

NOTE   Most countries now have ATMs (automated teller machines) from which cash can be withdrawn as required.

TA26 FOREIGN CURRENCY

Travellers should carry at least a small amount of the host country's currency for transportation costs from airport to hotel, tips, refreshments, etc. Most financial institutions carry U.S. dollars but order other foreign funds well in advance of the departure date to ensure their arrival in time. Other sources of foreign funds are foreign currency exchange services, such as the Bank of America Currency Exchange, which can exchange your Canadian dollars for the required currency. Rates of exchange offered can vary, so compare rates if time permits. You can purchase foreign currency at airports, but the rate of exchange may be higher than the norm.

Outside North America, you can exchange money at banks and frequently at major hotels. The customer may be required to present a passport as proof of identity.

If the need for an emergency supply of money arises, money can be telegraphed to the traveller.

TA27 EXPENSE REPORTS

Because expense reports must be accurately completed, the traveller should make notes and keep all receipts for business expenses incurred. Use a company form, such as the one illustrated on the next page, or take advantage of a computer spreadsheet program to build a template for an expense worksheet. You can enter data frequently and the computer will automatically update totals, or you can record all of the figures once a month and then print out the hard copy for approval and submission to the accounting department.

TA

TA28 TRAVEL INSURANCE

Health, life and baggage insurance additional to that provided by carriers is obtainable from travel agents or insurance company booths at airports and railway stations.

Travellers to international destinations can take the precaution of buying medical insurance in case of accident or injury while they are away from Canada. They can also purchase trip cancellation insurance on charter flights. This insurance is effective only in case of cancellation of the booking on medical grounds.

TA29 INTERNATIONAL TRAVEL

Making arrangements for international travel is similar to that required for domestic bookings. You may prefer, however, to rely more on a travel agent's specialized knowledge. Remember these points:

◆ Allow for jet-lag recovery time.
◆ Be aware of the host country's customs and national holidays (see Unit 18, S28).
◆ Know international time differences.
◆ Be familiar with airport names and cities.

Should you need assistance or travel advice while abroad, a list of Canadian missions is contained in the booklet *Bon Voyage, but...* published by the federal Department of Foreign Affairs and International Trade.

TA30 TRAVEL DOCUMENTS

▶ TA31 Passport

A passport is required for travel to all overseas destinations. It is available from the Passport Office, Foreign Affairs and International Trade, Ottawa, or from regional offices in all major centres in Canada, and is valid for five years. The application form must be accompanied by a birth certificate, citizenship certificate, or an expired passport, as well as two recent photographs, the signature of a professional person who has known the applicant for at least two years, and the appropriate fee. A passport can be processed within three days in a major centre or it may take up to two months if application is made from a remote area.

▶ TA32 Visa

A visa is a special permit required for visits to certain countries. Travel agents have information on these countries, the documents required when travelling to them, and the visa fee. Allow plenty of time for obtaining visas.

TA

TRAVEL EXPENSE REPORT

Name _____

Title _____ Department _____

Date(s) of Trip _July 19, 200--_ To _July 21, 20--_

Purpose _____

				Transportation					
				Auto			Other		
Date	From	To	km*	Own Car	Rental	Prkg.	Travel Method	Payment Method	Cost
July 19	home	airport	43	✓					19.35
	airport	S.W. city					air	cr. card	234.00
July 19-21	airport	in city			(3d)				162.00
" 21	airport	home	43	✓		cash 25.00			44.35
	Totals		86			25.00			459.70
	Total All Transportation Costs								459.70

*Claim 45¢/km

				Accommodation, Meals, and Other Expenses				
Date	Hotel Name	Amt.	Brkft.	Lunch	Dinner	Other (Explain)	Amt.
July 19	Delta Suites	95.00		7.50	21.50		124.00
20	Red Dragon Inn	73.00	4.50	6.75	13.00	(tip) 1.00	98.25
21			4.50	6.75			11.25
	Totals	168.00	9.00	21.00	34.50	1.00	233.50
	Total All Costs of Accommodation, etc.						233.50
	Total All Expenses						693.20

Signature _____ Date _____

Attach all receipts to this form

Company expense report

▶ **TA33   Health requirements**

Vaccinations and immunizations are required for some countries. Travel agents or local health officers can provide full details about the requirements and the documentation needed. Do not leave this until the last minute because certain vaccinations consist of a series of injections given over several weeks.

TA

TA34 CUSTOMS

Travellers are allowed to bring duty-free purchases back into Canada under the following circumstances.

Absence	Goods to a value of
Less than 24 hours	$ 50 (liquor and tobacco not permitted)
More than 48 hours (on an unlimited number of trips)	$200
After 7 days	$750

Included in the last two allowances are liquor (1.14 L [40 oz.], 1.5 L of wine or 24 355-mL [12-oz] bottles or cans of beer) and tobacco (200 cigarettes, or 50 cigars, or 200 grams of manufactured tobacco). Travellers may, of course, bring back additional items, provided they are prepared to pay the duty. The importation into Canada of some types of items is restricted or prohibited. Some items, such as certain food and plants, may not be brought into Canada. Check with your local Canada Customs office if you are in doubt about a planned purchase.

It is wise also to check Customs restrictions—especially regarding antiques, jewellery, art, animals, or agricultural products—before departing from Canada. Register any valuables (e.g., camera, jewellery) being taken out of the country with the Customs office prior to leaving so that no problems are encountered in bringing them back into Canada.

NOTE For more information, see Canada Customs and Revenue Agency Web site: www.ccra-adrc.gc.ca

TA35 MAKING TRAVEL ARRANGEMENTS

If your company does not have someone to look after travel arrangements, you could be asked to handle this for individual travellers.

Preparation guidelines

◆ Open a file for each business person for whom you are making travel arrangements.

◆ Prepare a travel arrangements worksheet (see example on page 535).

◆ Have up-to-date lists of airlines and hotels available for quick reference.

◆ Have an atlas available for reference regarding spelling names and other information, such as populations of cities/countries, climate, customs, etc.

◆ Have a contact person at a local bank whom you can call to get daily currency exchange rates.

◆ If one is not available, create a procedural manual for the company's travel policies, travel advance forms, expense claim forms, names of airports in Canada and the United States, etc. (Use the *Pitman Office Handbook* as a reference.)

TA

◆ When preparing itineraries, include the airline, flight numbers, and the terminal where passengers are departing and arriving. Include the names of hotels, and give confirmation and reservation numbers of hotels and car rentals. Provide names of individuals to meet with, phone numbers, meeting times, and meeting locations/addresses.

◆ Pay attention to details, and make your traveller aware of any changes that could affect his or her commitments at the destination points.

◆ Never assume that you are making the correct decision regarding changes; always check with the person for whom you are making the travel arrangements.

◆ Be aware of special needs for the traveller, for example, special diet, wheelchair assistance, smoking or non-smoking hotel rooms, etc.

◆ Confirm all airline flight numbers, departure and arrival times, hotel accommodations, confirmation numbers, and arrival times one week before and the day before the traveller is departing.

◆ Key or update the final itinerary the day before travel, and arrange a convenient time for you and the traveller to go over all the details of the trip.

Booking online

Airline and hotel reservations may be booked directly online by accessing specific Web sites.

- for airlines, major hotel chains, car rental companies, and particular distinations:

  Excite, Yahoo, Web Crawler, Infoseek, and Lycos

- for hotel and flight information for business travellers: TheTrip.com

  www.thetrip.com

- for locating the lowest airfares:

  www.Travelocity.com

  Excite's Fare Finder assists you in finding the lowest published airfares between two cities; information is updated daily.

- for access to more than 17 000 hotels around the world:

  Travel-Web

  www.travelweb.com

  www.biztravel.com

  www.tickets.priceline.com

  www.expedia.com

  www.airlineticketsdirect.com

NOTE Many major hotels have their own Web sites, for example:

> Radisson Hotels Worldwide
>
> www.radisson.com

- for information on city convention and visitors' bureaus and state tourism offices:

  www.city.net

  under the travel category at

  www.yahoo.com

TA

CORPORATION 2002

TRAVEL ARRANGEMENTS WORKSHEET   **DATE:** _____

TRAVELLER INFORMATION

Name	Corporate telephone	Corporate address
	Residential telephone	Residence

Purpose of trip/destination	Travel period (with alternative dates)

Travel counsellor's name and telephone	Method of payment

Travel funds required
  Cash (specify amount of lcurrency for each conutry) $
                                                           $
                                                           $
Traveller's cheques (specify denominations) $

Local transportation needed

Special requirements during trip

☐ food   ☐ reserved seating in flight

☐ non-smoking.smoking   ☐ movies

☐ passport/visa/birth certificate ☐ use of computer/telephone

☐ international driver's licence   ☐ car rental

☐ prescriptions

☐ location of accommodation: near airport or downtown

☐ Other

Arrangements prepared by

Travel arrangements worksheet

21 WORD PROCESSING

CONTENTS

Word processing means using a software program to capture ideas and information and to get them onto paper in an attractive, useful format in the most efficient and cost-effective way. This information can be input by support staff, managers, executives, professionals, writers, and others in their work and personal lives. Word processing is a major part of the integrated office automation process.

WP

WP1 WORD PROCESSORS

Word processing may be performed on computers or electronic typewriters.

Computers

Computers or microprocessors—from desktop models to electronic notebooks to terminals linked to a network—are used for word processing, databases, graphics, spreadsheets, and e-mail. In-depth information on networks can be found in Unit 9.

Electronic typewriters

These offer functions similar to those found on computers but not the versatility or the large memory. Electronic typewriters can be categorized into basically three types:

Simple correcting Most provide limited format storage and such automatic features as centring, underlining, bold, indent, and margin setting.

Limited storage Offer the features of the simple correcting type and also provide limited text-editing and storage capabilities. They might also provide storage for phrases and small amounts of frequently used information.

Sophisticated Offer advanced text-editing and storage. Most are equipped with visual displays and can perform functions close to those offered by computers, such as spelling checks and global search and replacement. Some permit the user to add functions, such as disk-storage capacity, with plug-in modules.

NOTE Some of these very sophisticated machines are called word processors by their manufacturers.

WP2 WORD-PROCESSING CYCLE

The stages through which a document passes from the original idea to its final destination are usually referred to as the word-processing cycle.

WP3 INPUTTING

When the original ideas and information have been combined into a document, inputting is needed.

Keyboard This is currently the most frequently used input device for word processing.

Mouse A graphical user interface (GUI) between user and screen allows a user to select menu options from icons (pictures of the applications and commands) using a mouse.

WP

Word-processing cycle

Other less frequently used input means are:

Scanner Keyed, printed, and even handwritten information can be scanned and stored without the need for rekeying.

TrackMan Marble® or TrackMan FX Marble® This is an upgraded mouse that eliminates the use of a mouse pad. This interface is designed for less wrist strain; for example, it has one-click scrolling (the digital ball has built in laser/optical technology).

TrackMan Marble® You manipulate the digital ball with your thumb.

TrackMan FX Marble® You manipulate the digital ball with your index finger.

NOTE *Gel Wrist Rest* This addition to the mouse pad is a wrist rest pad filled with a resilient gel that relieves wrist discomfort and strain.

Voice recognition The operator simply speaks to the equipment. This technology already has some applications and is one that will eventually become a major part of office life.

NOTE Consult Unit 2 for comments on the types of keyboards and monitors available for microcomputers. See Unit 3, "Efficiency, Time Management, and Ergonomics," for information about office ergonomics and its significance in word processing.

WP

WP4 WORD-PROCESSING SOFTWARE

Word-processing software packages range from extremely simple to extremely sophisticated and from cheap to expensive. They can vary from creating simple "words on paper" to creating documents that can support sound and video. All software provides basic editing and formatting; the more sophisticated packages contain a great number of additional features.

WP5 SOFTWARE FEATURES

Basic editing and formatting standard to all word-processing software

◆ Text may be edited (changed) by inserting, deleting, or striking over, and text may be moved to other locations.

◆ All software has default (inbuilt) settings for margins, starting line, line lengths, lines per page, and tabs appropriate for routine documents. These settings can be customized as needed.

◆ Centring, indenting, justifying (an even right-hand margin), underlining, boldfacing, and decimal tab are standard.

◆ Word-wrap and page breaks are routine, and spacing, font, and point variations are easily achieved.

◆ Storage and retrieval of text is routine, as is the ability to print in a variety of typefaces.

Additional possible software features

Calculating ability This feature allows you to calculate numbers you enter into columns of your document—subtotals, totals, and grand totals.

Conversion Some software can convert documents produced on another manufacturer's software.

Customizing You can customize your software in several ways. These include measurements (decimal or imperial) of lines and cursor positions, screen colours, symbols, and printer types.

Fonts Fonts are type styles. Most software allows you to change font styles and sizes at any point in the document.

Grammar check This permits the automatic checking of specific grammar, punctuation, and style points.

Graphics Some programs include their own graphics (clip art) collections and/or allow for the importation of others.

Headers and footers Pages may be automatically identified with a caption and with incremental page numbering either at the top or the bottom.

Hyphenation This feature tidies up the right margin by dividing words where needed. "Manual" lets you decide. "Auto" automatically hyphenates according to rules set in the software.

Line drawing This feature allows you to draw lines and create boxes. Lines can be horizontal or vertical, and both thickness and density can be varied.

WP

Line numbering This is useful for documents to be discussed line by line.

Logical operators Logical operators are used in formulas and functions where numbers are compared in two or more cells. The comparison will be either true or false, i.e., the conditions are met or they are not met.

Macros These allow short, frequently used expressions to be keyed, saved, and recalled with a single keystroke as desired.

Merge Form letters can be combined with a mailing list stored on disk to produce what appear to be original letters.

Newspaper-style columns These are particularly useful for desktop publishing applications, can be used for reports, and can speed up some tabulation tasks.

Redlining Where several people are working on a document, you can indicate parts to be added, deleted, or amended.

Search and replace The software can be instructed to find expressions or words and insert others in their place.

Sorting Some software will allow you to sort information alphabetically, and some alphabetically or numerically.

Spell-check Spell-check "reads" the text and identifies misspelled words for correcting.

Split screen Two parts of a document can be viewed on the screen at the same time.

Syntax checker This is a support feature that checks capitalization, grammar, phrasing, and other types of syntax errors.

Thesaurus This provides alternatives to words used and is a useful feature for writers.

Windowing Some software can display many screens (or "windows") at one time. You can work on a different file in each window, switching easily, without having to continually open and close files.

WYSIWYG (What You See Is What You Get) This feature allows you to view the document on screen before printing, so that positioning can be checked.

Among the other numerous features possible in word-processing packages are automatic leaders, automatic indent, and tabs that can be aligned right or left or decimal.

For report and manuscript production, software is available that permits automatic footnoting, and the automatic generation of index, outlines, table of authorities, and table of contents. Paragraph numbering and renumbering are also possible with some programs, and some will provide total word count.

WP

WP6 INTEGRATED SOFTWARE PACKAGES

Integrated software packages and suites are available for microcomputers that combine some or all of word processing, database management, spreadsheet, graphics, and communications. These can be invaluable for home or business use. See Unit 2 for more details on integrated software and suites. In addition, you can purchase desktop accessory software packages that provide simple word processing and such other features as calendaring, calculator, and communications.

While integrated packages are extremely convenient, ensure that the word-processing part of package has all of the features you need for business use.

WP7 CHOOSING WORD-PROCESSING SOFTWARE

Follow the points noted here if you are involved in choosing software:

♦ List your requirements and match what is available to what you need. You will need answers to these questions: Is the software to be used for correspondence? Reports? Science or mathematics applications where heavy use of equations, symbols, and tables is possible? Newsletters, publications, proposals going to clients?

♦ If the software is for office use, you should be aware of the capabilities of the hardware you have. It is also essential that the software be compatible with the software and/or hardware used in other systems or departments. For example, laser printers with PostScript (i.e., with a range of special fonts and the capability of handling high-resolution graphics) should be complemented with sophisticated software.

♦ Consider the advantages of word-processing software packages for Windows. These offer the user-friendliness of the GUI (graphical user interface). The operator uses a mouse to select menu options from icons, which are pictures of applications and commands. As well as offering a full range of word-processing features, many Windows packages also include a number of desktop publishing features. In considering these packages, be aware that they demand considerable computer memory and power. Be sure that your hardware can provide this. (See CO7, p. 121.)

♦ In evaluating a particular piece of software, ask:
  • Is it flexible enough? The integrated packages and suites described in the previous section are the most flexible because material can easily be moved from one module of the program to another, but some are not full-featured.
  • If it is not a Windows package, ask: Is it menu-driven (are you offered a list of options from which to choose?); command-driven (does it use function keys?); or a combination of both? Menu-driven programs are easier to learn but can be frustrating because they are slow. A command-driven package may require that you memorize a

WP

list of commands but the increased speed will be worth the effort. A combination of menu- and command-driven provides you with menus for more difficult or less frequently used tasks and commands for frequently used ones. Find out also if on-screen help is provided. This guides you through difficult tasks and saves you from consulting reference manuals.

NOTE Some software manufacturers and computer supplies companies provide templates to fit over keyboards that make the learning of commands very easy.

◆ Is the package a full-function one? Will it provide you with all of the features you would expect of a typical business-oriented word-processing package? In other words, is it powerful enough for you?

◆ Is it a clean-screen type or does a frame and a considerable amount of information appear? A clean screen means that you can actually *see* what the finished document will look like.

◆ Is it easy to learn? What kind of instructional material (documentation) is provided, are tutorial disks included, and does a hotline service exist that will support you with instant answers to your questions?

◆ What language assistance is provided in addition to the spell-check? Does it provide a thesaurus? Does it include a grammar check?

◆ Will it support a network?

◆ Will it support a laser printer? This may be important if you plan to do desktop publishing .

◆ Is there a saving on multiple-copy purchase (a site licence)?

◆ What happens in the event of upgrades of the package?

WP8 GETTING THE MOST FROM YOUR WORD PROCESSOR

The advantages of word processing are so obvious, it seems impossible that there could be a negative side. However, there is one; you must avoid problems such as the following to maintain cost-effectiveness.

Perfectionism The ease with which changes can be made can lead to unnecessary waste. Instead of one draft and a finished job, for example, some people produce multiple drafts.

Excessive paper use Printers are fast and powerful but more printing than is needed can occur if the paper is not aligned correctly, if the printer is not set up properly, or if only a casual on-screen proofreading was done.

Unnecessary records storage You will need increased storage if both disks and hard copies are kept on file when both may not really be necessary.

WP

Eyestrain and fatigue These problems can occur if you sit at a terminal for too long without a break or if the workstation or equipment is not ergonomically sound (see Unit 3 for information).

Duplication of effort Word-processing is not exclusively the domain of support staff. Supervisors and managers should take advantage of its time- and cost-saving benefits by keying rather than handwriting.

Not using the system to its full potential Learn all of the automatic features of your system. Word-processing equipment should not be used merely as an input tool with storage capability.

WP9 USING THE SYSTEM TO ITS FULL POTENTIAL

Use word-processing software to full advantage to achieve total cost-effectiveness. Study your manual carefully to see what your software can do for you. Tutorials on disk and training videos will help. Most software permits all of the following. Train yourself to use these functions well and watch your productivity improve.

Moving around the screen
- Use the cursor properly. Don't make manual moves around the screen. Learn the command that will take you to the beginning of a document or the beginning of a line in one move, for example.
- Use the delete/select keys properly (e.g., character, word, line, block). Don't delete one character at a time.

Use the automatic features
- Use the automatic date feature where appropriate. This saves many keystrokes.
- Use the automatic indent for numbered sentences and hanging indents. Don't space over.

NOTE You must, of course, use automatic indent with justified text. If you space over in this situation, your text will not align at the left.

Use the printer properly
- Use draft mode for rapid printing of something that is not required in finished form.
- Print only the pages you want. Identify particular pages. Don't print the whole document.
- Preview or view the document on screen before printing to make sure it is displayed on the page as you want it (i.e., not too high and not too low).

WP

Take advantage of the default settings
- Unless your organization's stationery is oddly shaped, work with the default settings provided. Key all documents on a 6.5" line and insert

lines of space (white space) as needed to provide balance. Change margins only in rare and exceptional conditions (e.g., for a widowed line).

◆ Use the default tab stops as much as possible.

Create new default settings and templates to suit your particular needs

◆ If your firm's stationery is different in shape from the software default, create a new default document. Don't make changes every time.

◆ Create templates of frequently produced jobs and save for future use (financial statements, for example). Templates can include a header and footer, call for a specific printer, print in a specific font, have a specified paragraph format, and have tab stops where desired.

Speed up your letter production

◆ Save and reuse as many form paragraphs as possible.

◆ Don't type envelopes. Use mailing labels or print envelopes from the inside address. Or, create a macro that automatically copies the inside address from a letter, puts that address in envelope format, and prints the envelope. In addition, you can include a return address on the macro. The procedure for doing this will vary with software. Your software manual will usually show the way.

◆ Make macros for letter endings (see below).

Use spell-check properly

◆ Create a personal dictionary in your spell-check by adding abbreviations, specialized terms used in your work, names of people, code names, brand names, and company names that you use frequently.

Be productive with reports

Many features speed up the production of reports and manuscripts:

◆ Use the automatic table of contents or outline feature.

◆ Use the binder feature to automatically move text over.

◆ Use block-protect to stop breaks in tables, quotations, etc.

◆ Use automatic page number and automatic headers and footers.

◆ Import tables from spreadsheets; don't redo them.

◆ Use widow/orphan-protect.

Use macros

Macros are amazing time-savers. Use them to automatically:

◆ provide the ending to your letters

◆ insert memo headings when you don't have preprinted stationery

♦ key headings that are used frequently (e.g., agendas, minutes)

♦ insert your name and address at the top of each personal letter you compose

> **NOTE** Some macros can repeat themselves, can pause for a specified time, or can pause to allow you to key in needed information.

WP10 STORAGE

The storage method and media you use will vary with the operating system and type of computer. Storage can be on 3.5" high-density formatted disks, CD-ROMs, or on an internal or external hard drive.

In-depth information on disk types can be found in Unit 2.

WP11 DISK CARE

Note the following points in protecting your precious software and storage disks:

♦ Do not expose the disk to any magnetic sources, such as telephones.

♦ Avoid extreme heat and cold.

♦ Print or write clearly on labels, and then attach them to disks.

♦ Invest in a disk file (see Unit 16, "Records Management," for assistance) to protect from dust, dirt, smoke, or spills.

♦ Protect disks against virus contamination (see Unit 2).

♦ Write-protect your disks (see below).

♦ Keep valuable disks in a safe, secure place.

♦ Create a software inventory. This will:
  • help take advantage of updates when they become available from the manufacturer
  • assist if security or copyright problems occur

♦ Make backup copies (see this unit, WP12).

♦ Become familiar with disk management techniques provided in the instruction manual or tutorial for your software.

♦ Get to know the operating system for your hardware. Operating systems vary considerably in the ways in which they format, copy, erase, rename, and display disk contents.

♦ Eliminate (purge) unnecessary files regularly.

♦ Learn to use a utility program to help organize files. These can also recover damaged or lost information, delete files, and copy files.

WP

Write-protecting disks

Write-protecting the disk preserves the data on the disk and keeps any other data from being written on it. For a 3.5" disk, slide the write-protect shutter.

WP12 DISK BACKUP

The term *backup* is used in two ways. It means copying entire disks and it means saving parts of your work on disk at regular intervals as you proceed.

Because of the danger of power supply difficulties, human error, or disk problems, make backup copies of both software and storage disks. Remember that copying commercial software without permission is an infringement of the *Copyright Act.*

Most software provides automatic timed backup of work at regular intervals. If yours does not permit this, back up regularly every 15 or 20 minutes. As well, make regular backup disk copies of what is on the hard drive—preferably on a daily basis.

WP13 DISK MANAGEMENT

Regardless of the computer type you use, you need a method of organizing files (the documents on your disks).

▶ WP14 Naming files

Word-processing software provides an index (or directory list) that acts as a table of contents for the files saved. Some systems permit many characters to be used in the file name, some as few as six. When work is saved, it is essential that the file name provide a reasonably clear indication of the content. A suitable code system must therefore be established.

The second of a series of sales letters sent to customers concerning chairs in February 20-- might be shown as:

Saleslet2 (chrs 29-)

| Dept. | Type of document | No. in series | Product | Month and year |

- ◆ If you key the file name onto your document, you create a useful cross-reference between document and disk.
- ◆ Identify files by date and time. Record them when you create and modify files, and they can be useful in tracking changes and in finding particular versions of files.
- ◆ Save all data files for a particular program on one disk. If you work with a spreadsheet and a word processor, for example, keep them separate.
- ◆ Keep all files related to a particular project on one disk.
- ◆ Label the disks clearly so that you do not risk overwriting valuable files.

▶ **WP15   Working with directories**

With DOS, you can organize files by placing them in directories and subdirectories. The main directory on the hard disk is known as the *root* directory. All other directories have to be created by the user. A tree structure, such as the one illustrated, works very well for DOS. You can open directories for each application software you use and then open subdirectories for the different kinds of documents that you create with each piece of software. This makes finding information much easier and keeps related files together. Your DOS manual will show you the steps to follow.

Windows enables you to create directories with the *File Manager* program or folders with *Explorer*.

Macintosh allows you to keep everything in order through the use of *folders*. As with Windows, you work with icons.

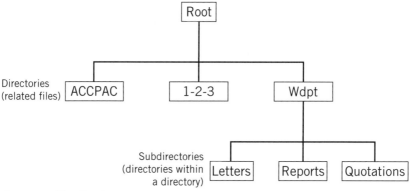

Tree-type file directory

WP16 PRINTERS

Printers for keyed documents range from low-resolution dot matrix to high-quality, near-typeset text with a PostScript laser. The quality of the output required will determine the one you use. Consult the chart on printers in Unit 2 for full details.

WP17   PAPER-HANDLING DEVICES

When you are working on very large word-processing printing jobs (such as many individualized letters), you can avoid paper-handling problems by:

Paper feeders These feed and align cut sheets into the printer automatically. On completion of printing, sheets are ejected into a hopper and automatically stacked.

Envelope feeders These are similar to paper feeders but with provision for the added thickness of an envelope.

WP

NOTE You can purchase low- to high-cost paper shredders to eliminate wasted paper, or you can contract independent firms for weekly/monthly on-the-spot recycling of paper waste in the office.

WP18 METHODS OF ORIGINATING TEXT FOR WORD PROCESSING

A number of choices are possible as methods of originating material for word processing, including original thought, handwriting and in-person dictation. The most cost-effective choice is machine (audio) dictation. Because dictation can take place at any time, it also offers the advantage of flexibility.

NOTE Many employers prefer inputting their material themselves. When this occurs, the main function of the word-processing operator is to "clean up" the material.

WP19 MACHINE DICTATION EQUIPMENT

Dictation equipment is of basically three types:

Hand-held portable units Similar to small tape recorders, these consist of a recorder, a microphone, and a separate transcriber. The dictator speaks into the microphone (or the entire unit if it has an inbuilt microphone). These small units are particularly convenient since they permit dictation anywhere—in the office, a car, a plane, etc. Some are voice-activated, use cue tones to indicate document starts, and come with clocks, alarms, and appointment reminders.

Desktop units These are designed for use in a workstation and need electricity. They offer controls on the microphone with such features as playback, interrupt, fast-forward, and end of letter. Some are voice-activated and offer cue tones to indicate end of document or special instructions. Many permit conference recording (i.e., recording conversations). Some provide a clock, alarm, and appointment reminders and can double as answering machines.

Centralized recording and transcribing units with a telephone hookup These systems permit dictation to a central location where transcription service is provided.

▶ WP20 Centralized recording units

Centralized recording systems allow for multiple recording, can be either analog or digital, and can permit productivity tracking.

Analog This older system uses magnetic audiotapes. Documents are retrieved by fast-forwarding through everything on the tape.

WP

Digital This translates the spoken word into binary language to interface with a computer. It can store more in less space, offers random access, and permits more efficient editing.

Automatic changer (also known as discrete media recorder) This type of equipment permits continuous central recording without the need for someone to insert a new cassette when one becomes full, because the recording medium is changed automatically. Long periods of dictation are possible and transcription can be under way while dictation continues.

Endless loop The recording tape is sealed into a tank and is not removed or touched. Such a system offers automatic, unattended use 24 hours a day. A supervisory console (or monitoring panel) enables dictation to be directed automatically to the person who can transcribe it most rapidly. With this system, transcription can occur just a short time after the dictation.

Telephone hookup Telephone hookup to a central recording device may be made through a private telephone system or through the regular telephone service. The telephone receiver is used for recording in both systems.

◆ *Private systems (purchased or rented)*: These are not supplied by the public telephone service. Three types are available:
  • *non-selector* equipment: Connected to one recorder only (if the recorder is in use, the dictator must wait)
  • *manual selector*: Dictator can select a vacant recorder
  • *automatic selector*: Dictator is automatically connected to first free recorder
◆ *Telephone company system*: Equipment provided by your local telephone service is connected with the centralized recording equipment. Access to the recording device is gained by dialling particular numbers, and dictation is possible from any extension telephone or from any outside telephone.

NOTE Advice on efficient dictation techniques is provided in Unit 1, "Communications."

▶ WP21 Transcription units

Transcription units are used by the word-processing operator to transcribe the dictated material. These units consist of a headset, a foot pedal, and the playback unit in which the recording medium is placed.

▶ WP22 Machine/Microtranscription

WP

Microtranscription is a valuable marketable skill in the workplace. This is a communication area where an employee's comprehension, grammar, proofreading, and spelling skills will surface. A good transcriptionist must also be a good listener. See Unit 18, S27, for more information on becoming a good listener.

Productivity techniques

♦ Make sure your equipment is working properly.

♦ Plan your work in advance; for example, determine how many items are on the tape, the approximate length of each item, and how long it will take to transcribe each item.

♦ Schedule time for transcription work (e.g., if possible, uninterrupted intervals of at least one hour).

♦ If you are not familiar with the dictator, listen through each tape to give you an idea of what to expect.

♦ If the dictator has a strong accent, listen through the tape a couple of times in order to become familiar with the voice.

♦ Listen and adjust the controls for suitable tone, volume, and speed.

♦ Listen carefully, and if after a few times you are unsure of what a word is or what has been dictated, then ask someone else to listen as well (if it is not strictly confidential material). If that person cannot decipher the word(s), then ask the dictator.

♦ Check the indicator (if one is provided by the dictator) for instructions and corrections.

♦ Listen to a complete phrase or thought, stop the machine, and key the phrase (keep a list of repetitious phrases or terminology for quick reference).

♦ Proofread the transcription carefully; run spellcheck for errors.

♦ Always check for enclosures or attachments (e.g., letters or memos); make sure they are included with the document before presenting it to your boss for a signature.

NOTE Some equipment will scan electronically to find errors, corrections, and special instructions.

WP23 ORGANIZATION OF WORD-PROCESSING ACTIVITIES

The size and needs of the firm will determine the way in which organizations set up their word-processing facility. This may range from a large, self-contained, fully equipped department (centralized) to a single, independent unit used by one operator (decentralized).

Centralized departments Separate departments that have their own budgets and report directly to management. Two forms typical of those used in a centralized word-processing department to control the flow of work are illustrated on the next page.

Decentralized departments (mini-centres) Small word-processing centres set up to serve individual departments under the direction of each department manager.

WP

Satellite centres Set up like mini-centres but exist only in firms that also have centralized word processing. The word-processing department handles the bulk of the company's output; satellite centres deal with any special requirements of a department (e.g., confidential or rush jobs).

Single units Used in traditional manager/assistant relationships.

WORD-PROCESSING DAILY WORK OUTPUT

OPERATOR_____ DATE_____

JOB NO.	TYPE OF WORK	ORIGINATOR	NUMBER OF LINES/PAGES	TIME USED HOURS	MINUTES

Operator's daily log

WORD-PROCESSING JOB REQUEST

DATE _____

JOB NO. _____

SECTION 1

ORIGINATOR	DEPT
WHEN NEEDED	SUBJECT OR REPORT TITLE

PAPER ❏ INTEROFFICE ❏ CO. LETTERHEAD ❏ BOND ❏ OTHER _____

ORIGINAL AND _____ COPIES	SPACING ❏ SINGLE ❏ DOUBLE ❏ ONE AND ONE-HALF

NOTE: TEXT WILL BE RETAINED ON TAPE FOR THREE WORKDAYS UNLESS REQUESTED OTHERWISE

SPECIAL INSTRUCTIONS

❏ SPECIAL RETENTION____/___/___
DATE

ATTACHED IS YOUR JOB PRODUCED IN ACCORDANCE WITH YOUR INSTRUCTIONS PLEASE ATTACH THIS FORM TO THE JOB IF REVISION IS REQUIRED

ASSIGNED TO	INPUT METHOD	
1. ORIGINAL	❏ MACHINE DICTATION TAPE NO. _____	
2. REVISION	❏ LONGHAND	
	❏ HARD COPY	
	❏ EDITED COPY	

PRODUCTION DATA	LINE COUNT _____	PAGE COUNT _____
REMARKS		

Job request form

PRODUCTION TIME

HARD COPY	DATE/TIME	MACHINE DICTATION	DATE/TIME
WORK SUBMITTED		WORK SUBMITTED	
PROOFING COMPLETED		PROOFING COMPLETED	
JOB DELIVERED		JOB DELIVERED	
TURNAROUND TIME		TURNAROUND TIME	

SECTION 2

COPY 1 ORIGINATOR'S COPY   COPY 2 SUPERVISOR'S COPY   COPY 3 PRODUCTION COPY

WP24 SERVICE BUREAUS AND CONSULTANTS

Word-processing service bureaus—which provide mail service, convert word-processing text to typesetting, and supply telecommunications, printing, and personnel—can be of use to organizations that do not have their own facility, as well as those that do. They are useful for:

◆ handling overload situations

◆ meeting tight deadlines—some will offer after-hours service

◆ projects requiring special knowledge or technology not available in-house

◆ conversions from other systems

◆ advice on word-processing applications

Consult the Yellow Pages for local bureaus.

WP25 TEMPORARY WORD-PROCESSING HELP

If your word-processing demands are high or you need short-term assistance, consider using the services of a temporary agency. To make best use of their services and ensure you obtain the most appropriate temporary help:

◆ Specify the make and type of equipment and type of software you use.

◆ Describe the type of application (letters, reports, statements).

◆ Name the kind of input (print, longhand, shorthand, audio).

◆ State the degree of proficiency and experience needed.

◆ Identify the length of time of the assignment.

WP26 CHANGING TECHNOLOGY IN WORD PROCESSING

Programs are available that incorporate audio, animated graphics, and video into an electronic letter. It will take office communications beyond paper and into electronics in a way that will not only speed the flow of information but also add to the scope of what can be conveyed.

WP27 TERMS

Bug: A defect in a program that causes a malfunction in the computer.

Command-driven software program: Instructions are given to the word-processing equipment by means of keystrokes (commands) that must be learned.

Continuous loop: See endless loop recorders (this unit, WP20).

WP

Cpi: A term that means characters per inch.

Cps: A term that means characters per second.

DDE: A term that means dynamic data exchange; the means by which a linked object is created.

Downtime: Time when equipment is not operating correctly because of some malfunction

Dumb terminal: A text-editing terminal of a computer-based system that relies on a mainframe or mini-computer for its intelligence

Electronic mail: The use of electronic means (telephone lines, private networks, or satellite networks) to transmit information

Embedded object: An object created by using OLE in which the embedded data is stored in the destination document.

Footer: Page identification used at the foot of a page

Formatting: Setting margins, indents, etc., for various business communications (e.g., letters and reports)

Global search and replace: The capability of word-processing software to locate a particular word or expression in stored information and replace it automatically with another word or expression

Hanging Indent: The first line of a paragraph begins at the left margin and the following lines are indented one-half inch.

Hard copy: A typed or printed document on paper

Header: Page identification used at the top of a page

Letter quality (LQ): The ability of a printer to produce high-quality print impressions

Linked object: An object created using DDE in which the linked data is stored in the source document

Menu-driven software: The program user instructs the word-processing equipment by selecting choices from a list of options (menu) shown on the screen.

Merged text: A term used to describe what appear to be individually keyed communications but are in fact letters or documents created from standard paragraphs.

Modem: A communications device (see Unit 2)

WP

Near-letter quality (NLQ): Print impressions produced by a dot matrix printer when the print head has passed several times over the paper

Network: A series of terminals and devices connected by communications channels

OLE: A term that means object *linking* and *embedding*; the means by which an embedded object is established.

Optical character recognition (OCR): Scanners, using OCR software, scan and enter keyed materials directly into the word-processing system without the need for rekeying.

Output: The completed document

PPM: Pages per minute

Peripherals: Items of equipment that may be attached to the system (e.g., printers, plotters, scanners)

Smart (intelligent) terminal: Terminal that has its own computer power but shares the printing and/or storage facilities of the computer

Text: Printed or written matter

Text editing: Revising recorded information

Transcribing unit: Playback component of a dictation machine

Turnaround time: The time taken between the beginning and the completion of a job once it has been given to the word-processing operator

Wizards: A feature that asks questions and uses your responses to automatically create a format layout for your document.

WP

····APPENDIX·····

This appendix contains important business-related reference material to supplement the information provided by this textbook.

▶ ABBREVIATIONS

Acceptable abbreviations for examples of academic degrees, as well as for Canadian provinces and U.S. states, are listed here.

ACADEMIC DEGREES

Bachelor of Arts	B.A.
Bachelor of Commerce	B. Com. or B. Comm.
Bachelor of Dental Surgery	B.D.S.
Bachelor of Engineering	B.E.
Bachelor of Education	B.Ed.
Bachelor of Fine Arts	B.F.A.
Bachelor of Journalism	B.J.
Bachelor of Laws	LL.B.
Bachelor of Library Science	B.L.S.
Bachelor of Music	B.Mus.
Bachelor of Philosophy	B.Ph.
Bachelor of Pharmacy	B.Pharm.
Bachelor of Science	B.S. or B.Sc.
Bachelor of Social Work	B.S.W.
Bachelor of Theology	B.Th.
Master of Arts	M.A.
Master of Applied Science	M.A.Sc.
Master of Business Administration	M.B.A.
Master of Dental Surgery	M.D.S.
Master of Forestry	M.F.
Master of Music	Mus.M.
Master of Philosophy	M.Phil.
Master of Science	M.Sc.
Master of Surgery	M.Ch.
Doctor of Divinity	D.D.
Doctor of Dental Surgery	D.D.S.
Doctor of Education	Ed.D.
Doctor of Literature	D.Lit.
Doctor of Library Science	D.L.S.
Doctor of Philosophy	Ph.D. or D.Ph.
Doctor of Science	D.Sc.
Doctor of Theology	D.Th.
Doctor of Veterinary Medicine	D.V.M.
Doctor of Veterinary Science	D.V.Sc.

See Unit 1, C110, p. 73 for college diploma designations.

For a list of standard business abbreviations, see Unit 1, C100.

▶ BUSINESS/FINANCIAL TERMS

Commonly used expressions that do not appear elsewhere in this handbook are listed below:

Affidavit: A statement made under oath

Agent: A person authorized to act for or in the place of another

Amortize: To set money aside in a special account or fund for the repayment of a debt in a specified period of time

Audit: Official examination of accounts and records of an organization

Bill of sale: Written evidence of transfer of ownership

Bond: Certificate acknowledging a loan

Cartel: Group of businesses formed to regulate prices, production, and marketing of goods

CEO: Chief Executive Officer

Chattel mortgage: Personal property used as security for a debt

CMA: Canadian Medical Association, Certified Management Accountant

Collateral: Property offered as security for a loan

Compound interest: Interest calculated on the principal plus the interest earned

Contract: Legally binding agreement

Debenture: Another term for bond, a certificate acknowledging a loan

Depreciation: The diminishing in value of assets over a period of time

Drawing account: A business account that enables the user to withdraw funds in advance

Equity: The dollar value of a business or property in excess of amounts owed in relation to it

Franchise: Authorization to sell a company's products or services

GM: General manager

Inventory: List of stock of a business

Liability: A debt for goods, services, or cash provided and owed to a business or individual

Liable: Responsible or bound by law to pay a debt or obligation

Lien: Signifies the right to another's property until debt has been cleared

M&A: merger and acquisition, i.e., corporate deals

Notary public: Person authorized to perform legal formalities

PAC: Pre-authorized contribution plan

PAD: Pre-authorized debit plan

Patent: Protection of an invention

Power of attorney: Legal authority to act on another's behalf

Promissory note (p.n., P/N): A written promise to pay or repay a loan at a future time

Share: Document proving part-ownership of a corporation

Sight draft: An order to pay on presentation of the draft

Statute of limitations: A law placing a specific time limit on the enforcement of claims

Title: The written right to possession of property

Void: Not legally enforceable

Voucher: A receipt or record of a business transaction

Warranty: Guarantee of quality of goods purchased

Write-off: Removal of a bad debt from an account

▶ INSURANCE TERMS

Adjuster: A person who adjusts claims for the insurance company

Auxiliary: Helping, assisting, or additional

Coinsurance: Joint insurance

Compliance: The act of complying or doing as another wishes

Comprehensive: Including other coverage

Demerit: Mark against a person's record

Disclaimer: Refuse to recognize; deny connection with

Discretion: The freedom to judge or choose; good judgment

Eligibility: Qualification for insurance

Endowment: The money or property given to provide income

Forfeit: Damages, loss, or penalty

Immune: Exempt; not liable for some duty or obligation

Indemnify: To compensate for damage, loss, or expense incurred

Indemnity: The payment for damage, loss, or expense incurred

Infirm: Weak or feeble

Insolvency: Unable to pay one's debts; bankruptcy

Insurable: Capable of being insured

Longevity: Long life

Monetary: Referring to the money of a country; a money award

Precedence: The act or fact of preceding; of greater importance

Prudent: Describes one who plans carefully ahead of time

`NOTE` The Financial Services Corporation of Ontario (FSCO) Insurance Ombudsman will investigate consumer complaints, but consumers must first contact an insurance company's ombudsman liaison officer.

A list of all firms and their liaison officers is available at: www.ontarioinsurance.com

► LEGAL TERMS

Affidavit: A statement in writing that is sworn to be true

Barrister: A legal representative (lawyer)

Contingency fee: A fee paid to a lawyer based on the percentage of the amount of money recovered in a legal action

Decedent/Deceased: A person who is dead

Decree: A decision ordered or settled by law

Defendant: The person who is accused in a lawsuit

Dissolution: The breaking up or termination of a legal bond, (e.g., the breaking up of a partnership agreement)

Executor: The person named in a will to carry out the terms of the will

Garnishee: To hold assests by legal authority

Garnishment: A legal action where possessions belonging to the defendant must be held until the plaintiff's claims are settled

Judicial: Having to do with the administration of justice

Notarial certificate: A document that contains facts that are sworn to be true and is witnessed and signed by a person legally authorized to certify the information in the document

Notary public: A person who is legally authorized to act on behalf of others and certify documents

Plaintiff: A person who brings legal action against the defendant

Proxy: Someone authorized or substituted to act or vote for a person in their absence

Solicitor: A legal respresentative (lawyer)

Substantiate: To prove or establish the truth

Summons: Notify formally to appear before a court or a judge

▶ REAL ESTATE TERMS

Amortization: The number of years it will take to pay off the entire amount of a mortgage

Appraisal: An estimate of a property's market value. This amount is used by lenders to determine the amount of the mortgage

Assessment: The value of a property set by the local municipality. The assessment is used to calculate property taxes

Assumable mortgage: A mortgage held on a property by a seller that can be taken over by the buyer. The buyer then assumes responsibility for making payments. An assumable mortgage can make a property more attractive to potential buyers

Blended mortgage payments: Equal or regular mortgage payments consisting of both a principal and an interest component

Bridge financing: Money borrowed against a homeowner's equity in a property (usually for a short term) to help finance the purchase or to make improvements to a property being sold

Broker: A real estate professional licensed to facilitate the sale, lease, or exchange of a property

Buy-down: A situation where the seller reduces the interest rate on a mortgage by paying the difference between the reduced rate and the market rate directly to the lender. A buy-down can make a property more attractive to potential buyers

CMHC: Canada Mortgage and Housing Corporation is the Federal Crown corporation that administers the National Housing Act.

Closed mortgage: A mortgage that cannot be prepaid, renegotiated, or refinanced during its term without signing penalties

Conventional mortgage: A first mortgage issued for up to 75 percent of the property's appraised value or purchase price, whichever is lower

Debt service ratio: The percentage of a borrower's gross income that can be used for housing costs (including mortgage payments and taxes). This is used to determine the amount of monthly mortgage payment the borrower can afford.

Easement: A legal right to use or cross (right of way) another person's land for limited purpose. A utility's right to run wires or lay pipe across a property is a common example.

Encroachment: An intrusion onto an adjoining property. A neighbour's fence, shed, or overhanging roofline that partially intrudes onto a property are examples

Equity: The value of property beyond what may be owed on the property, i.e., a house worth $200 000 with an outstanding mortgage of $100 000, creating equity of $100 000.

First mortgage: The first security registered on a property. Additional mortgages secured against the property are termed "secondary"

Gross debt service ratio (GDSR): The percentage of pre-tax income needed to cover payments related to housing, including mortgage, taxes and other household costs

High-ratio mortgage: A mortgage for more than 75 percent of a property's appraised value or purchase price

Listing agreement: The contract between the listing broker and an owner, authorizing the realtor to facilitate the sale or lease of a property

Mortgage: A contract between a borrower and a lender where the borrower pledges a property as security to guarantee repayment of the mortgage debt

Mortgage term: The length of time a lender will loan mortgage funds to a borrower. Most terms run from 6 months to 5 years, after which the borrower will either pay off the balance or renegotiate the mortgage for another term. Payment is calculated using the interest rate offered for the term, the amount of the mortgage, and the amortization period.

Multiple Listing Service (MLS): A comprehensive system for relaying information to realtors about properties for sale

Open mortgage: A loan in which the borrower can repay all or part of the debt without being charged a penalty (as distinct from a closed mortgage)

P.I.T.: (Principal, interest and taxes). The regular mortgage payment that includes payment against a portion of the principal, the interest, and the municipal property taxes

Pre-approved loan or mortgage: One that is approved, based on the borrower's financial circumstances, prior to the purchase, which will be made possible by the loan

Term: The length of time a specific interest rate is paid on a mortgage.

Total Debt Service Ratio (TDSR): The percentage of pre-tax income required to cover all payments for housing and all other debts, i.e., personal loans

NOTE   This information was provided by local realtors and the Ontario Real Estate Association (OREA) for the benefit of consumers in the real estate market.

▶ FOREIGN WORDS AND PHRASES

Many foreign words and phrases have been assimilated into English usage. Some of the more frequently used ones appear below.

ad hoc	temporary; for a specific purpose
ad infinitum	without limit or end
ad nauseam	to the point of disgust
ad valorem	according to value
bona fide	in good faith
caveat emptor	let the buyer beware
carte blanche	full discretionary powers
circa	about
coup d'état	a sudden and decisive political measure
cum laude	with honour, praise
exempli gratia (e.g.)	for example
esprit de corps	team spirit, team work, co-operation
et cetera (etc.)	and so forth
ex officio	by virtue of an office
fait accompli	something already done
faux pas	false step, error
id est (i.e.)	that is
incognito	in disguise
in toto	altogether, entirely
je ne sais quoi	indefinable quality
kudos	praise
laissez faire	the principle of letting people do as they please
modus operandi	method of operating
modus vivendi	way of life
nota bene (N.B.)	note well
ne plus ultra	the highest degree
non sequitur	does not follow, irrelevant
objet d'art	a work of art
per annum	each year
per capita	each person
per diem	each day
per se	itself
persona non grata	an unacceptable person
pièce de résistance	an outstanding item or event
prix fixe	set price for a complete meal
pro forma	done as a matter of form
pro rata	in proportion to
raison d'être	reason for being
répondez s'il vous plaît (R.S.V.P.)	please reply
sine qua non	something essential
status quo	current state of affairs
verbatim	word for word
via	by the way of (a route)
videlicet (viz.)	namely

▶ OTHER TERMS

AIDS	acquired immune deficiency syndrome
ATM	automated teller machine
AV	audiovisual
CD	compact disk
GNP	gross national product
PR	public relations
R & D	research and development
SRO	standing room only/sold right out

▶ HOLIDAYS

Statutory national and provincial holidays for Canada and the United States are listed here.

NATIONAL

New Year's Day	January 1
Good Friday	Varies
Victoria Day	Monday prior and closest to May 24
Canada Day	July 1
Labour Day	First Monday in September
Thanksgiving Day	Second Monday in October
Christmas Day	December 25

Government offices are also closed on Boxing Day (December 26), Easter Monday, and Remembrance Day (November 11). Banks are also closed on Remembrance Day.

PROVINCIAL (IN ADDITION TO NATIONAL HOLIDAYS)

Alberta	Boxing Day	December 26
British Columbia	British Columbia Day	First Monday in August
	Boxing Day	December 26
Manitoba	Civic Holiday	First Monday in August
	Boxing Day	December 26
New Brunswick	Boxing Day	December 26
Newfoundland	St. Patrick's Day	March 17
	St. George's Day	April 23
	Commonwealth Day	May 24
	Discovery Day	June 26
	Memorial Day	July 1
	Orangeman's Day	July 12
	Boxing Day	December 26

(continued...)

Northwest Territories	Civic Holiday	First Monday in August
	Boxing Day	December 26
Nova Scotia	Boxing Day	December 26
Ontario	Civic Holiday	First Monday in August
	(Simcoe Day in Toronto and some other municipalities)	
	Boxing Day	December 26
Prince Edward Island	Boxing Day	December 26
Quebec	St-Jean Baptiste Day	June 24
Saskatchewan	Civic Holiday	First Monday in August
	Boxing Day	December 26
Yukon	Discovery Day	Third Monday in August

U.S. NATIONAL HOLIDAYS

New Year's Day	January 1
Martin Luther King Day	Third Monday in January
Presidents' Birthday	Third Monday in February
Good Friday	Varies
Easter Monday	Varies
Memorial Day	Last Monday in May
Independence Day	July 4
Labor Day	First Monday in September
Columbus Day	Second Monday in October
Veterans' Day	November 11
Thanksgiving Day	Fourth Thursday in November
Christmas Day	December 25

▶ METRIC SYSTEM

The metric system adopted by Canada is Le Système international d'unités, or SI. Because the system is international, units, prefixes, and symbols must be used properly. Rules for keying metric expressions can be found in Unit 12, "Keying and Formatting Documents," K79. To obtain publications on metric practices, contact the Canadian Standards Association, 178 Rexdale Blvd., Rexdale, ON M9W 1R3.

METRIC UNITS

Name	Unit of	Symbol
metre	length	m
litre	volume	L
gram	mass	g
second	time	s
degree Celsius	temperature	°C

MOST FREQUENTLY USED METRIC MEASUREMENTS

Quantity	Unit	Symbol
Length	millimetre	mm
	centimetre	cm
	metre	m
	kilometre	km
	(1 m = 100 cm or 1000 mm)	
Area	square centimetre	cm2
	square metre	m2
	square kilometre	km2
	hectare	ha
Volume	cubic centimetre	cm3
	cubic decimetre	dm3
	cubic metre	m3
	(1 m3 = 1 000 000 cm3)	
	millilitre	mL
	litre	L
	(1L = 1000 mL)	
Mass	milligram	mg
	gram	g
	kilogram	kg
	tonne	t
	(1 kg = 1000 g)	
Time	second	s
	minute	min
	hour	h
Speed	metres per second	m/s
	kilometres per hour	km/h
Temperature	degree Celsius	°C

CONVERSION CHART FOR COMMONLY USED MEASURES

Length	1 inch	= 2.54 cm or 25.4 mm
	1 foot	= 0.305 m
	1 yard	= 0.914 m
	1 mile	= 1.609 km
Area	1 square inch	= 6.452 cm2
	1 square foot	= 0.093 m2
	1 square yard	= 0.836 m2
	1 acre	= 0.405 ha (hectare)
	1 square mile	= 2.590 km2 (259 ha)
Volume	1 fluid ounce	= 28.413 cm3 (28.4 mL)
	1 pint (imperial)	= 0.568 dm3 (0.57 L)
	1 quart	= 1.137 dm3 (1.14 L)
	1 gallon	= 4.546 dm3 (4.546 L)
	1 cubic inch	= 16.387 cm3
	1 cubic foot	= 28.317 dm3 (28.32 L)
	1 cubic yard	= 0.765 m3

(continued...)

Mass	1 ounce	= 28.350 g
	1 pound	= 0.454 kg
	1 ton (short 2000 lb.)	= 907.185 kg
Speed	1 mile per hour	= 0.447 m/s
		= 1.609 km/h

Temperature: $\frac{5}{9} \times$ No. of degrees Fahrenheit -32 = degrees Celsius

or

Converting °F to °C	*Converting °C to °F*
Subtract 32	Multiply by 1.8
Divide by 1.8	Add 32

Example: 80°F	*Example:* 27°C
$80 - 32 = 48$	$27 \times 1.8 = 48.6$
$48 \div 1.8 = 26.66°C$	$48.6 + 32 = 80.6°F$

SOME EASY-TO-REMEMBER MEASUREMENTS

◆ The standard doorway is about 2 m high and 0.75 m wide.
◆ An average chair seat is roughly 0.5 m high.
◆ A paper clip is about 3 cm long.
◆ There are about 200 mL in a cup of coffee.
◆ The width of a small fingernail is 1 cm.
◆ A coin is approximately 1 mm thick.

METRIC EQUIVALENTS

A few common comparisons are listed for quick reference.

1 centimetre	= 0.3937 inch
1 inch	= 2.54 centimetres
1 litre	= 35 ounces
1 pint	= 0.571 litre
1 metre	= 1.0936 yards
1 yard	= 0.9144 metre
1 kilogram	= 2.20 pounds
1 pound	= 0.4536 kilogram
80 km/h	= 50 mph
100° Celsius	= 212° Fahrenheit
0° Celsius	= 32° Fahrenheit

▶ ROMAN NUMERALS

◆ Use upper-case numerals for major divisions in outlines and in literary publications (volumes, books, chapters, appendixes, etc.).
◆ Use lower-case numerals for preliminary pages in reports and subsections.

Arabic	Roman	Arabic	Roman
1	I	30	XXX
2	II	40	XL
3	III	50	L
4	IV	60	LX
5	V	70	LXX
6	VI	80	LXXX
7	VII	90	XC
8	VIII	100	C
9	IX	200	CC
10	X	300	CCC
11	XI	400	CD
12	XII	500	D
13	XIII	600	DC
14	XIV	900	CM
15	XV	1 000	M
16	XVI	5 000	$\overline{\text{V}}$*
17	XVII	8 000	$\overline{\text{VIII}}$*
18	XVIII	10 000	$\overline{\text{X}}$*
19	XIX	30 000	$\overline{\text{XXX}}$*
20	XX	50 000	$\overline{\text{L}}$*

* A horizontal line over a number multiplies its value by 1000.

Build combinations of roman numerals by prefixing or annexing letters. A letter prefixed to another is subtracted from it; a letter annexed is added:

$$\overset{\overbrace{\quad}}{40}$$

49 = L – X + IX = XLIX

$$\overset{\overbrace{\quad}}{60}$$

62 = L + X + II = LXII

Do not repeat a roman numeral more than three times:

337 = CCCXXXVII
(437 = CDXXXVII not CCCCXXXVII)
1988 = MCMLXXXVIII
1990 = MCMXC
2000 = MM

▶ TIME ZONES AND AREA CODES

CANADA

Canada is divided into seven time zones. There is one hour's difference between each zone as you move across the country. Newfoundland time, however, is only one-half hour different from Atlantic time.

Subtract one hour for each zone moving from east to west. Add one hour for each zone moving from west to east.

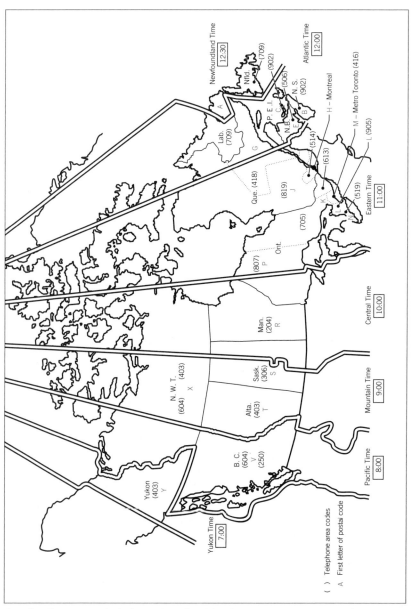

Canadian time zones and telephone area and postal codes

NOTE See Unit 19, TT13 Area Code Overlays for more information.

UNITED STATES

The continental United States is divided into four time zones, with one hour's difference between adjacent zones.

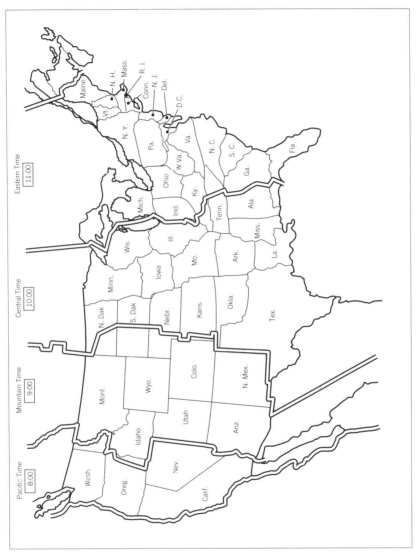

U.S. time zones

INTERNATIONAL TIMES

Add or subtract from Eastern Standard Time the hours shown to find Standard times in these countries.

(Ottawa, Monday 6 p.m. = Tokyo, Japan, Tuesday 8 a.m.)

Argentina	+	2	India	+	$10\frac{1}{2}$
Australia (East)	+	16	Iran	+	$8\frac{1}{2}$
(West)	+	13	Iraq	+	8
Austria	+	6	Israel	+	7
Belgium	+	6	Italy	+	6
Bermuda	+	1	Japan	+	14
Bolivia	+	1	Korea	+	$13\frac{1}{2}$
Bosnia-Herzegovina	+	6	Kuwait	+	8
Brazil	+	2	Netherlands	+	6
Bulgaria	+	7	New Zealand	+	17
Chile	+	1	Norway	+	6
China	+	13	Philippines	+	13
Colombia		0	Poland	+	6
Costa Rica	–	1	Portugal	+	5
Croatia	+	6	Russia	+	8
Cuba		0	Singapore	+	$12\frac{1}{2}$
Czech Republic	+	6	Slovak Republic	+	6
Denmark	+	6	South Africa	+	7
Egypt	+	7	Spain	+	6
Finland	+	7	Sweden	+	6
France	+	6	Switzerland	+	6
Germany	+	6	Syria	+	7
Ghana	+	6	Turkey	+	7
Great Britain	+	5	Ukraine	+	8
Greece	+	7	Uruguay	+	2
Hawaii	–	5	Venezuela	+	$\frac{1}{2}$
Hong Kong	+	13	Zimbabwe	+	7
Hungary	+	6			

INDEX

The boldface numbers in this index refer to page numbers; the lightface letter and number combinations are the locator codes on the pages. (References made to information contained in the appendix show page numbers plus the letter A.)

Please note the following points as you use this index:

• The references shown indicate the points at which information starts in each case.

• Use the code letters that identify each unit to help you quickly locate the kind of information you want. For example, if you want information on keying letters, use the K (Keyboarding and Formatting) references rather than the C (Communications: language skills) references. On the other hand, if you want information on writing letters, then use the C references.